CW01508696

Lauderdale

in the

20th Century

EDITED BY

NORRIE McLEISH & FAY MACKAY

This book was produced by the Lauderdale Development Forum
to celebrate the 500th anniversary on the 21st December 2002
of Lauder receiving its present Royal Charter.

The Forum would like to take this opportunity to thank the following
organisations for their financial help with the cost of producing the book.

**Scottish Power   Dunlaw Wind Farm Committee
Lauder Common Good Fund   Oxton Bovial Society**

Printed in the Scottish Borders by Buccleuch Printers, Galashiels.

This book is dedicated to the people of Lauderdale, past and present, who lived, loved, worked and died, in the Dale, and for those very special people who died for us.

Breathes there the man with soul so dead
Who never to himself hath said
This is my own, my native land!

Sir Walter Scott

Acknowledgements

The idea that this book might be written was born, when it was decided to reprint the book Lauder and Lauderdale, by A. Thomson, as part of the celebrations to mark the 500th anniversary of the granting of the present Royal Charter, to the Burgh of Lauder by King James IV in 1502.

The Lauderdale Development Forum had taken the decision to have the book reprinted, when it was suggested that it might be a good idea to try to have a follow up book written on the twentieth century in Lauderdale. As is usual if someone suggests that it would be a good idea to do this or that, they are given the task, so a small group was formed with Bill Walker as Chairman. The other members of the group were Trevor Burrows, Jean Landells and Andrew Mercer. Being complete amateurs to the art of writing books we decided that we must recruit some experts fairly quickly. Fay Mackay joined to help with research, Norrie McLeish with writing and editing and Tom Davidson to supply the artistic touch.

We have tried to make the book as interesting and as informative a possible, however we quickly realised that writing about events that have occurred over a period of one hundred years taxes the memory somewhat, especially if the particular subject has not been recorded before. We now know from our experiences that writing about the past has its pitfalls, as memories become dim with age, and that time can play tricks even with the best of them. So if there are, and we feel sure that there may be a few, inaccuracies, please look on them as the fault of bungling amateurs. If you do find some this we hope might just add a little pleasure to the reading of the book. We have tried to cover as many aspects of life in Lauderdale, over the past hundred years as possible, but if you find that your particular interest is not included, then we can only say sorry, but we really have tried. For various reasons people have either been unable or unwilling to supply us with the necessary information to complete certain subjects.

So many people have helped us in so many ways with the production of this book that it would be almost physically impossible to name everyone who has helped. Virtually everyone who was asked was so eager to assist that it was really very heartwarming, especially when information was proving difficult to obtain. However, after much heart searching it was decided that we would also include the names in this acknowledgement of the people who gave us a written piece, and who are not otherwise given credit in the book, they are: Colin Adamson, Jeff Aitkenhead, Stuart Allister, Bobby Anderson, May Anderson, Jim Archibald, Elspeth Boland, Michael Braithwaite, Eugene Brandeschi, Christine Brotherston, Agnes Cockburn, Elma Cunningham, Graeme Donald, Margo Douglas, Jack Dun, Ray Entwhistle, Lyndsay Fairbairn, Arthur Fairbairn, Anne-Marie Falcone, Julie Furness, Jimmy Gilchrist, Irene Gilchrist, John Gilchrist, Anne Hogarth, Tony Hogarth, Anna Hunter, Frances Jarvis, Barbara Jessop, Brian Jones, Jack Jones, David Long, John Mackay, The Hon. Gerald Maitland-Carew, Logan McDougal, Ian McLaren, George Megahy, Angela Mercer, Jon Mercer, Sandy Mercer, Mrs. P. Mitchell, Rosemary Murray,

David Quinn, Elizabeth Rae, Oliver Scott, James Sharp, The Rev. John Shields, David Smale, Ian Stevenson, Graeme Sutherland, Tommy Syme, Kath Thomson, Grace Whellans, David Wilkinson, John Wilkinson, Derek Wilson.

We must also mention, Arch Anderson and Walter Brotherston who were responsible for a lot of the modern photographs and for reproducing some of the old pictures that were in frames, therefore could not be disturbed. Also John Connell, Robin McTaggart and Jim Paterson for the many hours that they spent on computers, scanning in the pictures, transferring them to CD's and printing them out for us to view. To all of these people and many, many more I, on behalf of Jean, Andrew and Trevor would like to record here our very grateful thanks for all their help and forbearance.

Bill Walker

The picture on the cover of this book is from a painting by

TOM DAVIDSON

The Gallery, High Street, Earlston

Tom is also responsible for the illustrations in the book.

Introduction

This book is basically about the twentieth century. However, as we are writing about a community that has been in existence for many hundreds of years, we feel it necessary at times to set the scene as it were for our readers, and this will happen on occasion throughout the book.

Let us start then by explaining to any passing stranger who may read this book exactly where the Dale is situated. It is in the north west corner of the Scottish Borders, twenty five miles south east of Edinburgh. The A68 trunk road runs right through the valley of the river Leader to where the river joins the Tweed at Leaderfoot. The Leader rises on an area of land known as the Dass, once known as the Oxton Common. The nearest habitation is a farm called Threeburnford. The valley of the Leader is not of a regular shape but widens and narrows as the gentle, rolling hills on either side permit. To the north east we have the Lammermuir Hills, to the south west we have much smaller hills between the Leader and Galawater valleys.

Lauderdale's northern boundary is on Soutra Hill where the A68 crosses the Lammermuir Hills, here the traveller going south gets his first view of the Dale. You then carry on down the Dale passing the village of Oxton off to the right and then Carfraemill to the left, on through the Royal and Ancient Burgh of Lauder and shortly afterwards the village of Blainslie is off to the right, we then arrive at the point where the debate begins as to where Lauderdale ends. Let us just say that it finishes somewhere south of the southern entrance to Blainslie.

Lauderdale must be some eight to nine miles long and at its widest between six and seven miles wide. The valley floor at its widest won't be much more than two miles, but it reaches quite a distance into the Lammermuir Hills to the north and east.

The history of Lauderdale stretches way back into the mists of time. We know that the Dale was populated long before the Romans arrived some 2000 years ago, and that warfare and danger was never very far away evidence the number of ancient hill-forts and defensive camps and towers in the area. Not only was there regular warfare with the Romans, Normans, Vikings and English, etc., but there was also danger from within from the local War Lords, Highland Marauders and Border Reivers. We think today of any conflict lasting only months and at the most a year or so, but these people had to be in almost constant readiness to defend themselves, never knowing by whom or from where the next attack might come. Probably the last big set piece battle in this area would be on September 21st 1745, when the Jacobite army routed General Cope's dragoons at the Battle of Prestonpans. After the battle the Jacobite army is reputed to have followed Cope through Lauderdale, we doubt if this would be a pleasant experience for the inhabitants of the Dale even then.

Lauderdale was at one time, like large parts of the Borders, covered by an immense forest. However it seems that the continual conflict and fires of invading armies destroyed most of it during the middle part of the second millennium.

Having had such a violent and unpredictable past strangers would be forgiven even today for giving Lauderdale a very wide berth, or passing through as quickly as possible, but they would be wrong. The people in the Dale today are completely different from what you might expect given their past. You might expect them to probably be cunning, even secretive or maybe withdrawn and resenting of strangers. They are in fact the very opposite, being of an open, kindly and gentle nature always ready to hold out the hand of friendship to any strangers in their midst.

That is a brief glimpse of the Lauderdale of yesterday and today, we hope that you enjoy reading about a community that is more than just a place to stay. Anyone who would wish to acquaint themselves with the history of Lauderdale pre-1902 would do well to read Thomson's *"Lauder and Lauderdale"*.

BY ANCIENT RIGHT
LAUDER BURGH COAT OF ARMS
THE OLDEST BURGH COAT OF ARMS IN THE BORDERS
ADOPTED IN 1105

Editors' Note

Thomson published the original "Lauder and Lauderdale" in 1902, the Lauderdale Development Forum reproduced a handsome version in 2001. Thomson's book has long been the standard reference for all those wanting to research the history of Lauderdale as well as extensive chapters on ornithology and entomology as well as local literature. Thomson drew extensively on an unpublished MS of Thomas Broomfield, a solicitor in Lauder. He developed these notes added his own research and drew on the knowledge and expertise of others to produce a comprehensive account of Lauderdale up to the end of the 19th century.

A hundred years have now passed since the original publication. The Lauderdale Development Forum decided that it would be a good idea to follow this up by producing an account of Lauderdale in the 20th century It was an ambitious project.

At an early stage it was agreed that the composition, form and tone of the book would reflect, as well as record, the social changes of the 20th century. Possibly the most important change has been the rapid spread of democracy, certainly at local and central government level, but also in the basic structures of society. In rural Scotland of the 19th century power and influence was concentrated in the hands of local landowners and the gentry. Thomson's book reflected these social structures and it is to be hoped that this account reflects the changes that have taken place in the 20th century.

The material for this book has been drawn from people the length and breadth of Lauderdale. Organisations were invited to give details of their clubs and societies and it has been a fascinating experience for the editors to see how closely they related to changes that were taking place throughout the century. It is not however, an objective, academic view of Lauderdale; it is an account of the area from the people who are part of it and who lived and worked in it. The editors have strived to reflect the diversity by trying to retain the original voices of the people of Lauderdale.

As well as accounts of aspects of the physical changes that have taken place in the valley, there are a number of short biographies of some of local people. These are based on transcripts of interviews carried out by Fay Mackay over a number of years. In each case we have tried to capture the way the person spoke and sounded, sometimes at the cost of grammatical exactitude.

We hope that all this has helped make a book that is an accurate and comprehensive account of Lauderdale in the 20th century as well as evoking the lives and experiences of those who lived through this momentous century. What is certain is that the life in Lauderdale will continue to change in the 21st century. We wish those who will produce "Lauderdale in the 21st Century" our best wishes.

Fay Mackay and Norrie Mcleish
June 2003

Contents

*Extracted from "History of Blainslie, Roxburghshire"

by Col. W.H. Oliver

by kind permission of the Oliver family.

LIST OF ILLUSTRATIONS

The Town and Burgh of Lauder

Like the history of all of this area, the past of the Town and Burgh of Lauder, is hidden in the mists of time. Nothing was written down, so therefore no one can tell us when the first habitation was established, or where it stood. Some have speculated that the Common could have been in community ownership since before Roman times, and if that were the case there must have been some form of habitation then. Others have suggested that the main settlement was up on the Common in earlier times, and this of course would have been entirely sensible, the higher ground would have afforded the people a better defensive position, and they would also have been nearer to the centre of their ground, to be able to oversee it. However, it would be pure speculation to suggest, even a century, when the present site became the recognised settlement of Lauder Town. We would hazard a guess that it would probably be in the first millennium, possibly in the latter part of it.

"The study of old burgh seals, now their "seal" emblazoned coat-of-arms, settles definitely which towns have the claim to the greatest antiquity. I find, after much research among old records, that Lauder has the foremost claim to antiquity. The Burgh coat-of-arms is plain and simple, showing the Virgin standing with the Holy Child in her arms.

This seal is similar to that granted to Selkirk, but lacking the shield of the Scottish Lion Rampant within a double tressure. Lauder's seal dates from 1105, that of Selkirk from 1115. Thus we find that Lauder and Selkirk bear the palm for ancient pedigree"

"Antiquity of Border Towns" – James Aitken

We must therefore assume that the Town has been in existence for some considerable time before 1105. When the title of Burgh was first used.

A. Thomson in his book "Lauder and Lauderdale" says. "In ancient times, burghs were usually either of the Sovereign, or of a lord of regality - lay or spiritual. An early historian says, *"Lauder as a kirk town is as ancient as the reign of King David, if not older."* David I. (1124-53), indeed, gave "duo burgagia in Villa de Laweder" to De Norville, who appointed Bailies, but in the previous century the ancestors of the Lauders of Lauderdale fixed their residence in that part of the present Burgh which is known as the Tower Gardens." The statement of "Lauder as a 'kirk town'" creates obvious confusion in some minds. At a Town council meeting held on the 5th. April 1938, the Council was discussing, the petitioning of the Lord Lyon to grant the matriculation of the Royal Burgh Coat-of-Arms, where they state, *"That the Royal Burgh of Lauder (which was anciently known as Kirktown) has been a Royal Burgh since time immemorial"*. We understand that from around the period of 1000 AD when towns were having churches, castles and mills built by the local overlord, all towns with a church were known as kirk towns, so perhaps this is where the confusion arises.

During the fist half of the second millennium it appears that there were various spellings of the name Lauder; Lawdir, Lawder, Laweder, Lawedre, Lowedre, Louweder,

Lowedre and of course Lauder. There has also been a debate as to the origin of the name. Robert Romanes in his papers (1903) states that *"Camden in his Britannia says that the name of Lauder or Leader is derived from "Laudur", a Celtic word signifying the Lesser river, or river which breaks forth"*. It seems logical that there should be a connection between Lauder and Leader, therefore this explanation makes more sense than most. In the 1502 Royal Charter the spelling of the name was Lawdir, but by the time that J. Blaeu the famous Dutch mapmaker (1571-1638) drew his map of Lauderdale, the spelling that he used was Lauder.

During a large part of the second millennium Lauder had a disproportionate influence on the affairs of Scotland in contrast to its size. Many Royal Courts were held here, and also courts of Law. The fact that the Maitland family were involved at the highest level in the affairs of the land must have been a contributory factor of course. Again from Robert Romanes's papers we have: *"Lauder has been the seat of the Commissary Court of Berwickshire from very early times, and from the year 1581, at all events, the Register of Sasines (Land Writs) for the County of Berwick was kept there, until all the County Registers were removed to Edinburgh."* This was done in 1869.

It would seem that by the start of the 18th. century any influence that Lauder had on affairs of state was definitely on the wane, and that people had to be content to look after their own affairs.

In 1866 according to "Rutherfurds Southern Counties Register and Directory," the population of the Burgh was 1137, and the Parish (including the Burgh), was 2198.

In 1901 the figures were Burgh 724, Parish (with Burgh) 2185.

In 1951 the figures were Burgh 623, Parish (with Burgh) 1813.

In 1971 the figures were Burgh 604, Parish (with Burgh) 1551.

In 2001 the figures were Burgh 1091, Parish (with Burgh) 1414.

These figures were arrived at by maintaining the Parish boundary as it was at the start of the century, and also including in the Burgh figure, all new houses built in the new estates, whether they are within the old Burgh boundary or not.

It is fairly obvious that the mechanisation of the farms, and the fact that families are so much smaller today, has had a very big impact on the rural population generally.

These figures show very clearly the steep decline that the population of Lauder developed after 1866, and the decline only seems to have been halted sometime after 1971. No doubt supporters of the reorganisation of local government, which happened in 1975, will say that was the turning point, but was it? Between 1950 and 1975 Lauder Town Council built 98 Council houses and the "Veteran Gardens" Association built 2. In 1932 Berwickshire County Council built 2 for road workmen. Since 1975 no Council houses have been built in Lauder.

We can not say that Lauder has not benefitted from the reorganisation of local government; the Council built three nursery factories, where the Eildon houses now stand in the Orchard. Unfortunately they were under occupied during most of their lifetime, until Colour Box took them all over, but when Colour Box moved to the Smiddy, sadly they were empty again.

Where the increase in population has come from in the last 50 years or so has been, apart from the 100 Council houses, from the 222 private houses built in that time. We know that some people think that there are already enough houses in Lauder, but surely it is better to have a gradual increase in the population to keep pace with the infrastructure, than let the community decline, as it did in most of the last century.

The future is brighter for the Town of Lauder than it has been for a long time. The Community Council set up a committee in 1995 to seek the views of the people on how they wanted the community to go forward, and much has been achieved. Many fresh initiatives have been undertaken, and few towns the size of Lauder have a leisure centre like the one we have. Fresh ideas and new projects are being worked on all the time, and it is very encouraging to see so many of our new residents so willing to become involved. Lauder Town/Burgh has a very long proud and honourable past, we are confident that it has a long and happy future ahead of it.

Lord Provost Sir William Sleigh (Edinburgh) having been created an Honorary Burgess of the Royal Burgh on the 19th April, 1924.

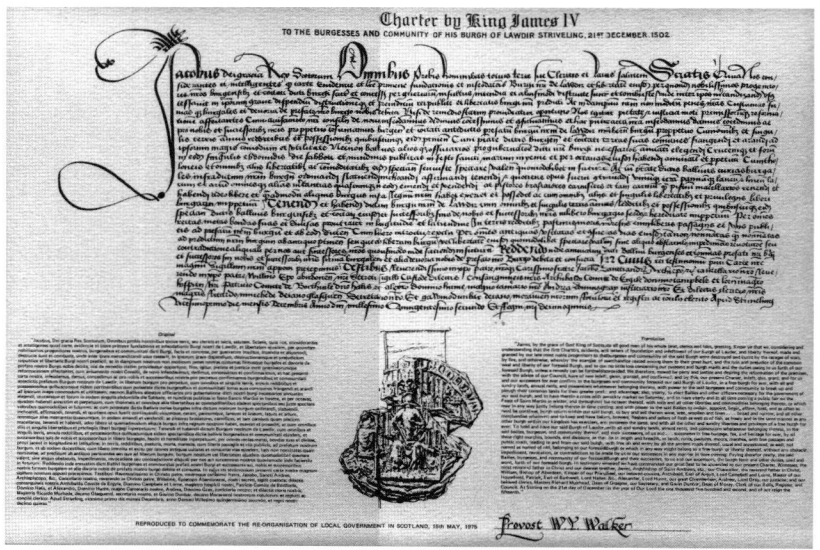

A copy of the 1502 Charter presented to members and officials at the last meeting of the Town Council on 15th May, 1975.

H.M. The Queen taking her leave of Provost Jolly in July 1956.

Lauder Town Council

Although Lauder Town Council has been in existence for some hundreds of years, its early functions and responsibilities were limited. As is indicated in the section on "Lauder Common", until the passing of the Great Reform Act of 1869, which increased the number of those who could vote, only Burgesses were invited to join the Town Council. The franchise was restricted to men, until 6th. February 1918, when the Representation of the People Act: gave the vote to women at 30; and then on 7th. May 1928, the Equal Franchise Act: gave the vote to women between the ages of 21 and 30. However it was not until 7th. November 1947 when Mrs. McLean Stone was elected, that Lauder had its first woman Councillor. She was followed eventually by Mrs. J. Rutherford, Mrs. C. Morgan and Mrs. M. Douglas.

The two main acts that regularised the functions and duties of the Town Council were the "Local Government (Scotland) Acts" and the "Burgh Police (Scotland) Acts". It was under the latter, of 1892 that Lauder Town Council was for the first time able to elect a Provost.

At first we had some committees with long winded names that were outwith the control of the Town Council, like the "Police Commissioners Local Authority Public Health Committee" and the "Police Commissioners Local Authority Water Works Committee", both of whom seem to have been made up entirely by members of the Town Council. These bodies seem to have come into being on 13th. January 1868, and disbanded at the end of the nineteenth century. the implementation of their decisions, was carried out by by the local Constabulary.

The advent of the "Local Government (Scotland) Act 1889", which saw the introduction of County Councils, meant the Town Council would take on the load of the ever increasing work passed on to them by Central Government.

The main contribution of the Local Government (Scotland) Act 1929 was to build on the existing pattern of Burghs and County Councils, by conferring on them, as strengthened multi-purpose authorities, a wide range of functions previously shared between them and a number of single-purpose bodies. Thus the 1929 Act, abolished not only parish councils, but also separate district committees (for highways and public health), standing joint committees (police), district boards of control (lunacy/mental health) and the separate education authorities etc.

There was also a pattern of District Councils which had some minor powers.

Although the 1929 Act was repealed and replaced by the Local Government (Scotland) Act 1947, no change was made to the general structure of local government between 1930 and 1960, so the activities of the Town Council did not change a great deal in this time.

In 1966 the Labour Government appointed a Royal Commission under the chairmanship of Lord Wheatly, to undertake a full review of Local Government in Scotland, and that sounded the death knell of Lauder Town Council.

As with a number of the older institutions in Lauderdale it is difficult, if not impossible, to put a date on the inception of the Town council. We do know that from the wording of the Royal Charter dated 21st. December 1502 the community had the right *"to elect Bailies and other officers necessary for the government of our said burgh,"* and also *"Know ye that we, considering and understanding that the first Charters, evidents, and letters of foundation and infestment of our Burgh of Lauder, and liberty thereof, made and granted by our late most noble progenitors to the burgesses and community of the said Burgh were destroyed and burnt by the ravages of wars, by fire, and otherwise,"* These two excerpts from the 1502 Charter make it very clear that a town council must have been in place for some considerable time before 1502, but for how long, that is the question no one seems to be able to answer. As has been said in the chapter on Lauder Common, up until the year 1869 to become a member of the Town Council a man had first of all to become a Burgess. The rather curious way in which the members of Lauder Town council were chosen is described for us by the Late Robert Romanes Town Clerk of Lauder from 1859 until his death in 1898:-

"The Town Council of Lauder, prior to 1852, numbered seventeen.

How the first Council was chosen, or appointed, does not appear from the records, but the Town Council, prior to 1832, was kept alive in this way. Yearly, in September or October, the Town Council, at a meeting called for the purpose, elected four Burgesses to be new councillors for a year. After these new councillors took their seats, and at the same meeting at which they were elected, the Council – New and old – chose six of the members of the Town Council as a leet out of which the Bailies (two) were to be elected. The leet retired, and the remaining Councillors chose the two Bailies from the Councillors on the leet, and thereafter the Bailies and the other four members of the leet returned to the council and the two newly elected Bailies made choice of fifteen other of the council to form with them the Town Council for the following year. The only restriction on the selection by the Bailies seems to have been that the four Burgess who were just elected by the Council should be retained, but burgesses who had only served as Councillors for one year might be dropped and other Burgesses be continued who had served for many years". By an Act of Parliament on 30th June, 1852, the number of Councillors on Lauder Town Council was reduced to nine including two Bailies, and the numbers remained at that until 1975, when all the Town Councils in Scotland were abolished. During this period the senior of the two Bailies was recognised as the Chairman of the council".

The following is an extract from the Minutes of a Meeting of the Town Council on the 9th. November 1894:-

"The minutes of the meetings held on 16th. October and 8th. November having been read and approved of were signed by the Chief Magistrate".

"The Clerk called the attention of the Council to the 36th Section of the Burgh Police (Scotland) Act 1892 under which it is provided that in a Burgh with a population of less than 10,000 a Chief Magistrate to be Called Provost shall

be elected and two other Magistrates to be called Bailies and it was resolved to elect a Provost and two Bailies in terms of the Act".

"Mr. Murray proposed and Mr. Munro seconded that Bailie Black be elected Provost, and the motion was unanimously carried. Bailie Black however stated that he was unable to accept as he was a good deal from home and felt he could not therefore discharge the duties properly, The meeting thereupon unanimously elected William Moore, and the said William Moore having taken of the office and taken the declaration de Fideli administratione officii were invested with the office".

EXTRACTS FROM LAUDER TOWN COUNCIL MINUTES

18th. May, 1897.

"A letter was read from George Cockburn dated 12th inst resigning his post as Town Officer and Scavenger. It was agreed to increase his wages by one shilling per week with which he expressed himself satisfied and withdrew his resignation".

Meeting 17th July 1900

"The Clerk reported that he had now heard from the Solicitors of the Lauder Light Railway Coy that the Company proposed to form a road along the south side of the line from the Edinburgh road to the road to Whitlaw beyond where the Railway crossed it. This was considered satisfactory and the draft of the claim by the Council for the land to be taken was approved of".

Meeting 25th. September 1900.

"The clerk stated that the roll of the council at present stood thus: -

A. G. Bain	*elected in Nov.*	*1897*
William Murray	*do.*	*1897*
William Moore	*do.*	*1897*
D. W. Harvey	*do.*	*1898*
John Hardie	*do.*	*1898*
Thomas Gray	*do.*	*1898*
George Rutherford	*do.*	*1899*
George Watson Anderson	*do.*	*1899*
Robert Symington	*do.*	*1899*

and that D. G. Bain William Murray and William Moore therefore fall to retire in November".

15th. January, 1901.

"All meetings of the Town Council shall be held in the Town Hall at 7 o'clock evening unless in the requisition to the Clerk to call any special meeting another place or hour shall be specified".

"The meeting appointed George Logan Broomfield Solicitor Lauder to be Treasurer and collector at the salary of £15 per annum with £5 per annum for collecting the water rate and 2¹/₂ % on the sum collected on the Railway

rate, the whole to run from 15th May last under deduction of the proportion of the salary included in the account to 15th October last. The foregoing to cover all work as Treasurer and collector including attendance at all meetings of the Town Council and they fixed £300 as the sum for which he is to find security for his intromissions".

"The meeting also appointed the said George Logan Broomfield to be Burgh Prosecutor and the Town Clerk to be of the Police Court both to be paid by fees as at present till Martinmas next".

Meeting 26th January 1901.

"It was moved by Provost Moore that the following address to the King should be forwarded to the Secretary for Scotland to be presented.–

Unto His Most Excellent Majesty King Edward VII

May it please your Majesty

We your Majesty's most dutiful and loyal subjects the Provost Magistrates and Councillors of the Royal Burgh of Lauder in Council assembled at a special meeting beg leave to offer our heartfelt sympathy and condolence with your Majesty and the Royal Family in your heavy bereavement and to express our own feeling of deep grief at the death of our beloved and gracious Queen who will ever be kept in affectionate remembrance by her people. We humbly and respectfully beg to assure Your Majesty of our loyalty and we pray that your Majesty may be long spared to reign over the Empire.

The motion was seconded by Bailie Harvey and unanimously carried".

Meeting 5th March 1901.

"The clerk read the following letter which the Provost had received from the Secretary for Scotland:-

> *Scottish Office*
> *Whitehall*
> *25 February 1901*

Sir

I am commanded by the King to convey to the Provost, Magistrates and Councillors of the Royal Burgh of Lauder His Majesty's thanks for the expressions of sympathy with his Majesty and the Royal Family on the occasion of the lamented death of her late Majesty Queen Victoria and also for the loyal and dutiful assurances on the occasion of His Majesty's succession to the Throne contained in there address which I have had the honour to lay before his Majesty.

I am

Your obedient Servant

(Signed) Balfour of Burleigh.

Meeting 10th September 1901.

"A circular from the Scottish Office dated 26th ult was submitted sending an amendment under the Locomotives on Highways Acts 1896 raising the maximum speed for a light locomotive from 10 to 12 miles an hour".

Meeting 8th November 1901.

"A letter from the Secretary of the Lauderdale Agricultural Society dated 26th ult was read as to the proposed resuscitation of the Spring Hiring Market in Lauder and it was agreed on the recommendation of the Society to fix the Tuesday before the last Monday of February as the day for holding the Market".

Meeting 7th. January, 1902.

"A letter from Mr. Andrew Thomson, Galashiels dated 3rd. ult was read asking permission to have the Burgh Charter lithographed for a book on Lauder and Lauderdale which he proposes to publish, and permission was granted".

Meeting 4th. February 1902.

"It was resolved to allow Craims and Shows on the Streets at the Hiring Fair, Craims to be charged 6d. and Shows 1s. each, the stances to be fixed by the Burgh Officer and no stances to be occupied before noon of the day preceding the fair nor after noon of the day following the fair".

"The Burgh property Committee were authorised to fence in a part of the Common beyond Mustruther for hay and if they thought proper to use the blown down wood on Chester Hill for the fence".

Meeting 1st. April 1902.

"A letter from the General Board of Lunacy dated 18th ult was submitted intimating that the Burgh's proportion of the estimated expenditure in connection with the District Asylum for the Current year was £12:1:10. and the Treasurer was authorised to pay the sum".

Meeting 6th. May 1902.

"Councillor Symington who became a member of the Town Council in 1873 and who had been almost continuously a member since then and who had filled the office of Junior Magistrate for ten years and that of Chief Magistrate for nine years having died on the twenty seventh ultimo the Council resolved to record in their minutes an expression of there sorrow at his death and of their appreciation of the great services he rendered to the Burgh and the clerk was instructed to send an excerpt of the minute to Mrs Symington and to express to her their sympathy with her and her children in their bereavement".

"On the motion of Councillor Shepherd seconded by Bailie Rutherford the Council unanimously elected Mr. James Cossar, Draper, Lauder to be Councillor ad interim in room of the late Councillor Symington".

Meeting 6th. May 1902.

"The licenses for the Slaughter Houses of Mrs. Henderson and Mr. James Reid were renewed for the year to Whitsunday 1903 and also for Mr. Brodie's Slaughter House when the Sanitary Inspector was satisfied that it had been put right".

Meeting 1st. July 1902.

"The drainage Committee reported that they had a meeting with the Sanitary Inspector who did not approve of the construction of dams on the burn but suggested that the settling bed from the Peatman Road downwards be cleaned out and that for a distance of 40 or 50 yards below the road the bed be contracted into a drain narrow at the bottom and four feet wide at the top and be paved with stones and also that, if Lord Lauderdale desired a small portion say 15 yards might be constructed in the same manner, where the settlement bed begins inside his grounds. The Clerk was instructed to inform the Local Government Board of what the Sanitary Inspector suggested and ask them if they would be satisfied with it".

Meeting 30th. September 1902.

"The Clerk was instructed to write to Mr. Robert Dickinson, Farmer, Longcroft the Director of the Lauder Light Railway Co. Elected by the Town Council & County Council of Berwickshire and request him to bring under the notice of the Board of Directors the necessity of providing more shelter accommodation for passengers and a better urinal at Lauder Station".

Meeting 6th. January, 1903.

"It was resolved to stop the letting of the Upper Loan Park to Muggers and let it in future along with the Under Loan Park by the season for grazing".

Meeting 6th. January 1903.

"The Clerk was instructed to write to Lord Lauderdale's Factor and call his attention to the state of the footpath between the west end of Lauder and the New Mills Road and ask him to have it gravelled and the kerb stones put right".

Meeting 2nd. June 1903

"An application by the Lauder Volunteers for permission to put up a new Magazine near the 700 yards firing point on the shooting range was read and it was remitted to the Standing Committee to deal with as they thought proper".

Meeting 8th. September 1903.

"It was agreed to join with the West and Middle Districts of Berwickshire in having an Hospital for Infectious Diseases at Gordon and the Clerk was appointed to represent the Town Council on the joint committee formed to arrange for the erection of the hospital".

Meeting 7th. March 1905

"It was agreed to allow the Good Templars to have the use of the Town Hall for meetings on Friday evenings for £1:5:0.per annum including gas and coal but exclusive of the remuneration to be paid to the Officer for his trouble. The charge to run as from 1st. inst".

Meeting 6th. June 1905.

"A letter from Thomas Cossar, Mid Row, dated 5th. inst complaining of the occupiers of three houses belonging to the Earl of Lauderdale on the opposite side of the street putting refuse water down the grating at his side was read and remitted to the Streets Committee to attend to".

Meeting 4th. July 1905.

"A letter from the Treasurer of the Sheep Co. dated 30th. ult as to the removal of the stock belonging to Mr. Charles Smith & Mr. George Rutherford on the ground that they were not now resident in the Burgh and as to increasing the stents was submitted. The Clerk was instructed to write to Mr. George Rutherford & Mr. Charles Smith and ask them to say if there was any reason why their sheep should not be removed from the Common as they were not now resident in the Royalty".

"The application by Mr. John Mackay Wyndhead to be regarded as a Cowkeeper and the report by the Sanitary Inspector thereon were submitted".

Meeting 5th September 1905.

"The Clerk reported that he had written to Mr. George Rutherford and Mr. Charles Smith as to the removal of their sheep from the Common and he read a reply he had received from the latter claiming to be a resident Burgess. All the members present with the exception of Councillor Munro were of opinion that Mr. Smith was not a resident burgess and that under the old law and usage of the Burgh that no burgess resident beyond the Royalty thereof is entitled to the privileges of pasturage on the Common and the Clerk was instructed to write to Mr. Smith to this effect and request him to have the sheep removed by Martinmas. It was agreed to increase the stent of each Burgess and Widow to the extent of one sheep".

"Councillor Bain in terms of notice given by him at last meeting called attention the carting of manure through the streets during the day and the Council fixed that from and after this date it shall be lawful to remove manure from any premises within or into or through the Burgh as follows Viz.. during the months of June, July August and September from the beginning of the day up to 8 o'clock a.m. only and during the other months of the year from the beginning of the day up to eleven o'clock a m. only. The Clerk was instructed to give public notice of this by hand bills posted in the Burgh".

Meeting 10th. November 1905.

"The Clerk was to write to Lord Lauderdale's to have the portion from the head of the Town to the bridge over the Washingburn, of the footpath at the side of the road put into a proper state of repair before the end of this month".

"The Streets and Lighting Committee were instructed to have gravel put down on any other parts of the footpaths within the Burgh where they considered it necessary".

"A circular from the Convention of Burghs as to the Motor Car Commission dated 1st. inst. was submitted and the Clerk was instructed to reply that the Council were of the opinion that eight miles an hour should be fixed as the maximum speed in towns and villages and that the punishment for all offences under the Act should be imprisonment without the option of a fine".

Meeting 5th. December 1905.

"As Mr. Charles Smith had not removed his sheep stock in terms of the minute of the meeting held on 5th. September last it was remitted to Councillor Munro and the Treasurer to see him on the subject".

Meeting 2nd. January 1906.

"It was resolved to relieve Mrs. Cuthbertson of her Burgh Assessment 5s.10d. on the grounds of poverty and to reduce the Burgh Assessment on the Salvation Army to an Assessment on a rental of £3. as part of their premises was used solely for religious purposes".

"It was resolved to refuse to pay the Voluntary Assessment imposed by the County Council for the Highland Society's Show at Peebles".

Meeting 6th. February 1906.

"The Treasurer submitted a letter he had received from Mr. Charles Smith as to the removal of his sheep stock, in which he stated that he did not consider that he was bound to remove his sheep. The Clerk was instructed to take proceedings against Mr. Smith to have the sheep removed".

Meeting 6th. March 1906.

"A letter was read from Mr. Charles Smith dated 19th. ult. withdrawing his refusal to remove his sheep stock from the Common".

Meeting 2nd. October 1906

"There was submitted a letter from the County Clerk dated 17th. ult. with a copy of a report by the County Analyst of a sample of butter taken in the Burgh to the effect that it was genuine but low class. The Clerk reported that he had seen the merchant from whom the sample had been got who explained that he had asked the Inspector to take a sample of the butter which was Siberian butter as he wished to have it tested and that the sample that he had got was nearly finished and that he did not propose to get any more of it".

Meeting 2nd. October 1906.

"The Clerk reported the further progress made in the adjustment with Lord Lauderdale's Agents of the draft Nomination of Valuators in connection with the new drainage scheme. Amended plans of the lines of sewers and of

the purification tanks and a report by Mr. Atkinson in terms of 103 of the Public Health (Scotland) Act 1897 that it was necessary to carry sewers through lands belonging to the Earl of Lauderdale and through the properties of Mr. William Burnside and Mrs. Agnes Symington were submitted and approved".

Meeting 4th. December 1906.

"The nomination of Valuators by the Council and the Earl of Lauderdale Trustees in connection with the Drainage Scheme was submitted and signed by the Provost and the Clerk. A revised estimate of the cost of the works according to which they would cost £1685. and the general conditions and specifications of the work were submitted and approved. The Council resolved to execute the works and the clerk was instructed to advertise for tenders".

Meeting 12th. February 1907.

"The drafts of a notice to owners of premises calling upon them to form connections with the new sewers and of an explanatory circular to be sent with the notice were submitted and approved and the Clerk was instructed to have these sent out".

Meeting 26th. March 1907.

"It was resolved to put up a notice prohibiting setting fire to the whins on the common and warning persons taking dogs on the common to keep them under proper control".

Meeting 1st. October 1907

"The plans and specifications for the new public necessaries were submitted".

Meeting 3rd. December 1907

"A letter from Mr. W. D. Aikman dated 13th. ult. was read stating that after examining the plans of the proposed necessaries he still objected to the one in the Avenue being placed so near his garden wall".

Meeting 6th. October 1908.

"A letter from the Secretary of the Leadervale Football Club dated 30th. ult. was read asking permission to play matches on Mustruther. As the ground was in the meantime let to Mr. Waldie for grazing the clerk was instructed to see if the Club had got permission from Mr. Waldie and if his permission had been got it was resolved to give permission to play matches up to 1st. April next on the understanding that the goal posts are removed and the ground made safe after every match".

Meeting 1st. June 1909.

"It was reported that the Earl of Lauderdale had been taking stone from the Quarry on the Common without leave and it was resolved to ask his factor to furnish a note of the quantity taken in order that an account might be made of the sum to be paid for the stone".

Meeting 6th. July 1909.

"It was reported that stone was also being taken from the Quarry for building at Lauder Haugh and the clerk was instructed to ask Lord Lauderdale's Factor for a note of the quantity taken and to inform him that no stone was to be taken from the quarry hereafter with the permission of the Council".

Meeting 10th. November 1911.

"Submitted letter from the Local Government Board of 8th. inst. as to the statement in the Sanitary Inspectors Report for 1910 that some of the houses in the Burgh have no drains. The Clerk was instructed to reply that the Council had the matter under consideration and would try to get the owners of the houses to put in drains".

Meeting 23rd. February 1912.

"The applications, which had been received for the situation of Burgh Officer & Scavenger were considered, and it was resolved to appoint Mr. William Hardie, High Street, Lauder on the condition that he gives his whole time to his work, except Saturday afternoons after 12 o'clock, to enter on his duties on Sunday 10th. March the engagement to be terminable on one months notice on either side, the duties to include:

1. *Lifting refuse from houses, and carting to depot every day except Sunday, this work to be done by 9 o'clock in the morning during the months of April, May, June, July, August and September and by 10 o'clock in the morning during the other months of the year.*

2. *Lighting and extinguishing street lamps.*

3. *Ribbing of the roads and cleaning them.*

4. *Attending to the Sewage purification works and public necessaries.*

5. *Keeping the Town Hall and attendance at all meetings held therein.*

6. *Collecting all sums due to the Council for stances on the streets or elsewhere and for stone taken from the quarries".*

Meeting 2nd. April 1912.

"Applications from the following keepers of premises as places for public refreshment between the hours of 8 o'clock at night and 5 o'clock of the morning, or at any time on Sunday, to be registered were laid before the meeting viz:-

Mrs. Bowie , Temperance Hotel.
Mr. William Shaw, Market Place.
Mrs. Lauder, Market Place.
Mr. Alexander Trotter, High Street.
Mrs. Wilson, Market Place.

and the Council instructed the Clerk to get a register, and register the applicants in it".

"It was reported that in consequence of the scarcity of coal Mr. Robert Watson, the Contractor for the lighting of the streets, proposed now to stop the lighting of the streets for the season, of which the meeting approved".

Meeting 2nd. July 1912.

"A circular from the Local Government Board dated 25th. ult. and a copy of the regulations therein referred to made by the Board providing for the compulsory notification as from 1st. August next of cases of Pulmonary Tuberculosis were submitted. The Clerk stated that he had arranged with the Medical Officer to have copies of the regulations sent to all Medical practitioners resident or practising in the Burgh and he was instructed to have the necessary advertisements made".

Meeting 16th. August 1912.

"A letter dated the 8th. inst. received by the Provost from the Committee in charge of the Annual Riding of the Marches was read stating that the Committee proposed to present to the Council the new Burgh Standard they had acquired on condition that the Council will annually fix a date and appoint a Standard Bearer for carrying the flag round the Burgh Marches, and that the flag will be kept in the special custody of the Provost for the time in his own house, and suggesting that the flag might be presented to the Council at the concert to be held by the Committee this evening. It was unanimously agreed to accept the flag on the conditioned mentioned".

Meeting 8th. November 1912.

"The Council elected Councillor Lindsay to be Provost and Councillor Monro to be a Bailie".

"The Council elected Provost Lindsay as a member of the County Council, and a representative on Gordon Hospital Board, and the Magistrates elected him a member of the County Licensing Court".

Meeting 7th. January 1913.

"A letter from the Burgh Officer dated 2nd. inst. was read stating that his horse had died, and expressing the hope that the Council would make some alteration on the terms of his engagement. It was resolved to make no alteration on the terms of his engagement but to give him £5. to recoup him for the loss of his horse".

Meeting 1st. April 1913.

"Submitted letter from the Medical Officer dated 12th. ult. as to the Burgh joining with the County Council in any arrangements the County Council might make for providing a Health Visitor, and the Clerk was instructed to write to the County Council that the Town Council would join in any such arrangements".

"Submitted a letter from the Officer Commanding "A" Company Of 1st. Cameron Highlanders dated 31st. ult. asking permission to use the high

ground on the road from Stow to Lauder as a manoeuvring ground for one day between the 18th. and 20th. inst., no entrenching or digging to be done. The Clerk was instructed to reply that as the shooting on the ground was let permission cannot be given without consent of the tenant of the shooting, but that if the consent of the tenant of the shooting was obtained the Council would give permission on the understanding that the manoeuvring is confined to the open moor".

"The Committee on the Burgh Property submitted the following list of charges proposed to be made for the use of the Town Hall as from Whitsunday next

Masonic Society £3. per annum.

Lauder Yearly Benefit Society 2/6. per annum.

Sales of Property 2/6 each.

Justice of Peace Courts and Old Age Pension Committee, Rural Insurance and Agricultural Society Meetings 2/6 each.

For Bowling Club, Curling Club, Fishing Club, Golf Club, Quoiting Club, and Horticultural Society Meetings 1/: each.

Any other meetings to charged as the Committee on the Burgh Property may fix. These charges to be in addition to the payment of 1/: to the Burgh Officer for attendance at each meeting".

Meeting 6th. October 1914

"Submitted circular from the Local Government Board dated 19th. ult. as to finding accommodation for the recruits now responding to the national call to arms".

Meeting 4th. May 1915

"Submitted letter from Lord Maitlands Factor dated 3rd. inst. requesting to be allowed to cart manure through the Burgh up to 10 o'clock a.m. The Clerk was instructed to reply that, as the bye-law on the subject had been confirmed both by the Local Government Board and the Secretary for Scotland, it would be impossible to extend the time without incurring the considerable expense of having the bye-law altered".

Meeting 4th. April 1916

"The Clerk was instructed to have the fire insurance of the Burgh buildings extended so as to cover damage by aircraft"

Meeting 26th. March 1918

"The Town Clerk stated that he proposed with the consent of the owners of the ruinous house at the east corner of the churchyard, if the approval of the heritors is got, to take down the house and continue the wall of the churchyard from the Mill Wynd were it adjoins the house in a curve to the Session House, so as to remove the sharp corner on the road, according to a plan he produced. The Council approved of the work proposed to be done".

Meeting 4th. February 1919

"The Committee appointed at the last meeting reported that they had met with representatives of the Parish council and the Kirk Sessions of the two churches in Lauder, and come to an arrangement that there should be a War Memorial for the Burgh and Parish, and the report was approved of, and the Provost and Bailies were appointed to be representatives of the Town council on the Joint Committee to arrange for the erection of the Memorial".

Meeting 1st. July 1919

"It was arranged that the members of the Town Council should consider among themselves as to the manner in which the peace was to be celebrated, and that a meeting should then be called to make arrangements for the celebrations".

Meeting 5th. November 1920

"It was reported that the result of the poll under the Temperance Act had been as follows : -

For no Licence   123.

For Limitation   6.

For no change   146".

Meeting 15th. March 1921

"The Council elected Councillor Anderson to be Provost in room of the Late Provost Lindsay".

Meeting 3rd. September 1924

"The Clerk was instructed to write to the Ministry of transport and make application for a Regulation restricting the speed of motor traffic through the Burgh to 10 miles per hour in terms of Section 9 of the Motor Car Act 1903".

Meeting 7th. July 1925

"It was reported that on the 5th. ult. the fountain and lamp erected in front of the Town Hall had been knocked over by a motor car driven by Mrs. Scott-Aiton, Ledgerwood, Earlston and that intimation had been made to the Insurance Company with whom the car is insured. After discussing the matter generally it was agreed to postpone consideration of the re-erection until it is seen what sum the Insurance company are agreeable to pay".

Meeting 12th. November 1929

"Councillor Watson gave notice that at the next Meeting he would move that the Burnmill Haugh be made open to the public, that children be allowed to play there, and picnic parties be allowed in without restriction, and with this end the present tenant be offered the Calfward Park in lieu of the Haugh, when the let of the grass parks come up in the spring".

Meeting 2nd. December 1930

"It was agreed that notwithstanding the usual practice, on moonlight nights the street lamps should be lit when any night was dark and cloudy".

Meeting 5th. September 1939

"It was agreed to procure a lorry load of sand in connection with the A.R.P., and have this laid down at three points in the Burgh for the use of the inhabitants. A circular to be issued advising householders to remove two pailfuls to their premises in case of emergency".

Meeting 7th. November 1939

"In view of the Town Hall having been taken over by the military Authorities, it was stated that the meetings of the council would meantime be held in the School".

Meeting 2nd. June 1942

"It was noted as a matter of interest that General Sikorskie, the Prime Minister of Poland, presently resident in Great Britain had visited the Burgh on the 30th. ulto., and had officially met the Provost, as representing the Town Council".

Meeting 4th. January 1944

"The Provost reported on damage being caused by the Polish Forces cutting down and burning growing timber in the Stell Wood. It was decided to write to the Unit that this practice must cease".

Meeting 7th. May 1946

"Arising out of the decoration and other work carried out in the Town Hall, it was agreed that the opportunity should be taken to instal electric light (4 lamps) since it is already available in the Tower for the Town clock".

Meeting 1st. June 1948

"Before proceeding to the general business of the meeting, the Provost welcomed the new Town Clerk, Mr. Andrew Y. Henry, and Mr. Henry suitably replied".

Meeting 6th. November 1951

"Letter from the Territorial and Auxiliary Forces Association asking permission to build a Drill hall, Garages and House. This was agreed".

Meeting 2nd. November 1954

"The Town clerk reported that the Medical Officer of Health recommended that Lauder Old Churchyard be formally closed for internments. The Town Clerk was authorised to take the necessary proceedings in the Sheriff Court".

Meeting 3rd. July 1956

"Mr. R. Kelly Burgh Officer indicated his decision to retire, he was to be retained to clean the Public Conveniences. The Council also agreed to appoint Mr. Kenneth Gray as Burgh Officer with effect from 6th. August 1956".

Meeting 2nd. September 1958

"There was read a letter dated 26th. August 1958 from the Chief Commercial Manager, Scottish Region, British Railways, Glasgow, intimating that the Lauder Freight Branch Railway would be closed on and from Wednesday 1st. October 1958. This Was noted".

Meeting 9th. April 1963

"There was submitted a letter from the Secretary of the Lauder Bowling Club intimating that it was proposed that the Green should be open for play on Sunday afternoons and asking for confirmation that the Town Council has no objection to Sunday Bowling. It was decided to take no objection provided the interests of residents in the neighbourhood were safeguarded".

Meeting 6th. September 1966

"Under reference to minute of meeting held on 5th. July 1966, (Para.15.), Bailie Hardie reported that the proposed Motor Trial had not taken place owing to the recent outbreak of Foot and Mouth Disease".

Meeting 7th. July 1970

"It was reported that Mr. William T. Wilson had commenced duties as additional Burgh workman on Monday 29th. June, but had taken ill the same day, and had been obliged to terminate his employment at the end of the same day".

Meeting 18th. April 1972

"Hon. Treasurer Brown, seconded by Bailie Walker moved that offers be invited from tenants for the sale to them of all Council Houses. This was unanimously agreed to".

Meeting 4th. May 1973

"It was unanimously resolved to convey the warmest congratulations of the Town Council to Miss. Jean Cook, of the Black Bull Hotel, on her winning the Egon Ronay Award for The Top Country Pub in Scotland and the British Tourist Authority's Award for British Publican of the Year".

Meeting 4th. September 1973

"It was agreed to grant permission for the use of the Avenue from 6 p.m. on Friday, 21st. September until the evening of Saturday, 22nd. September, 1973, in connection with the Medieval Fayre which is being held as part of Lauder Church Tercentenary Celebrations".

Meeting 4th. February 1975

"There was read a letter dated 30th. January, 1975, from the Chief Executive Officer, Ettrick and Lauderdale District Council, in which it was stated that it had been reported to the District Council that there was a

possibility of the Town Council giving consideration to a suggestion that the Town Council allocate the 38 houses which are at present under construction at Lauder prior to 16th. May, 1975 even though the properties are not likely to be completed until after reorganisation of Local Government. It was further stated in the letter that the report had caused some concern to both members and officials of the District Council, since, if true, it would cut across the whole spirit of regulations and proposals relating to the transfer of functions from outgoing to incoming authorities. In addition, the allocation of houses in advance by outgoing authorities need not necessarily be in the best interest of the area of the outgoing authority and the immediately surrounding district. It was agreed to inform the District Council that it had been the practice of the Town Council to allocate new houses well in advance of their completion, and it was their intention to do so in the case of the present development. It was further agreed to advise the District Council that the Town council do not accept that the allocation of the houses by the Town council as outgoing authority might not be in the best interests of its area, as the Council feel that they are in a very much better position to do this from their intimate knowledge of the area and the housing needs of the Burgh".

Provosts of Lauder (1894-1975)

William Moore From 9th. November 1894 until 4th. November 1910.

Mr. Moore had joined the Council prior to October 1875. He was Headmaster at Lauder Public School as it was then called, until his retirement in 1904, he was Session Clerk and also Registrar for the area.

James Cossar From 4th. November 1910 until 8th. November 1912.

Mr. Cossar joined the Council on 6th. May 1902 at a bye-election. He was the James Cossar, of the shop, James Cossar and Son and it was what was widely known in those days as a Draper's Shop.

The shop also provided millinery, tailoring and dressmaking, and is today known as the Flat Cat Gallery. He was father of a later Provost, Ronald Cossar.

Simon H. Lindsay From 8th. November 1912 until 15th. March 1921.

Mr. Lindsay joined the Council on 8th. November 1900, and appeared to have been a Gentleman of leisure. He lived at No 4 The Loan with his two sisters, one of whom was a teacher at Lauder School.

Mr. Lindsay died in office.

George W. Anderson From 15th. March 1921 until 4th. November 1932.

Mr. Anderson first joined the Council on 6th. November 1896, and was the local Joiner and Undertaker, he was also the Truancy Officer for a number of years.

He was Grandfather of a later Provost, William Hardie.

Ronald Cossar From 4th. November 1932 until 4th. November 1938.

Mr. Cossar first joined the Council on 10th. November 1922 and attended his last meeting on 17th. June 1938.

Jeremiah Halcrow From 4th. November 1938 until 7th. November 1941.

Mr. Halcrow joined the Council on 6th. November 1936. He was also Headmaster at Lauder School from 1932 until 1942.

John Dinnie From 7th. November 1941 until 7th. November 1944.

Mr. Dinnie joined the Council on 6th. November 1936. He became manager of the Government Food Stores that were built near the Railway Station at the start of the 39/45 War. They have been used for many years since then to rear chickens and produce eggs.

James Watson From 7th. November 1944 until 4th. May 1951.

James or Jimmy as he was affectionately known by all joined the Council on 8th. November 1925. He had a Saddlery where the Mace Shop now is in the Market Place and it was something to behold, how he ever found anything in that shop was a complete mystery to anyone else. It is rumoured that many unofficial council meetings were held in that shop.

Harry J. C. Smith From 4th. May 1951 until 7th. May 1954.

Dr. Harry Smith joined the Council on 7th. November 1947, after returning from the Far East where he had been a Captain in the Army Medical Corps. While he was in forces his wife Joan, also a Doctor, ran the practice until his return, he remained in practice until his retiral in 1988.

Arthur R. Jolly From 7th. May 1954 until 6th. May 1960.

Mr. Jolly joined the Council on 8th. May 1946. He was a man of many parts, Postman, Electrician, Plumber, Radio repairer, Seller of Sunday Newspapers and Shopkeeper. Alas the old shop is no more, it became no's 24 and 26 West High Street. He also had the honour of being presented to Her Majesty The Queen as Provost of Lauder on her visit in July 1956.

John H. G. Scott From 6th. May 1960 until 9th. May 1969.

Jack Scott as he was known to all joined the Council on 1st. September 1953 at a Bye-election, when he retired from the Council in 1969 he became Lauder's one and only Master of Works, and helped a great deal to prepare the Burgh for the coming changes in Local Government.

He is pictured left with his son Ian, 1967 Lauder Cornet.

William Hardie From 9th. May 1969 until 6th. May 1972.

Bill Hardie as he is known joined the Council on 2nd. September 1958 at a bye-election. His Mother had a Shoe Shop in East High Street, which when it closed became part of his mother's house, and subsequently became his house. Bill worked for some time for Ferranti particularly at their Dalkeith location. After the demise of Lauder Town council Bill was elected onto Ettrick and Lauderdale District Council, on which he served, eventually becoming leader of the Council, until it's demise. He was then elected onto The Scottish Borders Council, on which he still serves today.

William Y. Walker From 5th. May 1972 until 15th. May 1975.

Bill as he is known joined the council on 14th. November 1961 at a bye-election. Like Bill Hardie he remained in Local Government after the demise of Lauder Town Council, being elected to Borders Regional Council. However he found it impossible to give the necessary time to both his business and council work, so after two years he retired from Local Government for good. He did join the Lauderdale Community Council on 14th. November 1994, and has been heavily involved in the Affairs of the Burgh since.

It is worth a mention here of the men who have served the Town Council as Town Clerk's, and especially the family Romanes.

On 6th. December 1797 Robert Romanes was elected Town Clerk and he served until 1810 when his son became Town Clerk, he then served as Town Clerk until 1859, when he handed over the post to his son Robert. who served as Town Clerk until his death in 1898. The family connection did not end there though because Robert's son-in-law George Rankin became Town Clerk and served until he retired in 1923, 126 years service by one family. On 4th. December 1923 Allan Gordon Doughty became the new Town Clerk, serving until his retirement on 1st. June 1948, when his successor Andrew Yule Henry took over the position, which he held until Lauder Town Council ceased to exist on 15th. May 1975.

At the start of the century the Burgh Officers title was Burgh Officer and Scavenger, fortunately the Scavenger part was eventually dropped. The men who filled this post from the start of the century were:-

George Cockburn 1900	William Hardie 1914
Robert Forest 1921 followed by his son	Richard Kelly 1944
Kenneth Gray 1956	William Herkes 1973

George Scott as a second Burgh workman 1964.

Last Meeting of Lauder Town Council

Town Hall Lauder

Thursday 15th May 1975 at 7:15pm

A meeting of the Town Council having been called for this time and place.

PRESENT   Provost Walker in the Chair

Bailies Hardie and Rhind

Hon Treasurer Brown

Dean of Guild Mrs. Morgan

Councillors Baxter, Mrs. Douglas, McLaren and Miller

ATTENDING   The Town Clerk   Andrew Y Henry

Burgh Chamberlain   Stewart Harcus CA

Master of Works   John H. G. Scott

MINUTES   1   The minute of the meeting held on 13th May 1975, copies of which had been handed to every member, were held as read and as amended at Paragraph 7, signed as a correct record on the motion of Bailie Hardie, seconded by Bailie Rhind.

Conveyances of The Smithy and Bowling Green   2   Authority was given for execution of the following conveyances;

(i)   Disposition by the Provost, Magistrates and Councillors in favour of William T H Turnbull of the Smiddy, Old Causeway,

and

(i)   Disposition by the Provost, Magistrates and Councillors in favour of Lauder Bowling Club of the Bowling Green and adjoining ground at Stow Road Lauder.

3   The Provost was authorised to confirm and sign these minutes.

Andrew Henry Remembers

"I first came to Lauder from Westmoreland, where my aunt lived, in May 1939. I had failed my 11 plus exam and was about to take up bookkeeping lessons when a vacancy arose in Mr. Home's legal practice. I got the job there at the enormous salary of six shillings a week. I had to go to Nelson's in Edinburgh to learn shorthand and, as the classes cost about a guinea a time, it was not particularly profitable.

Encouraged by my aunt, I studied to be a solicitor. I managed to pass the entrance exams and eventually succeeded in the solicitor's examination. By that time though, the war had broken out and I was in the RAF, but I got time off to study.

After the war I came back to Lauder and joined the firm of Romanes and Rankin I took on the duties of Town Clerk about 1947, at that time the population of Lauder was just over six hundred.

There were lots of 'characters' though. I remember Mrs McConnachie who lived at Cottisbrook at that time. She had whist games every Saturday night. Mrs McConnachie was the widow of the parish minister. She was quite a character, much travelled and quite a musician. The other whist players were myself and a Mr. and Miss Young. He was with a firm of jewellers in Princes Street and every now and then he would go to Holyrood Palace to submit items of jewellery for the Queen's inspection.

Then there was Peter Burns. He and his wife used to run the shelter in the Mid Row. She was coloured and was always known as Nancy, though her real name was Julia. After them in the mid Row came Ruby Strachan who used to give dancing lessons. Her notice said that Miss Ruby M. Strachan would be opening her dancing classes on a certain day and that she was a pupil of "Mrs Van Dyke of Buchan." Of course no one had the faintest idea of who Mrs Van Dyke was. She had a good reputation as a dancing teacher though, but she didn t like to be called 'Strachan'. She always corrected people who called her 'Strachan', said her name was pronounced 'Strawan.'

There was Mrs Stone who was a town baillie. I remember her saying to me, as we watched a group of people gossiping, *"What a marvellous memory the Lauder people have about things happening."* When I said, *"Indeed they have."* She retorted, *"They still remember things that never happened."* A local story claimed that her house had an underground link to Thirlestane Castle. It is however, rather a long way from the castle for such a passage.

Alexander Kelly worked for Romanes and Rankin. He worked hard for his finals and when he passed them he went off to the First World War and he was killed. His name is on the town war memorial. He was a contemporary of Duncan Watson, one of the Watson brothers. The others were Jimmy and Dave. Dave was quite a character, he always did the creels at weddings. I have a photograph of him putting the basket over a bridegroom's head. No doubt after he was paid he would spend it all in the Black Bull.

The Hutchisons were another well-known family. They lived in the corner house going on to Church Wynd. The father had come to Lauder as a sort of cashier with Romanes and Rankin. He got involved in an odd bit of speculation, however and was relieved of his post. It was very odd. After his dismissal from Romanes and Rankin he got a job on the golf course. His son went out to India, where he later died. He did come home on a visit though and went up to the golf course. His father was with a crowd of people and apparently did not recognise his son. He shouted out, *"Who is that black bugger over there?"* He was referring to his own son. They were very droll were the Hutchisons."

Fountain and Lamp in Market Place from 1911 to 1925

Lauderdale Initiative Group

The key objectives of the Lauderdale Inititive Group are to enhance the local, economic, social and cultural environment so that Lauderdale is a better area in which to live and which will attract and retain visitors for longer periods of time.

The small group has been working steadily towards its goals over the last eight years.

- enhancing and increasing the community environmental facilities and services.
- increasing the use of surrounding natural features.
- improving the visual appearance of the area.
- promoting and sharing the culture an d heritage of the Royal and Ancient Burgh of Lauder for both local people and visitors.

Successes to date include:

- A Town Study by Edinburgh College of Art
- The Mini Guide
- The Walking Festival and all its connected events.
- A Booklet and Audio Town Trail
- Floodlighting the Church and Town Hall
- Christmas Lights.
- Encouraging floral displays for Britain in Bloom competitions.
- Hopefully, encouraging and helping to make people more aware of how they can enhance the area.

One project a year is all that the group try to achieve, but sometimes red tape and lack of funds can prolong projects. However determination and motivation is the name of the game.

The Old West Port.

The Row in early times.

Lauder Community Council

With the demise of Lauder Town Council, due to the reorganisation of local government, due to take place on the 15th. May 1975, discussions were held in Lauder as to how we should prepare for the change. Knowing that a Statutory Community Council would not be in place for some time after the changeover it was decided, with the help of Lauder Town Council and Berwickshire Council of Social Services, to press ahead immediately to form, what was to be known as the Lauder Provisional Community Council. A postal ballot was held with the Returning Officer, being A. Y. Henry, Town Clerk Lauder Town Council. The ballot had a 70% response. The setting up of this Provisional Community Council was a pilot project for Berwickshire. The Office Bearers and members of the Council were:-

Chairman:	Bailie J. Rhind.
Vice-Chairmen:	Mrs J. Rutherford and Mr G. Dodds.
Secretary:	Mr G. Megahy
Treasurer:	Mr W. Brown.
Committee:	H. Deans, I. McLaren, J. Murray, Col. W. H. Oliver, R. Runciman, I. Stevenson, G. Young.

This group did sterling work for the next three years filling what would have been a vacuum at a very important time in the life of the community. They produced their first News Sheet in September 1974. The final meeting of Lauder Provisional Community Council took place on Wednesday 16th. March 1977.

The inaugural meeting of what became known as Lauderdale Community Council was held on Monday 14th. February 1977. It seems rather strange to us now to have called it Lauderdale, as we understand that Oxton and Channelkirk Community Council was formed in the same year, being also part of Lauderdale. According to the (Local Government Scotland) Act 1973, the purpose of a Community Council is: *"In addition to any other purpose which a community council may pursue, the general purpose of a community council is to ascertain, co-ordinate, and express to the local authority for its area and to public authorities, the views of the community which it represents, in relation to such matters for which those authorities are responsible, and to take such action in the interests of that community as appears to it to be expedient and practicable".* At this first meeting of the Lauderdale Community Council the following office bearers were elected:-

Chairman:	Mr. G. W. Dodds.
Vice Chairman:	Mr. W. Y. Walker.
Secretary:	Mr. I. K. McLaren.
Treasurer:	Mrs. A. R. McDougal.
Members:	The Hon. G. Maitland-Carew. Mr. G. W. Megahy, Mr. J. D. Murray, Col. W. H. Oliver, Mrs. C. A. Scott-Aiton, Mr. I. Stevenson, Mr. D. S. Thomson, Mrs. I. H. Wilson.

It was agreed that future meetings would be held on the 2nd. Monday of each month excepting August, and this remains the case today.

Quite a change in the composition of the Council took place at the A.G.M. held on the 12th. December 1978, no less than six members did not stand for re-election. The new Council was composed of:-

Chairman:	Mr. G. W. Dodds.
Vice Chairman:	Mr. I. Stevenson.
Secretary:	Mr. I. K. McLaren.
Treasurer:	Mrs. A. R. McDougal.
Members:	Cap. The Hon. G. Maitland Carew, Mrs. I. Scott, Mr. D. S. Thomson.
Co-opted.	Mr. W. Hall, Mr. J. D. Murray, Mr. T. Ross. Mrs. S. Towers was co-opted onto the Council and appointed secretary at the meeting on Monday 13th. November 1979.

At the A. G. M. on Tuesday 15th. December 1981 the following were elected: -

Chairman:	Mr. G. W. Dodds.
Vice Chairman:	Mr. I. Stevenson.
Secretary:	Mrs. S. Towers.
Treasurer:	Mrs. A. R. McDougal.
Members:	Mr. W. Hall, The Hon. G. Maitland Carew, Mr. T. Ross.
Co-opted:	Mrs. A. R. McDougal, Mr. I. K. McLaren, Mr. J. D. Murray, Mrs. I. Scott. Mr. R. McLeod (from June 1983).

At the A. G. M. on Tuesday 18th. December 1984. the following were elected:-

Chairman:	Mr. G. W. Dodds.
Vice Chairman:	Mr. I. Stevenson.
Secretary:	Mrs. S. Towers.
Treasurer:	Mrs. A. R. McDougal.
Members:	Mrs. E. Fullerton, Mr. I. K. McLaren, Mr. R. McLeod, Mr. J. D. Murray, Mr. G. Renfrew, Mr. T. Ross, Mr. C. Tucker, Miss. L. Yeaman.
Co-opted:	The Hon. G. Maitland Carew.

At a meeting of the Community Council on Monday 14th. September 1987, it was agreed to a merger with Oxton and Channelkirk Community Council. This would mean an increase of three members, the merger to take effect from 27th. November 1987, then we would truly have a "Lauderdale Community Council".

The first meeting of the new Community Council was held Monday 7th. December 1987 in the Town Hall Lauder, at which the new Council was formed:-

Chairman:	Mr. I. Stevenson.
Vice Chairman:	Mr. T. Ross.

Secretary:	Miss. C. Mackie.
Treasurer:	Mrs. A. R. McDougal.
Members:	Mr I. K. McLaren, Mr. J. D. Murray, Mrs. S. Towers, Mr,. C. Tucker.
Co-opted:	Mr. G. Bell (Oxton), Mrs. E. Fullerton, Mr. G. Gilchrist (Oxton), Mr. W. Hall, Miss. C. Mackie, The Hon. G. Maitland Carew.

The election of Office Bearers and Members was held on 12th. November 1990 and are as follows:-

Chairman:	Mr I. Stevenson.
Vice Chairman:	Mr. J. D. Murray.
Secretary:	Miss. C. Mackie.
Treasurer:	Mrs. A. R. McDougal.
Members:	Mr. G. Bell, Mr. G. Gilchrist, The Hon. G. Maitland Carew, Mr. T. Ross, Mrs. S. Towers, Mr. C. Tucker.
Co-opted:	Mr. W. Hall, Mr. K. Nicol.

In the minute of the meeting of Monday 11th. May 1992, under any other business, Item 1 it states:-

"Some members of Oxton community have applied to the District Council for reinstatement of Oxton and district Community Council"

Again in the minute of Monday 12th. July 1992:-

"A decision on the reinstatement of an Oxton and Channelkirk Community Council has been deferred until 1993".

Then again in the minute of the meeting of Monday 13th. September 1993:-

"Ask the Chief Executive to ensure any proposed changes to the current status of Oxton within the Lauderdale Community Council are adequately advertised before the forthcoming Community Council elections".

There were no further reference's to the association with Oxton in the minutes of the Community Council.

Officers and Members elected at meeting on Monday 8th. November 1993 were:-

Chairman:	Mr. I. Stevenson.
Vice Chairman:	Mrs. A. R. McDougal.
Secretary:	Miss. C. Mackie.
Treasurer:	Mrs. S. Towers.
Members:	Mr. J. Bartlett, Mr. W. Hall, The Hon. G. Maitland Carew, Mr. A. Mercer, Mr. J D. Murray, Mrs. G. Whellans.
Co-opted:	Mrs. K. Runciman (13th. June 1994). Mr. W. Y. Walker (12th. December 1994). Mr G. Megahy (12th. June 1995).

At the meeting on Monday 9th. September 1996, there was tabled the "Review of Schemes for the establishment of Community Councils - Section 22 of the Local Government, Etc. (Scotland) Act 1994". This meant that as we were having another reorganisation of local government in Scotland, and that the then Community Councils would cease to exist. After some discussion it was agreed that the Lauderdale Council would carry on in office, until such time as a new scheme was implemented. This meant that in effect the then members served for a period of four years instead of the customary three.

At a meeting on Tuesday 10th. June 1997 held in the Town Hall Lauder, the returning Officer for the election of members to the New Community Council reported that the following had been elected:

Mr. J. Gilchrist, Mr. W. Hall, Mr. D. Hope, The Hon. G. Maitland Carew, Mr. G. Megahy, Mr. A. Mercer, Mr. I. Stevenson, Mrs. K. Runciman, Mr. W. Y. Walker.

Appointment of Office Bearers as follows:-

Chairman:	Mr. I. Stevenson.
Vice Chairman:	Mr. W. Hall.
Secretary:	No nomination an appeal to be made for a volunteer.
Treasurer:	Mrs. S. Towers to be asked to continue.

Name of Community Council: It was decided the name should remain the same. "Lauderdale Community Council". At the meeting on Monday 14th. July 1997, it was agreed to Co-opt Mrs. A. Hogarth on to the Community council and appoint her Secretary.

At the meeting held on Monday 13th. November 2000, the returning Officer reported that there had been no election, as twelve candidates had put their names forward for the twelve seats, and that the twelve new members were: Mr. I. Fallas, Mr. J. Gilchrist, Mr. W. Hall, Mr. H. Lawrie, Mrs. C. McGee, Mr. G. Megahy, Mr. A. Mercer, Mr. K. Smith, Mr. I. Stevenson, Mrs. S. Towers, Mr. W. Y. Walker, Mr. D. Younger.

The appointment of Office bearers followed:

Chairman:	Mr. I. Stevenson, after a ballot.
Vice Chairman:	Mr. W. Y. Walker.
Secretary:	Mrs. A. Hogarth.
Treasurer:	Mrs. S. Towers.
Co-opted:	Mr. G. Donald, The Hon. G. Maitland Carew.

To celebrate her Golden Jubilee HM the Queen accompanied by the Duke of Edinburgh visited Lauder on 29th. May and signed a scroll which was inscribed:

> *"This document records the Gratitude and*
> *Loyalty of The People of Lauder to*
> *Her Majesty The Queen*
> *on the occasion of the Golden Jubilee of*
> *Her Majesty's Accession to the Throne*
> *which was commemorated by the Visit which*
> *Her Majesty paid to Lauder on 29 May 2002*
> *to mark the 500th Anniversary of the*
> *Granting of a Royal Charter to the*
> *Burgh of Lauder*
> *by King James lV on 21 December 1502"*

H. M. The Queen leaving the Town Hall during her visit in June 2002.

Planting a tree during the Royal Visit 2002.

LAUDER PROVISIONAL COMMUNITY COUNCIL

NUMBER ONE

News Sheet

SEPTEMBER, 1974

THIS IS THE FIRST of what is hoped will be a series of NEWS SHEETS which will be used from time to time to keep you informed about the work your Provisional Community Council is carrying out on your behalf, and to give you details about any interesting activities being run by the many Clubs, Associations, etc. in our community. In the case of the latter, Secretaries are invited to use these News Sheets to publicise their current activities and any future events they may be arranging. Material for inclusion in the News Sheets should be sent to Col. W. H. Oliver, Blain, Blainslie. Telephone number: Blainslie 228.

YOU MAY BE INTERESTED in the way in which your Provisional Community Council has organised itself to expedite its work. The twelve elected members have unanimously chosen the following as their chief officers:—

Chairman: Baillie J. Rhind;   **Vice-Chairmen:** Mrs J. Rutherford and Mr G. Dodds;
Treasurer: Mr W. Brown;   **Secretary:** Mr G. Megahy.
Committee: I. Stevenson, R. Runciman, Col. Oliver, G. Young, J. Murray, H. Deans, I. McLaren.

There are at present four sub-Committees of which the Chairman and Secretary are ex-officio members, viz:—

Country Fayre: (Convener Mr I. McLaren) and Messrs G. Dodds, G. Young and W.T. F. Brown, assisted by many local organisations.
Lauder Face Lift Scheme: (Convener Mrs J. Rutherford) and Messrs H. Deans, G. Dodds and J. Murray.
Publicity: Col. W. H. Oliver and Mr I. McLaren.
Fireworks Display: (Convener Mr J. Murray) and representatives of the Football Club and Ex-Cornets' Association.

Also, the following Liaison Officers have been appointed:—
Berwickshire Civic Society: Mr H. Deans.
Central Borders Council of Social Service: Mr G. Dodds and
Sports: Mr D. Young.   Col. W. H. Oliver
Youth Club: Mr G. Dodds.

AT THE PRESENT TIME there are two functions which are engaging the attention of your Provisional Community Council. They are:—

LAUDER COUNTRY FAYRE; You will know from the advance publicity that a Costume Ball and Banquet Supper has been arranged on Friday, 27th September, 1974, at the Black Bull, and the following day a Country Fayre will be held in the grounds of Thirlestane Castle, by kind permission of Capt. The Hon. G. Maitland-Carew. Stalls, sideshows and sporting events have been arranged and the band of the Argyll and Sutherland Highlanders will play in the morning and afternoon. It is the intention that any profit arising will be ploughed back into the community by helping to finance community activities in the future when funds may not be so readily available.

 ★ COME TO THE....

Country Fayre

SOMETHING FOR EVERYONE

There are still a few tickets for the BALL on Friday, 27th September when the Graham Ford Trio will play for your pleasure

and on Saturday, 28th September within the grounds of Thirlestane Castle and in the Avenue you can see and hear The Military Band of the Argyll & Sutherland Highlanders, the Lauder School Maypole Dancers, the Kelso Laddies' Pipe Band, the Margaret Crawford School of Dancing from Stow, the Earlston High School Country Dance Team, and numerous stalls. *And in the evening in Public Hall* The Bobby Jack Broadcasting Scottish Dance Band. 8.45.

Lauder Provisional Community Council News Sheet September 1974.

Lauderdale News

On the 30th May 1996, as a result of a questionnaire sent out by the Community Council, a meeting was held in the Black Bull with a view to setting up a group who would produce a local newsletter. The meeting was successful and the first issue of the Lauderdale News was delivered to households the following July.

It was decided that the newsletter would come out four times a year and that it would be funded by advertising revenue as much as possible. The newsletter is delivered by volunteers who go out in all kinds of weather.

The first seven issues of the news were contained in four sheets of A4 except for the Special Millennium Edition, which had twenty full colour sheets. This was quite an achievement for a bunch of amateurs! During 1999 the group applied successfully through the Development Forum to the 'National Lottery Awards for All' scheme for funding to purchase their own equipment, which is now held in the Old Smiddy at the Leisure centre. Initially the group was funded by £150 from the Community Council, £100 from the Development Forum and £720 from Scottish Natural Heritage. Since then the advertising support from the local business community, which we appreciate very much, has kept us going.

Karen Runciman was our original Chair and John Connel has been a hard working editor from the start. For 1999-2000 Bill Walker was Chair.

The committee work hard to produce the newsletter as do the volunteers who distribute it. Unfortunately it has not been possible, so far, to get volunteers to deliver to the farms around Oxton. So if you do have some spare moments...

Lauder Common Riding at the Watering Stane – 1933.

No's 28 & 30 West High Street in earlier times.

Ex-Provost Jimmy Watson in his saddler's shop. Mr. Watson was a former Cornet of the town.

Lauder Smiddy early in the century.

Lauderdale Development Forum

At a Lauderdale Community Council meeting on Monday 15th May 1995 Trevor Burrows from the Borders Regional Council planning department asked the members of the Community Council if they would like to be one of the 12 areas in rural Scotland to become involved in a regeneration programme being organised by the Corrom Trust. According to their brochures the main objectives of their programme were to provide a framework for long term physical, social and economic regeneration in those rural communities where the need was greatest. After some discussion it was agreed to take the next step.

The next meeting was held in the Kirk Session House Lauder on Monday 19th June 1995. Present at the meeting were members of the Community Council, two representatives from the Corrom Trust, representatives from the Regional and District Councils, the Borders Tourist Board, Eildon Housing and the Local District Councillor.

The two representatives from the Corrom Trust gave a more detailed talk on the procedures involved and it was agreed to move on to the next stage of the programme; this was to be a half-day seminar in the Public Hall on Thursday 13th July between 12.30pm and 4.30pm.

People were invited to this meeting from all the local agencies, including the Community Council and local authorities and many more Lauder people. In the first part of the seminar, the Corrom Trust representatives gave a detailed talk on how they would carry out the first part of their programme of consultations. This would consist of an in-depth survey on the strengths and weaknesses in the infrastructure of the Community and also to get the opinions of the people. The second part of the seminar was conducted in small groups discussing what they saw as the problems facing the community, with one member reporting back to a question and answer session. The cost of the project was to be in two parts. The Corrom representatives then informed the meeting that the first part of the programme would be a preliminary study costing £9440 excluding VAT. The second part would be the main study costing £33,000 excluding VAT.

The Community Council then received a detailed report from the Corrom Trust on the seminar in which it was suggested that the Community Council respond within four weeks.

The Council decided to hold a public meeting to hear the views of the community. This meeting was held on Monday 18th September 1995 in the Public Hall. No representative from the Corrom Trust was present. It was a very well attended meeting and a full discussion took place. The final decision being that the Community Council should suspend for the time being the programme suggested by the Corrom Trust, and that the Council should set up a sub-group to carry out a survey of their own.

At the next meeting of the Community Council held on Monday 16th October 1995 four members of the Council were elected to form a committee with powers to co-opt. The members were Bill Walker (Chairman), Gerald Maitland-Carew, Rosemary McDougal and Grace Wheelans.

Their first meeting was held on Monday 6th November, at which it was decided to name the committee 'The Survey Sub Group' and to co-opt Trevor Burrows, George Megahy, Jim Sutherland, Liz Maddock and David Murray. The last three names being in the Channelkirk Community Council area as it was felt that the survey should cover the whole of Lauderdale.

During the course of subsequent meetings it was decided to draw up and implement a questionnaire, which would be sent to every household and that, it be designed that each person in the family from the age of eleven upwards would be able to participate. There were forty-one multiple-choice questions.

The subjects included housing, employment, education, countryside and environment, health and social services, emergency environmental and other services, retail services and other facilities, sport, social and entertainment, transport and highways, information and communications and local government. On the last page there was space for the families to write what they saw as the five main problems in Lauderdale and also the five main opportunities this presented. There was also space for any other comments. There was a request on each questionnaire that it be returned by 12th February 1996.

735 questionnaires were sent out and 351 were returned completed, of those over 70% had extra comments on the back page. At the same time, 38 organisations in the area were contacted and representatives from the survey sub-group attended meetings with 35 of them to remind the organisations about the survey and gather their ideas first hand. Two of the meetings were with the Primary Schools in Lauder and Oxton. There were also 38 businesses contacted to request their views - 18 responded.

The Community were fortunate to have had the help and support of Colour Box Miniatures and Lauderdale Engineering for the use of their computers and to Susan Sutherland, Grace Whellans, Andrew Burrows, Trevor Burrows and Jim Hunter for transferring all the information gathered onto discs.

A report was then produced entitled Lauderdale Appraisal "The Community Views". The report and an accompanying paper with the numbers and percentages of people who answered the questions was prepared and printed by the Borders Regional Council Planning Department, again in this the community had the unstinting help of Trevor Burrows, Lindsay Glasgow and Alison Clifton from that department. The hard work was now all completed. It had cost £632.56 of which Scottish Natural Heritage contributed £540.20. Lauderdale Community Council funded the remaining £92.36.

The next step was to hold a public meeting to discuss the report. This was done on Monday 29th April in Lauder Public Hall at which approximately 95 people were present. Copies of the report had been made available for some time before the meeting and were also available on the night. The chairman of the Survey Sub-

Group spoke to the report, then a general discussion took place. The main items identified were Sport/Social Facilities, Housing, Tourism, and Environmental Issues/ Public Rights of Way. The main issue was, without doubt, looking at the feasability of turning the old Colour Box factory at the Smiddy into some kind of Sport/Social facility. The other important issue seemed to be how the community could improve Lauderdale's appeal to tourists. The idea that the Avenue area be enlarged for parking and that a view and entrance to the Castle be created, found a lot of support. The question of housing received a good airing and it was hoped that the new estate proposed by Eildon would provide a good mix of housing and in particular it was suggested that the needs of the young single person should be catered for.

At the meeting of the Lauderdale Community Council on Monday 13th May 1996 Bill Walker proposed formally dissolving the Survey Sub-Group and this was agreed to. It was then agreed to form a new group to co-ordinate all the new initiatives and to take forward the concerns and ideas expressed by the community in the Lauderdale Appraisal, The Community's Views. This was approved and George Megahy was elected convenor to be assisted by Grace Whellans and Bill Walker. So the Lauderdale Development Forum was born.

At its inaugural meeting on Tuesday 28th May 1996 in Lauder Youth Trust Hall present were: George Megahy (Convenor), Irene Bonnar (Secretary), Grace Whellans (Treasurer), Trevor Burrows, Graeme Donald, Karen Runciman, Ogilvie Mathieson, Bill Walker and Bill Hardie.

At the Community Council meeting on Monday 10th June 1996 Gerald Maitland-Carew proposed that the Lauderdale Development Forum be considered a separate group from the Community Council. This was seconded by Rosemary McDougal and approved,

In the last six and a half years members of the Forum have been involved in helping to establish the wonderful new leisure centre which is the envy of many larger communities. Some have been involved in the very good work that the Initiative Group do to make Lauder more attractive.

The Forum has also been linked with the setting up of the very successful Lauderdale News newsletter, with After-School Care Club, with the planting of trees on the Common to celebrate the millennium, with the new Lauderdale Library in the old Smiddy courtesy of the Leisure Centre. There is a small group who continue to monitor local transport provisions. A few of these organisations have benefited from pump priming with initial cash injections from the Forum. So far there are only two initiatives that are proving difficult to progress, namely the Avenue area and the Lauder - Oxton Pathway. However, with determination and drive they will be overcome.

A public meeting was held by the Forum on 15th May 2000 in the Leisure Centre to see if there were any new initiatives that needed to be looked at. To help gather further information a form was inserted in the June edition of the Lauderdale News, with a very satisfying response and from those two sources six main issues were identified; Traffic and Parking, Public Transport, Crime Prevention, Walking and Cycling Routes, Teenager Activities and Tourism. Some of these are being actively tackled already.

The objectives of the Lauderdale Development Forum are:.

2.1 To promote the general good of the community in Lauderdale and to assist the work of statutory authorities and voluntary organisations engaged in advancing education, economic regeneration, furthering health and welfare.

2.2 To engage in the preservation, promotion and improvement of the environment, relieving poverty, sickness or distress and pursuing objective, which now or hereafter may be deemed by law to be charitable.

2.3 To promote and organise cooperation in the achievement of the above objectives and to that end bring together in the Forum representatives of the authorities and organisations engaged within Lauderdale in the furtherance of the above objectives or any of them.

2.4 To facilitate participation by all sections of the community in the development process and do all such things as may seen incidental or conducive to the attainment of the above.

Membership of the Forum as from AGM – 18 September 2000

Bill Walker	Nominated by Lauderdale CC	Convenor
Andrew Mercer	ditto	ditto
George Megahy	ditto	ditto
Graeme Donald	Nominated by	Leader Leisure Centre
Jean Landells	ditto	The Initiative Group
Wendy Perry	ditto	Newsletter Group
Frances Dickman	ditto	Channelkirk Community Council
Ruth Moir	ditto	After School Care Club
Eb Rooney	ditto	Lauder-Oxton Pathway Group
Ogilvie Mathieson	Representing Blainslie	
Joan Stevens	Representing Rural Transport	
Trevor Burrows	Co-opted as an individual	
Bill Hardie	Co-opted as an individual	

Bill Hardie Remembers

I was born in this house. My parents moved in here when they got married My father was a bootmaker and there was a shop with a workshop at the back. So I have lived all my life in Lauder.

I went to Lauder primary school when I was five. It has changed a lot since my day, then there were railings all around the outside and there were gates to get in. The railings were removed during the war to be melted down in order to build tanks and guns.

There were five teachers there; Miss Gill, Miss Kelly, Miss Bain, Miss Christie, Mr Wallace and the Schoolmaster Mr Harvey. Mr Wallace took what was called the Qualifying class. In my time you could stay on at Lauder and leave when you were fourteen. If you passed the 'qualy' you went to Duns. There was a prize giving ceremony at the end of term. Pupils got books as prizes for attendance and diligence and the Dux got a medal as well. It was called the Dickenson Medal.

We were always kicking a ball around in the playground and sometimes we played hopscotch or marbles. It was good for marbles for the playground was rough and soily not the smooth tarmacadam you have today. I remember that we started to play at rounders when Mr Harvey came, very keen on rounders was Mr Harvey. He also had gardening classes for the boys. We all had plots usually with an older boy and a younger sharing. I shared with George Runciman. The area where the plots were has now been either built on as part of the school or is part of the road.

When I travelled to School in Duns it could sometimes be quite exciting. I went by car to Earlston and then I got the train to Duns. At night we got away five minutes early to catch the west train to Earlston. At the same time there were people getting the east train to Berwickshire. When floods took away the railway line we had to travel by bus, it went by way of Westruther so it was quite a long journey. I remember one winter when we had no sooner arrived at school we were sent home again. We couldn't get the Westruther bus so we had to take the one to Greenlaw. On the way we met a bus coming the other way full of Canadian airmen based at Charterhall, and both buses got stuck in the snow. That was exciting when you were young. When I left the school I worked in my fathers shop for a while and then went into the Post Office. Working there you got to know most of the people and there were quite a few characters or 'Worthies' as we would call them back then. There was Dave Watson who did the creelings. On the day war broke out Dave opened the kirk doors in the middle of the service and shouted out, 'Air raid!!" Well, you can imagine that put paid to the service that day. Then there was

'Black Nancy' and her husband Jimmy Brown. She ran a lodging house for tramps. Folk said that she had been a tramp herself and that she had decided to settle down. But I don't know if that is true. Dick Kelly was the dustcart man. He collected the rubbish every day, well not Sunday, and took it to the dump. Refuse collection was taken over by the county in nineteen seventy five and the dump was closed. We have an awful lot more rubbish nowadays and its collected only once a week.

I became a Lauder town councillor in 1958. At that time Lauder was wee enough to be run by the Council without any committees. Later I became Dean of Guild and then a Baillie and then Provost. The council was made up of seven councillors, two Baillies and the Provost. I remember the Queen visited Lauder in 1956 when Bob Jolly was the Provost. Princess Anne has visited us twice recently.

I can remember the Maitland girls of Thirlestane castle. There was Lord and Lady Lauderdale, Captain Gerald's grandmother . She survived her husband for a good long time. The heir to the title Colin, was killed in the war.

There used to be a smiddy just across the road from this house. I can remember horses being shod there. In those days the blacksmith had to bend the metal and punch it into the shape of a horseshoe. Nowadays they are ready made and they shape the hoof to the shoe rather than the shoe to the hoof as they used to do. I remember watching Willie Turnbull, the blacksmith, bending the metal to make the trim for the carts. Sometimes carpenters would come over if they had to respoke a cart. There was always a fire on in the smiddy so it was nice and warm in the winter. Folks would gather there and that was when a lot of the local news was passed about.

Lauder Common

It would be useful to start by explaining the position and extent of the common. If we start in Edinburgh Road, immediately past the garage turn left into Whitlaw farm road, and then after passing the new Fire Station we reach a cattle grid, crossing the grid we found ourselves on Lauder Common. As we travel the boundary Trabroun and Whitlaw farms are on our right, and to the north. When we reach the western boundary we are then looking into the Parish of Stow, about half way along this western boundary we reach the watering stane on the road between Lauder and Stow. After reaching the Southern boundary which separates us from the farms of Allanshaws, Muircleugh and Woodheads, we reach the road from Lauder to Galashiels via Woodheads, the golf course being on the Southern boundary here but of course still part of the Common. We then follow the boundary along the road to the dyke behind the golf course club house, then follow the dyke along to the small gate on to the Common, we continue to follow the dyke from there down at right angles to the fence at the Burnmill, then follow this fence back to the Lauder Galashiels road, across the road and follow the verge up to the cemetery. From here we follow a dyke down to and across the Burnmill Burn for a short distance then back along to the road and across the road to the corner of the housing estate at Lauderdale drive. We now follow the boundary past this estate, past the old Manse Glebe and past the acres on the right then we turn sharp right up and over the hill to Lauder Hill across the Lauder to Stow road down and across to the cattle grid on the Whitlaw farm road and that is the boundary completed. Encompassed in that area are some 1700 acres of land.

If you read the various books and papers written about the history of Lauder and Lauderdale, and the sections on the common lands, you will find that the writers all agree on one point, and that is their inability to determine exactly when Lauder Common came into existence as a common.

In the booklet 'Lauder, it's Kirk & People' by the late Rev. Richard F. James, M.A. he suggests that these common lands were probably inherited from the days of our Guotodin forebears, some 2400 years ago. Also in a series of papers written by the late Robert Romanes, Harryburn, Lauder, and printed for private circulation in 1903, he states that, *"the history of Lauder provides, as we have said, a vista, extending over past centuries, wherethrough one may, in imagination, see the early inhabitants, smeared with lard and painted with ochre, loafing about on the banks of the Leader, when not engaged in hunting for food over the forests out of which the Common arose, and assembling in their families and tribes in their wattle huts and villages, prior to the time when the invasion of the Romans opened up the country and introduced the first seeds of civilisation; and thereafter settling down in their village community in the peaceful possession of their common lands"*. From 'Lauder and Lauderdale' by A. Thomson, printed in 1902, we have on Burgh Lands. *"As early as the thirteenth century, the inhabitants of Lauder owned arable land and meadow land. There is, however, difficulty in fixing a date for the initiation of the present Burgess system.*

It is the growth of century on century. The property of the Burgh is extensive and valuable, say 1700 acres. Individual owners are termed Burgesses. The holding is known as an "acre," though without reference to measurement. The name is derived from German acker, synonymous with ager (L), a field. In primitive times, the village-community – a brotherhood of self styled kinsmen – settled on a space of land. This may be called an adaptation of the Patriarchal Theory, which originated in separate families being held together by the authority and protection of the eldest valid male ascendant.

The Horde Theory, on the other hand, grew out of isolated families. Both theories are founded on the strongest of all instincts, common to even the lower animals, viz., love of their young offspring. It was stated by Sir Henry Maine, in a Parliamentary Return of 1870, that originally all land was held by the Community in common, but was under the management of the "Headsman" of the village. Headship or Leadership arose only from selection by the community. All were born alike, but all were not alike gifted.

Even the principle of trial by jury may be traced to this archaic source. The transference of ownership from the community to the individual may have been the process of many generations.

Gradually, individual members were allowed to break up portions of land apart from one another. This might have led to undue appropriation of land, and therefore the extent of each separate holding or tillage was fixed, while the *remainder was used in common for the pasturing of cattle. The principal of this arrangement is still maintained in so far as the management of the burgh lands is partly in the hands of the individual and partly in the hands of the Magistrates and Council.*

Lauder thus perpetuates the system of joint ownership by groups larger than the families, which is still common in India, especially in that earliest home of the Aryan race, the Punjab. In the realm of land ownership it is a self-governed village-community. Thus, further proof is borne that the early inhabitants of the town had not yielded to Roman influence, which had a tendency to cause the cultivating groups to take the manorial form. The ancient village-assembly closely resembled the Court Baron, held by the lord of the manor. The coincidence will appear from the following epigram, - Everything which the lord can do can be done by the council of village elders, or by the village-headman, -being responsible to the community."

Finally we quote, Professor Sir John Rankine K.C.

"There came the era when the only landowner was the community massed in a village by the chance of war, by necessity of mutual protection and the scarcity of food caused by increase of population. There was no such right as that of individual ownership in any part of the soil. In the breaking up of this system, first the house then the adjoining acre.......fell under absolute ownership, the rest remaining common, subject to the tillage of part at regular intervals by the families composing the community whose lots in these hill parts were fixed by cut and cavil".

These are the thoughts of a number of people who have researched the origins of Lauder Common, and as you can see from these few comments recorded here none seem able to say clearly when precisely the common became a Commonty.

They do all indicate though in their writings that they are of the opinion that there has been a Commonty in that place for a very long time.

What we do know for certain though is that Lauder had common lands on and before the 21st. December 1502, as shown in the Royal Charter granted to the Burgh on that date by James IV. We say on and before, as this Charter specifically states that it is replacing earlier charters that *"were destroyed and burnt by the ravages of wars, by fire, and otherwise"*. How many other charters and when they were granted is not known.

We are now at the start of the sixteenth century, when a number of books become available for the discerning reader. However, before we turn to the twentieth century there are a few more points to try to clarify.

That the title Burgess was in use at the start of the sixteenth century is not in doubt, as it is referred to in the Royal Charter, however when it was first used in that context in Lauder is again hidden in the mists of time. Incidentally the word Burgess is burgeis in old French or Bourgeois meaning in French, a French citizen; one of the mercantile or shopkeeping class.

This leads us then to the understanding that to be a Burgess a man (and remember only a man can be a burgess even today) must be of some standing in the community and have a certain amount of wealth. First of all he must buy an acre, then he must approach the Town Council and ask to be enroled as a Burgess, with the Council's approval he must then purchase a Burgess Ticket, the price of which has varied over the years, (having been as low as £10. at one time), he is now entitled to graze a number of cows and sheep on the common. He and the other Burgess are charged each year by the Town Council a set amount to cover the costs of the administration of the town's affairs. Apart from his own acre and the right to grazings on the common he was also entitled to part of the common to cultivate, the size of this area was dependant on the number of Burgesses entitled. There was never any more than 105 acres available, and no matter how many acres a burgess owned he was only entitled to graze and cultivate as one.

Every Burgess, was bound to attend the three head courts of the Burgh, held after the feast of St. Michael, Yule and Easter, and another imperative duty was that of "Watching the Burgh". An officer appointed by the Burgh went his nightly round, and with a stout staff struck the door of each house which was bound to provide a watchman for the night, who was expected to step forth, fully equipped with two weapons, ready to watch the Burgh, "wisely and busily from curfew to sunrise". One rather strange feature of the rather unique relationship between the Town Council and the Burgesses was that to be a Town Councillor you had first of all to be a Burgess. In fact, this situation remained until the Great Reform Act in 1869. The obvious result of the Act was that a greater number of non burgesses began to be elected to the Town Council, and then disagreements arose between the Council and the Burgesses. Unfortunately from then on a lot of money that could have been better spent improving the lot of the people of Lauder was wasted on litigation by both parties. In 1940 in Duns Sheriff Court at the last piece of litigation between the two parties Sheriff Burn-Murdoch concluded and hoped that "disputes about the Commonty have smouldered too long and it would enhance the dignity of the ancient and Royal Burgh if they could be satisfactorily ended", and in fact they were. Perhaps as a recognition of their weakened position, following the passing of the 1869 Act. The Burgesses and widows of Burgesses entered into a voluntary agreement for the common management of their cattle and sheep on the Commonty and for the division of the net profits amongst themselves. The Association thus formed remains known as the Lauderhill Sheep Company. This agreement is confirmed by a Town Council Meeting minute dated 8th. November 1878.

"Mr. Symington moved in terms of the motion given by him on 20th. September, that the Council should resign the charge of the herd of Cattle grazing on the Common, as well as the flock of sheep, which they have already resigned the charge of, and the hiring of the Shepherd and Cowherd; and all charge of the Flocks and Herds on the Common, from and after the 22nd. day of November curt., to the owners of the flock and herd, by a Committee to be appointed by them, or otherwise, reserving to the Council power to fix the stints, and to charge for the grass mail, such sums as the requirements of the Burgh may render necessary; which motion was seconded by W. Rae: and W. Henderson moved that no change be made on the existing system, & W. Henderson's motion, not having been seconded, & no other motion having been made, W. Symington's motion, was declared to be carried; and the Clerk was directed to send an extract from this portion of the Minute to Mr. Broomfield, who acts for the Committee of Burgesses in charge of the sheep on the Common."

It may be appropriate to mention at this point that a Burgess can not pass on his rights and privileges to any other person except his widow. Another very important aspect of the rights and privileges of a Burgess is that he must live within the bounds of the Royalty to be able to exercise those rights. There have been quite a number of occasions when people have been asked to remove their animals from the Common after moving outwith the Burgh, which they have done.

The last person asked to remove his stock from the common was Mr. John Middlemiss after he had moved to Wiselawmill, the following is a Minute of the meeting of Lauder Town Council dated 3rd October 1961, and it shows how amicably this problem was solved. *"The Town Clerk reported that he had been informed by Mr. John Middlemiss, that without making any admission that he is no longer entitled to grazing rights on the Common, he was arranging for his son, James, to apply for admission as a Burgess, and that it was proposed that the latter would take over his father's sheep stock at the end of this year, when Mr John Middlemiss would cease to exercise the right of grazing on the Common. This was noted."*

After 1975 and the changes in Local Government it was no longer possible to purchase a Burgess ticket therefore there are now only four people who hold Burgess Tickets. Also in 1975 Ettrick and Lauderdale District Council took over the administration of the Lauder Common and the Lauder Common Good Fund in accordance with the 1973 Local Government Scotland Act.

The District Council obviously found Lauder Common difficult to deal with and decided on drastic measures as is evident from the following extract:

General Purposes Committee – 3rd December, 1985
Private Business
Non-Delegated Matters

16 Lauder Comon

With reference to paragraph 13 of the Minute of Meeting of this Committee held on 17th January, 1984 there was submitted a further report by the Chief Executive on the legal position regarding Lauder Common, together with a report prepared by Messrs. John Sale & Partners, which concluded that if the Common were available for let by tender to a new single tenant a rent far in excess of that presently received from the Lauderhill Sheep Company under the existing formula could be expected. Such a lease of the Common would amount in law to "disposal" and accordingly the report recommended:-

(a)   that the Council agree in principle, that Lauder Common be disposed of by long-term lease; and

(b)   that, in pursuance of this decision, an application under Section 75(2) of the Local Government (Scotland) Act 1973 be presented to the Court of Session in order that the Council's entitlement to dispose of might be determined.

After discussion the Committee recommended approval of the recommendations contained in the report and it was agreed that a report on the outcome of the application to the Court of Session be submitted to this Committee whenever it was available whereupon further consideration could be given to the question of disposal of the Common.

It is not really very reassuring when these people say that disposal does not necessarily mean to sell, it does however mean that if you have the authority of the court to dispose then you have the authority to sell, then where would our Common Riding be.

Happily for some reason or another the District Council did not proceed to dispose of the Common, but what of Scottish Borders Council who took over administration of the Common in 1999, are they just waiting until there are no Burgesses left.

Lauder Common has been intertwined in the lives of the people of Lauder for many hundreds of years it would be very sad indeed if the present generation let it slip from their grasp by inactivity.

German field Gun

The photograph shows the carriage of a German field gun which lay at the top of the Burnmill Haugh in Lauder from the end of World War 1 to the start of World War II.

Locally known as the cannon, it was brought to Lauder as a relic of the Great War and was placed on Chester Hill near the sixth green on the golf course. This upset some young men, some just home from the war, and they went up one night and pushed it down through the whins and it ended up near the burn at the bottom. The barrel, about six feet long, broke off and was left half way up. Several of the party were summoned to appear at Duns Sheriff Court, among them Norman Murray, builder, Ecky Rutherford, grocer and John Middlemiss, farmer. They were fined 7/6d each for their part in the ploy.

Both pieces were removed for scrap about 1940 to help with the war effort.

Pictured playing on the gun carriage about 1937 are Jim and Dave Middlemiss with Bill Cranston and Aggie Shaw in charge.

German Field Gun.

Lauder Common Riding

Thomson, in his book "Lauder and Lauderdale" (1902) mentions the ancient origins of the Common Riding as involving Burgesses and supporters checking the boundary cairns marking Lauder Common. He makes no mention of the function of a "Cornet" and notes that the custom fell into disuse almost a hundred years before he was writing. The Reverend Dick James in his book "Lauder - Its Kirk and People" (1973) also refers to the cessation of the Common Riding in the early 1800s, brought about by order of the Town Council for reasons of public safety. (Excessive amounts of alcohol and galloping of horses down the High Street seemed to be involved.)

However, in 1911 there was a desire, as a way of marking the coronation of King George the Fifth, to resurrect the tradition and help was sought from Selkirk as to the best way of achieving this. Since then the ceremonial aspects of the Common Riding have remained unchanged up to the present day; including the annual election of a Cornet, the Kirking of the Cornet, the Night Afore the Morn Concert where the Cornet is presented with his commemorative cup, and the route taken round the town and the marches. The only thing which has altered from time to time is the actual date of the event. In ancient times, as mentioned by Thomson, this was Ascension Day. The present arrangement of the first Saturday in August was arrived at after the Second World War probably to accommodate the increasing number of town festivals being marked in the Borders.

Along with the main object of riding the marches a variety of other events has always been included to make a festive week in the Royal Burgh. Horse racing used to take place at the Castle Haugh and, later, on the Common above Greenwells, after the ride out. Foot racing also provided entertainment with the Professional Games held in the public park for many years until 1986. At the same time a gymkhana took place in the Castle Riggs. A public dance was always held on the night of the Cornet's election in May, and since 1931 another, organised by the ex-Cornets Association, following the mounted gathering at Threepwood crossroads with the Gala Braw Lad and Lass and their supporters. It is notable that the Lauder Cornet who inaugurated this gathering, Jimmy Shaw, celebrated the seventieth anniversary of the occasion aged 91 last year (2001) when the gathering was, at Lauder Town Hall due to the serious outbreak of foot and mouth disease that year. It was also from 1931 that the Cornet was required to choose a Cornet's Lass to accompany him at Threepwood and on other social occasions.

The organisation of the Common Riding and its associated events have always been the responsibility of the Common Riding Committee although up till the reorganisation of Local Government in 1975 the Provost, as civic head of the Royal Burgh, played an important part in the ceremonial of the day, as well as representing the Burgh at the festivities of other towns. These duties are now carried out by the Chairman of the Common Riding Committee

The other group which plays a large part in Common Riding affairs is the ex-Cornets Association. Since 1911 there have been seventy seven Lauder Cornets -

gaps having occurred during the two World Wars. It is a remarkable fact that in recent years the number of ex-Cornets meeting at the Waterin' Stane each Common Riding day has always exceeded forty! It is the ex-Cornets as a group who choose a suitable candidate for the position of Cornet each year and pass their recommendation to the Common Riding Committee. (Many ex-Cornets also serve on the Common Riding Committee.) A very popular event is the ex-Cornets' annual dinner on the Monday of Common Riding week.

There is also a Ladies Committee which does sterling work in many ways, both fund-rasing and promoting events during the week. The office bearers of this committee now sit on the parent Common Riding Committee.

Long and loyal service is a feature of the organisation of the Common Riding. Ex-Provost Bill Hardie served as chairman for twenty years; ex-Provost Jackie Scott served almost as long in the same role, and ex- Cornet Ian Brotherston for nine years. Recently retired treasurer George Dodds gave twenty one years to the job and present secretary Ian McLaren has now done twenty years. His predecessor Miss Ruby Strachan was in post for sixteen years. A glance at the list of ex-Cornets will show similar loyalties running through families, many of which have provided multiple Cornets.

The ancient and cherished tradition of the Common Riding today continues to contribute much to the life of the Royal Burgh, increasing the sense of pride and cohesiveness in its people, while at the same time providing a wonderful experience for each young man lucky enough to serve as Cornet.

List of Lauder Ex-Cornets

1911	H. P. Webster	1951	J. Mackison	1977	G. W. Masson
1912	W. Watson	1952	J. R Weatherley	1978	S. R. Gryczka
1913	I. White	1953	D. T. Middlemiss	1979	I. Middlemiss
1914	D. H. Watson	1954	J. A. Middlemiss	1980	R. J. R. Ker
1923	J. M. Graham	1955	R. B. Landells	1981	J. F. Threadgall
1924	C. O. Cant	1956	S. Threadgall	1982	R. A. Kerr
1925	J. M. Paterson	1957	D. S. Thomson	1983	S. Thomson
1926	G. Wilson	1958	A. D. Whellans	1984	J. C. McNeil
1927	T. Shaw	1959	D. M. Wilson	1985	R. E. Landells
1926	J. Nivison	1960	A. P. Turnbull	1986	P. F. Middlemiss
1929	T. H. Scott	1961	W. T. F. Brown	1987	A. Middiemiss
1930	J. Brodie	1962	J. D. Murray	1988	D. Wilkinson
1931	W. J. Shaw	1963	W. Middlemiss	1989	R. Wilkinson
1932	A. Brown	1964	D. S. Waldie	1990	A. Gilchrist
1933	R. T. Landells	1965	J. T. Brotherston	1991	J. Fairbairn
1934	J. Watson	1966	D. N. White	1992	A. Strangeways
1935	A. Brown	1967	I. H. W. G. Scott	1993	D. Wilson
1936	J. C. Delahunt	1968	C. G. A. McHutchon	1994	M. Middlemiss
1937	J. T. Robson	1969	I. W. M. Anderson	1995	R. Millar
1938	F. Tocher	1970	D. A. E. Elrick	1996	M. Bryson
1939	A. Landells	1971	G. I. Jones	1997	R. Wilson
1946	A. L. Thomson	1972	G. Threadgall	1998	S. Smith
1947	B. Redpath	1973	M. Johnston	1999	G. Gilder
1948	W. Johnston	1974	P. R. Riddell	2000	A. Crombie-Smith
1949	J. Johnston	1975	G. S. Riddell	2001	I. Fallas
1950	J. B. Dagg	1976	S. Threadgall	2002	D. Megahy

Lauder Common Riding returning to the Town Hall – 1920s.

Lauder Common Riding Platform Party – 1955.

Lauder Common Riding – Town Hall 1926.

Lauder Common Riding passing the Smiddy – 1928.

William Anderson Remembers

"I was born in 1917 at Middletown farm up the Gala Water road from Fountainhall. My parents were married in 1909 and had set up house in a cottage there, about a mile from the source of the Leader. That's where I was born. The farm was owned, at that time, by people named Steadman and my father was the shepherd there. Our cottage was about a mile up from the farm steading.

The nearest town was Stow and I started school in Fountainhall when I was six. It was a walk of four miles and I was too young to manage it at five so they waited till I was six. All the children from the farm walked down to school together. We left the Middletown farm cottage in 1924 and went right into Gala Water to Cathpair which marches with Lauder Hill on the Midlothian boundary. From there I went to Stow school and stayed there until I left just before my fourteenth birthday.

My first job was shawing turnips on a neighbouring farm. I was paid three pence for every hundred yards I did. After that I helped with the lambing at Corshope near Heriot. I was paid eight pounds for the eight weeks and I lodged with the shepherd's people. They must have thought I was alright because they took me back the next year, and I got a pay rise. In between times I did some shepherding at Blackadder Mains in Berwickshire. In 1933 my father took over the farm of Headshaw, from then on most of my life was spent in the Leader valley.

In 1937 I started to become involved with the Oxton Dog Trials. They were started by Andrew Brown of Rigside. He supplied the field and the sheep were from Longcroft and Tollishill. During the war they moved to a larger venue at Headshaw when we ran a sheep show along with it to make money for the Red Cross. They were held at Headshaw until 1971 and all the time the sheep came mostly from Tollishill. They were driven down by the shepherd, Willie Renwick. He would start out the day before and spend the night at Hillhouse. He arrived at Headshaw along with his dogs the next morning. They were held there till 1971 when my nephew thought he would plough up the field, so we ran out of that good field. By this time I was working for Andrew Sharp Harvest Limited and managing the farms of Carfrae, Kelphope and Tollishill, about six thousand acres in all. When I moved to Addinston in 1966, it was held there until 1982 when I left Addinston and went to Lauder Hill. With the exception of two years, when we had it at Bowerhouse, it has been held at Lauder Hill ever since.

It is held in a part of Lauder Hill known as "The Racecourse". It is a flat piece of land on the left hand side of the hill to the south of the grid going onto the Common. I read that this part of Lauder was known as " The Racecourse", because in the days after the Common Riding they used to have horse racing on it. It was long before my time, I know that.

Some of the really big names used to come to the trials. There was Johnny Wilson who twice won International Sheepdog Trials. Bobby Dalziel has won the international trials at least twice. Then there's Bobby Henderson from Heriot, he competes and he has been an International winner. We also had some very high-class judges such as the late George Brown who had also been an International winner. He was Andrew Brown's brother who started the trial here. Bill Merchant from Inverness has come and judged the trial quite a few times. He was often the man on the microphone at the Scottish National Sheepdog Trials and he announced the competitors as they came on. He came here through Jimmy Gilchrist and judged the trial when it was held at Headshaw. He's been a good friend of mine that man, because I got to know him through that trial.

I started work as sheep manager for the sheep company at Lauder Hill in 1944 and I am still there yet. When I started, it was war time and there were a lot of Polish soldiers training with tanks up in the hills. They just drove though all the stone walls and fences. It made it very difficult to get a shepherd to come and shepherd the sheep with the place in that state. The hill was all churned up by the tanks. We put up with it till the end of the war and wrote several letters to the War Department about it. Eventually we got a letter back telling us that if there were any complaints more about this common land, then they would just relieve us of the thing and take it over themselves. We thought we had better draw our horns in after that. I had to employ stone wall dykers to rebuild the dykes, though the War Department paid the Company the money for it. They also paid for tractors and excavators to level out the ground. We decided not to re-seed it as we hoped the heather would establish itself again, and it did. The heather landed its first roots because we kept it well burnt. We have now got the best managed heather moors in the Lammermoors because the heather is burnt in rotation and its good for the sheep. The march dykes were all complete, they were alright after the tanks. The sheep pens had all to be rebuilt, but that was paid for by the War Department.

Our first shepherd was Jackie McDonald, who was with me for two years, before he went to Gairsmuir. I was very fortunate with him because his dogs were so good, they could handle sheep on this open wilderness. That first year we had to take the sheep up to Whitlaw to be dipped. Some were dipped in the autumn and by the next year, we had kind of got the pens built up and rigged up the dippers or something. It was quite an ordeal. The next was Tom Young, he came in 1946 and stayed fourteen years. His lassies were brought up on Lauder Hill. We were fortunate that all these years we had first rate shepherds. Tom Aitchison came after that, he was quite a few years. Then there was Wattie Nichol, he was with me fourteen years until I retired. Aye, they were the very best of shepherds".

From the Scottish Farmer dated 21st September 2002

Scotland is noted for the loyalty and dedication of its farming community. However, not many can match the 'shift' put in by 85-year-old William Anderson of Woodlea, Haughhead Rd., Earlston, who this week handed in his notice as farm manager for the well-known Blackie outfit run by the Lauderhill Sheep Company after a stint of some 58years, which commenced in February 1944.

Clubs and Societies

Lauder After School Club

Lauder after school club opened In August 1998. A group of working parents whose children attended Lauder Primary School at the time planned and developed the club.

The club is managed by a committee of parents Mrs. J. Fox, Head Teacher at Lauder Primary School and all her staff support and assist the club. One of the club's benefits is that children do not have to leave the school premises to attend the club. The club runs every school day in the school hall from 2.45pm-6.00pm.

It is staffed by a co-ordinator and play leader allowing up to 16 pupils to attend. The service is flexible and the childcare provided can be full-time, part time or occasional depending on families needs. The club is open to any child from primary 1-primary 7.

As well as a variety of indoor activities and games the club is able to make use of the school play ground (weather permitting!), and can also access the public park for more adventurous play.

Over the years the club has organised various fund -raising events to allow the continued up-dating and extension of equipment and resources. The events have included, a jumble sale, family, ceilidh (shared with the P.T.A.) a sponsored walk, Christmas hamper raffle and a potted plant stall at a P.T.A. event The main focus of the fund raising events has always been to allow the children attending the club to be involved in the planning and organising of each event.

Lauder Amateur Dramatic Society

Harry McDonald tells us that as a young teenager he used to get piano lessons from Margaret Alchin in Lauder. One week, after lessons, following a visit by several of Lauder's youngsters to a festival of three one act plays in Selkirk, Harry had said to Margaret that it was a pity that Lauder did not have a Drama Club of its own. Margaret must have mentioned this conversation to her father, Willie, for in a very short time a meeting had been called to discuss the possibilities of forming a club. This first meeting was held on the 5th. June 1949, in Lauder Parish Church Hall. According to the rather old, and slightly tattered, minute book a committee was formed, consisting of a President: Mr. A. J. Holmes, Vice President: Willie Alchin, Secretary: Margaret Alchin. Treasurer: not known.

From the early minutes: *It was decided to begin rehearsals soon. The question was raised how to obtain funds for the Club. It was decided to approach the Educational Authority to obtain use of Lauder Primary School for meetings and to enquire if any grant was available for the encouragement of Amateur Dramatics.*

Meanwhile during the summer months we have permission to use this Hall on Wednesday evenings the charge being three shillings each meeting.

Wednesday 15th. June; Attendance twenty six. The second meeting of the L.A.D.C. was held in Lauder Parish Church hall on the 15th. June 1949. After reading the minutes of the previous meeting the President Mr. Holmes gave a resumé of the Committees efforts to obtain assistance from the Educational Officer. It was proposed that the Club remained independent. The question of a membership fee was raised and Mr. McDonald proposed that this be fixed at 2/6. per year seconded by Mr. Graham. It was decided to increase the Committee to five members and Miss Strachan was appointed.

The third meeting of the L.A.D.C. was held in Lauder Public School on 29th. Sept. 1949. Mr. Holmes opened the meeting and after the minutes of the previous meeting had been read, the President gave a short description of a recent visit paid by some of the members to a course of lectures held in the Academy Hall, Galashiels on the 11th. September. Mrs. M. Whellans was elected to the committee to fill the vacancy caused by the resignation of Miss Strachan. Mr. Spaven stage lighting expert of the Galashiels Dramateurs gave an interesting talk on stage management and lighting. Miss Spaven followed with a short talk general affairs connected with Amateur Dramatics.

The fourth meeting of the Lauder Amateur Dramatic Club (note it started out as a club), was held on the 6th. October, and it again met in the school, and continued to do so for quite some time. At this meeting the members taking part in the first production were given their scripts and the first readings were held.

Their first public appearance was at a Scottish Community Drama Association Festival in Selkirk on 31st. January 1950, where they performed a one act play "The Wee Comic" by John Donald Kelly. They did so as Lauder Amateur Dramatic Club.

Their next public appearance was in the spring of 1950 in the Public Hall Lauder where they performed three one act plays, as Lauder Amateur Dramatic Society. The Plays were: "Limericks" a farcical comedy by Christine Orr. "The Spider Ring" a drama by Mabel Constanduros and Howard Agg, and of course "The Wee Comic" By John Donald Kelly. It says a great deal about the members confidence and ability that they were prepared to enter a S.C.D.A Festival on their first venture on to the stage. The experience certainly did not deter them in any way, as they went from strength to strength, entering many more festivals in the succeeding years, and winning a fair number in the process.

We owe a great debt to those early pioneers of the L.A.D.S. who started what is now something of an institution in Lauder and we must also praise the members who have followed in their footsteps, who have given so much pleasure over the years to the people of Lauderdale. We know that it can not be easy at times to persuade new members to take part, especially with so many distractions these days, but we know that we speak for a lot of people when we say that we really do enjoy your productions.

Productions : -

1950 Three One Act Plays	1968 Ten Little Niggers	1985 Scarlet Ribbon
1951 Bachelors Are Bold	1969 See How They Run	1986 Two One Act Plays
1952 Two One Act Plays	1970 The Chiltern Hundreds	1987 Two One Act Plays
1953 The Ghost Train	1971 Pools Paradise	1988 Big Bad Mouse
1954 Flare Path	1972 White Sheep Of The Family	1989 Sailor Beware
1955 Two One Act Plays	1973 No production	1990 Cat On The Fiddle
1956 No production	1974 No production	1991 The Campbells Are Coming
1957 Pitfall	1975 Cat On The Fiddle	1992 Lucy For Some
1958 Two One Act Plays	1976 What's Cooking?	1993 On The Verge
1959 Rebecca	1977 Bonaventure	1994 Wedding Of The Year
1960 Doctor In The House	1978 Keep In A Cool Place	1995 A Tomb With A View
1961 Two One Act Plays	1979 I'll Get My Man	1996 Ski Whiz
1962 Love Is A Luxury	1980 Wild Goose Chase	1997 Cambusdonald Royal
1963 Reluctant Hero	1981 Shock Tactics	1998 Two One Act Plays
1964 Maiden Ladies	1982 Two One Act Plays	1999 No production
1965 Wanted One Body	1983 The House On The Cliff	2000 Kindly Keep It Covered
1966 Such Things Happen	1984 Breath of Spring	2001 Touch And Go
1967 Post Horn Gallop		

A very good record only four missed productions over all those years.

Lauder Amateur Dramatic Society. "Touch and Go" 2001.

Lauder Amateur Dramatic Society. "Johnny Jouk the Gibbet" 1958.

Lauderdale Amateur Horticultural Society

The first minutes are dated 1885.

Originally the committee seem to have met three times a year in the Black Bull Hotel. The annual show is held on the last Saturday in August and although the number of entries has recently declined the usual high standards have been retained.

There are now 9 hard working members of the committee this contrasts with ten years ago when Jim Fullerton was secretary, treasurer as well as being chairman.

Lauderdale Angling Association

The waters of The River Leader and its tributaries have always run clean and clear with a population of brown trout and grayling, supplemented during the winter months by a spawning run of salmon and sea-trout and Tweed brown trout which use the Leader to maintain the life cycle.

The Leader has long been a venue for sport fishing for trout, salmon being protected to ensure their continued existence, and although numbers are less than in the past, sizeable trout can still be found in the pools and riffles, living alongside the shoals of juvenile trout and salmon. For a few pounds a year anglers have access to over 20 miles of the Leader and its tributaries during the angling season which extends from 15th March to 5th October. This is all thanks to a few locals who met in Lauder Town Hall on 11 April 1906, namely Mr. George L. Broomfield (chair), Mr Bertram, Addiston (President), Mr Dickinson, Longcroft (vice- chairman) and Mr Scroggie (secretary and Treasurer) and members W. Brodie, G. H. Broomfield, Rev. Turner, Wm Wilson and George Aitken.

The committee approached Lord Lauderdale for permission to fish for trout in his waters, which was granted after consultation with those who had shooting interests on the water. Reports of illegal fishing led to the appointment of a "river watcher" at 20 shillings a week! His job lasted only two years as a lack of funds meant his departure in August 1908. Poaching was rife in these days as an extract from the minute book shows. It states that *"Alexander Knox and Adam White were found fishing by illegal means on 21 June 1908, taking trout. Their punishment being to forfeit their permits to fish and their crime was reported to the police".*

The first angling competition was also held this year, but no catch returns remain. In the same year the river was polluted by a septic tank overflowing from the Boondreigh water, the farmer was ordered to restock the river by the courts. The first record of a competition was in June 1936 when Mr. R Bruce won an evening competition with 7 1/2lb of trout and earned a new rod, with other prizes consisting of a jar of tobacco for the heaviest fish caught and a currant loaf for the heaviest half dozen. A full account of activities and personalities of the association can be found in the minute books now housed in the library in Lauder.

Lauder Bowling Club

At a meeting of the Lauder Town Council in February 1888 an area of 40 square yards in the Loan Park was set aside for a bowling club. It was conditional on a rent of ten shillings, which had to be paid to the Burgh every Martinmas. The following month a meeting was held to investigate ways of raising funds to start a bowling club. The Rev. W. Martin was given the fund raising responsibility and he estimated that it would require £10 to get the project off the ground.

Within a very short time he had gathered subscriptions totalling £146. A committee was formed and the Town Council gave permission to cut approximately 1600 square yards of turf from the Common to lay the green. The first match was played on Thursday 27th September 1888. The following April the first clubhouse was opened having cost the grand sum of £26 and 5 shillings. The latest clubhouse cost £54000.

Lauder Bowling Club – Opening Day 1932-33.

Lauder Bowling Club – Opening Day 1988.

As the membership grew, the club played in leagues and played for cups donated by members. In 1914 Lauder became a member of the Border Bowling Association and in 1922 was accepted into the Scottish Bowling Association. In 1924 Mr W. Sleigh, who was a Lauder boy, brought 3 rinks from Edinburgh Corporation to play. He later became Lord Provost of Edinburgh and was knighted. He presented the club with a silver cup, which is still played for today as the Lord Provost Sir W. L. Sleigh cup. During the war years the condition of the green had deteriorated so much that it had to be re-turfed. The cost of this was estimated at a considerable £585. Members were asked for interest free loans and a sale of work was held. So successful was this fund raising that, after much hard work, the new green was opened by Provost J. Watson on the 30th June 1945. During local government reorganisation in 1975, one of the last acts of Lauder Town Council was to convey Lauder Bowling Club to the members without any transfer of money. In 1979, the original clubhouse was replaced with a larger one. The following year the club applied for a licence, which was granted in May 1980. In 1988 the club celebrated its centenary with a dinner dance held in the Public Hall. In 1996 it was decided to build a new clubhouse with all the latest equipment. Members worked hard to raise the funds and they even constructed the building itself under the supervision of two experienced builder members. In June 1997 the clubhouse was officially opened by the President of the Scottish Bowling Association, Mr J. Renwick of Hawick

At the present time the club has about 90 members. Current subscriptions are £45 compared to the 3/6d in 1888. The club has produced a number of champion players and has been represented in the Scottish finals in Ayr, most recently in 1999. Lady members have played a huge part in the running of the club. In 1993-94 Mrs N. A. Turnbull was President of the club.

Lauderdale Curling Club

It is the oldest associated club in Berwickshire having been constituted in 1850 with 20 members.

On the 6th April 1850 a petition was presented to the Lauder Town Council requesting a part of the Burgh ground for the construction of a pond. The council was asked to, "..encourage the club, got up for the promotion of this truly national pastime, and which they hope will enhance the health and happiness of all those who may join it".

Part of the Calfward park was given free of charge and a pond was built. A few years later a skating pond was made with a path separating the two. Two years later the club became a member of The Royal Caledonian Curling Club. In 1855 a wooden clubhouse was built for the protection of the stones, but in 1890 it was replaced by a larger stone built building. In 1902 the club had fifty members. The records have been lost after this date and it appears that sometime between 1903 and the 1930s the club ceased to function. We do know that Lauder youngsters were skating on the pond in the 1930s and 40s. The Calfward park is now partially covered by the old rubbish dump at the Burnmill which also engulfed the two ponds. A footbridge was constructed over the Burnmill Burn and there is still a right-of-way passing the east side of Millburn Park housing estate and entering Factors Park beside the house newly built on the site of the old Territorial Hall.

Lauderdale Curling Club – Winners of Border Province Challenge Trophy 17th January 1903. The Club didn't win this trophy again until 2003.

Lauderdale Curling Club at Kelso Ice Rink 2002.

On the 25th July 1950 a meeting was held in the Carfraemill Hotel. The original aim of the meeting had been to revive the defunct Heriot Club, which had disbanded some years before and many of whose ex-members now played at Stow, which was becoming too big. At the meeting however, it was decided to name the club the Lauderdale Curling Club. Exactly one hundred years after it was founded the club had been reborn.

The club curled at Haymarket in the early years with limited success. In 1956 there was great excitement when they won their first trophy. The club started to curl at the Kelso Ice rink from the season 1964-65. The following year the club won the first Border Bonspiel at Kelso.

The victorious rinks at the Borders Bonspiel of 1965, were;

Frank Wilson (skip), Willie Sharp, Jessie Wilson and Joyce Sharp.

Allan Forrest (skip), Frank Forrest, Jack Dun and Bob Bennett.

At that time the club played in most of the local competitions; the Border League, Berwickshire Kettle and the Laidlaw, with several successes. Jack Dun passed on the secretaryship to Mrs. Obie Sharp in 1972.

In the year 2000 the office bearers were:

President: Jean Ker   Vice-President: Ogilvie Mathieson
Secretary: Elaine Robertson Treasurer: Jill Ledingham

Lauder & Oxton District Rifle Club

The Lauder & Oxton District Rifle Club was founded on the 15th December 1944 by the local branches of the Home Guard. In those days the club was called The Lauder & Oxton Home Guard Rifle Club, and membership was limited to members of the Home Guard.

The founding members were:-

President	Major Graham Munro
Secretary & Treasurer	Mr W Stevenson
Committee	Messrs. Cranston, Dobson, Nelson, McKerrow, Leeming and Blashnee.

The Club in those days, shot on Tuesday and Thursday evenings on outdoor ranges at Braefoot, Oxton and the Chesters, Lauder. The cost of ammunition was 3d for 10 rounds and a target cost the princely sum of 1d.

In 1945 the Club was opened to members of the armed services and civil defence, the membership fee being set at 2/6d per annum. In November 1946 it was decided that any person over 15 could become a member.

After some time spent trying to find premises, 1946 was the year that the club acquired their first indoor 25 yards range, this being donated to the club by the Earl of Lauderdale and located in the loft of the Castle Stables. The members spent a good deal of their time in early 1947 converting the loft into a rifle range, and negotiating a suitable electricity supply from Southern Electric Company at a cost of 4 1/2d per unit.

1948 was quite a memorable year for the members, as this was the year the club acquired the use of the Eagle Haugh within Thirlestane Castle grounds as their outdoor range. The Countess of Lauderdale officially opened the range by firing the first shot. The club also received two trophies that year, one from the Earl of Lauderdale and the other from Major Munro.

In July 1955 the name of the club became Lauder & Oxton District Rifle Club following instructions from the T.A.A. that all clubs using Home Guard in their title, must stop doing so.

In December 1957 Mr W. Stevenson was awarded the N.S.R.A. (National Small Bore Rifle Association) Medal and bar for more than 10 years service to the sport, in his capacity of Secretary and Treasurer.

At the beginning of 1970 the club moved from their old range at the Castle Stables (no doubt with a little regret, when one listens to them reminiscing about the loft) to the range within the Territorial Hall in Factors Park. In 1979 Mr W Stevenson retired from his post as Secretary & Treasurer after 35 years of loyal service to the club. The members presented him with a clock suitably inscribed, as a small token of their heart-felt appreciation.

In March 1994 the Territorial Auxiliary Volunteer Reserve Association (TAVRA) closed the Range down and that meant that the Club had no range of their own. However, Selkirk Rifle Club came to their rescue and now the Lauder & Oxton Rifle Club shoots every Friday night on the Selkirk Range. In 2002 the annual membership fee is £35.

Lauder & Oxton Club had the honour of hosting the Scottish National Meeting on their outdoor range in 1986, 1989, 1992, 1995 and 2002. The N.S.R.A. Centenary Meeting in 2001 had to be cancelled due to Foot and Mouth Outbreak, but this

Meeting was rescheduled in 2002. At each of these meetings 300-400 competitors and their families made their way to spend a week in the Scottish Borders.

Lauder Ex. Cornets Association

The Association was restarted in 1911 after being defunct for a number of years.

The association elect a Cornet and forward his name for approval to the Common Riding Committee. The earliest extant minutes are from 1946. The Association links with its sister association in Galashiels to hold the Threepwood Night. It is now held on the last Friday evening in May, having previously been held on the last Wednesday in May. A group of horses led by the Cornet makes its way to Threepwood where they meet with a similar group led by the Gala Braw Lad and Lass. Medals and speeches are exchanged and then all ride back to Lauder where a Cornet's Reel Dance is held outside the Town Hall. On the Common Riding morning the Association has a private breakfast in the Lauderdale Hotel. They then march down the High street behind the Silver Band before taking up their duties for the morning. The ex-cornets gather at the Waterin' Stane where toasts are made including ex. Cornet G.Masson's quaich and a rendition of 'Jeanie's Black Ee' is sung

You can only become a member after being the Lauder Cornet. There are between 30 and 40 ex-Cornets who gather together each year.

Football in Lauder

Enquiries have shown that football has been played in the Burgh for over 120 years. An extract from a Town Council meeting of the 14th November 1881 reads *"The Clerk read a letter from Mr Laidlaw, asking the use of the field next to Mr Broomfield's house for the purpose of playing football during the winter months, and the Council unanimously granted the use of the field if the Club got the consent of the Tenant."* It would appear that the piece of ground in question would be in an area around the bowling green. At a further meeting, on the 6th of March 1882, on the motion of Mr Aikman, the Council unanimously agreed to allowing the curling pond in the Calfward Park being extended westwards as to afford space for skating and sliding and the remit to Mr Aikman to grant the permission authorised, *"when arrangements are made to do what is necessary without putting the town to any expense in any way and at seasons to do as little harm as possible".* A reservation as to the above to be put into the articles of let. Also inserted in the conditions was a clause that the Football Club be entitled to use the Loan Park for their games between the 1st of December and the 1st of March.

The next information we have is a minute of a Town Council meeting on the 30th of October 1893. The Chief Magistrate reported that he had received an application from the Football Club to be allowed to play on Mustruther. Bailie Symington moved that the request be not granted which motion was seconded by Mr Murray. Mr Moore moved that the application be granted for the period till the end of March on the footing that the Club arrange with the Tenant; seconded by Mr Bain. Three voted Mr Moore's motion, four voted Mr Bailie

Symington's motion, one declined to vote and the application was refused accordingly.

Whilst football was played through the early part of last century, little written evidence can be found. During the mid thirties Mr D. Harvey, being a keen supporter of the then football team, wrote reports for the local press. The following is an extract from his note book.

24th Nov 1934
Border Juvenile League.
Gala Red Triangle V Lauder Leadervale.

Lauder Leadervale still keep top place in the Border Juvenile League by defeating Gala Red Triangle at Gala on Saturday.

Brisk play ruled in this game in the opening minutes, and Riddle gave the Vale the lead from a nice pass by R. Landells. Gala retaliated but failed badly in front of goal, and soon the Vale went further ahead, R. Landells being the marksman this time. Gala made determined efforts to reduce the lead but the backs held firm, Lothian especially standing the vale in good stead during the period of stress.

The second half opened with a rush by the Vale forwards and Riddle struck the post when he had a great chance to put the vale further ahead. The Gala left wing had a fine understanding and carried play into the Vale half and reduced the lead, through a great drive by the Gala right half.

End to end play followed now and Baird sent in a nice header which was tipped over the bar. But Riddle scored the Vale third goal, the Goalkeeper this time having to retrieve the ball from high up in the net. Both teams played hard right up to the final whistle but no further scoring took place.

Mr H. Kerr Referee.

Team. *Cumming, Redpath, Lothian, A Landells, D Harvey, Brown, R Whellans, J Landells, R Landells, Baird and Riddle.*

The next mention of the Football Club comes from an extraction of Council Minutes dated 7th June 1949 and it quotes *"A letter from Mr Thos. O.B. Wilson, Secretary of the Lauder Leadervale Amateur Football Club, dated 27th May, intimating that the Club had been reformed and enquiring to what extent the Town Council were prepared to carry out grass-cutting and general maintenance of the playing field at the public park. The Town Clerk was instructed to reply that the Council will undertake the cutting of the grass as often as they think necessary but if the Football Club decided that additional cutting was desirable it would require to be done at the Club's expense."* The park in question is the Public Park as we know it today. A further meeting of the Town Council on the 28th of July 1949 states permission was granted to the Lauder Leadervale Amateur Football Club to use the football pitch at the Public Park for all home fixtures during the coming playing season and to mark the field in regulation style.

The Public Park was now being recognised as an excellent facility for playing football. This led to the Border Amateur Football Association requesting permission from the Town Council to use the Park for the final of the Dudley Cup on the 29th of April 1950 and to take a collection at the match.

The Lauder Leadervale Football Club disbanded in the early Sixties, therefore for a period of a few years in the Sixties there was no Football Club in the town. The present Club, Lauder Amateur Football Club, was formed in 1967. In 1968 the Football Club purchased the Library, 48 West High Street, from the Town Council and Trustees and converted it into meeting and changing rooms. These premises were used as clubrooms until the Ettrick and Lauderdale District Council, in 1980, bought and renovated Woodcote House to be used as a clubhouse, adjacent to the park The new clubhouse was officially opened by the Manager of The Heart of Midlothian Football Club Mr Bobby Moncur prior to a friendly match against a Hearts eleven on Sunday 28th September 1980.

During season 69/70 Lauder AFC were successful in winning the South of Scotland cup, an achievement unequalled by any Lauder team since.

The committee of the Football Club invited the ex-Hearts footballer Mr Jim Jefferies, who lived in the town, to become team manager for the new season 1986/87. He accepted and had a successful spell as manager. This didn't go unnoticed and before long was moving on to bigger and better things which cumulated in being the manager of The Heart of Midlothian when they won the Scottish cup in 1998. The club are at present competing in the Border Amateur "B" division and also have a healthy junior section representing the Town at various age groups.

Lauder Football Club – Winners of Border League under-18s sections 1972.

Lauder Football Team 1996.

Lauder Golf Club

There is some doubt as to when the Club was actually first formed. Until quite recently it had been believed that the first record of any mention of the Golf Club had been in a minute of the Town Council of 31st. March 1896. However, further research has shown that the following minute appears in a meeting of the Town Council of 17th. July 1885:-

> *"The Clerk read a letter from Mr. Laidlaw, Lauder, asking the Town Council to grant permission to the Golf Club to play golf on the Chester Hill, which was granted unanimously."*

What happened to that earlier Club? Why did they stop playing on Chester Hill? Why, in 1896, did Provost Moore recommend to the Council that they be allowed to play on Lauder Hill, and to improve the ground for that purpose? Why, in 1897, did Provost Moore bring before the Council an application by certain of the inhabitants who proposed to form a Golf Course once again on Chester Hill? Intriguing questions, however the answers may be quite simple, it may be that the first attempt at forming a Golf Club in 1885 failed.

The initial layout of the course was supervised by Mr. Willie Park, Jnr., British Open Champion 1887 and 1889. The professional course record of 70 is held by him and has stood since 1905.

Minute of Lauder Town Council 2nd. April 1901:-

> *"Permission was given to the Lauder Golf Club to put up a shelter house on the Course."*

An extract from A. Thomson's Lauder and Lauderdale states that:-

> *"This Club was formed in 1896. The course is on Chester Hill. Everything is being done to make it attractive. The situation itself is bracing, and the view from the Hill is charming, especially looking towards Thirlestane Castle on the way home to the "new" green. Some of the holes are "short." The "approach"*

in most cases is too easy. But these are faults capable of correction without very great expense. The Club, which has already a membership of 42, has entered into the spirit of the game with enthusiasm. "Players are ever ready to welcome "visitors," and to take them in. Mr. J. Logan of Birkhill is Captain of the Club, and Mr J. H. Scroggie, Chemist, is Secretary and Treasurer."

Minute of Meeting Town Council 2nd. February 1909:-

"An application by Lauder Golf Club for permission to put up a tool house was considered and permission granted."

At a meeting of Lauder Town Council on 7th. February 1911, there was a letter from Lauder Golf Club seeking permission to build a Clubhouse at the Golf Course. Plans were submitted showing the layout and design and also asking permission to alter the entrance to the Course. Permission was granted on both counts.

After the building of the Clubhouse there seems to have been a relatively quiet period in the life of the Club, until in 1936 when the Town Council was asked to takeover the Management of the Club. This was, perhaps, due to the depression, and the fact that there was a considerable decline in the Lauder population at this time.

From a Town Council minute of 7th. May 1940 we find that, John F. Robson was appointed Green Keeper on a wage of £2:5/- per week. He was appointed on a weekly basis only, as he could be called up to the forces at anytime. He was, as he ceased duties on 3rd. August 1940. Perhaps this was when the Course went into recession, so to speak.

After what seems to have been a ten year rest we find a letter dated 9th. May 1950 from the Lauderdale Golf Club to the Town Council asking for permission to carry out an experiment, consisting of burning clumps of rushes and some cutting of grass to ascertain if the course could be put in playing condition. Permission was granted.

Next was a letter from Mr. J. D. Clark Solicitor Duns, to the Town Council at a meeting on 6th. July 1954 asking the council to let the Golf Course to a client of his. The Council agreed to let the Course for a sum of £5. per annum on a lease of 20 years with a break at 10 years. A letter from Mr. J. D. Clark Duns, to the Town Council at a meeting on 1st. February 1955, stated that if his client could not obtain full grazing rights on the Golf Course he would not be interested in taking it over as a Golf Course. The Clerk was asked to repeat an explanation of the position, ie. The Golf Course being part of the Lauder Common the Burgesses already had the grazing rights.

Town Council meeting 3rd. June 1958.

'An enquiry had been received from a Mr. G. M. Brydone Edinburgh, regarding leasing the Golf Course and Club House. It was agreed to inform Mr. Brydone that the Council were prepared to lease the Golf Course and Club house to him for an annual rent of £5, subject to the grazing rights of the Burgesses'.

Town Council meeting 7th. June 1960.

'It was agreed to hold an informal meeting of the Council to consider the reinstatement of the Golf Course, at the Golf Pavilion on Tuesday 14th. instant, at 7.30 P.M.'

Town Council meeting 6th. July 1960.

'It was reported that the informal meeting had taken place on the 17th. instead of the 14th. June due to inclement weather. A number of suggestions were made and it was agreed to approach Mr. A. T. Harrison, Superintendent of Parks, Edinburgh City Council, about the loan of gang mowers for cutting the course, and about the price of various types of mowers to be obtained.'

Town Council meeting 26th. July 1960.

"There was read a letter dated 14th. instant, from Mr J. H. Scroggie, 116 Greenbank Crescent, Edinburgh 10, to the Town Clerk, stating that he had come to know that the question of re-opening the Golf Course was being considered, and that a number of years ago he had indicated that he would very much like to help financially if the Town Council should decide to put the course in order again."

"Mr. Scroggie further stated in his letter that his offer of financial assistance was still open and that he was prepared to contribute the sum of £500. towards the re-starting of the Golf Course in memory of his father who, he understood was one of the founder members of the Lauder Golf Club in 1896 and who was Secretary and Treasurer until he retired and left Lauder for Edinburgh. Before parting with the money, Mr. Scroggie added that he would like to require assurances that the venture has the backing of the Town Council and that it was placed on a sound and permanent footing. The warmest appreciation was expressed of Mr. Scroggie's most generous offer of support."

"There was also read a letter dated 19th. instant from Mr. A. T. Harrison, Superintendent of Parks, Edinburgh, stating that whilst he had not had an opportunity to examine the conditions prevailing at the Golf Course, he would recommend that his department lend a Hayter Rotary Cutter for the initial cut. Thereafter they might consider letting the Council have at very small cost, three of his departments old gang mowers which were being replaced. Mr. Harrison considered that it would probably be better that he inspect the course first and he would endeavour to come to Lauder for this purpose sometime during early August."

Town Council Meeting 6th. September 1960.

"It was reported that Mr.A.T.Harrison had inspected the Golf Course on 18th. August, along with his assistant Mr. Ford, when Dean of Guild Hardie, Councillor Gilbert Mitchell and the Town Clerk had been present. It had been arranged to inform Mr. Harrison when the Council's tractor would be available for grass cutting on the course, when he would arrange for a Hayter Rotary Mower being sent on loan for the initial work. Mr. Harrison had indicated that a set of three gang mowers which were being disposed of by his Department would be available for purchase at a cost of £15. and it was agreed that these should be purchased."

Town Council Meeting 9th. May 1961.

"It was resolved that notices should be posted up inviting applications for the position of Greenkeeper at the Golf Course, the wage to be at current Joint Industrial Council Rates."

Town Council Meeting 7th. November 1961.

"The Town Clerk reported that Mr. George Scott, had commenced work at the Golf Course on Monday, 23rd. October 1961."

Town Council Meeting 8th. May 1962.

"It was decided that when the Golf Course was opened for play, the charges for the current year to 15th. May 1963 would be as follows:- 3s. per day (Sundays 5s.) 10s.per week 30s. for period to 15th. May 1963. Youths under 18 years 10s."

Town Council Meeting 3rd. July 1962.

"It was agreed that the official re-opening of the Golf Course should take place as soon as it could be arranged, Wednesday, 11th. Instant, being suggested as a provisional date. It was unanimously agreed that Mr. J. H. Scroggie, C.T.E., O.B.E., should be asked to perform the opening ceremony, and that an exhibition match should also be organised."

Town Council Meeting 11th. May 1971.

"Permission was granted for secondary pupils from Earlston High School, approximately eight in number, to receive golf instruction at the Golf Course on Friday afternoons without charge."

"It was agreed that the annual charge for persons under the age of sixteen years playing golf at the Golf Course should be 50p."

With the approach of 1975 and the drastic changes to the form of Local Government, Lauder Town Council's management of the Lauder Golf Course was coming to an end, the management being handed over to the incoming Ettrick and Lauderdale District Council.

However, the membership was growing and the members were becoming restless with the situation, several plans were put to a vote by the membership, but narrowly defeated. In the early part of 1991 the Club again began serious discussions with the District Council, and at an Extraordinary General Meeting in April, held in the Public Hall, in an overwhelming vote of 81 for and 4 against, the committee were able to finalise their discussions with the Council. This meant that in June of that year the members of Lauder Golf Club were able to take over and run their own course again.

Since then the Club has celebrated its centenary, which was apparently a very successful one for the Club. The Club has gone from strength to strength, continually making improvements to both the course and to their equipment. In the year 2000 the club were able to carry out a major innovation by installing a simple watering system, the great benefit of this will be their ability to have a consistent water supply to the greens during dry spells of weather.

The Office Bearers during the year 2000 were.

Gents		Ladies	
Captain:	Mr. R. Wilkinson	Captain:	Mrs. C. Hughes
Vice Captain:	Mr. E. Forsyth	Vice Captain:	Mrs. J. Kerr
Hon Sec/Treas.:	Mr. D. Dickson	Secretary:	Mrs. L. Wilkinson
Assist. Secretary:	Mr. R.Towers	Treasurer:	Mrs. C. McGee
Comp. Secretary:	Mr. M. D. Smith	Handicap Sec.:	Mrs. M. Houston
Green Convenor:	Mr. I. Scott	Comm. Members:	Mrs. A. Thomson
			Mrs. J. Moffat
		Junior Organiser:	Mrs. M. Houston

The opening foursome with Mr. Scroggie on the day Lauder Golf Course was re-opened.

Lauder Golf Club Elderly Gentlemen's Golfing Society 2002.

Lauder Guides

Guiding in Lauder has spanned decades with numerous local volunteers enabling girls (aged 10-16 years) from Lauder and neighbouring farms and villages such as Blainslie, Oxton and Westruther to enjoy the thrills, excitement and challenges that the Guide movement represents.

Having been known as the girl guides for many years, in 1989 the movement was renamed The Girl Guide Association (Scotland). The whole movement undertook major changes with uniforms being updated by well-known designer Jeff Banks. The promise badge changed shape, the promise and the laws were reworded and there were changes in the programme itself. It was at this time that I took over the running of the unit, undertaking to ensure that Lauder kept up to date with the changes. With the help of the then Colourbox factory, the girls involved in the unit at the time stuffed envelopes to raise money to buy neckerchiefs, sashes, handbooks and badge books.

For many years now, the girls have enjoyed the challenges and activities offered by the guide programme, and have in particular shared my love of the outdoors, with most taking part in at least one camp each year. The girls enjoyed taking part in joint camps with other Guide units and at least three Guides enjoyed the challenge and camaraderie of International Camp – with more than 800 Guides from all over the world, some as far afield as The Bahamas, New Zealand and Japan. I myself was able and proud to take part in 4 International Camps, 2 in Scotland, 1 in Wales and 1 in Ireland.

Badges came and went, and many new Brownies joined the unit, feeding up from 1st Lauder Brownies. Everyone seemed to enjoy the three year cycle of "adventurous" activities such as skiing, snowboarding, rock climbing, abseiling, trampolining, swimming and ice skating (one group of Guides even became enrolled during a fire drill whilst at the ice rink!). It is amazing to see the change in a 10 year old – welcoming her to the Guide Unit on her first apprehensive night, helping her feel her way through the Guide programme and seeing her leave with the confidence and knowledge gained from their time in Guides. Some stayed only a few months, while others stayed for years – one in particular stayed for nine years, and that must say something for the Guide Movement!

As a unit we have tried hard over the years to work in harmony with the community by ensuring the Guides took part in important aspect, such as Remembrance Sunday Parade and Thinking Day services at church in February. In 1998, Lauder Guides decided to go "big" and attempt to be Santa – we started the Guide Christmas Post – the first year we delivered almost 800 cards – over the next few years the number of cards delivered steadily grew and in 2001 we delivered an amazing 2521 cards – not bad going for 20 Guides and 1 Guider to deal with! As another Community activity the unit experimented with running a soup kitchen immediately after the Remembrance Sunday Parade, the first year was slow, but the word had obviously got out – home made soup after a cold march – meant that the soup was sold out the following year.

A new and updated Guide programme was launched with a UK wide advertising campaign in 2001/2002 with it came Go-for-it's, Unit Guidelines and more freedom for the girls to make their own decisions and plan what they wanted to do. This was exactly what the girls wanted and needed – Guiding was keeping up with the times, and is always growing with the girls requirements. It has been fantastic to see Guiding go from strength to strength in Lauder over the years and I have enjoyed each and every meeting over the 13 years I was involved with the Unit. I am proud to have been involved with 1st Lauder Guides, and hope that they continue to go from strength to strength.

Elspeth Boland
Lauder Guide Guider
1989-2002

Lauder Guides with the Black Bull Charabanc 1920s.

Lauder Guides 2003.

Lauderdale Hunt

In 1889 Charles and Joseph Scott-Plummer of Sunderland Hall formed a pack of hounds which they kennelled at their home. In 1910 their pack was bought by Lt. Col. A. Mitchell and Maj. A. Paton. The hounds were then moved to Maj. Paton's kennels at St. Boswells.

This was still a privately owned pack. When the hounds were meeting north of Stow the Colonel would load hounds and staff on the train at St. Boswells and transport them to Fountainhall, returning home again after the meet by the same way.

It was at this stage the hunt became known as the Lauderdale Hunt.

In 1930 Col. Mitchell took a lease at Thirlestane Castle stables and moved the hounds there. In 1935 at the point-to-point meeting at Blainslie Col. Mitchell's sons presented the hounds to the country.

1940 and the hounds again moved, this time to Threepwood, home of the new master, Mr. A. Cunningham. During World War II Mr. Cunningham kept a nucleus of hounds to enable the Hunt to restart after the war.

In 1947 the Hunt became a subscription pack. Trustees were appointed and a constitution drawn up. Previously only landowners had subscribed.

Trabroun was bought in 1951. The money was raised by donations from members and from the sale of shares left to the Hunt by Col. Mitchell. The Hunt continues at Trabroun until the present day.

The longest serving employee was Will White, who retired in 1971 after some 53 years service.

Lauderdale Hunt Supporters Club

It was decided at a meeting in the Black Bull Hotel on the 20th February 1967 to form a Hunt Supporters Club.

The first fundraiser was a dance held in the Black Bull Hotel in June 1967. A second dance was arranged for the following December but had to be cancelled due to an outbreak of foot and mouth disease. We now hold about six fundraisers in a year, one of which donates all proceeds to charity. In a good year we can hand over £5000 to the Hunt.

In its first year there were 97 paid members. The longest serving committee member is Mrs Irene Griffiths from Blythe. She was originally elected to the committee in June 1976.

Lauderdale Limpers Running Club

Founded in November 1997, its aims are to promote the sport of running and provide a focus for members to have the support of others for competition, fitness and health.

Despite its short history, club members have competed in such diverse events as: the New York Marathon, the Earlston Black Hill Race, the Edinburgh New Year's

Day Triathlon and the Wild Nan Endurance Race in Wolverhampton. They have also competed in many local races and fun runs.

Our own events include; The Mad March race, a four mile race within the Burgh, The Christmas Handicap, a three mile sprint around all the 30 mile an hour signs in the village, The Two Pubs Race, a five mile cross country run between The Lauderdale Hotel and The Tower Hotel in Oxton. In 2000 we held our first Cross Country event for adults and children on Lauder Common. Our biggest event is The Thirlestane Castle Run held in the Castle grounds. In October 2000, the second year it was held, it attracted over 300 runners and raised a four figure sum for charity as well as lesser amounts for other local groups. It is now a firm fixture in the national running calendar.

Club membership is free and open to all, young and old. There are currently around 30 members. While all members have achieved impressive personal goals, notable members include; John Wilkinson, former Scottish Hill Running Champion, Gary Gardiner, multiple medal winner at various games for disabled athletes and George Runciman, a sub- 3 hour marathon runner.

A group of Lauderdale Limpers Running Club 2002.

Lodge St. Luke No 132 Lauder from 1901-2002.

As stated in the original book 'Lauder and Lauderdale' by A Thomson, excluding the church, Lodge St. Luke No 132 is probably still the oldest organisation in Lauder. It was founded in 1772 and sponsored by Lodge Melrose No.1 and Lodge Dunse No.23. The original Charter, granted by The Grand Lodge of Scotland in December 1772, is still on view in the Lodge, as is the 'Intrant Book' containing the names of the ten founding members plus every member who has joined the Lodge since the Charter was issued.

The twentieth century started quietly for the Lodge. The minutes were very brief, as on January 24th 1901, *"The Brethren met by command of the RWM for the Degree of Entered Apprentice. It was proposed by the RWM, and unanimously agreed that a minute be recorded expressing the deep regret of the death of Her Majesty*

Queen Victoria". 101 years later the same regret was expressed on the death of Her Majesty Queen Elizabeth, the Queen Mother.

During World War II, the Kirk Hall, in Castle Wynd was used to billet soldiers. They were reputedly caught in the act of burning papers etc which they had removed from cupboards in the hall. Unfortunately it was too late to save the minute books from 1772 until 1877, which had already been destroyed.

The Bi-centenary celebrations were held in December 1972. They consisted of a re-dedication ceremony in the Public Hall and Dinner in the Lauderdale Hotel. The week ended with a Church service conducted by the Rev D. A. Tosh and the Rev R. F. James. A bench seat was also presented to the Royal and Ancient Burgh, suitably inscribed, and placed in Edinburgh Road.

Over the years meetings have been held in the Town Hall, the Public Hall, the Kirk Hall, the West Church Hall, the Session House, the School, the Black Bull Hotel and the Eagle Hotel. Then in 1979 the two houses at 53 and 55 West High Street became available. They were bought and converted into a Lodge suitable for Masonic purposes. After over 200 years, and having met in the aforementioned known places Lodge St. Luke finally had a home of its own. The Lodge will be eternally grateful to the small but very committed band of volunteers who, over a period of four years, gave up their time, money and effort to carry out the conversion. The first meeting took place on 5th October 1983, and the Dedication service on 11th May the following year. In 1994 improvements were made to the front of the building with new windows and sandstone surrounds. In 1998 further improvements were carried out internally. The building dates from around the inception of the Lodge in 1772, and, we hope, will be sound for another two hundred years.

Lodge St. Luke meeting in the early part of the century.

Lodge St. Luke 132 Charter. Original document dated 19th Dec. 1772.

Lauder Playgroup and Mother and Toddlers Group

The group was started in 1970 as an informal gathering of young mothers and their children between the ages of two and a half and four and a half. They met in the Territorial Hall on Factors Park.

Shortly afterwards the Lauder Playgroup became a member of the newly-formed Borders Playgroup Association. It immediately became more formalised with official playleaders who were trained in providing a more structured learning environment for the youngsters.

The Territorial Hall was large and was so cold that many of the children kept their hats and coats on in the winter. In 1973 the playgroup moved to the Scout Hall, now the Youth Trust Hall, where it still is today.

As time went by it became apparent that there was a need for somewhere for the mothers of pre-playgroup children to meet for support and friendship and a place for the young ones to play together. A mother and toddlers' group was formed which met on alternate days in the Youth Trust Hall. In 1992 the group moved into the cosy Church Centre within the Church grounds.

Today the Playgroup meets on Tuesday, Thursday and Friday mornings. To reflect the changes in pre- school education, the Playgroup now caters for the pre-school syllabus and offers funded places for qualifying three year olds and above. There is a permanent Playleader supported by mums who help out on a rota basis.

The Mother and Toddlers group meets every Wednesday and Friday. Mums can have coffee and a chat while their children learn to mix with their peers who will accompany them through their future school careers. There are currently 10 children in the Playgroup. There are around ten mothers with their children who regularly attend the Mothers and Toddlers Group

Lauder Playgroup 1970

The Probus Club of Lauderdale

The inaugural meeting was held on the 22 September 1992 in the Black Bull Hotel. It took the form of a lunch, which had been organised by the Rotary Club of Lauderdale. From the founding members present, Dr Harry Crombie-Smith was elected President with Charles Hollinshead as Secretary and Arthur Gillon as Treasurer. A constitution was adopted and a programme of monthly lunchtime meetings arranged.

The President's Medallion of Office was jointly gifted to the Club by the Lauder Rotary Club and Dr. Harry Crombie-Smith. John Manson, a founder member, gifted a Chairman's gavel which he had made.

Past Presidents:

1992-93	Dr. H. Crombie-Smith
1993-94	Bill Walker
1994-95	Arthur Fairburn
1995-96	Arthur Gillon
1996-97	Charles Hollinshead
1997-98	Walter Scott
1998-99	Alister Kerr
1999-00	Harvey Binnie
2000-01	David Gurney

The word Probus is an acronym for, Professional and Business but membership is not restricted to these two groups. It can include others who have had some measure of responsibility during their working life.

Membership is open to retired and semi-retired men who appreciate opportunities to meet others in similar circumstances and of a similar level of interest. Meetings of the Club are held on the second Tuesday of each month for lunch, between 12.30 and 2.30 pm, in the Lauderdale Hotel.

Rotary Club of Lauderdale

The club was formed in 1987

The aims are expressed in the Rotary motto: "Service before Self."

We have supported all the main promotions of Rotary International including:

eye camps - cataracts worldwide

Water wells-India

Eradication of polio

Emergency boxes for any disaster

International student exchange

Eurotary International (Lauder hosted)

Lauderdale members have raised funds for many local charities and causes including the sponsoring of the Young Entertainer of the Year Competition which covers the Borders area. Recently the club helped sponsor the new Dialysis Unit at the Borders General Hospital.

Winter meetings generally take the form of a meal followed by a guest speaker. Talks have been given on a huge range of subjects and sometimes include speakers from visiting Rotarians from around the world. In the summer activities include, barbecues, sponsored walks and barn dances.

Membership is drawn from the Royal Burgh as well as the Earlston and Stow areas. Membership was as high as 32 but currently is about 21. Meetings are held in the Lauderdale Hotel every Wednesday evening from 7.00 pm. All of the members are allocated to a committee in order to get everyone involved. The current President is James Cullen.

The 24th Berwickshire Lauder Scout Group

It was founded in1921 with 23 scouts and with Mr H D Fraser who was the head teacher at Lauder Primary School as Scoutmaster. The group was officially registered with the Scout movement on the 14th April 1925 with J.M.Bell as Scoutmaster. The Cubs were also founded in 1925. The Beaver colony was started in 1986 as a result of an increased interest in the Scout movement by younger children.

The Beavers are for boys and girls aged 6-8, the Cubs for boys between 8 and 11 and 11-16 for the Scouts.

At first the group met in the primary school hall. In 1960 they moved to the Youth Trust Hall, formerly the Old Church Hall, after it had been bought by the people of Lauder. Over the years summer and weekend camps have proved both enjoyable and memorable. Venues for weekend local camps over the years have included Burnmill, Burncastle, Pyatshaw and Inchkeith. Summer camps have been held as far south as Scarborough and in the north of Scotland as well as many sites between. In 1989 the group represented the Scottish Scouts in Zellhof in Austria, for the 25 Scouts and 6 leaders it was a memorable experience. Since 1921, two Scouts have been chosen each year to appear with the Lauder Cornet as Halberd Bearers at the official ceremony outside the Town Hall on Common Riding Day. When the Queen visited Lauder in 1956, the Scouts formed a guard of honour.

Current membership is: Beavers 22, Cubs 24 and Scouts 18. Without the hard work of the voluntary leaders and helpers the group would not have survived. Some of the longest serving members include; Rev. D A Tosh (1933-1952), Ian Brotherstone (1975-1990) and David Wilkinson (1988-present).

Lauder Scout Troop 1940s.

Lauder Scouts 2001.

Lauder Beaver Scouts 1996.

Lauder Tennis Club

Lauder Tennis Club was founded in 1922 and play commenced in May 1924 on land donated by Miss Romanes of Harryburn. The first ball struck was preserved in a little glass case, which, up until two or three years ago, resided in the clubhouse. Anyone knowing of its whereabouts, please let the club know.

The Club thrived then declined and was restarted in the early 1970s, on a very bumpy surface. Several fund raising schemes, together with Grant Aid from the Scottish Sports Council and the Lauder Common Good Fund, resulted in a new surface being laid by 'En-Tout-Cas' in 1979.

The Club continued to have its ups and downs until in the late 1980s, there was a move to resite the club behind the football pitches. The lack of time, effort and mostly finance put paid to that idea.

In the spring of 1991, and new 'Gragreen' surface was laid by 'En-Tout-Cas' at a cost of £10,000. This together with running repairs, lasted until the present day. At the time of writing, the courts are in dire need of resurfacing.

The Club today is run by a handful of members, providing a useful amenity fo the town of Lauder, but as with most of its life, Lauder Tennis Club continues to struggle to survive.

Minute of Meeting of Lauder Town Council, 16th March 1885.

"There was read a letter from G. L. Broomfield, proposing to lease a part of the Under Loan Park, for the purpose of playing Lawn Tennis there; Mr. R. Henderson reported that he, and Mr. Wilson, had examined the ground with Mr. G. L. Broomfield; and they recommended that a strip across the field of

*35yards wide from the West Wall should be let for the the purposes of the
Tennis Club, on condition of the Club properly enclosing the ground and
making a suitable entrance and paying a yearly rent to the Burgh of One
Pound Ten Shillings, which was approved of; and if this offer is accepted the
necessary reservations will be made in the conditions of Let of the Park."*

The Berwickshire Advertiser August 24th 1937

Tennis

The Lauderdale Sports Club

*There was a large turnout of spectators at the American Tournament. Lord
and Lady Maitland visited the courts during the afternoon and watched the
play for a considerable time. In the semi-final, Mr and Mrs. Millar, Hawick,
beat Miss Paterson and Mr. E. Duthie, Lauder, 6-2; Miss Bunyan and D.
Clark, Duns, beat Miss Scott and G. Fairbairn, Stow, 6-5. Final; Mr and Mrs
Millar beat Miss Bunyan and D. Clark, 6-2.*

Opening of Lauder Tennis Courts 1920s.

Women's Rural Institute

Lauder WRI

The first meeting was held in May 1919 and Miss Gibb was the first president.

In the early days meetings were held at the time of the full moon. This was
because the ladies had to walk to the meeting, no cars or telephones in those days!
There was probably a great deal more chatting and gossip exchanged than you get

nowadays. Talks and demonstrations on countryside matters made up the programme. Popular subjects were goat husbandry, butter making, girdle baking, knitting, sewing, rug making and homemade remedies for a variety or ailments. Nowadays the latter would be called 'alternative medicine,' Originally meetings were held in the school, but when the school was being rebuilt we moved to the Parish Church Hall.

We used to have regular whist drives including a Charities Whist Drive which was held in February and 30 years ago raised as much as £375, a considerable sum of money in these days. At the meetings before Easter, eggs were collected and gifted to a local hospital. Toys were collected before Christmas and distributed to the children's ward at Peel Hospital. We also used to have an annual summer outing on the first Monday in June. The bus would pick us up at 6 am to leave for places like Oban or Aberdeen. Today things are different; we no longer have whist drives or day trips.

We do, however, have an enthusiastic core of ladies who support the WRI at its monthly meetings and spread the word of our talks and activities. We still bake and do crafts for "Home and Country."

Lauder Young Woman's Group

The Lauder Young Wives and Mothers Group was formed in 1970.

The aims were to encourage young wives and mothers to meet together on a monthly basis in fellowship and to listen to a variety of speakers on a wide range of topics. Now the aim is for any woman whether married or single to join in fellowship.

Membership has fallen and it has not proved possible to form a committee. It is now run more as a social gathering with a very varied syllabus organised by two or more members. Numbers were usually around 12 rising for a while to 20 but declining latterly.

Youth Trust Hall

The Youth Trust Hall came into being on the 2nd April, 1993, before then it was known as the Scout Hall. The hall was used by the Scouts and the Cubs and by the Lauder Playgroup. The Group Scout Council previously ran the hall for the Scouts, Cubs and took care of the overall running of the hall. In 1989 it was decided within the Group Scout Council that repairs and alterations had to be made to the hall. It was then decided at a public meeting that a Youth Trust be set up in order to attract grants for improvements, and a steering committee was appointed. An agreement was reached between the previous Trustees and the newly appointed Trustees to call the hall The Youth Trust Hall.

The new Trustees are John Wilkinson, Nora Turnbull, Ann Strangeways, and William Middlemiss. It was also agreed to have a Management Committee to run the day to day details, lets etc. The main purpose to help and run the hall for the Youth of Lauder.

The hall was previously owned by the West Church (formerly United Free Church). It was sold to John Monteith Ltd in 1956 then to John Wilkinson and James Derek Wilkinson in 1959 and then to the Trustees for Lauder Boy Scouts and Cubs Committee in 1960. It was then sold for a nominal amount to the Youth Trust Hall Trustees in April 1993.

Over the years a number of people have worked hard to keep the hall running for the youth of Lauder and it is to those people that many thanks must go for their great support. It is hoped that in years to come that the youth of Lauder will always have somewhere to hold all manner of activities, and thus ensure that it helps to keep a community together.

Youth Trust Hall 2000 (Scout Hall).

Andrew Mercer Remembers

I was born at Whitslaid Farm at about nine o'clock in the morning on the 12th of May 1938. I suppose I was a leftover, there is five years between me and the next youngest. The eldest was born in 1922 and the rest of them up to 1933. My oldest brother was killed in the war and my oldest sister died in the early 50's. I started Lauder school in 1943 and I am still friendly with some of the laddies that I met on that first day at school. My earliest jobs were feeding the hens and shutting them in. I stayed at Lauder school till I was twelve. I was brainy enough to go to Berwickshire High School, but that would have meant leaving the house at quarter to seven in the morning and not getting home till somewhere after six at night. I didn't like that idea and my father didn't like it either, so I went to Earlston Junior Secondary school. When I left school I worked on the farm but my brothers and me just did not get on. So I left after the harvest. I finished on the Friday or Saturday and had another job on the Monday.

I went to work with Tom Purves, the engineer in Earlston. They had nothing in the way of tackle. He used to buy odd cars and if they had a tool kit with them, well that was more tackle. He was a really good engineer and I learned lots of things from him. Hand him a bit of metal, a drill and a file and a hacksaw and he could make it into anything It was just as well, because you just couldn't go and get a thing off the shelf for the stuff we worked on. You had to learn how to adapt and make. They went bust about 1958 but I soon got another job as a blacksmith welder, though it was only temporary. Then I went along to King's in Earlston. They looked at me and said, "Oh well, sign here. You are in". Then they gave me some steel plates, a scraper and a wire brush and told me to clean them. That was my job.

My grandfather, who was a saddler in Galashiels, took over the tenancy of Whitslaid in 1910. In 1921 my father married a housemaid to the neighbouring farm but various things happened and he got a job as a steward at a farm down in Burnmouth. He was there for three years when his father became very ill and the family asked him to come home. He came home for a few months but the family would not accept my mother. So he said, "Right, I'm off again!" He got a steward's job at Lennel Hill at Coldstream. It was with Leitch who was a stock dealer among other things. It was my mother's job to milk the cows. On some mornings she would go out and there might be as many as twenty cows and other mornings there were none at all. My mother had gone to Kilmarnock Dairy School and she used to make an awfully good cheese with this milk. She was allowed to keep the milk as long as she milked all the cows. She sold the cheese to the shops in Coldstream. People used to come to buy the cheese while it was still green. My mother would tell them, "It's still green. You will get it when it is ready." My mother made more cheese than most people because she had access to all this milk. Other people could only use what was surplus to the farm and you might only have three cows on a farm.

My father went back home in 1926 and when his father died in '27 or '28, he got the tenancy. His oldest brother was a driver on the railway and his other brother and sister couldn't do anything on a farm so he took it over. It was part of the Carolside Estate until we bought it in 1959. The rent we paid in 1959 was just the same as the one we had been paying in 1910. But the tenancy was on what was called a 'strongbow' lease, which meant that we couldn't sell straw off it without permission. The estate had real control over you, they virtually told us how to farm. We were not allowed to put up barbed wire fencing but the estate put in hunting gates free of charge. All the timber belonged to them, if a tree blew down, we had to ask them if we could cut it or if they were going to come up and cut it. The farm had to be kept in good repair. The estate used to do all the fencing on a regular basis then we paid half and they paid half. The effect was that the rent started to creep up by other means.

We had to buy all our own equipment and machinery. We had a threshing mill for grain, which was built by Hogarth of Kelso. So it's a Hogarth mill. They built it and maintained it even after they had retired. The first time my dad came home he bought a tractor. It drove the mill as well as doing outside work. We had the mill right up to '63 when we bought a combine. But it had too small a capacity for the acreage we had and it just couldn't get through the crop. Some of the neighbours used to come in with their combines and help us out.

When the Hogarths came up I remember they used to bring a wooden box marked 'ball bearings' with them, but inside it was fitted to take two-dozen eggs. Now you have to remember that this was during the war and just afterwards when we had food rationing. You couldn't sell anything except through the Ministry of Food. We were contacted to send ninety dozen eggs a week to the packing station at Earlston. The ministry didn't accept that hens only laid for so long. It was, "How many hens do you have?" and then they told you your quota."

When we sold up in 1990, the auctioneers came up to see what we had and they asked us what was on hire and what was on lease. Everything was bought and paid for. We didn't believe in leasing or hiring, though nowadays everything is geared to that. We had about four hundred and fifty acres. We had sheep from early on, close to two hundred ewes and thirty to forty cattle. We had about ninety acres of grain and anything up to forty acres of turnips to feed the stock. We bought a space seeder which planted the turnip seeds at a rate of one every inch. It meant we didn't have to buy nearly as much turnip seed. So that was a great saving.

We started getting more and better chemicals, which kept the weeds down and stopped the turnip seedlings from getting strangled. During the war they had these War Agricultural Committees, right little Hitlers they were. They could put you out your farm for any reason or tell you to plough up a field even though it was totally unsuitable for ploughing. You had to plant it with whatever they said. I suppose the idea was right but the folk that got the top jobs were not the right people. We were reported for having a 'dirty field', in other words 'too many weeds.' They came down to look at the field in question and they all said how terrible it was. Now my father was a very easy-going person but he had some strange quirks of nature about him. He said to the Chairman, *"Well before you say o'er much, there's another field, you had better come and have a look at it too"*. So they crowded into that field, looked around and said that it was even worse. *"Well dinna be sae hasty,"* said my father, *"this field's his,"* pointing to a member of the Committee. Another time my father bought a load of heifers and asked his neighbour if he could get a loan of his bull. *"I'm not having my bu'l near your cows,"* was the answer. Fair enough, said my dad. He then put the heifers in the field next to the bull and, of course the bull came straight through the fence. *"Right,"* says my father to the neighbour, *"I am going to sue you for damage to my heifers."*

At that time there could be anything up to eight working on the farm. Most manual work was at hay and harvest and then there was the singlin' and shawin' of turnips. When you hired a man to the farm, he made an agreement with you. This was his wages, plus so much for the harvest plus maybe a thousand yards of a tattie drill.

I started collecting a few farm artefacts probably because I hated to throw stuff out. Then I started to collect stationary engines. At one point I had forty-two engines and had also acquired twenty-four tractors and I don't know how many tons of spares, hand tools, bygones and other rubbish. I collected them from varying farms and usually they were in a bit of a mess. I had a lot of repairs to do and that is where the engineering side of things came in handy. Sometimes we were given stuff and sometimes I swapped with other people who liked collecting. I go to auctions too. Sometimes in the pound boxes, they used to be five bob boxes, in among the rubbish you would find something special.

One of my greatest finds was on the tractor side. A fellow came up to me and said, "What's an International 1020 worth?" I said that I couldn't put a figure on it but that it would be a fair amount. The upshot was that I went through to Fife and it was the steward on the farm that I saw because the owner was away in America. The steward showed me the tractor. It was a bit sad looking but it was really something. Anyway I went through to see the owner when he came back. After I had a close look at it he asked me what I would do if I got it. *"No way,"* I said, *"if I get anything like that it's a captive."* He thought for a while and then said that he had decided not to sell it but would pay me for doing it up. I told him that that would not work, as I might do it different from what he wanted. So I says, *"I will tell you what I will do I will take it, do it up, treat it as my own but the ownership remains yours, and when you want it back, you just say so."* Well, he looked at me as if I was daft, which I probably am. *"You mean to say, folk do that?"* And I says, *"Aye and it works. Aye." "Right. That's a better deal as I could get ony other way."* I heard just a few days after that, he'd been bothered with folk going looking at it and trying to buy it. He was sick o' thae folk an' I got it, just like that. And I've still got it.

Another thing I was awful pleased with was my 1870 washing machine, which I paid £3 for. I got it at a farm sale at Silloth. It was in an old airfield and the stuff was laid out all along the runway. The farmer had retired and was going off on a world cruise. He had been in the game since I don't know when. I bought two or three good pieces at that sale. I don't have as much stuff now as I used to because of problems of space. The last really good acquisition I made was a 1920's pass seed system, which I bought at a local farm sale.

I am usually away every weekend to show them at vintage car rallies. I suppose there are four of us who are considered experts in this line. What one doesn't know, the other does. There's Jock Gibson from Elsrickle, Eric Moodie from Leaming and, well it used to be Bill Brown from Wooler but he died, and me. Joan Middlemas from Duns came in. She's very good and she makes a really good job of the stuff. Though she has the disadvantage of being a female; folk think it is her husband's stuff. So she has to put them right, so she's actually had to go further than us.

Somebody asked me once about the purpose of our collections and the only thing I could think of was 'cos the loonie-bin wouldn't take us."

Utilities

Lauder Water Supply

Administrative Arrangements

1900 - 1968:

In common with most rural water supplies the Lauder supply was a locally managed service during the majority of the twentieth century.

Lauder Town Council was responsible for the public water supply until the South East Scotland Water Board was formed in 1968.

Although Lauder Town Council carried this responsibility there was significant reliance on the services of the Water Engineer of Berwick County Council. Lauder, as a relatively small community, could not justify employing a full time Water Engineer.

1968 - 1975:

South East Scotland Water Board (SESWB) assumed responsibility for public water supplies in its' area in 1968. Initially the Lauder supply continued under the local management of the Town Council under an Agency Agreement. This agreement ceased on 15 November 1969 and SESWB took on the management and direct responsibility for the operation of the Lauder system.

1975-1996:

Accountability for the public water supplies in Scotland was once again devolved to local administrations in 1975 upon the formation of the Regional Councils. The Regional Councils (9 across mainland Scotland) were large enough to provide the required economy of scale in operating and maintaining water resources, treatment and distribution systems. Borders Regional Council Water and Drainage Services Department took over the management of the Lauder water supply along with all other public supplies across the region.

1996 - 2002:

East of Scotland Water, one of three public water authorities in Scotland, was formed on 1 April 1996 as part of a restructuring of local government. European directives on water quality, waste water treatment and other environmental matters were placing a considerable financial burden on the Regional Councils. In rural areas such as Borders, Dumfries and Galloway and the Highlands it was becoming increasingly difficult to fund the required investment programme without significant price rises to customers. The economy of scale offered by consolidating the administrative arrangements in three water authorities became irresistible.

In April 2002:

> Management of all public water supplies will pass to a single organisation to be known as Scottish Water in April 2002. This further consolidation of the industry will offer additional economies of scale and will enable the delivery of a £2 billion investment programme over four years in the most efficient way. Significant efficiencies in operational costs will be pursued in order to minimise the price rises needed to find the investment programme.

Developments in Lauder's water supply arrangements

Throughout the first half of the twentieth century Lauder was served by spring water supplies from Lauder Common.

Reference is made in correspondence held in water authority files to a spring on Muircleugh Farm dating back to 1895. Further, more extensive springs on the common to the North West of Muircleugh are shown on plans held by East of Scotland Water, the current public supply authority. A 4" fireclay pipe from these springs fed a collecting well, labelled on the Ordnance Survey map as a "cistern", to the east of the access road to Muircleugh. From the collecting well a 3" cast iron pipe ran to a storage tank located at Lauderhill south west of Allanbank and indicated by the OS as "Reservoir (Lauder Corporation Water Works)". A 3" cast iron pipe continued from this storage tank into Lauder. These springs, collecting well and storage tank still exist. A second "small tank" existed to the north of Stow Road, west of the bowling green, but this was presumably demolished when housing was developed in the area.

Water authority files from the early part of the twentieth century contain hand written notes of measured flow rates at the Lauderhill tank dated 2 June 1910.

Records suggest that by the 1930's the 3" pipe feeding Lauder was in need of reinforcement. A priced tender dated 21 September 1932 was submitted for the construction of an additional 4" pipe from Lauderhill tank to the junction of Stow Road, Edinburgh Road and High Street. The total length of the proposed new supply pipe was 1,100 yards and the tendered price was £568 and 16 shillings. This represented a price of 10 shilling and four pence per yard (or 52 pence in today's currency). Interestingly there is a reference in the tender to the pipes, which were of asbestos cement construction, being specified in 4 metre lengths - metrication in 1932!

Despite this reinforcement of the supply system dry weather in 1939 resulted in water shortages to certain properties in Lauder. The Berwick County Council Water Engineer was engaged by Lauder Town Council to carry out an examination of the Lauderhill storage tank. There was obvious leakage from the tank and the Engineer made recommendations on repair methods and materials to be used in rectifying problems with mortar joints and cracks in the floor.

The supply system appears to have worked satisfactorily for a few years but by the mid 1940's was again giving cause for concern. In 1946 there were further difficulties with the supply during periods of dry weather. The Town Council hired the services of two Waste Inspectors from Edinburgh City Council to carry out a leak detection exercise. Given that the the spring resource was becoming inadequate for the demand there was clearly significant advantage in minimising the amount of water lost through leaking mains.

In 1947 there were continuing problems with the adequacy of the supply. The Berwick County Engineer was again engaged and following a survey of flow rates coming from the springs he recommended the clearance of roots from the 4" fireclay pipe from the springs to Lauderhill tank. Root growth within the pipeline was considered to be responsible for impairing the quality of water flowing into the storage tank. Later that year a Consulting Engineer was employed to report on Lauder's supply system and recommended that the existing supply be augmented by a ditch intake and filter bed.

This reference to a filter bed is the first recorded indication of any attempt to improve the quality of the water supply. All concerns previously had been in relation to the adequacy of the quantity.

During the late 1940's and into the 1950's a number of larger water supply schemes were planned and implemented in the Borders. Berwickshire County Council developed two schemes: the Watchwater Scheme to serve Eastern Berwickshire and the Earnscleugh Scheme to serve Western Berwickshire. The Watchwater Scheme included the Watchwater Reservoir and a water treatment works at Rawburn along with trunk mains to the demand centres of Eastern Berwickshire. The Earnscleugh Scheme included a river intake at Bermuda and a raw water transfer pipeline to a new water treatment works at Wanton Walls to the North of Lauder.

When the Berwickshire County Engineer was invited to comment on the 1947 Consulting Engineer's report on the Lauder Water Supply he did not agree with the recommendations, suggesting instead that the Lauder Town Council should consider connecting Lauder to the Earnscleugh Scheme which was then in its early planning stages.

It is not known what the costing arrangements might have been but in any event Lauder was not connected to Berwickshire County Council's Earnscleugh Scheme. The water treatment works at Wanton Walls, just 2 miles North of Lauder, was commissioned in 1954 but it would be many years later that it finally came to serve the Lauder community.

From 1948 to 1969 there were continuing intermittent problems with the adequacy of Lauder's spring supply. Waste and leakage detection exercises were carried out by Berwickshire County Council staff on behalf of (and chargeable to) Lauder Town Council.

1967 seems to have been a difficult year in which the supply to the Hamish Morrison poultry units at Stow Road ran out. Morrison's premises were inspected and they were advised to increase their own water storage capacity. Morrisons used a combination of their own private spring supply and a feed from the public mains system. They were instructed to alter their pipework arrangements in order to comply with the Water Bylaws and prevent the risk of their private supply contaminating the public mains supply. Morrison subsequently removed the private supply altogether, which presumably placed an added burden on the already stretched public supply.

With the advent of the South East of Scotland Water Board in 1967 several opportunities were taken to rationalise water supply arrangements in the Borders by linking previously self- sufficient communities to the strategic schemes that had been constructed during the 1950's and 60's.

Hence plans were finally laid to link Lauder to the Earnscleugh supply from the Wanton Walls treatment works. In May 1968 tenders were sought for the construction of 660 yards of 6" PVC pipeline from Peatman Corner to East High Street along with 180 yards of 3" PVC main in Loan View. The lowest tender was from H Thomson (Selkirk) Ltd., in the sum of £4,791-3s-1 id.

Delays were incurred in seeking to obtain grant assistance from the Scottish Development Department and it was not until April 1969 that the tender from H Thomson (Selkirk) Ltd was finally accepted with a 4% enhancement on the previously tendered rates as an inflation allowance. The value of the contract was £4,982-16s-10d. The mainlaying work was certified as completed on 30 November 1969 and the final measurement of work done was valued at £5,407-5s-3d. The completion date was just two weeks afier the agency agreement between South East Scotland Water Board and Lauder Town Council ceased on 15 November 1969. The SESWB had assumed full responsibility for day to day operation of the water supply as well as for strategic planning.

Even though Lauder was connected to the Earnscleugh supply the town was zoned, with part still fed from the springs via Lauderhill tank. In 1971 the fireclay pipe from the springs to the storage tank was once again choked by root growth coming in through the pipe joints. In addition a substantial loss of water was occurring due to the dilapidated state of the manholes on the pipeline. To overcome these problems a length of 2,133 yards of 2" PVC pipework with glued joints was inserted inside the fireclay pipe. This sleeving work was completed by late 1971.

Some mains replacement work was carried out in The Row in 1972. Further mains replacement in Edinburgh Road in 1976 was completed to accommodate housing at Brownsmuir Park and industrial development of the Old Station Yard. Little else appears to have been done during the 1970's and 1980's.

The European Dimension

In 1980 the European Parliament passed directive 80/778/EC - "The Drinking Water Directive" - which was to have a very significant impact on all UK water supplies.

As a member of the EU the UK government was obliged to convert the Drinking Water Directive into law and so The Water Supply (Water Quality) (Scotland) Regulations 1990 came about.

Earlier legislation (Water (Scotland) Act 1948 and 1980) had placed a duty on water utilities to supply "wholesome water" without defining what was meant by "wholesome". Whilst water utilities did pay due regard to the quality of their product, often relying on World Health Organisation guidelines as quality targets, they were not held to account for any variations in water quality.

The Drinking Water Directive and the statutory Regulations that were based on it defined for the first time the meaning of "wholesome". Numerical water quality standards were set for over 60 parameters covering microbiological, physico-chemical and aesthetic aspects of quality. Where existing supplies could not consistently meet the newly defined standards water utilities had to give legally binding undertakings to the government to carry out improvement works within set timescales to ensure compliance with the Regulations.

There were huge implications for water supplies across the country and a significant impact for the Lauder supply.

Investing for quality

The Earnscleugh Scheme had always been very reliable in terms of sufficiency of water supply. Indeed its sufficiency was further augmented during the 1970's by the addition of a raw water feed from the Boondreigh water via a pumping station constructed at Dodmill. Unfortunately the quality of the supply has always been very variable, particularly with regard to colour. Originating from peaty moorland the Earnscleugh water becomes heavily stained during wet weather. The Wanton Walls treatment works as originally designed and built was unable to cope with the sudden huge variations in colour. Consequently the water going into supply was often quite brown. Many Lauder residents will recall that as recently as the early 1990's the bath water often looked dirty before getting into it!

During the late 1980's and early 1990's Borders Regional Council's Water and Drainage Services Department carried out a thorough review of the regions water supply arrangements. This review was driven by a number of issues: drought conditions in the early 1980's had exposed the limitations of some of the regions supplies; the Water Quality Regulations required significant improvements to a number of supplies; much of the water supply infrastructure was ageing and in need of refurbishment or replacement; the need to rationalise arrangements wherever possible to minimise the cost of improvements.

Various alternative treatment technologies were trialed at Wanton Walls but the cost of developing a sophisticated treatment plant to cope with the extreme variations in raw water quality proved to be prohibitive.

At the same time as the Earnscleugh water quality problem was being investigated plans were being drawn up to augment the Central Borders water supply. An opportunity arose when a large industrial water user in Selkirk decided to withdraw from the public supply network and use a private borehole source. This left a significant quantity of water available for use elsewhere.

A number of options for increasing the available water resource in the Central Borders were subjected to a very detailed financial appraisal. The resulting strategy, implemented during the 1990's, involved making early use of the spare resource from Selkirk by constructing a trunk main from Selkirk to the east side of Galashiels. From there water could be moved through an existing pipeline to Earlston. A new main was laid up the Leader Valley to enable the transfer of water from Earlston to the Lauder area and into Western

Berwickshire via the Wanton Walls storage tank. A pumping station was built near West Mains, Lauder to lift treated water to Wanton Walls.

Subsequently further work was carried out to develop additional boreholes at the Howden Wellfield near Selkirk, provide a new treatment works at Howden and a pumping main to a new tank in the Thornbush Quarry overlooking Selkirk. This project, at a cost of £5 million provided high quality water in sufficient quantity to serve Lauder's needs at the same time as significantly augmenting the available supplies to the Galashiels and Earlston areas.

The Wanton Walls treatment works is now used only when the raw water quality is high. Any deterioration in the colour of the water is detected and triggers an automatic shutdown of the works with associated initiation of pumping from the Central Borders supply. This arrangement meets all water quality criteria and the ongoing use of the gravity feed from the Earnscleugh, when it is suitable, helps to keep costs down.

Having resolved the problem of producing a high quality water supply the focus of investment turned to maintaining water quality in distribution. The old cast iron mains in Lauder had reached the end of their working life and were replaced in 2000, having served the community for the whole of the twentieth century.

The water supply arrangements now in place in Lauder look set to provide a reliable high quality service for the 21st century.

Public Electricity Supply

The long-awaited Public Electricity Supply arrived in Lauder in 1932. Citizens of the Royal Burgh, together with Councillors and Officials, had become increasingly frustrated knowing that electricity was enjoyed in other towns in the Borders.

Repeated requests from the Burgh Fathers to the Scottish Southern Electric Supply Company for an electricity supply to be made available in the Burgh had been unsuccessful. In late 1929, through 1930 and into 1931, continued pressure on the Electric Supply Company had resulted in several responses from the General Manager, Mr W S Sawtell, at Galashiels. These responses varied from, *"The Company's programme does not include Lauder at the present moment"* (November 1929), to *"I have been instructed to prepare an estimate for making a supply available"* (October 1930). Then, in February 1931, a further letter from Mr Sawtell stated that no further action could be taken until the result of a review of an Electricity Scheme for the South of Scotland was known.

Clearly, Councillors were extremely frustrated at the continued delay and the Burgh Clerk was instructed to write to the Electricity Commissioners in London to enquire if anything could be done to expedite the installation of electricity into Lauder. This action certainly proved rewarding in that, in a letter dated 7th April 1931, just two months later, the Company intimated that an extension of the Company's cable for a supply to Lauder would be considered and dealt with without any undue delay.

In March 1932, formal letters from the Scottish Southern Company's Head Office at 10 Melville Street, Edinburgh, requested the Council's permission to erect an overhead low-tension distribution network within the Burgh, were received. The Council agreed to grant the necessary permission, so far as the Town Council had interest and authority.

Later that same month, another letter from the General Manager at Galashiels was received offering to install street lighting at a cost of £5 per lamp and intimating the unit charge for the electricity to supply the lamps of five pence per unit. The lamps would be attached to brackets on the Company's poles and would be controlled via a switch-wire and a solar-dial time clock. The estimated cost of 21 street lamps with all the ancillary equipment totalled One Hundred and Five Pounds. (£105).

Lauder had, of course, street lighting in the form of gas lamps with the gas supplied by The Lauder Gas Company. The Council instructed the Streets Committee to submit details of the cost of supplying gas and repairing street lamps over the preceding five years. On submission, the Council would consider the respective costs, and no doubt the relative merits, of street lighting by gas and by electricity.

On the 6th September 1932, the Scottish Southern Electric Supply Company was granted permission to connect an Earth Wire for the present electricity supply to the main Water pipe near the Schoolhouse. Electricity had at last arrived in Lauder although it is possible that, at sometime before September 1932, the network had been commissioned and had relied on conventional earth-rods that had eventually been proved inadequate.

Extensions to the Lauder distribution network continued after September 1932 with the erection of poles in Station Road and Manse Road. It is interesting to note that in February 1933, the Streets Committee was authorised to expend the sum of £1 to carry out repairs on several gas lamps and put these lamps in full working order to complete the remainder of the Lighting Season.

With the aforementioned reports and estimates in connection with future Street Lighting made available to the Council, a Special Meeting was held on the 8th July 1933. The proposals from both the Lauder Gas Company, to repair existing lamps and install further lamp standards, and the Scottish Southern Electric Company to install 28 lamps on pole brackets was debated. It was a close run decision. Two Councillors voted for the Gas Company's proposal two voted for the Electric Company's proposal with one Councillor abstaining. It was on the casting vote of Provost Cossar that the electricity scheme won the day.

The new form of lighting must have been speedily installed for it was in September, just two months later, that the Clerk was instructed to formally write to The Lauder Gas Company intimating the discontinuance of gas for the lighting of the streets.

It was in January 1934 that the account for the installation of the Street Lamps, amounting to £145, was passed for payment. Apparently the quotation by the Electric Supply Company discussed at the Special Meeting in July 1933 was for 28 lamps totalling £140 but an additional lamp installation had been requested thereby raising the account by a further £5. At the same meeting, the Streets Committee was authorised to purchase three-dozen, 100-watt 'bulbs' to be kept in reserve for use in lamps as required.

Electricity was not cheap, either in the wiring of homes and commercial premises or the cost per unit of consumption. Numerous letters were appearing in the Borders newspapers in the early thirties complaining bitterly that the price of electricity was too high and beyond the reach of ordinary folk. As such, it was clear that only the more affluent people could afford the luxury of electric lighting and power in their homes. It is interesting to note that a far-sighted correspondent wrote a letter entitled 'Cheap Electricity', to the Southern Reporter of March 24 1932, claiming that further Government powers were required to address the high price of electricity and those powers should include the complete nationalisation of the electricity supply industry! For the record, nationalisation took place in September 1947.

Even so, consumers continued to be connected and by 1936, complaints of the system voltage being inadequate in the Burgh were increasing and the Town Clerk was further instructed to draw the attention of the Electric Supply Company to the general drop in illuminating power of the street lamps. With the high-voltage network now extending to places such as Gordon, Westruther, Greenlaw and beyond to Coldstream, Duns and Eyemouth, the maintaining of the system voltage had become a problem the Electric Supply Company simply could not address through lack of capital and financial restraints.

By the 1950's, after the Nationalisation of the Electricity Supply Industry, farms and smaller settlements in the vicinity of Lauder, such as Langshaw and Blainslie were being connected and the problems of low voltage not only continued but also became exacerbated. The age of television was now with us and a voltage drop of more than the permissible limit of 6% caused screens to shrink and, in many cases, pictures to collapse altogether.

During the 1950's and 1960's, extensions and reinforcements of lines into Lauder were carried out by the nationalised South of Scotland Electricity Board. By this time, three overhead supply lines met the demand for power into the Burgh. The re-built Blainslie line from Earlston, the Langshaw line from Galashiels and the Westruther line from Gordon. The results of extensive works on these lines barely justified the expenditure and by the early 1970's, matters were becoming desperate. The Langshaw Line, for example, crossed high terrain and was prone to damage through high winds, ice and snow. This resulted in repeated supply interruptions for many consumers in Lauder. The line was known in engineering circles as a 'Rogue Circuit' although money was continually poured into maintaining the line.

Also at this time, the residents of Stow and beyond to Heriot were suffering the effects of low voltage. Consequently the planners had little choice but to design a bold and imaginative scheme for a major reinforcement to address all these problems. It was in 1975 that a 17 kilometre, 33,000-volt line of stout construction was built from Galashiels Grid Station to Lauder with a new substation built on the outskirts of the town housing a 6,500-kva transformer and ancillary equipment. A further line of 9.1 kilometres, constructed again to 33kv standard, but operated at the secondary distribution voltage of 11kv, was built from Lauder to Torsonce to interconnect with the Galashiels/Stow line. The total capital investment was in the region of £200,000. A far cry from the estimate 43 years earlier of £140 for 28 street lamps?

This major investment benefited some 2,000 electricity consumers by resolving the problems of poor supply voltage (by as much as 15% in some cases) and improving the reliability of the public electricity supply.

It does seems quite incredible to us today that, electricity, such an essential part of our life, twenty four hours a day, only arrived in Lauderdale as recently as 1932. Just think what life is like without it for just a few hours, and then think again what it must be like in a country where a natural disaster or war has struck and there is no electricity for weeks on end. It also seems rather strange when you realise, that that other great source of power, heat and light, gas, was here in Lauderdale almost one hundred years before electricity. Could that situation have had anything to do with fact that the inhabitants of Lauder themselves were able to make the necessary arrangements to have the gas installed?

Gas for Lauder

The Lauder Gas Light Company was formed in 1842 with a nominal capital of £1,000. Shares were issued at £5. per share, and there were 37 subscribers. The Burgh of Lauder purchased £50. worth of stock.

On the 18th. June 1844, a piece of ground at the Burnmill was sold by, Public Roup to the Lauder Gas Light Company, for ten shillings with a ground annual of two shillings and six pence Sterling. It was bought by David Broomfield, John Romanes, Robert Scott, James Hay, Alexander Crawford and Archibald Valance.

At a Town Council meeting on 28th. June 1880 permission was sought by the Gas Light Company to erect a tank and gasometer at a cost of £47:15:0.

At a Town Council meeting on 3rd. May 1910, a letter was discussed from Robert Watson and Hugh Clarkson, proposing to buy the Gas Works from the Company, provided that the Council pay the full price for gas for street lighting at a maximum sum of 6/8d (six shillings and eight pence) per 1,000 cubic feet, and pay the full price for any other gas used by the council. At a further meeting of the Town Council on 5th. August 1910, the Council having had a letter from the Lauder Gas Light Company stating that they wished to sell the business, the Council decided after a vote to elect a representative to the meeting of dissolution to vote in favour of the sale. The disposition of the Gas Works to Watson and Clarkson was duly signed, having paid £450. for the works.

In 1912 Hugh Clarkson sold his share in the Gas Works to Robert Watson for £300, and in 1940 Robert Watson conveyed the Gas Works to William Watson.

On the 1st. May 1949 the gas industry was nationalised, and the Scottish Gas Board acquired the company from William Watson. On that date there were 195 operational gas works producing town gas throughout Scotland. Of the operational gas works, only four (Comrie, Kilbirnie, Lauder and West Wemyss) were privately owned companies. Of these four, only Comrie and Lauder were owned and managed by private individuals. Lauder was one of the smallest gas works in Scotland. The works had two beds of retorts, each with two stop ended retorts, capable of producing about 5,000 cubic feet of gas per day, without (uniquely in Scotland) the use of an exhauster.

The works was finally closed in 1965 when the gas supply was taken from the supergrid through a 2" diameter gas pipe to Lauder.

One of the first if not the first, natural gas pipeline supplying Natural Gas (ex North Sea) entered Scotland at Oxenrig Farm, Coldstream to traverse North Westwards through Berwickshire skirting Gordon up to Boon Hill and thence down to Lauder Barns, Wyndhead and through nearly all the Burgess acres past the Manse and through the valley up to Oxton, Mountmill, Channelkirk and over Soutra to Gilston to its final destination of Airdrie. The first supplies of Natural Gas reached Lauder on 12th. October 1970.

Upon its closure Lauder Gas Works attracted attention as, for a time, there were plans to preserve the works as a museum. In the event the proposal was not accepted, and the site was cleared in 1965.

Burnmill Farm and Gasworks

Lauder Fire Brigade

During the 1980's Lauder experienced the second largest population growth in the district at 36%.

As a result of a review of standards of fire cover, a report was sent to Lothian and Borders Fire Board in 1997 indicating that the Brigade was unable to meet its required response times to the Burgh of Lauder and the surrounding area. The report recommended that the practicalities of establishing a retained station within the Burgh of Lauder should be examined in detail.

It was estimated that it would be possible to sustain a retained fire crew and with the Board's approval and support from Scottish Borders Council the recruitment programme began early in 1999.

Lothian and Borders Fire Brigade held a recruitment day in Lauder Public Hall, to which approximately Fifty local residents attended, and recruited 12 men and 3 women to be the first crew. The crew spent the following year attending training courses.

January 2000 saw work start on the station on the industrial estate at the north end of the Burgh. It is a single storey building of traditional construction with a steel frame in the appliance bay and concrete floors throughout The building has an appliance bay, kitchen, watch room, lecture room, workshop, drying room, muster/changing area and toilet and shower facilities for both men and women fire-fighters. A training yard, training tower and parking facilities are at the rear of the building. The official opening of Lauder Fire Station was on Friday 1st September 2000 by her Royal Highness the Princess Royal.

The First Lauder Fire Crew.

F/F Stephen Baker	F/F Maxine Bamford
F/F Brian Bell	F/F Aldo Falccne
F/F Mary Fallas	F/F Christine Jaffray
F/F Kenneth Lindsay	F/F Bernard Quinn
F/F Douglas Scott	F/F David Wilson
Leading F/F John Connell	Leading F/F Andrew Cook
Leading F/F John Riva	

Wholetime officers on secondment for the 1st year operational.

Sub Officer Kenneth Taylor
Sub Officer Kenneth Wilson

Official opening of Lauder Fire Station in 2000.

Lauder Fire Brigade.

Dr. Crombie Smith Remembers

"I was born in Edinburgh. My father was a pharmacist who had his own wholesale manufacturing factory where he made medicines. My memory goes a long way back. During the First World War we had a retail shop as well. I started to learn about medicines when I was a small child. I remember working in the front shop and being lifted on to a high stool behind the dispensing counter. My job was to stamp the corner of the prescriptions that dad made up. I was about two years old at the time. I attended a private school and then went on to Daniel Stewart's College until 1931 when I left and went to Edinburgh University. I didn't have many hobbies as I had to work in the factory. It was very busy and I learnt lots of skills. I remember I got a handicrafts prize for building a railway engine out of wood. I still have it upstairs but it is a bit of a ruin now.

When I finished my medical degree I was due to go back to the university and do research. I had gone on holiday to Orkney and had just arrived there when I got a telegram from my father telling me to get home straight away. At first, I ignored it, but when I got another I phoned home. My father told me he had met someone who was looking for a locum for a doctor in the Borders who was unwell. My dad insisted that I come home and follow it up. In these days you did what your parents told you. I arrived back on Thursday and contacted Dr Georgeson, who was ill on his yacht in Kirkcaldy. On Friday I travelled to Kirkcaldy and chatted with Dr Georgeson and we seemed to hit it off. It was agreed that I would come down to Lauder and take over from the temporary assistant. On the Sunday morning, it was the 31st July 1938, as I was getting ready to go to Lauder, the telephone rang. It was Mrs Georgeson to tell me that her husband had died,

However, she said that I had just to carry on with the agreed arrangement. I didn't have a car then but I had passed my driving test so I collected Dr Georgeson's car from a garage that he had rented in Leith and drove down to Lauder on the Sunday morning. There were flags out everywhere. I had assumed that they had heard I was coming and had put them out for me! I knew nothing about the Common Ridings then. I booked into the Eagle Hotel and on the Monday morning walked down the street to start work.

Later that day Mrs Georgeson came in to see me and said that her husband had taken a notion to me and that I was to be given first refusal in getting the practice. Now, in those days doctors weren't appointed to practices, they had to buy them. It was really quite difficult for a doctor to get into a practice, they usually didn't have the money or the opportunity. I was wondering about this when Dr Georgeson's lawyer phoned me. He said that he knew what the doctor's views were and that he had been instructed to make arrangements that would suit me. I thus became owner of the practice and also of Dr Georgeson's house, the Red House.

I got married in 1940 and was conscripted into the army in 1941. After some square bashing and a few weeks training in tropical medicine I was shipped off to

India and then to Burma. I was not to come home until 1946. My wife had run the practice under the name of Dr Campsie. I came home on the Winchester Castle and my wife was on the quayside waiting for me. Before I was demobbed I was put in charge of a small hospital at Drygrange. It was quite handy because I was able to stay at home. I was demobbed from this hospital to York and came back from York as a civilian. I got the train to Edinburgh then the bus to Lauder. I got off the bus at twenty past five and walked down to the Red House, Mrs Smith said to me, *"I'm finished. Surgery's at six o'clock"* My demob leave had lasted for about thirty-five minutes.

At that time there was National Insurance, which had been started by Lloyd George about 1910. Employed people earning less than £250 a year were entitled to free medical attention and free medicines. Their wives and children were considered to be private patients. Workers were referred to as panel patients. If you were a worker getting more than £250 a year then you were a private patient and weren't eligible for National Health Insurance Benefits. This produced a rather curious situation at places of consultation which for most doctors was our own home. Private patients sat in the dining room. They came in by the front door and sat in the dining room at the dining room table, The panel patients, who might be the husband or father of those in the dining room, sat in the kitchen. I didn't like this arrangement, but it was fiercely protected by the patients themselves. I altered the house slightly and turned the washhouse into a kitchen and the kitchen became a waiting room. The private patients didn't like this change, they thought they should come in the front door and not by the side door like panel patients.

The new health service came into action in 1948 after a great deal of acrimonious wrangling. Everyone was entitled to free medical care and prescriptions. For this the doctor got 8s.6d a year for looking after each person. The local Co-op pharmacy dispensed medicines until it closed in 1969. I just started dispensing them and, of course this came quite easy to me, as I had been brought up in the trade. There was no general hospital then, Edinburgh was the nearest one. We had only one ambulance and it was stationed at Gordon, attached to the fever hospital. The matron of Gordon hospital acted as the attendant and a local Gordon man was called in when necessary to drive the ambulance. If someone needed hospital attention for more ordinary things like a broken arm for example, then they went by bus. When the Health service came along in 1948 we got an ambulance, which was stationed at Earlston. A few years later the hospital at Peel, near Clovenfords, which had been an emergency hospital during the war, became available for civilian use. It was much handier being only ten miles away. Few people had cars then, indeed only a few had a telephone. Everything moved at a slower pace. If somebody required a doctor to visit, a relative or friend would cycle in to the surgery and wait their turn in the waiting room to ask for a visit to the sick person. I remember one occasion when a man came in after sitting in the waiting room. *"It's not me that's ill doctor, but would you come and see the wife."* I asked what was wrong with her. *"I think she's needing you,"* he replied. This was the euphemistic way of a husband saying that his wife was about to have a baby. *"When is it?"* I asked. *"Now, doctor."* This man had cycled in from Pilmuir about four miles away, waited his turn in the waiting room, then asked me to go and see his wife who was busy having a baby.

I hurried up and closed the surgery and set off up to Pilmuir. When I got there the nurse had her head stuck out of the bedroom window of the cottage and shouted, *"Quick, quick!"* I ran in and there was the baby half born It was a breech delivery. The body was out but the head had still to emerge. It all went fine but it was very different from what happens nowadays.

Being a country doctor I became skilled at driving in all kinds of weather conditions. In those days we had some very heavy snowfalls in winter, with the snow reaching the tops of telegraph poles in some places. Sometimes you had to make a circuitous route to get to the place you wanted to go. Quite often I travelled on a sledge with a horse pulling me. It was quite an experience, sitting on a bale of straw on the sledge being pulled by an enormous Clydesdale whose hooves were never more than a foot from your face. Of course, if somebody required hospitalisation who lived far out in the hills, then they would be put on the sledge to get down to the nearest available road. It is all very different nowadays and people are much more knowledgable. In those days people waited for the doctor and accepted what the doctor told them."

Lauder Town Council Final Meeting 15th May 1975.

The Leader Leisure Centre

Background

Part of the buildings at Old Causewayend now known as 'the Leisure Centre' formed 'the Smiddy' from the early 1800s to the late 1970s by which time the buildings and the business had grown into a blacksmith and engineering works.

The Bronze Age/Colour Box factory, which produced miniature ornaments that became collector's pieces, occupied the blacksmith buildings during the 1980s before moving to a purpose built factory to the north end of the town. In 1992 a report was prepared for the owner of the factory and the Chairman of Ettrick and Lauderdale District Council but lack of funds meant no action.

The idea of converting the former factory into a modern leisure centre was resurrected in 1995 during a community appraisal exercise promoted by the Planning Department of Scottish Borders Council, as part of a community regeneration study. One feature of the appraisal revealed that people's perception of facilities for leisure pursuits was one of poor provision. The majority thought that indoor facilities for social, sporting and recreational education were poor for all age groups. The opportunity identified most often remained the potential use of the former factory and Smiddy as 'a community centre, tourist office and static library'.

The public meeting held in 1996 resulted in the formation of a 'Steering Group' with Leadervale Leisure Limited formed in 1997, as a Company limited by guarantee to manage leisure opportunities in and around Lauder, including the management of the Leader Leisure Centre. The Company had two Directors and up to 19 members, all volunteers. The Company employed part time staff to manage the Centre and liaise with the tutors of a number of clubs and classes.

The main objectives of the Company were:

* To build and operate the Leisure Centre
* To encourage recreational activity
* To engage in joint management of other social and leisure facilities

The total cost in converting the former factory was £230,000 with £107,000 secured from the Lottery, £53,000 from the Scottish Executive, £48,000 from Scottish Borders Council (who also leased the building to the company) and £22,000 from community raised funds. The Leader Leisure Centre opened to the public in November 1999 just over three years after the formation of the Steering Group. The Centre was officially opened by HRH The Princess Royal on 13th March 2000.

From 2000 the Company widened the programme of the Centre by encouraging the development of the Health and Fitness Suite; a Cyber Corner and Computer Suite; the Social Library and Information facilities; a range of Sports Clubs, a Learning

Centre offering classes linked to further education; an After School and Holiday Club and a system for the casual booking of the facilities.

Discussion with members of the Centre indicated a need to increase the size of the Fitness Suite, develop the Social Facilities and provide a quiet area for reflective activities and meetings of community groups. The Executive Committee of Leadervale Leisure Limited therefore considered a further application to the National Lottery and the possibility of a closer working relationship between the agencies responsible for other community facilities in the town, particularly the Public Hall, the Town Hall, the Youth Trust Hall and the Primary School.

Princess Royal officially opening the Leader Leisure Centre 2000.

The fitness suite in the Leader Leisure Centre.

Lauder Primary School

The 20th century made an inauspicious start as far as Lauder primary school was concerned. Mr. Moore, the headmaster, noted that the attendance was *"not very satisfactory"* when the school reopened on the 3rd of January 1900. The following week Friday drill had to be cancelled as the *"Sergeant was unwell"*. From the middle of February through well into March, Berwickshire was hit by storms that blocked many of the country roads. Attendance at school, particularly by country pupils was a major cause of concern to Mr. Moore who noted that after a particularly rainy night and morning not one child from the country had attended school. However, in June they got an unexpected holiday to celebrate the capture of Pretoria in South Africa from the Boer Republic. In that same year the Upper Department was certificated as a Secondary Department. A year later the school roll stood at 196.

In 1904 Mr. Moore retired and Mr. Armit became headmaster. He left in May 1907 and was succeeded by John M. Duthie. The following year a school garden was laid out in plots. The school timetable had to be altered slightly in order to allow extra time to be given to the school garden. It paid dividends though, for the next year the pupils won several prizes at the Lauder Flower Show. Unusually, in June of 1910 the school was closed early on account of the *'extreme heat'*. In addition to recurring outbreaks of whooping cough and chicken pox, the school had to close in 1915 *"due to the prevalence of influenza"*. In March 1918 the school was closed for three weeks then it re-opened, only to be closed again for a further two weeks, this time because of an outbreak of measles. In October of that year the school was closed for almost a month as result of the influenza epidemic that swept through Lauder and engulfed Europe at the end of WW1.

In January 1919 Mr Duthie resigned and Mr. H. D. Fraser became headmaster. The school continued to be affected by recurring outbreaks of sore throats, colds and impetigo. The school garden was a great success and when it was too wet to work the children were sometimes taken to observe and transplant some wild flowers. In 1922 scarlet fever was causing great concern. A number of children went down with it and many parents kept their children at home for fear of infection. It was a serious outbreak that saw the death of one pupil from Whitlaw. Happier times prevailed though for the schoolchildren whose summer holidays started early after they had cheered the King and Queen as they passed through Lauder. However, in 1927 the school was once again affected by illness, this time it was an outbreak of mumps.

As well as disruption to school attendance due to infectious illnesses and bad weather, many parents kept their children off school particularly when their labour was required on the farm, a constant source of irritation to the school authorities.

Mr Jeremiah Halcrow became headmaster in September 1932. In the following session the school children heard visiting lecturers on 'The Savings Movement', and

'Temperance'. The school also closed for 'Empire day' on the 24th May after a patriotic address by a local dignitary. On January 15th 1936 George W. Anderson resigned as janitor of the school after 55 years of service. In the following March William Hardy was appointed as the school cleaner. Attendance – or lack of it – continued to exercise the mind of the headmaster. In December 1939 he noted that, *"Many very young children from long distances have been in regular attendance while other older pupils from shorter distances have been absent."*

In October 1938 the school buildings were utilised for the distribution of gas masks to the population of Lauder. The national emergency continued into 1939. That year opened with another kind of tragedy when young Robert Plenderleith of Class Senior II was drowned in the flooded Leader. The school was dismissed on the day of his funeral. The unsettled international situation was felt in the school when the children were given a talk on how to protect themselves from an aerial gas attack. The start of the war in September saw the school roll increased by 47 evacuee pupils.

The appointment of two evacuee teachers relieved the pressure on teachers somewhat. Some of the evacuees only stayed a few months before returning home. The school garden became more important and the school was urged to cultivate as much ground as possible. As part of this one of the teachers attended a course in potato inspecting and on completion acted as official potato inspector. Scarlet fever continued to cause scares but immunisation against smallpox and diphtheria became common. Petrol rationing sometimes curtailed the visits of specialist teachers, as did the advent of blocked roads in winter.

In December 1942 Mr. Halcrow retired and was succeeded by Mr. D. W. Harvey. The end of the war in Europe was celebrated by giving everyone two days holiday. When the new school term started in January 1946 the school roll had dropped to 88. Much of the first half of the year was taken up by planning for the introduction of the 'Meals in schools' scheme and of the raising of the school leaving age. In June the Moderator of the General assembly of the Church of Scotland, the Rt. Reverend John McKenzie visited the school and addressed the children. In that same year the last of the evacuee children left. The following year opened with an outbreak of measles followed by some terrible weather. Snowstorms continued throughout February and March causing considerable disruption in the school with many roads in the area blocked. This year saw the introduction of a Child Welfare Clinic and the start of the School Meal Service. The school roll dropped even further in 1948 when all the secondary students were transferred out of Lauder, causing the roll to drop to 72. The aggrieved headmaster was informed that all itinerant teachers would be withdrawn and that no teacher would be appointed to take needlework. The following February the Director of Education personally supervised the removal of a quantity of Domestic and Rural science equipment. However, this bitter pill was sweetened somewhat when he allowed the headmaster to buy a splendid upright piano at a local furniture sale.

Outbreaks of mumps and chickenpox continued to cause problems, but new lavatories were installed to replace the *"the outworn ones so long in use"*. The school received the benefits of electricity and then central heating. In 1954 the school roll had risen to 99, by 1958, mainly as a result of the closures of country schools the roll had risen to 125. In 1965 the public and church halls were used for classes as well as temporary classrooms being installed in the playground, while major rebuilding work was carried out. They moved back into the refurbished school in May 1966. By 1971 the school roll had plunged to 87 and in November 1974, strike action by teachers caused the closure of the school.

Mr Harvey retired in 1976 after 30 years of service; his successor was Mr Robert Towers MA. Mr Towers oversaw a number of changes in the operations of the school. He introduced educational outings and set up a parent-teacher association as well encouraging a range of extra-curricular activities. In 1980 an HM Report stated: *"I have the feeling this is a very happy school"*. The buildings suffered a bit over the years though. In 1993 a severe frost over the holiday period resulted in burst pipes and severe water damage was sustained. It was decided that a 'frost alert' heating would be run over the holidays. In 1987 a new classroom was being built over part of an existing classroom and corridor. Unfortunately, when the existing roof was taken off it started to rain. There was considerable excitement as pupils ran about with buckets and mops. After the school suffered a number of break-ins, a burglar alarm was installed. Mr Towers was called out a number of times in the middle of the night by the police only to discover that the culprits were currents of air, crawling spiders or sometimes wall displays falling. The 80s and 90s was a period of rapid change for the school. The buildings were improved but curricular changes were even more pronounced. It was a challenging time for headteachers to manage major curricular change as well as look after the welfare of the school.

Mr Towers retired in 1997 and Lauder Primary School had its first female headteacher. Mrs Jeanette Fox had previously been the headteacher at Channelkirk Primary School in nearby Oxton. A pre-school programme established for 3 and 4 year olds has proved successful. The playground was extended and a new garden area established. A computer suite was introduced with pupils able to access the Internet. In 2001 the school roll stood at 150 with another 24 in the nursery.

The changes that the school has seen in the 20th centuries are huge but I suspect that the 21st century will see even greater changes in primary education in Lauder.

David Harvey – Head Teacher Lauder 1943 - 1975.

Lauder School 1957/58.

*Lauder School and Schoolhouse
in the early 1900s.*

Lauder School before alterations.

Lauderdale Path Network

In November 2001 there was an appraisal of the various paths and walks in and around Lauder and Oxton, where people walked, rode and cycled. This was organised by Scottish Borders Paths together with Scottish Borders Council and carried out by an independent consultant. As many people as possible were asked to participate either by answering questions in the street or by going to the Leader Leisure Centre or Oxton Village Hall at the advertised times. All landowners were invited to contribute. From this the consultants produced a document with actual and possible paths marked on maps along with comments made. The Access Officer from SBC, Phil Waite, called a public meeting in Lauder at the beginning of February to present the findings of the appraisal and to find out if there was any interest in forming a local paths group. He explained that through 'Paths for All' £10,000 had been granted to this area for the appraisal and to begin to establish a good path network that took into account the needs of all the community and would be done in close collaboration with farmers and landowners. The catch was that £5,000 had to be spent before the end of May, £3,000 of which has gone on the initial appraisal.

The people from Lauder and Oxton who attended that meeting agreed that they were keen to form a group and held the first meeting of the Lauderdale Path Network on the 24th March. 12 people attended this meeting, including walkers, horse riders and landowners, they elected a chair, treasurer and secretary – principally to get a bank account opened. It was agreed that the money should be spent, as soon as possible, and therefore a project had to be chosen that could be done almost immediately and would benefit most people. From the information gained in the appraisal, and local knowledge, the group decided to improve the path at Burnmill to give proper access for pushchairs and wheelchairs, at least part of the way.

It turned out that the Access Officer had already looked at this path and had drawn up specifications and got some estimates. The local group have subsequently had a site meeting with Phil Waite and reassessed these specifications to suit what was felt to be needed by the community and was within the money available to us. Anyone in Lauder who has been to Burnmill recently may have noticed the mess that Richmond Homes have made of that end of the path – this has been brought to their attention by the Community Council, the Access Officer and SEPA. The result of this is that, hopefully, Richmond Homes will not only make good the damage but also bring that section of the path up to a much better standard than it was.

The overall plan of the LPN is to create a network of access routes in Lauderdale, which meets the needs of both landowners and users. The objective is not just to focus around Lauder, and with this end in mind the group is keen to have more input from Blainslie and Oxton. We are very keen to hear from anyone in Blainslie, Oxton and Lauder who would like to become involved either in discussions or in the more practical aspects of creating a path network. You don't have to have any special skills, just an interest in walking, cycling or riding in Lauderdale.

Break time for members of Lauderdale Paths Network clearing the path at the quarry in the Burnmill.

Lauder Millenium Community Woodland

Early in 1999 the Community Council posed the question 'What should the Burgh do to celebrate the Millennium?' To find out what the community felt there was a meeting in Lauder Public Hall to which representatives of all the groups, clubs, societies, the school, the Church and other notaries from Lauder were invited. There were a number of suggestions amongst which was one from James Hepburne-Scott. He suggested that it might be a good idea to restore some of the derelict pieces of woodland on Lauder Common. This idea was expanded upon and developed into a plan to have a community woodland for the Millennium, it also turned out to be one of the most popular of all the suggestions put forward.

A group of interested people, including James and three Middlemiss brothers - Dave, Jim and Bill, of the Lauderdale Sheep company which grazes the Common - duly met in the Eagle Hotel to discuss taking the project forward. It must be said that this project was a fortunate one from the outset. Within days of starting out the chance arose to acquire 1000 very special Scots pines, at no cost. These trees had been grown from cuttings taken from a remnant of the ancient Caledonian forest in Glen Loyne, Invernesshire, the parents being too old to produce seed. The Forest Authority reared the saplings at the Bush Estate, with the intention of creating a seed nursery with which to eventually reforest the original Highland sites. However, an ideal site had not been located, and this was where our luck was in, as James was asked if he knew of one almost as soon as we had decided to plant woodland. The proposed site on the western edge of Lauder Common proved perfect for the purpose. However these trees were by now 4 years old and needed to be planted that spring and we still needed some funding to get fences erected to keep sheep and rabbits out. By some Herculean effort James managed to get a grant application through and accepted by the Forestry Commission in record time. Funding was obtained through the Woodland Grant Scheme and Community Woodland Supplement with interim financial support from the Common Good Fund, which will in the long term benefit from the woodland through seed royalties. Further bonuses arrived in the form of 200 oak trees from Aaron Barnes and Neil Bowes, both of whom helped with planting, as well as 50 junipers from the Borders Forest Trust.

Dave and Bill Middlemiss were invaluable in the work they put in. In particular, they spent several days drilling 1100 holes in which to plant the trees as at 4 years old these were not small trees, some up to 5 feet tall and all in 2 litre pots. All those who braved the showers on the planting day were very grateful for that, and would never have been able to complete the planting in a day if this had not been done. Dave, Bill and other stalwarts had endured even wetter weather on the previous Thursday when the trees were unloaded and laid out on the Common. This was far more complicated than it sounds, since the trees had to be planted in a particular order to avoid potential cross-pollination between closely related individuals. The trees were laid out according to a computer-generated plan devised by Sam Samuels of Stow.

Saturday 8th. May 1999 dawned dull and very wet - a wonderful day for the planting of Lauder Millennium Community Woodland, for the trees, anyway! Fortunately for the people planting, the rain eventually stopped, the sun came out, and a new woodland was created. Lauder should he proud of the community spirit displayed on planting day. The new Cornet, Gordon Gilder, climbed the hill with his supporters in the pouring rain on the morning after, Picking Night to plant the first tree, together with re-elected councillor, Bill Hardie, in his best suit, and sporting a large umbrella. A list of the 60 volunteers who helped to make the planting such a success has been made for posterity and all the children were given a certificate to commemorate the occasion.

In the autumn a further 1000 trees (for the second millennium) were planted. These were a mixture of native broadleaved trees oak, ash, willow, cherry, rowan & holly. Again there was a good turn out of volunteers of all ages. We were all very grateful on both occasions to David Wilkinson and the Lauder Scouts who sustained the workers with an excellent barbecue.

By early 2002 the Caledonian pines had a crop of cones ready to he harvested to get the seeds to produce saplings that will become a new generation of native trees ready to regenerate the Caledonian Forest. On Sunday 2nd March 2002 members of the Lauder Cub pack led by Jon Mercer carefully collected the ripe cones under the watchful eye of James Hepburne-Scott. The cones were then soaked and carefully dried so that they dropped the seeds hidden within. These would then be allowed to germinate under carefully controlled conditions to produce, hopefully, hundreds of seedlings that can be returned to Glen Loyne for planting.

In the spring of 2001 the original group of enthusiasts led by James Hepburne-Scott got back together again to discuss the next project. This time it was decided that restoring an existing piece of woodland on the Common would be a good idea. The chosen wood was Cuckoo Wood as it has significance in the Common Riding traditions and it was within good walking distance of the Millennium Wood and Lauder.

On Saturday 29th September 'phase 2' of the Lauder Millennium Community Woodland was begun and planted. After an unpromising start in the morning when Jim Knight, James Hepburn-Scott, Jon and Angela Mercer begun to remove 400 turfs where the trees were to be planted, the day brightened into a beautiful afternoon. Along with the sunshine came all the willing helpers, young and not so young. They all got enthusiastically to work digging holes, hammering in stakes, heeling in trees and tying on tree guards. Within two hours all 400 trees were planted. All the trees were cell grown by Alba Trees so we were able to plant them before winter, and are a mixture of Scots pine and broadleaved trees. The fencing, rebuilding of the dyke and the purchase of the trees were all made possible with grants from the Forestry Authority and Borders Forest Trust.

The view from Cuckoo Wood is spectacular with the Eildon Hills to the right and Thirlestane Castle rising over Lauder to the left. It makes a glorious walk from the original Millennium Community Woodland (growing well) across the Common to Cuckoo Wood and then dropping down to the Lauder Burn before returning through Burnmill. Taking in some of the best views in the Borders. The completion of the Lauderdale path appraisal and the formation of a group to look at creating a network of paths around Lauder and Oxton is great news for the future of the Community Woodlands. This will mean that there is a very strong possibility of finding funding and support for improvement of the Burnmill area and the creation of a circular Millennium Woodland Walk in the next couple of years.

Planting day at the Millennium Wood on Lauder Common.

Lauder Parish Church.

U. P. Church in Kirk Wynd.

The Church in Lauder

Religion in Lauderdale, down the centuries, has, as might be expected, reflected the ongoing life of Scotland. With St. Cuthbert as one of the formative influences, Christianity in Lauderdale followed the traditions of the Celtic Church, so influential in the development of the faith in Scotland. However, the Celtic Church, especially in the south of Scotland soon gave way to Roman Catholicism after the Synod of Whitby and by the time of the Reformation, there were a number of churches and chapels in Lauderdale.

After the Reformation, the geography of Lauder Parish was established. It covered an area largely as it is to this day, with the one alteration to which reference will be made later. 1673 saw the completion of the present Church building which continues to dominate the centre of the Burgh 330 years on. Together with Channelkirk, it provides the focus for church life and pastoral care within all of Lauderdale north of Blainslie. It is worth mentioning Channelkirk at this point, because there is no doubt that it had been 'the Mither Kirk' of Lauderdale. It is highly probable that Lauder had been given its own independent status before the Reformation (See: Lauder It's Kirk and People - Rev Richard James). The links between these parishes were still strong, however, so strong that they were served by one minister after the Reformation (1560), until in 1611 the Reverend Allan Lundie was finally inducted into the parish of Chinilkirk (one of the many variant spellings which that parish has endured over the centuries) (See: History of Channelkirk - Rev Archibald Allan).

The first hundred and thirty years of Scottish church life after the Reformation was dominated by the struggle to determine the form of Church government which would hold sway within the National Church. Sadly, no sooner had Presbyterianism been finally *'By Law established'*, than other cracks began to appear within the fabric of Church life. Among a number of issues which haunted the Scottish Church over the next 240 years was the subject of patronage - the method by which ministers were appointed to their parishes - and as early as 1733 the first secession took place. Lauder, although never being at the heart of these disputes, was not immune to the problems affecting the harmony of the National Church. There were a few disaffected parishioners, and Mr Thomson [Lauder and Lauderdale] records that they walked regularly to Stow to worship. The 'Original Secession Church' itself split in 1747 (Burghers or Associates from Anti-Burghers or General Associates) and the Lauder Seceders, who had been walking to Stow, found a natural home with the Anti-Burghers who worshipped in Earlston.

After a few years, the connection with Earlston was broken. This was followed by six years during which the Lauder contingent found a home with the like-minded Presbyterians in Oxton, but eventually, an Anti-Burgher congregation was formed in Lauder (1757) and a Church was built in the area opposite where the Lauderdale Hotel now stands, in front of the site occupied by 'Inchkeith'. In typical fashion, once Lauder had acquired an Anti-burgher Church, it was only a matter of time before a congregation representing the Associate (Burgher) Church was created and in 1794 it was born; with a Church, to serve this small group, being built, a year later, in The Rotten Row. In 1825, these two congregations united as part of the reunion between the Burgher and Anti-Burgher Churches, when the United Presbyterian Church was formed, and they chose to worship in the Anti-Burgher Church. The building in The Rotten Row became, first a school-house, and then a manse, until the United Presbyterian Church eventually disposed of the property.

In the meantime The Church of Scotland had, as far back as 1752 suffered yet another secession when the 'Relief' Church left the fold. This Church made little impact on Burgh life, although it would not have been Scotland, if a few disaffected folk had not associated with this movement, and indeed they did build a Church in what is now called Crofts Road, but it only ever had one minister The United Presbyterian Church (opposite the Lauderdale Hotel) became an extremely active and energetic Church, which certainly rivalled the Parish Church in numbers and influence in Burgh life. A new Church was built by this Congregation in 1841 just before an enormous Church building programme began, which, not without cause, coincided with the creation of the Free Church, which itself came into being following the great Disruption of 1843, when the National Church was divided once more; this time a split which tore the Church of Scotland apart.

Lauder was not unaffected by 'The Disruption' and land was gifted adjacent to where Castle Wynd meets Kirk Wynd; there a Church was, very quickly, built (now housing Lauderdale Coachworks). It was opened in 1843 with a service at which the guest preacher was Dr John Wilson of Bombay, one of Lauder's truly great sons.

During its lifetime the Free Church in Lauder had only had three ministers. After the union between the Free Church and the United Presbyterian Church, forming the United Free Church, Lauder was left with two U. F. Churches (East and West). Clearly this was one too many and a local union took place in 1908 which saw the closure of the old 'Free' Church, leaving the West Church, i.e. the original 'United Presbyterian' Church, as Lauder's only United Free Church. This in turn was absorbed into the National Church (The Church of Scotland) with the great union of 1929 - a union which saw the mainstream of all those various schisms, secessions and disruptions dating back to The Original Secession Church, return within the fold of the established Church. [As a post-script to this, the Earl of Lauderdale, purchased the old 'Free' Church and gifted it to the parish church as a church hall, which purpose it served until it was sold in 1971 to Messrs Walker and Williamson of the Lauderdale Garage.]

The immediate impact of this union between the two United Free Church congregations was that Lauder, as from 1908, had only two churches. As already observed, in 1929 the Church of Scotland formed a union with the United Free Church and Lauder's remaining United Free Church became the West Parish Church of the Church of Scotland; a situation which continued for the next 25 years until in 1954, when after repeated attempts to negotiate a union between these two parishes, the West Church opted to dissolve rather than unite with the Old Parish Church.

So it was, that in these very unhappy circumstances, Lauder, after 196 years, found itself, once more with one Church; the Old Parish Church. Throughout all these years, whilst secessions and disruptions had wrought their destructive influence upon the Church life of Scotland, the Old Parish Kirk had continued to exercise its ministry within the Burgh, and although, others may have felt that at times it was overshadowed by a more dynamic presence exhibited by at least one of the other churches, it was, finally, the 'Auld Kirk' which survived in the face of all the difficulties confronting Church and state.

Since 1954, the same 'Old Parish Church', has continued to exercise the only ministry in Lauder; indeed, there can be few parishes in Scotland where over the centuries, no other denomination has sunk roots apart from the 'Auld Kirk' and its separated children. The Lauderdale family, although traditionally Episcopalian, continued to worship in the Church of their ancestors, and with the arrival of Captain (The Honorable) Gerald Maitland-Carew, and his family as the occupants of Thirlstane Castle, that tradition continued. Indeed, Captain Gerald is now an Elder in the Parish Church, and so the link between Thirlstane Castle, the Maitland family and the Kirk is, if anything, even more solid than it has been in the past 300 years.

In 1967 The Presbytery of Melrose after due consideration decided to alter the boundaries of Lauder Parish. This alteration brought within the parish, the Blainslies and the land to the south as far as Kedzlie and Chapel-on-Leader. This deprived Melrose Parish of a considerable area, but in effect it rationalized a situation which had existed from the period of the Reformation, since it was accepted by all the interested parties that the people of Blainslie and the surrounding area had always looked to Lauder as their Church.

The one other major change which has affected Lauder Kirk in more recent times is that since 1973 it has been linked with the Parish of Channelkirk, and shares a minister - in this, it will be noted, we have gone full circle, since, during the initial fifty years after the Reformation these parishes had done just that - shared a minister. In practical terms this reflects much that has been experienced by parishes all over Scotland, and not just in rural areas, but also within urban communities. However, it is confidently expected that the 21st Century will herald many more changes in the life and structure of the Church, but given that the Kirk in Lauder, and indeed Lauderdale, has survived so many changes in days past, the hope is that with the faith and industry of the people, Lauder and its Kirk will continue to witness to the Christian faith for many years to come.

The Glebe (Lauder old Manse)

The original Manse of Lauder was built around 1660 and was on the site which is now occupied by the Red House in East High Street. A new manse was built in 1812 at a cost of £1080 and is now known as the Glebe, set in 11 acres of Glebe land. The garden can often be at its best in February/March with the wooded areas covered in snowdrops and aconites.

The Glebe is owned by Ray and Babs Entwistle, and they, with their son James, spend a great deal of their time maintaining and improving the garden, the orchard and a productive vegetable patch, as well as looking after hens and sheep.

The house has seen many occupiers, many ministers, from Peter Cosens, William Smith, Donald Macleod, James Middleton, Adam B.S.Watson, Thomas Martin, Walter Lamb, William McConnachie, David A. Tosh and Richard F. James. Then in 1982 the congregation sold the Manse because of the escalating cost of maintaining such an old building, to Alan and Alison Cunningham, when they sold Threepwood farm, which they had farmed since the late 1930's.

Life is full of chance – of luck – and a wrong road on a bitterly cold day, drew Alan Cunningham and Ray Entwistle together. Ray had been to a craft fair at Ingliston, had seen some fine bronzes produced by Peter Fagan of Bronze Age and agreed to visit the factory in Lauder. He set off from Edinburgh on a winter's day in 1980 and reached Stow on the A7 before realising that he was on the wrong road. He decided to cross the moor and came across Alan Cunningham with two assistants and a hundred sheep on the road. They talked, Alan accepted a few minutes warmth in the car, Ray and Babs went for tea to Threepwood, for very many years, and later, when Alan and Alison sold the farm and moved to the Glebe, they went for tea again. One beautiful summer afternoon, Alan promised Ray first option on the Glebe if he ever decided to sell, and, even after his death, his son Andrew rang Ray in 1992 and fulfilled his father's promise.

Alison often went back to the Glebe for coffee or tea until her memory began to fail. Other members of the Lauder community would stroll through the park to the house in which their marriage ceremonies took place in the War years.

The property has changed internally, but externally is much the same as in a picture by John Blair, painted in 1892 and presented as a prize at the Lauder Bowling Club, and now hangs in the house.

Lauder Church Guild

The centenary was celebrated in 1995 with an exhibition of wedding dresses held in the church along with a flower-arranging exhibition. The funds raised from this together with a concert given by the late Bill Sharp, enabled the guild to commission a specially designed table. The table sits at the back of the church and has been much admired by both visitors and members. The name of the guild was changed from that of Church of Scotland's Woman's Guild in 1997 to encourage male membership and to broaden the basis of our membership. We changed from holding our meetings in the evening to the afternoon in order to allow our more senior members to attend.

Currently there are 22 members including one male.

West Church – Free Presbyterian Church and Manse.

Rev. Thomas Martin
1876-1904.

Rev. Walter Lamb
1905-1906.

Rev. William McConachie.
D.D. 1906-1931.

Rev. David A. Tosh B.D.
1932-1961.

Rev. Richard F. James M.A.
1961-1982.

Rev. John M. Shields
1997-.

THE CHURCH IN LAUDER - Annex A

Ministers in Lauder through the 20th Century:

United Presbyterian Church

(From 1900 became the West United Free. Church)

The Reverend Thomas Keir (resigned 1908)

Free Church

(From 1900 it became the East United Free Church - In 1900, The Free Church and the United Presbyterian Church united to Form the United Free Church)

The Reverend Duncan Turner (Died 1907)

United Free Church

(1908 The East and West Churches United - The East Church ceased to be a Church)

The Reverend George McNab (1908 - 1918)

The Reverend John Robertson (1918 - 1929)

West Parish Church

(In 1929 the U.F. Church united with the Church of Scotland)

The Reverend John Robertson (1929-1947)

The Reverend John Meikie Gray (1947-1952)

The Reverend James Mudge (1953 - 1954)

Old Parish Church

The Reverend Thomas Martin (1876 - 1904)

The Reverend Walter Lamb (1905 - 1906)

The Reverend William McConnachie (1906 - 1931)

The Reverend David Alexander Tosh (1932-1961)

The Reverend Richard Forbes James (1961 - 1982)

The Reverend Duncan I McGregor (1983-1996)

The Reverend John M Shields (1997-

Lauder Library Facilities

It Is more than probable that a library existed in the Burgh in the early part of the nineteenth century. However owing to the disappearance of old minute books, it is impossible to acquire accurate information of its management.

It would appear however that according to a booklet "Rules and Catalogue" of Lauder Reading-Room and Library dated 1898 that the Library was instituted in February 1862. It is also mentioned in "Rutherfurds Southern Counties Register" in 1866 that the Office Bearers at the time were.

President.	Mark Liddell.
Vice President.	James Whitton, Thirlestane Castle.
Secretary.	W. D. Aikman.
Treasurer.	J. McPherson.
Number of Volumes	436

A course of lectures was given during the winter in connection with the Library.

In 1876 funds were raised by means of a public subscription for the purpose of providing a building to house the Library. By a disposition dated 6th. April 1876 and recorded in the Particular Register of Sasines for the Burgh of Lauder on 12th. April 1876, William Lowrie Sleigh sold to the Members and Subscribers of the "Lauder Subscription Library" a tenement and yard now known as 48 West High Street Lauder for the sum of £150. Mr. Sleigh actually bought the property for £275. and sold it on immediately to the Library. He had a small cycle shop almost opposite the Library in West High Street. On leaving Lauder for Edinburgh he went on to form the famous Rossleigh Motor Co. When he became Sir William Sleigh, Lord Provost of Edinburgh he was admitted an Honorary Burgess and Freeman of the Burgh on the 19th. April 1924.

It is not known exactly when the billiard table was acquired for the Library, but it must have been sometime before 1886, as there are references made to the Billiard table in the minute book immediately after that date.

Extract from the Minute Book of Lauder Subscription Library.

This book commencing with the Annual Meeting Minute of 13th. January 1886.

"At the Annual General Meeting of Members of Lauder Library Mr. Moore Pres".

The meeting audited the Treasures accounts and found the same correct and showing a balance of £14:3:4.stg due to the Library. The Office Bearers were appointed as follows viz:-

Mr. Broomfield	*President*	*December*
Mr. Moore	*Vice President*	

Mr. Aikman Treasurer
Mr. Hogarth Secretary

Committee
Messrs.	*Anderson*	*October*
	Purves	*April*
	D. Watson	*February*
	Small	*May*
	Henderson	*June*
	Jolly	*July*
	Booth	*August*
	Westwood	*January*
	Murray	*March*
	Wm. Graham	*September*
	Jas Graham	*November*
	Cossar	

The sub Committee were appointed as follows:-

Messrs	*David Watson*
	George W.Anderson
	George Purvis.

It was agreed that the binding of the Magazines be remitted to the Sub-Committee and that about £2. be expended for that purpose.

It was also resolved that about £2. be expended on new books. The choice of the same was remitted to the Sub-Committee & Messrs Moore & Aikman. It was proposed and seconded that the 'Nineteenth Century' be added to the Magazines in the Library, there being an amendment that it not be added if it costs more than 1/3 monthly and on a vote being taken the amendment was carried by a majority of votes, this remitted to the Sub-Committee. The papers and magazines were continued as formerly. The papers were then sold as follows.

Evening News	*Mr. Anderson*	*9d.*
Scotsman	*Mr. Richardson*	*2/6.*
Kelso Mail	*Mr. D. Watson*	*6d.*
Ils.Lon.News	*Mr. Romanes*	*4/6.*
Punch	*Mr. Aikman*	*1/-.*
Courant	*Mr. Hogarth*	*1/10.*
Graphic	*Mr. Jolly*	*3/3.*

It is assumed that the month shown opposite the Committee members name signifies the month when they were responsible for the Library.

In a "Guide to Lauder and Lauderdale" Published by J. H. Scroggie, Chemist and Stationer in 1911 is the following:

Library and Reading Room.

This building is situated on the South side of High Street a little to the west of the vennel. The Library consists largely of modern fiction. In the reading room several daily newspapers and weekly newspapers are supplied, with the most important illustrated weeklies. There is also a good selection of monthly magazines. A good Billiard table is open to visitors at a very small charge. Draughts, chess and dominoes may also be played. In 1904 the Public Libraries Act was adopted but nothing further has been done in the direction of providing more suitable accommodation for the Library.

This was the last entry in the old minute book:

4th. July 1924.

"A meeting of Committee was held in Mr. J. H. Scroggie's shop. Mr. John Robson was, subject to signing the agreement, appointed Librarian."

Signed J H. Scroggie   President

We complain today of ever more rules and regulations but obviously this is not a new phenomenon, in the Rules and Catalogue Booklet of 1898 there were only six simple rules. In the Rules and Regulations of Lauder Subscription Library revised, February 1925 the number of rules for the Library had reached 20, for the reading and recreation room 7 rules, for the Billiard room 20 rules and for the gas 3 rules, making a grand total 50 rules.

Some of the more interesting rules were:

Library Rules

Rule 14.   The institution shall be open every lawful day, Public Holidays excepted from 9 AM. - 10 PM.

Rule 17.   Visitors shall be admitted to the privileges on payment of the following charges:-
Two shillings per month.
One shilling and six pence per fortnight.
One shilling per week.
Two pence per day.

Rule 18.   The Librarian shall prevent the admission of any person who in his opinion is intoxicated, uncleanly or disorderly and shall require the withdrawal of any person who is noisy or causing disturbance by unseemly conversation or otherwise.

Rule 19.   No spirituous Liquors shall be consumed in the Public rooms.

General Rules.

Rule 3.   Spittoons are provided and any member found spitting on the floor will be liable to a penalty of sixpence.

Rule 6.   Betting, playing for money and all card games strictly prohibited. Any offender will be liable to a penalty of one shilling on the first offence and on a second offence of a similar nature will be reported to the Committee for its disposal.

Billiard Table Rules.

Rule 10.   No person under sixteen years of age shall be allowed to play.

Rule 18.   No person shall be allowed to play whose hands or clothes are in a state such as might be injurious to the cloth.

From 1925 details of the activities of the Subscription Library become a bit vague, as the new minute book is assumed to be lost or destroyed.

On the 11th. April 1950 at a Lauder Town Council meeting a letter was read from Mr. Edward Duthie, Chairman Lauder Subscription Library, applying for permission to have the front of the building harled in cement, windows painted and a wooden porch taken away.

Lauder Town Council Meeting 6th June 1950

"Letter dated 17th my 1950 from the Scottish Home Department intimating that an honorarium by the Town Council to a part-time Librarian under section 339 of the Local (Scotland) Government Act 1947 would not appear to be competent."

When Mr. J. Robson resigned on 13th June 1959 and the post was advertised in the Southern Reporter, eleven applications were received. There were applications from all over the Borders, even from one person as far away as Thornhill in Dumfriesshire. Even though the job had changed from Librarian to Caretaker, though perhaps the fact that a free house went with the job was the attraction. By this time the premises had ceased to be used as a Library, it was used mainly as a Billiard room and for Committee meetings. The books had all been disposed of, some to Messrs James Thin in Edinburgh.

Mr. and Mrs. Doug Whellans took over as caretakers and remained there until 1967.

Lauder Town Council Meeting 3rd October 1967.

"There was read a letter dated 5th September 1967 from Mr. A. S. Baxter Secretary of the Lauder Lodge of Freemasons about the disposal of the Library premises at 48 West High Street, which it was understood would soon become vacant. It was agreed that the Town Council was not directly concerned with as it was thought in the first instance. An approach should be made to the Secretary of the Library Committee."

In 1975 The Borders Regional Council assumed responsibility for Library services in the Borders, and they eventually introduced a mobile Library service to the Lauder area.

In 1984 Ettrick and Lauderdale District Council petitioned the Court of Session for approval of a scheme for the Future Administration of the Lauder Subscription Library, The Isobel Ormiston trust and the Reverend W. McConachie Bequest and the funds and assets thereof. In fact the Council were seeking permission to sell the premises at 48 West High Street to create a trust fund in conjunction with the

Ormiston Trust and the McConachie Bequest. The Ormiston Trust Fund came from the sale of a piece of land owned by the Trust where the Council Houses were built in what is now the Scott Road/Smithy Croft area.

The value of the land at the time of sale was £300. The McConachie Bequest was made by the Rev. William McConachie to the Library in his will on 2nd December 1931 of £100. The interest to be used to purchase books.

The piece of ground in Scott Road/Smithy Croft was conveyed by a disposition by Isobel Ormiston in 1824. The objective of the Isobel Ormiston trust was for the education of poor children in the Burgh of Lauder and to be administered by the Minister of the West Church. Permission was duly granted by the Court.

In August 1986 the Library Building at 48 West High Street was sold for £11,755.

At meeting of the Leader Leisure Centre Lauder held on 1st March 1999 part of item 3.8 of the minute read,

> "The Secretary intimated that Bill Walker had offered his voluntary services in securing a Library in the Smiddy. The meeting agreed that he should proceed with the idea of using an end wall in the Smiddy, meet with the Principal Librarian and report on progress in due course."

After a number of meetings and phone calls with John Beedle, Area Librarian, everything was agreed to start in the Smiddy as soon as the shelving was up. The Scottish Borders Council Library service would give 140 books, and change them every 6 weeks.

Leader Library Lauder

At the A.G.M. of the Lauderdale Library on 8th. November 2000 the Chairman reported that despite a few teething problems the first year of the new Library had been a success, with over 100 members using the facility, and that literally hundreds of books had been handed in by well wishers. However there was still a major problem on how to fund the Library in the long term.

The Officer Bearers elected were:-

Chairperson   Kate Hankey.

Secretary   Cathy Rooney.

Treasurer   Jill Brooks.

Committee Members:-

Helen Cranston, Rhona Neil, Jacqui Louden, Margaret Middlemiss, Grace Whellans, Fred Campbell and Bill Walker.

In the later part of 2000 it emerged that there was a fund called the Lauder Library and Ormiston Fund operated by the Scottish Borders Council with a capital value of £32,000. in it. Hopefully the financial problems are now over for the Library.

Oxton Station with the Station Masters house in the foreground.
By courtesy of Robert D. Clapperton Photographic Trust.

The crowd on Lauder platform on the day the last train ran in 1959.

Jimmy Shaw Remembers

"I remember the Hiring Fairs with the farmers in their bowler hats and their wives and bairns. I was just a laddie then. At night the shows all lit up and that tae me was the most exciting thing of all. It was kerosene lamps and was blazing with flames all afternoon. They had shooting stalls and hoopla and all the things you can think off. Coconuts and all the rest, it was a great time. Folk came from the top of Soutra right down, even to Earlston although Earlston had its own Hiring Fair too and St Boswells had one too. The Lauder one was always held round about August. Then Lauder was done away with and Earlston finished up and it was only St Boswells.

Folk couldna' travel in these days, not really. There were no buses or, well there were no cars or anything like that. There was a Miss Wood in Lauder, she had the governor's car, or the dog cart. My uncle had a dog cart and it had a seat at the front and a box seat at the back for keeping your dog in or something, that was called a dog case. In those days there were no lorries and the only way ye could travel was by train and that was expensive and a lang way round. When I was a laddie we walked the sheep from St. Boswells. Oh I thought that was great. Before we left St. Boswells we got a Featherstone's pie. We'd stop at Blainslie and I remember Beenie Park in the wee shop there. Beenie would make you a bolognese sandwich, by God it was as thick as her, and a bottle of lemonade. Oh yon was good! Champagne was never like that and the corned beef on days like that was real good.

Ye had your dances then, not like nowadays. Everybody went and ye had a master of ceremonies, and the ladies were down one side of the hall and the fellas the other side. He said, "Gentlemen take your partners for a," waltz, a one-step, a foxtrot or whatever. Ye'd dance across the floor with your eye on a girl and somebody would get in before ye. So ye'd had it chum! I always remember one guy, he was dancing away with a girl, going round the floor, and the lady says to him, "Mr Low, when do you dip?" "Oh," he says, "the back end where the fleas are bad." We were getting quite modern then. The foxtrot, the Charleston y'know, that sort of thing. My pal, Bob, had a motor bike and we went tae the dancing Westruther, Oxton, Blainslie and Lauder. I made a mistake once. I got taken with a girl and booked the last dance with her. Well, the last dance meant ye were going tae take her home ye see. Well, I didn't discover 'til we were leaving the hall at Oxton that she lived three miles away! I had tae walk the three miles there and I was that long in coming back that Bob didn't wait for me. After that I made sure where the girl stayed before I booked the last dance.

When I was about six I would go out and play with other boys on most Saturday evenings. Sometimes we went across the street and into Taits the grocers, a little shop up there. Mrs Tait and her daughter would be serving as her husband was out on the van. It seemed that Mrs Graham, who lived in the Rotten Row, was always in there, with her was her sister, Mrs Sanderson, and they would chat away. Always Mrs Sanderson would say, "I've got a pain, you haven't a pickle of baking soda Mrs Tait?" And Mrs Tait would go off and come back with a tumbler, stirring it with a teaspoon. She would give it to Mrs Sanderson who said, "that's grand." And suddenly there was an explosion! Oh I thought the whole ceiling was going to come in. Every Saturday when you would meet Mrs Sanderson there, this is what happened.

My Auntie Maggie and Auntie Betsy lived in a little house in the main street. You would maybe see a ponytrap or a bicycle on it but usually there was no traffic. I used to think it was the widest street in the world. Nothing on it and all the street lamps lit. I always remember my aunties wore these little lace caps, tight necks with brooches. There was a big family bible on the table but I wasn't watching that for there was always a tin of toffees. They had two box beds, I remember them so well. The curtains were drawn when they were not in use you see and there was a sofa in front of the beds. It was a different world then. I remember one Saturday evening sitting on the doorstep and I can still hear myself saying it, "What for did ye let them take away my auld Maggie? Ay ah'm no gaun in. A'hm no gaun in. She had died you see and I could not understand it. It was 1913 and I can remember from that day onward everything that ever happened, so it was like she was a marker to me.

We got up to all sorts of nonsense when I was a boy. One of the things we did was to get two doors opposite, of course there was no traffic on the street. We'd get a bit of string and tie it on the handle of that door across the road and tie it tae the other one. We'd get someone tae knock on both doors simultaneously, and of course both people would come to the door and they couldn't open the door. They were pulling against each other. The other thing bairns used tae enjoy was when there was a wedding. There was a scatter. The receptions used to be held in Lauder Hotel and the scatter would be, "Poor oot, poor oot…poor oot!" I remember one fella, Jimmy Watts, he'd been at a wedding and he thought he would play a prank on us bairns and he heated some of the pennies on a shovel on the fire! And another thing we used tae like was the Masons' Walk in November. They had a torchlight procession and they all wore lum hats. And oh' us bairns used tae love if there was snow on the ground and see how many you could knock off. We would hide behind the dyke, throw a snowball and woof!! Oh we were no angels us bairns.

Tramps used to come through the village and all us bairns, we sort of knew them. There was one tramp we were all terrified of; he was called Yorky. Ye'd hear "Yorky's on the road!", or "Yorky's coming!" and all the bairns would disappear. Why we were frightened of Yorky I don't know. There was another that we weren't very fond of either. Oh she was a fierce wumin! She was more down Kelso area but occasionally came up here.

In Lauder, ye had what ye called "the lodging hoose" which was a place where tramps stayed overnight. Now that was controlled by an old man called Peter Burns. We called him Captain Hook because he had one hand missing and a hook instead of a hand. Peter Burns and his wife, Jeannie, lived there. I don't know if she was his wife or not but the two of them sort of lived there and looked after it. They'd have various tramps come in there and stay overnight. The house is still there. Peter was also the town crier. Ye see he would go out round the town with a bell, "Tomorrow morning at eleven o'clock all water will be turned off so fill your pitchers and kettles." When somebody died ye'd get him tae come round and tell people round the whole town, Mr so and so has died, the funeral is at eleven o'clock and you are cordially invited."

After the Hiring Fairs there were the flittings. They were always on the 28th May and folk flitted from maybe Earlston to the other side of Lauder or round about Galashiels. Always on the morning of the 28th of May the flitting would begin. There would always be two carts for each family you see. On the front cart, which was the big cart, they had their good furniture. On the back cart they had their tools and odd boxes and things like that. But on the back of the last cart there was a sofa which was tied down very firmly. On the sofa in the end cart sat the mother and all the children. Up behind her were all her plants; aspidistras, geraniums and all kinds different. My pals and I watched very carefully but we weren't interested in the flowers. We wanted to see what laddies were there to play football, for we knew they would be going to Lauder school.

Boghall Smiddy.

Newbigging Walls Smiddy.

Lauder Cemetery

The Cemetery must have opened for internments in the early 1860's, a recent search found a headstone with the following inscription on it;

IN MEMORY OF
PHILIP TAIT
Who died 29th. Nov. 1864
Aged 16 years
The first buried in this cemetery
OF HIS FATHER
THOMAS TAIT
Who died 20th. Oct. 1867
Aged 72 Years

This was all that was written on, what was a very large but plain stone, and for its age remarkably easy to read.

From its opening until 1931, the Cemetery was under the control of the Parish Council. The Local Government (Scotland) Act 1929 did away with Parish Councils, separate district committees (for highways and public health), standing joint committees (police), district boards of control (lunacy/mental health) and separate education authorities. Lauder Cemetery then came under the joint control of Lauder Town Council and the West District Council of Berwickshire County Council.

"Minute of first meeting of Lauder Cemetery Joint Management Committee held in the Town Hall, Lauder, on Tuesday 3rd. March 1931 at 7.15 PM.

Present Provost Anderson and Councillor Allen representing Lauder Town Council. Captain A. R. McDougal representing the West District Council of Berwickshire County Council. Mr. A. G. Doughty, Town Clerk, Lauder and West District Council Clerk, in attendance.

Provost Anderson was elected Chairman of the Meeting, and took the chair.

"Mr. Doughty reported that in terms of the Local Government (Scotland) Act (1929) the two interested Local Authorities had agreed that the maintenance of the Cemetery shold be borne by the two Authorities on the basis of the rateable value of the Burghal and Landward portion of the Parish as appearing in the Valuation Roll from time to time, without taking into account any de-rating or other grants to be received by either of the Authorities."

The last meeting of the Joint Committee was held on 14th. May 1975. The number of meetings held each year were erratic, sometimes it would be only one, sometimes two, sometimes three, and sometimes four, none at all were minuted between 1941 and 1948, possibly because of the war.

After the reorganisation of local government in 1975 the administration of the Lauder cemetery was taken over by Ettrick and Lauderdale District Council, and in 1999, after further reorganisation it was then administered by Scottish Borders Council.

Even after the Cemetery opened, interments occasionally still took place in Lauder Old Parish Churchyard, this was available for people who already had family interred there. The following minute from a meeting of Lauder Town Council held on 2nd. November 1954 marks the end of this practice.

"The Town Clerk reported that the Medical Officer of Health recommended that Lauder Old Churchyard be formally closed for interments. The Town Clerk was authorised to take the necessary proceedings in the Sheriff Court."

Leadervale garage and petrol pumps.

Garage Services in Lauderdale

Perhaps it might be useful if we start with the people who were repairing two wheeled vehicles at the start of the century, and then take it from there. First of all there was William Sleigh who had a cycle shop somewhere in West High Street, near Alec Paton's garage. This was the same Mr. Sleigh who, when he moved to Edinburgh, in conjunction with a partner Mr. Ross, formed the prestigious motor company of Rossleigh, who sold only the best motor cars of the day. Mr. Sleigh joined Edinburgh City Council, and went on to become Sir William Sleigh, Lord Provost of Edinburgh. A minute of a Town Council meeting dated 19th. April 1924 States. *"In terms of the resolution come to at the meeting held on 5th. February last The Right Honourable William Lowne Sleigh, Lord Provost of the City of Edinburgh, was duly admitted an Honorary Burgess and Freeman of the Burgh and the Burgess Ticket, in an appropriate casket, was presented to him by Provost Anderson. The Record of Admission was signed by Lord Provost Sleigh".*

Next we have Sandy Currie who operated a strange combination of Cycle and Barber shop, in what is now No.9 West High Street. Sandy stayed here for a number of years, then moved to No.3 East High Street, eventually being taken over by George Deans sometime in the nineteen twenties. We were now really moving into the twentieth century when Mr. Deans purchased an open topped char-a-banc, which included in its travels, a trip to Edinburgh every Thursday (Lauder half day), leaving Lauder at 1 P.M. and was driven by Jessie, George's daughter. The cost of the return trip was three shillings and six pence. 'Midside Maggie' was the name given to the char-a-banc, based on a character in a 17th. Century true story told in A. Thomsons "Lauder and Lauderdale". At a meeting of the Town Council on the 5th. December the following appeared in the minutes, *"A further application by Mr. George Deans to erect the petrol pump referred to in last minutes, was submitted, along with sketch showing that it was now proposed to place the pump close to the wall of his premises. The Council granted permission for the Pump being erected in this position, on the understanding that it was erected at the sight and to the satisfaction of the Streets Committee."* It would appear that this was the first petrol pump erected in Lauder.

The next owner of these premises was Mr. Archibald MacNeilage, who expanded the repair side of the business. Mrs. MacNeilage at some time started to use the front room of the house as a tea room.

Eventually in 1932 Mr. MacNeilage managed to persuade the Town Council to allow him to move his petrol pumps to the edge of the kerb. The next owner Mr. Ian Forrest bought the premises in 1956, and changed the name of the premises to "Lauderdale Garage", he then sold it on to Mr. Tom Sharp in 1959.

Mr. Sharp seems to have been unsuccessful in his venture in the Lauderdale Garage, as the business closed in 1962. It was bought at a roup sale in 1963 by George Williamson and Bill Walker, who developed the repair side, and also secured a franchise to sell Austin Cars. Further development of the business took place during the 1960's, when they acquired the old Church Hall in Kirk Wynd, followed by the B.P. Filling Station at the Lauderdale Hotel. After which they obtained the lease of the Jed Service Station in Jedburgh from Shell.

In 1972 George Williamson moved to Jedburgh, and the partners decided to sell the property at No 3 East High Street and split the business in two, George taking the Jedburgh part, and Bill the Lauder part. This meant that Bill retained the old Church Hall and the B.P. Filling Station, and No 3 East High Street became a house again.

We must step back in time for a moment, back to 1928 when a new garage was built at the north end of Lauder, which is still there today. It was built by a James Shiels and was known as James Shiels & Son Leadervale Garage, it was built specially for the son Frederick, known to every one who knew him as Fred. Fred was trained and served his apprenticeship with the previously mentioned Rossleigh's of Edinburgh. This garage had, from an early time, the Morris, M.G., Riley and Wolseley franchises.

In 1969 Fred Shiels sold the business to Stuart Allister and Willie Fortune. The partnership lasted for four years, and in 1973 Willie Fortune left the business, leaving Stuart Allister as the sole owner.

By this time the writing was already on the wall for many small garages in rural communities. After lengthy discussions, Stuart Allister and Bill Walker decided to merge their businesses. By merging their Austin and Morris franchise when they did, they just managed to beat the manufacturers to it. The new firm became known as Lauderdale Garages, and the extensions and further building that had started under Stuart Allister and Willie Fortune were finished and continued, with a new modern coachworks being added. During this time there was the continual disruption, and expense, created by the seeming need for the manufacturer to keep changing the name of the company, finally settling on Rover in the 1980's. During this period also, L.P.G. was introduced, and conversions were carried out on the premises, but, it was not a success.

In early 1980 a Leyland Tractor Agency was introduced along with a new Partner, Ian Forrest. The same Ian Forrest who had served his apprenticeship in this garage, and who had at one time, (as mentioned earlier) owned the garage at No 3 East High Street. Bill Walker retired in 1987 and the business continued until 1993 when Stuart Allister and Ian Forrest retired, selling to Adam Purves & Son, Galashiels.

At the present time Messrs Purves have a busy filling station and shop, and provide a full garage repair and recovery service. During its most productive time, in the 70's and 80's, the Lauderdale Garage, at one time had a staff of 25. The old Church Hall is still used today as a car body repair workshop, the B.P. Filling Station closed in the early 1970's.

We turn now to the third premises in Lauder to have been used to repair motor vehicles, that is the one presently occupied by Alec Paton at 37 West High Street. This garage has never had a name, but has always been identified by the name of the owner, and these premises have been in continual use longer than any of the others. At the start of this article we mentioned William Sleigh and his cycle shop. With further information, obtained, we suspect that this is in fact the same premises, because in 1920 when John M. Broomfield purchased the premises the lower part of what is now No.39 West High Street was used as a cycle shop, and was then part of the premises. The building at the rear which eventually became, and still is the workshop, was we understand at the time of purchase, a hay shed. There are still tools in the workshop stamped with Mr. Broomfields name and the date 1922. Mr. Broomfield was in time joined in the firm by his son Ian, apart from the repairs that they carried out, they also ran a very memorable taxi service, the tales are legend. On one occasion while conveying a party to Westruther to a dance, a member of the party commented on the number of rabbits in a particular field, Jakie as he was affectionately known, replied that he had seen so many rabbits in that particular field at one time that the crows had to sit on the fence.

Minute of a Meeting of the Town Council on 5th. November 1926:

> *Applications from Messrs A. & J. Rutherford and John M. Broomfield were submitted for permission to erect Petrol Pumps at their respective premises in the High Street. It was agreed to grant permission in each case on condition that the pumps were placed close into the wall.*

Perhaps it would be appropriate to mention here that at one time during the 1960s, you could buy petrol at five different locations in Lauder.

Lauderdale Garage 3 East High Street:	National Benzole.
A.& J. Rutherford Market Place:	Shell.
John M. Broomfield 37 West High Street:	Regent.
Lauder Filling Station Lauderdale Hotel:	B.P.
Leadervale Garage Edinburgh Road:	Shell.

There was also a Filling Station at Boghall selling Shell. Today there is only one site selling petrol in Lauderdale and that is the Lauderdale Garage, owned by Adam Purves, selling Shell.

In 1971 John M. Broomfield died and passed the business on to his son Ian. Unfortunately, after a short illness Ian died in 1973.

The business was then sold in 1974 to Willie Fortune, the same Willie Fortune who had been a partner in the Leadervale Garage. In January 1979 a young lad named Alec Paton went to work for Willie Fortune as an apprentice. Willie Fortune died in February 1991, and Andrew Cunningham from Oxton took over the premises in April 1991.

On the 1st. August 1996 Alec Paton bought the business from Andrew Cunningham, and Alec is still running it successfully today, having worked there since 1979.

Lauderdale Garage.

Petrol pumps at Rutherford's Shop.

Summary Justice in Lauder

For three-quarters of the 20th century summary justice in Lauder was meted out by the Magistrates Court and the JP Court, the former dealt only with offences committed in the Burgh while the JPs dealt with the wider West district of Berwickshire. There was a sea change in 1975 when District Courts came into being covering a much wider area and from then on offences committed in the Lauder area were prosecuted in Ettrick and Lauderdale District Court sitting in the Sheriff Court building in Selkirk rather than in Lauder itself.

The Magistrates Court was presided over by the Provost and Bailies of the Burgh elected from among the Town's Councillors. The prosecutor in the Court was generally a Solicitor with the Town Council while the Clerk of Court was a Burgh Official as well. The Court's jurisdiction covered many minor common law offences, such as Breach of the Peace and Drunkenness. Fines originally were up to a maximum of £10, later put up to £50 or imprisonment for up to 60 days. The Bailies tended to be long serving and had a great deal of experience thus allowing them to deal quickly and efficiently with their case load. The more serious crimes could not be tried in the Court and these were dealt with in the Sheriff Court instead. At one time the Magistrates Courts dealt with a relatively small proportion of all criminal cases in Scotland but this has now changed to the extent that nowadays more than 50% of all cases are prosecuted in the District Court.

The origins of the Justice of the Peace Court can be traced back as far as Roman times in terms of the way in which justice was dispensed. The title itself can first be found in the Criminal Justice Act 1587 and holders of the office are described in the Justices of Peace Act 1609 as *"Godlie, wyse and vertueus gentilmen of good quality, moyen and rapport to be appointed by His Majesty for keeping his Majesty's peace"*. Today's JPs are of course of no less standing in the community! The right to confer the office of JP was originally vested in the Secretary of State for Scotland and latterly lies with the Scottish Executive. The Justices operated within the landward areas of counties as distinct from burghs with the primary aim of "keeping the peace". Until 1975 the Court also had a small debt function.

The District Court system came into being in 1975 covering each District Council or Islands area in Scotland. In Lauder's case this fell within Ettrick and Lauderdale District. While the District Court is an independent statutory entity, distinct from the local authority, there is an element of continuity between it and the old Courts in the sense that the office of JP is preserved. Although on the one hand Lauder lost its very own Court there is still a local feel to the dispensing of justice in the sense that JPs are resident in and knowledgeable about their local communities. JPs in this area sit alone but it is possible as in Berwickshire for the Court to be presided over by a bench of three JPs. There was a further change in 1996 when the whole of the Scottish Borders came under a single local authority and the Courts are now run by Scottish Borders Council.

Sentencing power has increased over the years to the extent that fines of up to £2,500 can be imposed although the maximum period of imprisonment remains the same at 60 days. The Courts can also impose compensation orders so that the offender pays back the victim for any damage such as broken shop windows, vandalised cars and the like. Again the more serious crimes are outwith the ambit of the District Courts although as indicated above they deal with a much greater volume of the criminal cases than their pre 1975 predecessors. The jurisdiction of the Court is limited to offences that happen within its own boundaries and in a lot of instances nowadays that can involve speeding offences on the A68 north of Lauder! The Court can also deal administratively with the collection of fines for offences committed in other parts of the country and vice versa. Cases are now prosecuted by the Procurator Fiscal who is completely independent from the Council, although the Clerk to the Court is still a Council Solicitor. At one time Councillors were entitled to act as JPs but the position has now changed since the enactment of Human Rights Legislation. The rationale is that since there is some financial benefit to the Council from the fines collected, the Councillor JPs might be more biased in favour of finding defendants guilty than otherwise. However, in most cases the Council only retains ten percent of the fine with the balance being paid to Central Government. At the time of writing (2002) a major review of summary justice in Scotland is underway and it remains to be seen what effect this will have on the District Court. By contrast to time gone by JPs now have a specially tailored training programme and although they remain unpaid there can be little doubt that the dispensing of justice nowadays is a more professional business than in the past.

JPs must retire from actively presiding over cases in the District Court at the age of 70 but they can stay on what is referred to as the Supplemental List for the purpose of authenticating various documents. In addition to the cases actually dealt with in the Court, staff deal with fixed penalty fines which tend in the main to relate to motoring offences. A new system of conditional offers has also been introduced recently, whereby the Procurator Fiscal can offer the offender the chance to pay a monetary penalty rather than be dealt with in Court. This has had the benefit of freeing up more time to devote to the more serious cases. On that point probably the most significant penalty that can be imposed by the Court is a driving ban of at least six months which usually takes effect when the offender has built up more than the 12 or more permitted penalty points on his or her licence.

Sadly, it is unlikely that the Royal Burgh of Lauder will ever see a Court sitting within its boundaries again. Finally, although this article is concerned with the dispensing of summary justice in Lauder, it is worth noting that at one time the Commissary Court also sat in the Royal Burgh.

Lauder Neighbourhood Watch

In 1993 Bill Walker distributed leaflets to residents of Brownsmuir Park, the majority of whom were in favour of setting up a Neighbourhood Watch Scheme. A meeting took place in the Town Hall and those present decided that a scheme would be of benefit to the estate. PC Forrest advised on how to set it up and a committee was formed under the Chairmanship of Eugene Brandeschi.

It was agreed that signs be placed at each end of the Lauder boundary and at the entrance to Brownsmuir Park. The Community Council paid for the signs, which were erected by Scottish Borders Council.

Over the years the Neighbourhood watch has grown but more volunteers are needed.

A History of Police in Lauderdale

At the beginning of the nineteenth century there was a general agreement throughout Great Britain that the issue of policing had to be addressed. Crime was perceived to be increasing at an alarming rate and public disorder was common place. These problems were acutely highlighted in the large cities but even in the counties of Scotland there were calls for a resolution to the problem.

In 1812 Walter Scott noted that *"A spirit of lawlessness and insubordination was prevalent in some parts of the country"* the complex consequences of the industrial revolution and the increased mechanisation of agriculture led to a large shifting population tramping throughout Scotland in search of work during the first half of the nineteenth century.

It was clear that the old system of maintaining law and order was inadequate. The parish constable was an official who served the justice of the peace. He served for six months in theory but in practice it was difficult to find replacements because there were many drawbacks.

In rural areas like Lauder the community had no cause to enforce game and poaching laws and a constable who was active in his duties was seen as a man betraying his neighbours. Only during the Napoleonic Wars, when constables were exempt from joining the militia, did men willingly apply.

The parish constables had powers of arrest and could require public assistance to quell disturbances. They were instructed to concentrate on *"The preservation of the public peace and to arrest vagrants and to prevent tumults and seditious behaviour"*.

Written records concerning parish constables that worked in Lauder are sparse, but a truncheon has survived. It has a hand painted crown and the letter "G1111R B of Lauder". This constable's baton or staff is a formidable weapon, made of wood and over 28 inches in length.

The transition from parish constable to the establishment of the new police in Berwickshire was not a smooth process. Many of the cities and towns in Scotland including Edinburgh had installed primitive systems of policing in the early years of the nineteenth century, but the establishment of the Metropolitan Police in London in 1829 set a trend and a template for policing for all of Great Britain.

The 1830's and 1840's in Lauder provided more evidence of the need for change. When the parish constables did make an arrest the facilities for detaining suspects were not very satisfactory. The Tollbooth in the town was effectively the police station. The under storey had three cells with barred windows and one cell referred to as the "black hole". In 1835 four men were in the cells awaiting trial charged with breaking into a wagon. They escaped by breaking down the inner door and removing the outer doorstep. People in Lauder saw them making off but without the assistance of an effective police force, they declined to try and stop them. In the same year a female prisoner enticed the jailer to get some whisky, made him a drink and escaped. Needless to say the jailer lost his job!!

In 1843 the prison was condemned. As the Inspector of Prisons opened the rusty lock he saw that the floor in the cells had grass on it.

In the 1840's a new *'lockuphouse'* was built in Mill Wynd, Lauder.

In 1845 the parish minister commented that with regard to the burgh prison *"it happily has seldom any inmates"*. Whether this was because of a lack of crime or lack of detection is not clear.

In 1847 another external influence affected the way the burgh thought about their system of keeping the peace. A group of navvies rioted at Galashiels because a shopkeeper from Lauder had refused to supply goods "on tick" to them and dragoons were dispatched from Edinburgh. The shopkeeper returned to Lauder followed by the rioters who were eventually quelled by the Dragoons. In this incident, the advantages of having a force that could effectively deal with public disorder was brought home to the inhabitants and may have accelerated calls for the establishment of the new police. A writer later commented *"the strong arm of the law gave security. The dragoons were a terror to evil doers but a praise and protection to the law-abiding community of Lauder"*.

It appears that the parish constables could cope with crimes committed by locals in the burgh but when outside influences intruded in the shape of visiting navvies and vagrants, the system was found wanting.

It is no exaggeration to state that vagrancy was one of the main issues that forced the creation of the new police in Berwickshire. The economic upheavals in Scotland in the early 19th century created large migratory groups of people on the tramp looking for work. The inadequacies of the Poor Law, with the abiding principle that each parish should look after their own poor, made vagrants unwelcome in the burgh.

In 1840, the Superintendent of the County Police of Edinburgh, A.J. List, wrote that *"a rural police is essential to the comfort and security of the respectable and peaceable part of the community."* He clearly equated crime with vagrancy and restructured the constables in the newly formed force to prevent crime and suppress vagrancy. His views influenced rural forces that were forming at that time and certainly the fledgling Berwickshire Constabulary.

The adoption of the 'new' police in Berwickshire appears to have happened unevenly over a number of years. By 1850 the force was officially formed, consisting of 16 men including an S. Underhill as Chief Officer based at Duns. However, there is evidence that a constable of Berwickshire Constabulary was active in Lauder in 1848. A local newspaper reported an incident involving a P.C. James Dobbie at Lauder. It was PC Dobbie that was on trial for assault following a prisoner trying to escape from his custody at Lauder Fair day. It was alleged that P.C. Dobbie had been attacked by two men and had reacted by striking them with his baton. The jury unanimously decided that he was not guilty and expressed the opinion that the men should have been locked up for six months!!

After this somewhat rocky start that exemplifies the suspicion in which the new police were initially held, the Constable at Lauder returned to more mundane police matters.

In December 1852 the hue and cry went up as it was discovered that a murder had been committed on the toll road near to Lylestane Cottages. The Toll Keeper at Cleekimin, Andrew Mather had been found dead lying by the side of the road. The accused John Williams was an American from Boston working as a casual labourer. He had been found near the body. Three local men initially detained Williams and word was sent for the constable. P.C. Dewar arrived and searched Williams and found a snuff box, tobacco tin and a pipe that all belonged to the dead man. P.C. Dewar then conveyed Williams, by cart to Lauder lockuphouse. Williams told P.C. Dewar that *"he did not think they could hang him"* and that *"he would see us all in hell before he was hanged"*. Despite his bravado he was hung in a public execution, on gallows erected in front of the Castle Hotel, Greenlaw.

There were plenty of more mundane crimes for the new police in Lauder to address. In 1852, the town council resolved to offer £10 reward for information that would lead to the discovery of a person who was committing fireraising in the burgh. Other instances from the 1850's include 'drunk and riotous behaviour', thefts of 'silver and copper monies' and domestic assault whereby the husband struck his wife "with his feet upon the thighs, ...and legs". Also with his hands upon the head and other parts of her person. These offences were to be a constant feature of the work of the police throughout the nineteenth and twentieth centuries. One particular incident in 1858 could have been written for a 'bodice ripping' tale by Catherine Cookson. P.C. James Robertson noted a complaint from a seventeen-year-old girl that a Lauder dignitary had been riding his horse on the Post Road between Lauder and Thirlestane when he had spoken to the girl. It was alleged that he had tried to 'put her down upon the road', with intent to ravish her. She had resisted and in the struggle the arm of her dress had been ripped off. As he went to find his horse, the girl ran off into a field and hid from the man who searched the field on horseback but failed to find her. The constable reported the incident to the Procurator Fiscal but despite the fact that the girl's mother had witnessed the attack, the fiscal decided that there should be no further proceedings. Decisions like that and the concentration of police activity on poaching officers and vagrants involving the poorest people in the burgh, led to resentment and the constable was seen as the representative of landed interests.

It has been written that because of this perception the local constable was probably the loneliest man in the burgh. The men that constituted the new police in Lauder were drawn from the same class as the people they prosecuted. They were deliberately recruited from outside the towns they policed, to avoid conflicting loyalties of family and friends

Of the police recruited in the second half of the 19th century, 77% came from outside Berwickshire. These men did not very often see it as a career but rather a stopgap job before finding a better position. The average length of service for a policeman in the second half of the nineteenth century was approximately 21 years. It was a steady, respectable job but the pay was low and the discipline harsh. The Chief Officer at Duns was an autocrat who expected his constables to be always smart and available 24 hours a day. The constable at Lauder was given helpful tips or Standing Orders on how to keep his uniform immaculate including using a mixture of ammonia and tea which could be used to clean the grease from collars of tunics and coats. Berwickshire constables were expected to attend the Kirk one Sunday in uniform and the next in civilian clothing.

The burgh constable had to meet other officers from neighbouring stations at 'conference points' and when on his beat he had to obtain the signatures of 'respectable' people to show evidence of his patrolling.

The constable patrolled on foot in all weather, carried a baton, handcuffs and at night a lantern and a cutlass. The chief officer had high expectations of his poorly paid men. They had to be literate and able to complete the ever-present paper work. The job had implications for the constable's wife, who was expected to clean the office and cells, prepare the prisoner's food and deal with female prisoners. With these harsh conditions and the social exclusion it is small wonder that so many looked for other jobs or sought refuge in alcohol which often led to their dismissal.

By 1891, the force had expanded to 28 men under Chief Officer G.List. The list of equipment issued to the constables included a whistle and chain and a 'forage cap'. This was a Kepi style cap. Every constable was required to be the owner of a 'respectable suit of plain clothes'!

From 1895 to 1897 Constable Nicoll was working from the Lockuphouse at Lauder and at this time nearly half of all the recorded crime in Lauder was a breach of the peace. The other most numerous offences were assault, theft, being drunk and incapable and malicious mischief. There were also 3 officers under the Burgh Police (Scotland) Act of 1892. This innocuous sounding piece of legislation regulated the police and statutory laws of burghs including Lauder. It forced the police to intervene in traditional activities and push the people towards a more decorous lifestyle. Lauder people were prosecuted for playing football in the street, throwing dirty water on the footpath in Mid Row and allowing a horse and cart to remain on the High Street unattended.

78% of the people that Constable Nicoll reported had been drunk when they committed their offences. Licensees that sold drink out of hours were also charged.

The Licensee of the Eagle Hotel was reported for supplying a *'pint of ale and a half mutchkin of whisky'* out of hours. The accused persons were all working class with labourers and peddlers constituting approximately 50% of the accused. Some of the occupations of the accused are jobs that have long since disappeared including rag collectors, skin collectors, umbrella menders and rabbit trappers. With 36% of the accused being of no fixed abode, it appears that PC Nicoll was continuing the catching and robust police action against vagrants urged since the formation of the force and reinforced by Chief Officer G. List, the brother of A. J List who complained of the *"very large mass of migrating tramps, vagrants and dangerous classes which daily infest the county."*

PC Nicoll also arrested 18 Irishmen all of whom were reported as drunk. They formed part of the army of cheap labour engaged as harvesters and in other agricultural occupations that had annually worked in the Borders since the late 18th century. Despite being indispensable for farmers, the locals resented them and the police were urged to keep a watch on them. Like vagrants the equation ran that Irish = drunk = crime. The navvy riots that periodically erupted during the construction of the Edinburgh to Carlisle roadway, had at Midlothian in 1846 led to the murder of a policeman and so the police were wary of the Irish.

By the beginning of the 20th century the police had become an accepted, if not always welcome, sight to the locals of the burgh. The police themselves began to see their occupation as a career and the introduction of pensions encouraged them to soldier on plodding the streets of the Burgh. By 1912 the average length of service of a policeman serving in Berwickshire Constabulary was 14 years and the way Lauder was policed changed.

During the nineteenth century there had generally been a lone constable in Lauder, but by 1912 the station was staffed with a Sergeant Charles Grant and a constable Alexander Nettie. It would appear that the sergeant was a permanent feature in the station with constables who had just joined the force receiving such training as there was under the tutelage of the sergeant.

The period 1909 to 1939 was dominated by 3 sergeants in the burgh: Charles Grant, Robert Geggie and William Murdoch.

Stories are still told of Sergeant Murdoch who stood no nonsense and ruled the town with a rod of iron. It is said that in the evenings he could look along the High Street from the east end and was able to tell if anything was amiss. He habitually wandered up and down the vennels and nobody knew where he would appear. He and his wife had a signaling system whereby she waved a white handkerchief in a particular way to let him know if he was wanted at the police station or whatever.

The Great War of 1914-1918 impacted on the people of Lauder in terms of the deaths of servicemen and privations on the home front. It also had a large impact on the way the police operated. The Official Secrets Act of 1911 allowed that any person committing an offence could be apprehended without warrant not merely by a constable but by any person whatsoever. Chief Constable Morren detailed in a series of memorandums the preparations by the police *"for action in the event of a landing by the enemy in this country"*. The role of special constable volunteer policemen came to the fore. Lauder had six special constables in the burgh and six in the landward sub-division. It was noted that two owned cars and one had a motorcycle. These special constables assisted the constable at Lauder as he tried to enforce a wide variety of emergency legislation. Horses were required for war transport and the constable had to ensure that their requisition was enforced. The police set up a system for reporting the sighting of enemy airships and all private wireless telegraph stations had to be closed and their aerials removed!! The fear of spies and invasion also prompted the police to issue permits to pigeon fanciers only after they had satisfactorily shown that there was no evidence of the pigeons being used *"for communication with agents of the enemy on the continent"*.

A resident of the Burgh was charged under the Defence of the Realm Act, which demanded national solidarity during wartime, with creating the offence of spreading disaffection or alarm amongst members of H M's forces or among the civilian population. During the war six army and navy deserters were rounded up by the burgh police.

An anaysis of the crimes detected in Lauder between 1909 and 1919 returns to a familiar theme. The people charged with being drunk and incapable or drunk and disorderly, made up 60% of the accused. Trespass still acounted for 16% of the accused and the ubiquitous breach of the peace 8%. There was a wide variety of other offences reported but one was very significant. In 1916 a general dealer of the burgh was charged with driving a motor vehicle without lights. The growth of use of motor cars and lorries brought a class of people, those who could afford the vehicles, into conflict with the police for the first time. These drivers were often the respectable and peaceable part of the community that A.J. List had earlier believed would benefit from the police. The driver was an exception. 40% of the accused persons were labourers and 29% were vagrants or pedlars.

By 1918 the Berwickshire Constabulary had adopted the cap that is still used today but without the diced band. Between 1929 and 1939 the crimes committed in the burgh were still dominated by drunken behavior with 25% being of the accused charged with drunk and incapable and drunk and disorderly and 25% for breach of the peace. This period showed a remarkable growth in two types of offences. Firstly, theft which had grown to 11% of the total. This was possibly because people had more property that could be stolen. Secondly motoring offences. In 1921 on what is now the A. 697 road between Lylestane and Huntingdon, a car had suffered a burst rear tyre. This had resulted in the occupants being "turned out onto the road" and a female died. It would appear that the police in Lauder treated motoring offences seriously. Between 1929 and 1939, 12% of all offences were related to road traffic offences and of these 7% were charged with drunk driving. In 1936 the Chief Constable D.W.S. Brown lamented that offences involving drunkeness had more than doubled in the county and he also expressed concern at the increase in motoring offences. During this period, labourers again made up the bulk of the accused and significantly, the threat of vagrants had declined to such an extent, that vagrants and pedlars only constituted 11% of the accused persons.

With the advent of the Second World War, the police in the burgh were again utilised to help the war effort. Locals were encouraged to always carry gas masks, to avoid the waste of any food, electricity, gas or water and to be ready to assist the constable if required. Despite the war, the business of policing continued and in October 1939, the Burgh Court in Lauder dealt with three men for breach of the peace, a woman who had been drunk and incapable and a man who had no current road fund licence. The theme of drunken behaviour in the burgh continued.

In 1940 the war arrived at Lauder when a resident, an Italian national, was interned at the police station as an "Enemy Alien".

At the start of the Second World War, the police serving in the Lauder Section were, Sergeant William Murdoch, Constable Robert Dougal and Constable William Campbell based at Oxton. The County of Berwick Police at that time numbered 32 officers, comprising of Chief Constable David W.S. Brown, Superintendent/Deputy Chief Constable Robert Brand, an Inspector, six Sergeants and 23 Constables.

The situation remained the same until 1948 when the three counties of Berwick, Roxburgh and Selkirk amalgamated to form the one force. After the Second World War a large percentage of officers recruited into the Force were ex-forces. This fact was clearly evident some thirty years later, in mid sixties, when the retiral of those officers caused a shortage, resulting in a large number of new officers being recruited.

Up to 1948 the police station in Lauder was situated at No.1 Millwynd, the *"lockuphouse"* that had been in use for one hundred years. It was replaced that same year by the new police station in East High Street. This new station took the form of a police office in the centre with a house at either end. It was one of the first of many buildings to have a flat roof, the type of roof that was to give endless trouble in the years to come. The sergeant lived in the left side house of the building with direct access to the police station and the constable in the right side.

A year earlier the legendary Sergeant William Murdoch was replaced by Sergeant William Miller. By this time a constable was earning £7.50 per week, albeit that they were in rent-free accommodation. The main mode of transport in those days was a bicycle and this situation later improved with the arrival of the much-loved BSA Bantam motor cycles.

In 1951 a new Chief Constable arrived, from the south to take over from David W.S. Brown. His name was John Willison and he was from Worcestershire. There is no doubt that Mr Willison was progressive as he completely transformed the force and effectively brought it into the 20th century. An example of what he was like was that in order to buy motor cycles that the force badly needed he sold two or three rural police stations.

As time went by and the volume of traffic gradually increased and the A.68 became busier, then road accidents became more prevalent and criminals more mobile. The need was identified to have a speedy response to situations and it was decided to have a patrol car based at Lauder. One of the first Traffic Officers to be stationed there was Peter Allan. Peter was 12 years on the patrol car, having been transferred from Duns to Lauder in 1952. The patrol car at that time was a Mk 7 Jaguar

On occasions, the traffic officers often became involved in local matters and Peter recalls a complaint being received from Thirlestane to the effect that someone was poaching trout on the Leader. Everybody knew who it was (Jackie Scott who lived in Lauder and worked with Roger Builders, Earlston.) Peter decided to visit Mr Scott and make him aware that he knew that it was him who was doing the poaching. Jackie of course denied all knowledge and the following morning Peter opened his back door to discover a polythene bag lying on the step with ten brown trout inside. This was Mr Scott's way of telling the police that *'yes it was me but you'll never prove it.'* It transpired that there were no more complaints of poaching on the Leader.

There were one or two characters in the force at that time and one in particular arrived from Northern Ireland with his wife and he was to go down in the annals of the force as one of the great characters. His name was Herbie Todd and he and his wife Ethel quickly settled down to life in the Royal Burgh. It must have been heaven compared to the turbulent times in Northern Ireland. Herbie was a joiner to trade having served his time in the Harland and Wolff shipyards in Belfast. He and his family were well liked in the town, even although he was strict and knew how to handle trouble.

In 1958, Thomas McCallum took over as Chief Constable and he was what could be termed as home grown having come up through the ranks in the Border Forces.

As a result of traffic officers now being based at Lauder more houses were required and a semi-detached block was built at the rear of the police station to house the two traffic officers. In 1967/68 a second block was built next to the first, to house the officers from Oxton and Gordon when the controversial practice of closing rural police stations continued.

Bob Beattie arrived in Lauder in 1960 and took over from Peter Allan on the patrol car. Bob and his family settled well in Lauder and made many friends. He joined Alec Gregory on the patrol car and they worked together until 1966. That year Alec was transferred to Jedburgh and was replaced by Bob Bell. One of Bob Beattie's favourite stories was the day he and Sergeant Eric Taylor attended a road accident at Broadwood Sheil on the A.68 between Lauder and Earlston. Constables Frankie Whyte and Ronnie Dalton from Earlston, who were on a motor cycle, joined him there. Frankie parked the motor cycle on the verge on the apex of the bend where the accident had occurred. He had no sooner done so when a Citroen motor car, travelling south, came round the bend, skidded on the icy road, hit the motor cycle and knocked it into the field. Frankie immediately went over to the vehicle and began to give the person inside the car a real telling off. It was not until he was finished tongue lashing that he realized that the car was foreign and therefore a left-hand drive. He had therefore spent some time giving the front seat passenger a telling off for dangerous driving. To make matters worse the occupants of the car were Belgian and couldn't speak a word of English. Frankie was not allowed to forget the incident for some considerable time.

Sergeant Eric Taylor was tranferred from Hawick to Lauder in 1960. In those days the force had only two woman police officers and the police officer's wives were still expected to help in dealing with female prisoners, without payment. Eric's wife recalls an occasion when a well-known woman of ill repute was arrested in Lauder and after the woman's appearance in court, Mrs Taylor accompanied her husband in transferring the prisoner to Saughton Prison Edinburgh. On their arrival there, the prisoner was placed in a detention room prior to being processed. At that point another officer arrived and on seeing a woman with a police officer assumed that she was the prisoner and took her by the arm and asked her if this was her first time in Saughton. Luckily the Taylors saw the funny side and still laugh about it to this day

Rae Hastings was transferred to the car in Lauder in 1971, replacing Bob Beattie, and he remained there until 1973 when he was transferred to the CID at Galashiels. Rae was one of the few people who could claim that he had been run over by a stagecoach The story was that a stagecoach sponsored by White Horse Whisky was making the epic journey from Edinburgh to London. On reaching Soutra it had cast a metal wheel band. The patrol car had attended and the wheel was duly repaired. At this point something had frightened the horses and the stagecoach had suddenly ran forward onto the patrol car and caused considerable damage. Rae had no option but to fill in an accident report and when it came to the part where it described the horsepower of the other vehicle he completed it in with the number four. After all the stagecoach was being pulled by four horses!!

One of the longest serving officers in Lauder was P.C. Adam Tindall who was posted to Lauder in 1952 and was there until his retirement. Adam has since passed away and is still remembered with affection by many of the older residents in the town.

Sergeant George Dodds, who retired in 1976, was the last Sergeant to reside at the police station. After he left the house it became an extension to the police station and included a muster room. George and his wife still reside in the town.

Sergeant Vic Pemberton was subsequently transferred to Lauder and travelled back and forth from his home in Bowden in his fibreglass Reliant Kitten. On one occasion when he had a slight accident with the car, his 'kind' colleagues left a repair kit on his desk, in the form of roll of sellotape.

Harry Scott, who incidentally is a native of Lauder arrived to work, or more accurately, take up employment in the Royal Burgh in 1973. He remained there until he was promoted and transferred to Galashiels in 1978. One story that Harry recalls was when a beer lorry shed its load on the bend at Thirlstane Farm. Most of the beer finished up in the field to the delight of the cattle and the local residents, including the polis. Initially the owners of the lorry stated that they were writing off the load and the villagers could help themselves. No further prompting was needed. and roadmen, farm workers, local residents, and of course the police, loaded up whatever transport they had in hand and carted the beer away. Later however the insurance company was to dictate otherwise, asking for proof that the load existed and the company was obliged to account for the load. So then the panic started because the police, before they could accept anything in the way of presents or gratuities, had to have the permission of the Chief Constable and needless to say most of the beer had been consumed and what was left was quickly removed from their homes.

In 1975 Berwick, Roxburgh and Selkirk Constabulary amalgamated with Edinburgh City Police and Lothian and Peebles Constabulary. This restructuring, reduced the number of forces in Scotland form twenty-three to eight. The three counties together with Peeblessshire combined to form what was to be called 'G' Division in the new Lothian and Borders Force. The Division, somewhat unkindly, was to be called the Tractor Division by some of the less informed city slickers. To those who had served in Berwick, Roxburgh and Selkirk Constabulary, the demise of such an efficient little Force was extremely sad but nevertheless the larger Division soon gained the reputation as being just as efficient as the other six Divisions of the new force.

Lauder had now became part of the Selkirk Section in the Galashiels Sub-Division, a very formal set-up compared to what it was pre-regionalisation. With wages now reflecting the shifts and unsociable hours that were being worked, officers we allowed to purchase their own homes within a certain mileage of their workplace. Inevitably this resulted in a number of police owned houses becoming vacant with little or no prospect of them ever being occupied by officers again.

The patrol car was finally withdrawn from Lauder in 1997 and based in Galashiels. The two blocks of houses at the rear of the police station were sold. The police authorities had therefore no option but to put them on the market. This situation of selling police houses radically changed the way the force was to be policed. Whereas before the police officers resided where they worked and they and their families were very much part of the community. It now transpired that officers were travelling as much as twenty miles to the station where they worked. This situation had distinct advantages and disadvantages. The advantages of living where they worked meant that officers knew everybody in the town and also knew what was going on. Officers who were now travelling from outwith were treated more like strangers and did not have the same rapport with the locals. Added to this, the officers were not Lauder officers as such but Selkirk Section officers with an area of responsibility stretching for many miles.

Police in the burgh were slow to adopt technology, often because of the expense. Constant foot patrols gave way to pedal cycles and then the motor car. The telephone gave the public instant access. In the nineteenth century the constable was contacted in person or spoken to when he was on his beat, by the twenty first century access and response was demanded immediately by the public.

The uniform and equipment used by the police has changed dramatically in the last ten years. The tunic, wooden baton and handcuffs, that Constable Nichol of 1895 would have recognised, gave way to a jersey, a side handled baton and rigid handcuffs. At the beginning of the twenty first century, C.S. spray and stab proof vests are routinely worn by patrolling officers.

At the end of the nineteenth century, road traffic offences accounted for 28% of all police reports. reflecting the increased use of motor vehicles particulary on the busy A.68 trunk road. Vandalism accounted for 16% of the reports, assault 14% and crimes of dishonesty 13%. Only 8% of police reports were for breach of the peace. It is difficult to analyse these figures and their significance compared to previous statistics but it would appear that the burgh had become a more peaceful place to live and although alcohol did feature in many of the offences recorded, it was not as important as it had been previously.

Lauder is also distinctive in that the officers that have served there have nearly all been policemen. Only two policewomen have worked in the burgh and only for very short periods.

During the past century, policing in the Royal Burgh has changed dramatically with policing pressures dictating that officers travel almost everywhere in vehicles. The days when crime figures were low and travelling criminals where virtually unheard of, have gone and we no longer have the familiar figure walking through the streets, passing the time of day with the locals thereby keeping the finger on the pulse of the community. Finally, a great many police officers have served in the Lauder area during the past century and it has been very apparent that the vast majority have enjoyed the experience.

Lauder Police Station 1840s - 1950s.

Lauder Police Station 1950s - 2002.

Oxton Police Station after the first world war.

Oxton Police Station mid 1930s to 1953.

Oxton Police Station 1953 - 1967/68.

Jim Fullerton Remembers

"I was born at Eastfield of Lempitlaw near Kelso. My mother was my father's second wife, his first died of the awful flu at the end of the war. My grandfather, on my father's side, came from Cairndinness near Haddington. But my father told me that the family originated just the other side of Duns.

My father worked on the farms and he moved about a lot. He would move for the sake of getting eight shillings a week of a difference in his pay. I remember my grandfather coming to stay. He made what they termed 'brose' away back. You took so much oatmeal and so much water, stirred it up, covered it and let it stand. He made a wee bowl for me - I never forgot that. We went for a wee walk and came back and I devoured the brose. I remember my father's first wife's mother. We termed her just granny you see. She was a wee body, maybe not five feet. She was the wee-est body I ever saw, wore clogs, and fed pigs the size of her. There were some other clog folk who came to the Newbiggin and some of the bairns at Fountainhall school wore clogs; but after a while nobody wore them.

I started Fountainhall Primary School when I was five. Walked the three miles to school in the morning along with the other bairns. Our first teacher was Miss Lumsden, she wore tweedy clothes and came to school on the back of her sister's motorbike. Another teacher was Mr Simpson, I remember he could keep order. When he came out of the schoolhouse into the playground things went quiet.

I left Fountainhall when I was coming on nine. We flitted in the May across to Hartside. We flitted by horse and cart; across the hill between Middletoun and Threeburnford, which was top of the valley up there at Channelkirk, then down the road and up to Hartside. The house we lived in was a single cottage at the steading. Other than that there was a well and a couple of other houses.

I went to Oxton School, which was just under two miles away. A Mr Cree was my teacher. He was a nice, wee teacher. I don't think he had a strap you know. I never saw it. He was quite a good teacher I suppose. When I left school I could read, write and count. I came tenth out of three hundred in the Berwickshire bursary exam. You could either go to Lauder or Duns. But of course it was hardly mentioned that you had to pay your way. I came to Lauder for a couple of months before the summer holidays. Then it was discovered that if I wanted to stay on at Lauder for the new term, there would have to be new books and it was going to cost a fiver. The other option was Duns where you had to stay in a hostel and that was money again. And of course, Duns was at the far side of the world as far as going for education there. So I finished my education at Oxton. I did very little in the last year because I was right to the very top, as far as you could teach.

While I was at school I used to nip into the bakehouse, run by Jimmy Bell and his wife, and do wee bits of jobs after school and at lunchtime. This had been going on for a while, so when my mother and father were on the move again it was more or less arranged between my father and Jimmy Bell that I'd go on as an apprentice. My father and mother moved at the November term so I was fourteen and three months when I was out in the wide, wide world to look after myself. The only advice I got from my father was, "Never get anything you can't pay for." Never ever in my whole life have I got anything that I couldn't lay down the money for.

As an apprentice in a bakery you had all the drudgery to do. But I learnt the job gey quick and I was as pleased as punch this day when the boss said, "I want two pints of eggs." I'll never forget it. Two pints of eggs you see? Well you had to crack your egg of course and open it up. They were country eggs and you had to make a right job of smelling them. In the bakehouse you had to clean tins and wire trays. You cleaned them and anything else that needed cleaning, Of course you weren't allowed near the ovens.

I picked things up pretty quickly to tell the truth and when I was about sixteen Jimmy Bell, my boss, turned ill. I was summoned up the stairs to the bedroom and he says, "Do you think you could manage the bread?" I said, 'Well I have watched what you did, Yes. I will have a go." And that was that. So I made dough myself for the first time. It was for two hundred and twenty loaves. The first loaf I put in, when it came out it was about two feet long. I had made a mistake and of course I couldn't shift it. But the rest of the batch was fine. It was nice. It was nice bread.

Times were hard then. Not long after Jimmy Bell spoke to me and says, "Could you manage the bakehouse?" He says, "The vanman's leaving and I'm thinking I'll do the van." So I never hesitated. I just said, "Yes. I'll do the bakehouse." I was eighteen, maybe a bit less. "Okay then. You'll do alright." So this day he comes to me after the bread was out the oven and he has this list written out. "You'll do that today. You see?" He must have had a wee bit look at my face because he says, "If you can't do it today, we'll do it tomorrow." And I thought to myself, "Well, I'm damned there'll be nothing left to do tomorrow." And I got everything done.

I worked about twelve hours a day. We made rolls in the morning, cookies, scones and everything else. In a short time I was making and decorating wedding cakes. I learned to do that by watching Jimmy Bell. When I made my first wedding cake; I cooked, mixed it, fired it and put marzipan and icing on to it. It had three tiers with solid silver pedestals between the tiers. It cost three pound ten shillings. The woman who ordered it thought she kept the silver!

The Bells were good to me and I really enjoyed working there. I got ten shillings a week to start with. Maybe it doesn't sound much nowadays but I had my keep. So I was twice as well off as most young men at the time. I worked there till 1963 twenty -seven years.

In summer I played at football in Justice Hall Haugh. In winter there was badminton and indoor bowls. Then there were the dances. There'd be a dance at Oxton one Saturday and Blainslie the next, Westruther the next. In between times they might have a Friday night dance. After Friday night dances I just went in and changed my clothes to start work at three in the morning.

I had not liked my short time at Lauder school. I tried to forget it when I moved. But there was one thing I never forgot a wee dark-haired lassie called Mary Waldie. That lassie's face stuck in my mind. When she left school she worked at Faughhill as a maidservant you see. Then her mother moved to Oxton along with Mary and her sister. Mary was a grand dancer and she kind of learned me some of the dances. Off and on I walked her home from dances. I think she had a wee bit of a notion of me at the time. This night I walked her up to the house. "Now," she says, "You'll have to stop this getting me home." I says, "What do you mean I'll have to stop it?" "I'm getting married." she says. Maybe I'll draw a veil over the next few years, but Mary became Mrs Galbraith.

This Don Galbraith was in the army, an Argyll you know: He went away. I went to a dance at Blainslie. I hadn't seen Mary, I'll guarantee, since she was married. Who should walk in but Mary? I danced with Mary and you know I suddenly realised that I was dancing every dance with her and she was giving me, you know, the lady's choice. It was that dance that night that is seemed everything turned. She did tell me that there was a difficulty in the marriage. I knew fine it broke the moral code as things were. I says, "We're not going to skulk about and hide in vennels. We're going to tell folk, we'll show folk that we're gaun thegither. Right!" That was late 1943 and I saw Mary practically everyday of my life till the day she died. That was 1996."

Mary and Jim married in 1957 when Mary's divorce finally came through. He and Mary opened up a hotel at Loanside, which they ran successfully for many years. In 1995 Mary took a stroke and was to spend 51 weeks in the hospital before she died. During this time Jim and Mary helped raise thousands of pounds for the hospital.

Cambridge Smiddy.

Making a metal tyre at Cambridge Smiddy.

Fitting the tyre to a cart wheel Willie Turnbull and Tommy Halliday.

Population and Special Buildings

In the mid 19th century, the recorded population of Lauderdale (the parishes of Lauder and Channelkirk) reached a peak of 2882, recorded in the Census of 1851. During the second half of the 19th century, the population of Lauderdale showed a continuous decline at every Census (see Figure 1). In contrast, over the same period, the population of Scotland as a whole showed a continuous increase. Clearly, this situation arose from the urbanisation of Scotland with the increasing economic prosperity and employment in the towns and cities, whilst areas like Lauderdale, largely dependent on agriculture, saw a decline in the number of jobs available as farms mechanised and needed less labour.

At the start of the 20th century, at the 1901 Census, Lauderdale's population had fallen by almost 30% from its peak in 1851 to stand at 2021. This decline was of growing concern locally, but the coming of the railway in 1901 was seen as the key to reversing it. Writing in his "History of Channelkirk" in 1900, the Reverend Archibald Allan commented that *"with the advent of the railway it is to be hoped that the drain on population will cease, seeing that there will be more employment"*. The work involved in the construction of the railway itself brought new people into Lauderdale, if only for a temporary period. The survey notes of the Census Enumerator for the 1901 Census recording that at the station site *"owing to Construction of Railway there is a hut in which there are keeper and family (1 male, 4 females) and 22 workers (male)."*

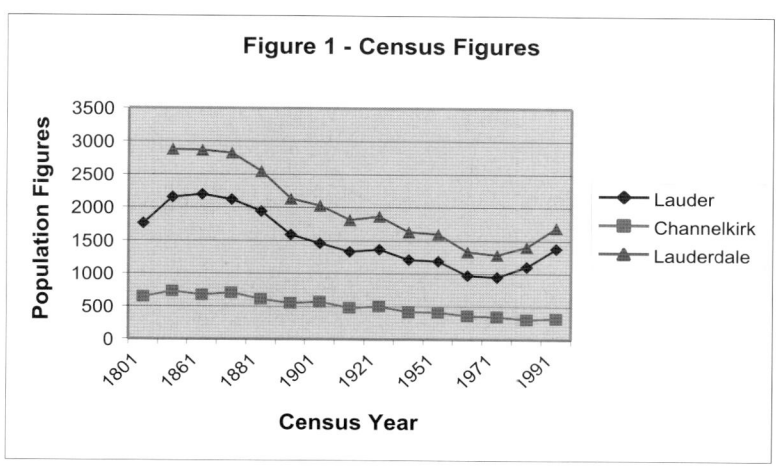

However, the Reverend Allan's optimism proved unfounded as the century developed, the railway eventually closing for passengers in 1958, and the population continuing to fall until the 1970s reaching 1288 in 1971, significantly less than half of the figure in 1851. Again, the contrast with Scotland as a whole continued with the national population continuing to grow through the 20th century, reaching a peak of 5.2 million in 1971, a reflection of the continued growth of the industrial towns and cities, whilst Lauderdale, like other rural areas, continued to decline. The growing congestion and poor housing conditions in urban Scotland, and the population decline of the rural areas, were major factors in the development of the Town and Country Planning system in Scotland.

PLANNING IN LAUDERDALE

Before the Housing and Town Planning Act of 1909, local authorities in Scotland had no right or power to control or regulate the development of land. Even after this, very few authorities made "planning schemes", which the Act empowered them to do, mainly because heavy compensation could be due to anyone sustaining losses as a result of a scheme. Growing concerns in the 1930s about industrial expansion, population growth, housing conditions, and a need to better co-ordinate the expansion taking place in many towns and cities, led to a call for new legislation. The Second World War delayed matters, but the need for reconstruction after the War accelerated the call for legislation and resulted in the landmark 1947 Town and Country Planning (Scotland) Act. This Act introduced a system of development control still largely intact today, and the concept of a Development Plan. This process and plan was to be administered at County level, in the case of Lauderdale by Berwickshire County Council.

So, for the first half of the 20th century, there was little or no control over development in Lauderdale. However, in the Burgh of Lauder, the minutes of the Town Council contain regular references to plans being considered for new buildings, and alterations and additions to buildings. New houses were limited largely to development along what was then Station Road, now Edinburgh Road. Some change was recorded by the Town Council, the most notable entries in the minutes on this subject being as follows:

2 May 1911:   - *"Following a vote, it was agreed by 6 to 2 that a water trough should be placed in front of the Town Hall. A design was selected incorporating a trough and lamp"*.

                     - Also *"plans of a double cottage to be erected by Mr William Murray to the west of Temperance Hotel"* were approved.

5 September 1911   - Approval was given to *"plans of a new house for the Headmaster of Lauder Public School to be erected in his present garden of the Schoolhouse."*

26 March 1918   - The Town Clerk stated *"that he proposed with the consent of the owners of the ruinous house at the east corner of the churchyard .... to take down the house and continue the wall of the churchyard from the Mill Wynd where it joins the*

house in a curve to the Session House".

4 February 1919   -   Agreement *"that there should be a War Memorial erected".*

4 May 1926   -   Plans of a house for Mr A G Doughty approved – *"This being the house known as the Grange".*

4 February 1930   -   Plans for *"the erection of two roadsmens houses in South Gardens on the Back Road"* approved.

2 July 1935   -   Application by the GPO to place a telephone kiosk on the south pavement in the Market Place agreed to.

11 November 1947 -   Plans of *"two new cottages to be erected by the Scottish Garden City Association on the Factors Park along the Upper Back Road"* approved.

6 May 1949   -   *"Four Agricultural Workers houses at South Backside"* approved.

4 October 1949   -   letter received from Mrs R. O. Lawson, Alberta, Canada, daughter of the late John H Scott owner of the upper storey of a derelict house in Mid Row, including £25 towards demolition costs. Agreed that the Town Clerk should arrange for this work to be carried out as soon as possible.

3 January 1950   -   agreed to name road on west side of which the four houses forming the Allanbank scheme – Manse.

6 November 1951   -   letter from Territorial and Auxiliary Forces asking permission to build *"a Drill Hall, garages and house"* in Factors Park agreed.

10 June 1968   -   approval for building 22 houses in what is now Scott Road.

16 February 1971   -   proposals for a development of 40 houses on the Upper Loan Park agreed in principle. Noted that *"this was the first time that private housing had been planned on this scale in Lauder".*

   -   also agreed to purchase a field at Crofts Road for additional Council Houses.

11 April 1972   -   agreed on opening of second development of Crofts Road Housing Scheme by John P Mackintosh MP on 28 April 1972.

3 July 1973   -   agreed to purchase ground at Factors Park for erection of Local Authority housing.

4 March 1975   -   new sewerage works operational.

13 May 1975   -   agreed to name second development at Factors Park site "Millburn Park".

LISTED BUILDINGS

From the 1950s, following the 1947 Planning Acts mentioned earlier, the Secretary of State for Scotland was empowered to recognise the importance of individual buildings or groups of buildings which were considered to be of architectural or historic interest by including them in a list of such buildings. These "listed buildings" were then afforded protection from demolition or alteration which would affect their character. The first review and listing of buildings in Lauderdale did not take place until 1971 when twelve buildings were listed. These were:

- Thirlestane Castle
- Eagle Lodge (Eagle Gates)
- Lauder Bridge
- St Cuthberts Church, Oxton
- Justicehall
- 1 East High Street, Lauder
- Lauder church
- Lauder War Memorial
- Black Bull Hotel
- 20-24 Market Place, Lauder
- Lauder Town Hall
- 6 Mill Wynd, Lauder

Since then, the list for Lauderdale has been reviewed, and enlarged, on a number of occasions. Today, there are 44 listed buildings in Lauderdale.

The listed buildings are classified as being of national importance (category A), regional significance (category B), and of local significance (category C). The buildings range from the magnificent Thirlestane Castle to the humble Lauder Telephone Kiosk. The following descriptions of the category A and B buildings are taken from the Listed Buildings Index, held by Scottish Borders Council:

LAUDER BURGH

East High Street, Lauder Church (Church of Scotland) – Listed Category A

Sir William Bruce, 1673; porches added 1820; restored 1969-72. Greek Cross plan church with low central tower surmounted by squat steeple and Gothic porches to NW and SE re-entrant angles. Harled rubble with rec sandstone ashlar dressings, including vertical margins at arrises, coped gables with beaked skew putts to each arm and architraved openings. Simple Gothic mullior and transom window with intersecting tracery and moulded architrave to gable of each arm; pair of wide rectangular windows with moulded architraves below.

Tower: 2-stages; square in plan to apex of roofs octagonal above. Single round-arched window with keystone and imposts anc louvred vents to alternate faces of upper stage. Two pigeon holes beneath eaves to each face. Squat spire surmounted by weather vane.

Arms: fenestrated to gable end only, apart from N and E arms, each of which have a single low wide window, built into upper section of original church entrance towards NE re-entrant angle (corresponding entrances formerly existed to SW re-entrant). Gable of N arm surmounted by small sandstone cross finial and its skew putts surmounted by sandstone obelisk finials (only pair remaining intact of those originally flanking each gable). Stone slab funerary plaques mounted on church wall to W side of S arm and N side of E and W arms.

Porches: of square plan. Eaves band with crenellated sandstone parapet with ridged coping above. Entrances to N side of that to NW re-entrant and S side of that to SE re-entrant. Each with round-arched doorway with hoodmould and replacement boarded timber door. Simple Gothic window to W and E sides respectively.

Multi-pane timber windows; some of lower ones with top hoppers; single stained glass window to N gable. Grey slate roofs.

Interior: Pointed arches spring from piers to each side of crossing. Late 18th century panelled pulpit of hexagonal plan and hexagonal sounding board with pointed apex surmounted by gilded spiked ball finial attached to SE corner of crossing; later pilastered back with incised lines. Boarded timber dado and panelled box pews to ground floor and lofts. Lofts installed at different dates from about mid 18th century onwards. Much refitting of interior in 1820, when porches added (to give covered access to lofts in place of external stairs which had preceded them) and 1860's. Stone flagged floor to each porch; half turn staircase with stone steps and timber handrail supported on plain cast iron balustrade; 6-panel internal timber doors at ground and upper levels. Stained glass window to N arm dedicated to daughter of former minister in 1901.

Entrance Gates and Churchyard Wall: pair of sandstone ashlar gatepiers. Rusticated piers on moulded bases to outer/N face; plain/largely rendered to gate reveals and inner/S face. Each with cornice decorated by 3 flower motifs to N/ outer face and moulded coping surmounted by obelisk with recessed panel to each face. Replacement cast iron gates. Whinstone rubble wall encloses churchyard, apart from at railed gaps at NE and SE corners; mainly with rubble coping; squared sandstone ashlar coping, largely replaced in concrete, to N side, where main section of wall was lowered in 1980's. Various gravestones incorporated into wall, including early 19th century red sandstone monument with moulded pediment and oval plaque and headstones of Romanes family tomb (Robert Romanes was distinguished local historian). Churchyard contains variety of 18th and 19th century gravestones.

References: David MacGibbon and Thomas Ross, The Ecclesiastical Architecture of Scotland, Vol III (1896, Reprinted 1991) pp582-85; A. Thomson, Lauder and Lauderdale (1902) pp76-84; Transactions of the Scottish Ecclesiological Society, Vol VIII, Part I (1925) pp121-25; George Hay, The Architecture of Scottish Post-Reformation Churches 1560-1843 (1957) pp66-67; Hubert Fenwick, Architect Royal (1970) pp48-49; Rev. Richard F. James, Lauder - its Kirk and People (1973) pp 9-20.

Notes: Ecclesiastical building in use as such. Built by John Maitland, Duke of Lauderdale to replace the original Lauder church which stood outside the Burgh and close to his residence, Thirlestane Castle. William Bruce was at the time engaged in remodelling the castle. In a letter dated 15 April 1673 the Duke requests that the church should be 'decent and large enough, with a handsome little steeple, if any of the timber of the old church will serve, it will be cheaper etc'. The aisle-less Greek cross plan with arms of equal length appears to be unique in Scotland and is thought to derive inspiration from the church of François Mansart at Balleroy in France (Fenwick). Originally, when the service was Episcopal, the church was probably without lofts and the east arm was the choir. Later, during Presbyterian worship, the choir appears to have been disused for a while and the lofts were erected. The Trabroun loft, over the S aisle, is known to have been existence by the mid 18th century; the Tweedale loft was constructed over the formerly disused choir in 1789; the Lauderdale (Maitland) and town lofts are first mentioned in 1820 in connection with their original external staircases. Stylistically the lofts are very similar and consistent with a mid/later 18th-early 19th century date, with the Trabroun and Lauderdale lofts being slightly the earliest in appearance. The Parish Minister applied to the church heritors for the enclosing of the churchyard in 1784. In 1820 the pulpit was lifted and set back to the east by one foot by taking the corner off a pillar and alterations were made to the pews. In 1835 a weathervane was erected. In 1862 the lofts were altered and a greater slope made to the galleries. In 1864 wooden floors were installed and the pews were altered and refitted. Restoration work carried out between 1969 and 1972 included the replacing of stonework to the windows and doorways, the renewal of the datestone and the re-harling of the exterior. The bell was the gift of Charles, Earl of Lauderdale in 1687 and has been recast twice, in 1751 and 1834.

War Memorial, Edinburgh Road – Listed Category B

1923. Memorial to First World War in form similar to that of market cross. Octagonal granite shaft set on stepped base of square plan with chamfered sides. Base inscribed '*ERECTED IN MEMORY OF THOSE FROM THE PARISH AND BURGH OF LAUDER WHO LAID DOWN THEIR LIVES FOR THEIR COUNTRY IN THE WAR OF 1914-1918*'; names are given on sides. Shaft surmounted by sandstone carving of lion rampant holding shield inscribed with cross and dates 1914 - 1918. Plaque commemorating those who died in Second World War added at base on East side. In design, it is similar to a mercat cross. Lauder's former mercat cross (of which nothing survives) was situated in front of the town hall and it is possible that it was based on this.

Black Bull Hotel, 9 Market Place - Listed Category B

Late 18th century, extended early 19th century with later additions. 2-storey and attic 7-bay former coaching inn with single and 2-storey rear (NE) wing and attached former stable block. Palladian window with Gothic astragals to principal (SW) elevation. Principal elevation rendered with incised lines in imitation of ashlar and painted ashlar dressings; harled elsewhere. Base course and eaves band to principal elevation; also architraved openings. Coped gables to either side of main block.

SW (Principal) Elevation: 6 regularly-spaced bays to original building to right: entrances to 2nd and 5th bays; that to left has 2-leaf 6-panel timber door; that to right has 2-leaf 4-panel timber door and ashlar cornice. Flanking windows. Window to each bay to 1st floor. Gabled dormers to alternate bays above. Wide bay added to left in early 19th century to accommodate function rooms. Palladian window with Gothic astragals to arch head. Tripartite window with narrower flanking lights above.

NE Elevation: gable end of former stable block projects forward to centre. Late 20th century single storey addition set back to left. 2-storey gable end of mid-19th century rear wing set back; 2 1st floor windows; piended roofed section adjoins to right.

SE Elevation: blank gable end of original block/byre to left. Mid 19th century wing to right largely obscured by later lean-to section with entrance and window to right. Late 20th century single storey sections to right flanking large recessed entrance. Former stable block/byre (2 separate ranges) set back to right; entrance and 2 inserted windows to left section; entrance and loft window to right section.

NW Elevation: adjoins 7 Market Place.

12-pane/multipane timber sash and case windows to principal (S) elevation (several have original hand blown panes). Grey slate roofs. 3 harled coped ridge stacks including 2 gablehead stacks to main body of building; harled coped wallhead stack to rear; harled coped stack to piended-roofed rear wing.

Interior: Adamesque plasterwork to ceiling of ground floor reception room; also panelled timber dado and round-arched niches. Otherwise most of ground floor altered and open-plan. Timber panelling with built in closets and bolection-moulded fireplace surround to 1st floor room to original section. Plaster cornicing to 1st floor room to early 19th century extension.

A substantial former coaching inn with a well preserved street frontage. It would appear to have been extended and upgraded in the early 19th century to include reception rooms. The main stabling appears to have been around a courtyard on the W side of the rear stable block/byre.

Telephone Kiosk, Market Place – Listed Category B

The K6 design is also known as the Jubilee Kiosk, commemorating the Silver Jubilee year of George V, during which the GPO set up a committee to re-design the telephone kiosk for mass production, with a Jubilee Concession Scheme providing one kiosk for each village with a Post Office. Scott was asked to design the new kiosk in March 1935, and after approval by the Royal Fine Art Commission, the K6 went into production in 1936. The same commission had, in 1924, decided on the colour red for the kiosk, being "easy to spot and giving and authoritative and official character" (Stamp).

Lauder Town Hall – Listed Category B

Later 18th century rebuilding of earlier structure. 2-storey and attic rectangular-plan town hall (ground floor originally occupied by prison) with clock-tower surmounted by spire and flight of steps to 1st floor entrance. Harled exterior with sandstone ashlar dressings. Rendered plinth to NE and SW sides. Coped gables with block skew putts. Ashlar cills to windows of upper 2 storeys.

NW (Entrance) Elevation: symmetrical arrangement. Central 1st floor entrance with Gibbs surround and pulvinated entablature with moulded cornice; boarded timber door; pair of blind oculi above with splayed voussoirs at cardinal points; flight of stone steps to ground level with cast iron handrails; entrance with boarded timber door to right return. Bottom of steps flanked by cast iron lamp standards, each with cross bar dated 1925; lanterns above are replacements. Clock-tower rises from centre of gable; square in plan with vertical margins at arrises and moulded eaves band; small square architraved window with louvred vents to each side; clock face above to this and SE sides; small recessed vent to NE and SW sides; squat spire surmounted by weathervane.

SW Elevation: entrance (to prison) to right of centre; heavy boarded timber door reinforced with iron strips. Small window with cast iron grille to right. Central window and one to right to 1st floor; 3 symmetrically arranged boarded windows to attic.

NE Elevation: 2 small windows with cast iron bars to ground floor. Single window to left of 1st floor and one above.

SE Elevation: adjoins No 1 Mid Row.

12-pane timber sash and case windows to 1st floor; 4 and 9-pane timber frame windows elsewhere, apart from attic windows to S, which are boarded. Grey slate roofs. Later shared coped coursed whinstone stack with sandstone quoins projects from SE gable; octagonal and round cans.

Interior: ground floor prison comprises 2 barrel-vaulted cells (larger one to W probably originally subdivided into 2 cells). Lobby to W formerly gave access to small window-less cell (known as 'the black hole') situated beneath steps to main entrance. Prison entrance opens onto small lobby with heavy boarded timber doors giving access to each of main cells. Stone flagged floor. Rebuilt fireplace with plain stone surround to E cell. 1st floor comprises single room (used as court-room and council-chamber); blocked fireplace to E wall. Entrance vestibule enclosed by masonry piers rising from ground floor to support clock-tower; timber staircase opens off this to S, giving access to attic, which rises into roof-space. Clock-tower contains bell, thought to have been renewed in 1790.

References: A Thomson, Lauder And Lauderdale (1902) pp33-34; Robert Romanes, Lauder (1903) pp64-67; Rev Richard F James, Lauder - its Kirk and People (1973); RCAHMS, Tolbooths And Town-houses (1996) P130.

Notes: B Group with Nos 1-5 and No 7 Mid Row (see separate list descriptions) as forming a prominent and complete terrace at the centre of the burgh. The town hall itself is a significant landmark building and a good example of early/traditional civic architecture. It appears that a town hall or tolbooth has existed in Lauder since at least the mid 16th century. In 'Pitcairn's Criminal Trials' there is reference to the *"burning of the tolbuth of Lauder"* in 1606. The building was thatched until 1770 when its roof was slated. It appears to have been more or less rebuilt around 1773, when contracts for its repair were put out. It ceased to be used as a prison in 1843, when it was condemned by a government inspector. A new clock was ordered to be *"sett up in the steeple of the tolbooth"* (one was already then in existence) in 1734 and this was replaced in 1859. The surrounds of the principal entrance and oculi above have been renewed in later 20th century (and so probably has the clock face).

6 Mill Wynd – Listed Category B

Early to earlier 19th century with slightly later addition. 2-storey 3-bay rectangular-plan villa with later 2-storey rear/W wing. Classical design with pedimented entrance bay to principal/E elevation. Coursed cherry caulking whinstone to principal/E and S elevations; coursed whinstone rubble elsewhere/whinstone rubble rear/W wing; droved sandstone ashlar dressings to main block. Base course; eaves course. Vertical margins with flanking quoins at arrises. Architraved windows with flanking alternate blocks and slightly projecting cills.

E (Principal) Elevation: symmetrical arrangement. Central entrance with later 19th century glazed timber porch with pilastered arrises; entrance with 4-panel timber door and rectangular fanlight to right return; tripartite window with narrow flanking lights to front; window to left return. Wide window above adjoins base of pediment supported on flanking brackets; blind lunette aligned above window. Single window to ground and 1st floors to flanking bays.

W Elevation: slightly lower wing adjoins to centre. Gabled dormer above to main block. Later polygonal dormer above/to left. Remaining fenestration not visible.

S Elevation: flanking windows to each storey.

N Elevation: blank.

Mainly 12-pane timber sash and case windows. Grey slate roofs, piended to main block; partially piended to rear/W wing. Shouldered sandstone ashlar wallhead stacks with moulded cornices to either side (N and S) of main block.

Interior: not inspected (1998).

Railed Wall: low whinstone rubble wall with rounded sandstone coping surmounted by cast iron railings with stylised finials bounds terrace to E of house; segmentally recessed in plan to W at centre; cast iron gate to N end.

3 The Row – Listed Category B

18th century incorporating earlier fabric; altered late 19th century when attic storey added. Single storey and attic 3-bay terraced cottage retaining remains of inglenook fireplace. Harled exterior; ashlar architraves to openings on principal (S) elevation; projecting sills to windows.

S (Principal) Elevation: entrance with boarded timber door with glazed panel to right of centre. Flanking windows with gabled dormers with rendered sides above. Short single storey section of coped wall (exterior of inglenook) extends to left.

N Elevation: entrance with boarded timber door to right; small window to left.

E Elevation: adjoins No 7 The Row.

W Elevation: adjoins No 3 The Row.

4-pane horned timber sash and case windows to principal (S) elevation. Slate roof with single rooflight to each pitch. Flanking ridge stacks; that to W (above inglenook) is of rubble with band course and round cans; that to E is harled and coped.

Interior: remains of inglenook fireplace in front room to left of entrance. Part of smoke hood beam or chimney bar visible and small remaining section of inglenook set back behind it; small storage recess to left side. Cupboard set into inglenook recess to right of fireplace. Early beamed ceiling. Simple rubble fireplace (flue partially replaced in brick) in kitchen.

References: Captain Armstrong's County Of Berwick Map (1771); 1" to 1 Mile; appears on First Edition Ordnance Survey Map; 25" to 1 Mile; 1859; Berwickshire Sheet XIX.8; late 19th century Photograph of The Row in possession of occupant; cottage shown as thatched and single storey; Robert Romanes, Lauder (1903) p62.

NOTES: B Group with adjoining No 1 and No 3 The Row (see separate list descriptions) as a traditional early burgh terrace. Notable for the remains of the inglenook fireplace, an uncommon survival at such a humble vernacular level. Prior to 1823 The Row formed part of a road which led to Thirlestane Castle and across to Norton.

43 West High Street – Listed Category B

Probably early 19th century with later alterations. Single storey 6-bay cottage, formed by merger of 2 3-bay cottages. Whinstone rubble with render-pointed repairs and end gable; large lintel stones.

SW (Entrance) Elevation: 3 bays to left; central entrance with boarded timber door; window to left and later canted window to right. 3 bays to right; central entrance with part-glazed replacement door; window to left and entrance with boarded timber door to former byre to right.

NE Elevation: largely blank with enlarged window to left, small, low window to right and timber-lintelled window to outer right.

NE and SW Elevations: blank gable ends.

Mainly 12-pane timber sash and case windows. Grey slate roof with rooflight to S pitch. Central rubble ridge stack; gablehead stack to SW rebuilt in brick.

Interior: survival of box bed with timber sliding shutter track top and bottom; shutters now missing; replacement bed base. Contemporary adjacent fitted panelled dresser intact. Timber beamed and boarded ceiling. Plain stone chimneypiece with simple bracketed mantelpiece. Broad boards to inner door. Byre to NE with cobbled floor and channel; bare rubble walls and joist holes from an upper floor now removed. New timber roof structure and sarking boards.

References: Appears on First Edition Ordnance Survey Map; 25" to 1 Mile; 1859; Berwickshire Sheet XIX.8.

Notes Listed in particular for survival of early internal features (box bed and dresser). Originally part of a row of cottages, those at the High Street end have since been demolished.

Lauder Parish

Thirlestane Castle – Listed Category A

17th century core with additions by Sir William Bruce 1673; Additions by William Burn 1840, and David Bryce, 1840. Ceilings by Robert Mylne, 1675.

Eagle Lodge, Thirlestane Castle

Gateway with rusticated piers topped by eagles; curved screen walls; ornamental wrought iron gates.

Lauder Bridge – Listed Category B

Single stone span, buttressed at one end with archway set in square recess; parapet additions at either end - Possibly 18th century.

Drummond Hall Bridge – Listed Category B

Possibly 18th century. Stone bridge across Earnscleugh Water; 2 arches with dry-stone rubble parapet, overflow arch smaller. Elongated voussoirs.

Harryburn House, including Stables, Chuckie Lodge, Gates, Gatepiers and Railings

Harryburn House

1834. 2-storey and basement, symmetrical 3-bay rectangular-plan house with billiard room and stable block to rear. Squared and snecked whinstone rubble with polished ashlar portico, plain architraves and angle margins. Band courses at basement and principal level; eaves cornice; quoins and long and short dressings at openings have droved tails.

SW (Entrance) Elevation: steps up to open recessed portico-type porch; 4 square columns of Greek anta order, in distyle in antis arrangement (2 outer columns engaged) supporting plain entablature with cornice and blocking course; recessed tripartite doorpiece behind. Single windows to basement. Tripartite windows in outer bays and above doorway. Cast-iron balcony to principal floor, supported on slim columns.

NW and SE (Side) Elevations: 3-bay; single windows to principal and 1st floors in each bay. Wing walls to left and right, surmounted by classical urns.

NE (Rear) Elevation: 3-bay obscured by later 2-storey piend-roofed bachelor wing accessed by bridge from 1st floor. Original 8-pane sash and case windows to rear and sides, replaced by 4-pane on main SW elevation at principal and 1st floors. Grey slate piended roof; corniced stacks; moulded octagonal cans.

Interior: 2 later wood and compostion chimneypieces; original decorative plaster cornices to principal rooms; panelled doors and shutters stone staircase; iron balusters and timber handrail

Stables: now converted for residential use; single storey piend-roofed stables and carriage house; segmental carriage arch to SE (partially blocked and glazed). 5 variously altered openings to NE elevation; hayloft above.

Chuckie Lodge: single storey, 3-bay lodge. Coursed pebbles set in cement framed in slim polished sandstone dressings. Base and cill courses; quoin strips.

Chuckie Lodge

SW (Entrance) Elevation: open timber porch in central bay; timber columns supporting open lattice frieze and pediment; panelled door; letterbox fanlight. Canted window in bay to right. Single window in bay to left.

SE Elevation: bipartite window.

NW Elevation: blank.

NE Elevation: regrettable flat-roofed addition obscuring original openings. 4-pane sash and case windows. Grey slate roof; rendered ridge stack; moulded octagonal can.

Gates, Gatepiers and Railings: 2 pierced cast-iron gatepiers with pyramidal caps and finials adjoining to SW of lodge; cast-iron gates with anthemion details; wrought-iron railings with fleur-de-lys heads flanking gatepiers.

Channelkirk Parish

Parish Church of St Cuthbert and Churchyard– Listed Category A

Dated 1817, original pulpit and fittings - Battlemented gables and pointed Gothic Windows. The Church of St. Cuthbert at Channelkirk has a long history and was referred to in the 13th Century as "The mother and parish church of the whole valley of Lauderdale". The church was rebuilt in 1817 following a long protest by the then minister Rev. John Brown about the poor condition of the existing building

Justicehall – Listed Category B

18th century - Simple rectangular building of coursed rubble patched with cement; centre gabled pediment and chimney, end gables have skewputts

Development Plans

As mentioned earlier, the Town and Country Planning Act of 1947 empowered County Councils, as Planning authorities, to prepare Development Plans for their areas. However, it was not until December 1960 that the first Development Plan for Berwickshire was published. The Plan was prepared on the basis that the steady population decline, which had been apparent for the previous century, would be arrested and the population could at least be retained, at the estimated 1951 figure of 25,753 for the County. However, the Plan included provision for population growth of 1,400 over the subsequent 20-year period, mainly in the four Burghs in the County – Coldstream, Duns, Eyemouth and Lauder, together with modest growth in Earlston and Chirnside. The target for Lauder was an increase from 580 in 1957 to 700.

In order to accommodate this increase, investment was proposed on the following:

- Road improvements on A68 to Carfraemill and realignment between Carolside and Birkenside and at Soutra Hill, but most significant a Lauder by-pass. This road was proposed to run from Harryburn Bridge between the town and Thirlestane Castle through the Castle grounds to rejoin the existing A68 south of Lauder.

- A new link road was also proposed to connect with the Avenue and 3.87 acres of land between the new by-pass and the existing built-up areas were zoned for commercial use *"for such development as Hotel, Motel, Petrol Service Station, etc."*

- Improvements were proposed at Lauder School, including the addition of a general purposes dining room, schools meals kitchen, staff room, cloakrooms, and toilets.

- The proposed increase in population required new sites for housing and industry. An area of 1.45 acres, adjacent to the grounds of Allanbank House, was proposed for "semi-industrial activities such as builders and contractors premises, workshops, etc." The Plan concluded that *"the attraction of new industries is important to the future economy of the Burgh."*

- Housing was not seen as an immediate problem, the Town Council, as Housing Authority, considered that *"the housing position is fairly satisfactory and their housing list comprises only two applicants."* Sites at Mill Wynd for 34 Houses, and Upper Vennel for 14 Houses, were included in the Plan for public housing, and at Loanend for 45 private houses, and Rotten Row (North) for 6 private houses, giving a total provision, over 20 years, of 59 houses.

- Finally, a caravan site was proposed on an area of 2.47 acres on the north side of Stow Road.

One consequence of the modest scale of development of Lauder was that the overall plan of the town, which was developed in mediaeval times, remained intact through the 20th century. Thus, in 1971, the National Trust for Scotland, following renovation work to both the Town Hall and the Parish Kirk, was able to write to the Town Council expressing its delight at these improvements and expressing the view that *"Lauder was still the best example in Scotland of the Street Plan and general form of the Mediaeval Burgh."* The Trust encouraged the Town Council to develop a full scale "facelift" on the lines of that carried out in Haddington. The importance of Lauder as a town of special architectural and historic interest was recognised in its designation as a Conservation Area in 1974 by the Planning Authority, Berwickshire County Council. Subsequently, the Secretary of State for Scotland recognised the Conservation Area as being of *"outstanding architectural and historical interest"*.

The County Council initiated a Lauder Facelift Scheme in January 1975. This was prompted by the availability of grants from the Secretary of State for Scotland for undergrounding electricity supply cables in areas of outstanding architectural or historic interest, and proposals by the South of Scotland Electricity Board to reinforce supplies in Lauder. At this time, the whole of the Burgh had many timber poles and overhead wires criss-crossing the High Street and Market Place, with electricity supplies entering properties via upper floors.

In May 1975, following the re-organisation of local government in Scotland, the County Council and Lauder Town Council ceased to exist and were replaced by Borders Regional Council and Ettrick & Lauderdale District Council. The Regional Council, as local planning authority, inherited responsibility for the Facelift Scheme, which proceeded during the autumn of 1975 with undergrounding of cables and new pavements in the Market Place, The Avenue, and part of West High Street. Unfortunately, due to a lack of financial resources, the rest of the undergrounding did not take place, and many overhead supplies remain to this day.

During the late 1970s and early 1980s, the new planning authority of Borders Regional Council prepared a series of Local Plans covering the whole Borders area. Lauderdale was included in the Ettrick and Lauderdale North Local Plan, published in 1985. The Plan noted that, over the previous decade, the population of Lauder had increased by over 30% with the development of private and local authority housing, much of it outwith the former Burgh boundary. The need for further land for private housing was recognised by the designation of a new site at Cottesbrook for 24 houses. Concern was expressed about the urgent need for upgrading some individual properties in the centre of Lauder, whose condition was *"seriously detracting from the recent facelift scheme"*.

The Council subsequently acquired by compulsory purchase properties at 13, 31 and 36 West High Street and restored them for housing use in partnership with the National Trust for Scotland as part of a joint Borders Little Houses Scheme.

The integrity and completeness of the street pattern of Lauder was later threatened by the dereliction of important properties at 22 – 26 West High Street, including Jolly's shop. These properties lay derelict for several years during the 1980s, eventually being held together by elaborate scaffolding, which was a detrimental feature of the High Street for some time. Again, after protracted legal procedures, the Regional Council secured the ownership and subsequent restoration of the properties by The Scottish Historic Buildings Trust.

The new Local Plan replaced the 1960 Berwickshire County Development Plan, which had included the Lauder by-pass proposal mentioned earlier. When consulted on the Local Plan proposals, Lauderdale Community Council expressed the view that a by-pass was undesirable. The Local Plan abandoned the by-pass proposal and ensured that Trunk Road traffic would continue to pass through Lauder's High Street for the rest of the century and into the 21st.

There had been some industrial development in Lauder with the development by the Scottish Development Agency of three village workshops in an area known as The Orchard, behind Scott Road. These were subsequently linked to accommodate the expansion of Colourbox Miniatures, a local company founded by Lauder resident Peter Fagan. The Local Plan proposed additional industrial development as part of an environmental improvement scheme at the Old Station Yard area. This was subsequently carried out by the Regional Council, with help from the Scottish Development Agency, and provided sites for local businesses including a new factory for Colourbox which allowed their Orchard premises to be redeveloped for housing by Eildon Housing Association. The Station Yard area also became home for the Council Roads depot and the new Lauder Fire Station completed in 1999.

Significant additional private housing was proposed at a new site at Brownsmuir Park.

The continued demand for housing in Lauderdale was recognised in the Borders Structure Plan 1991, which recognised Lauder as a local service centre. The Plan included provision for population growth in Ettrick and Lauderdale from 33,930 in 1989 to an expected 34,877 by 2001, and recommended that sites be made available mainly in the Central Borders, but also in Lauder and Oxton. The detailed proposals for additional development were included in a new Ettrick and Lauderdale Local Plan published in 1995. This Plan proposed significant new housing sites extending to 8.4 Ha in Lauder and 2.7 Ha in Oxton, as well as recommending that suitable "infill sites" in the existing built-up areas be developed. The following specific sites were agreed:

1.1 Ha at Burnmill for 20 houses

1.0 Ha at Lauderdale Drive for 20 houses

4.6 Ha at Millburn Park for 90 houses

1.7 Ha at Under Loan Park for 35 houses

1.7 Ha at Main Street, Oxton for 35 houses

1.0 Ha at Station Road, Oxton for 20 houses

The development of these sites has progressed in the final years of the 20th century and allowed further expansion of the population of Lauderdale with many new families moving into the area. Recent and proposed additional allocations of housing land to the south of Lauder are likely to ensure that this expansion will continue.

Oxton War Memorial Hall

In the early 1920's a number of meetings were held to consider how best to commemorate the men who gave their lives in the First World War. It was decided to build a village hall as a lasting memorial, and that the money should be sought by public subscription and other fund raising ventures.

The wording on the stone plaque on the War Memorial Hall reads *"Oxton War Memorial Hall erected by public subscription 1924 and dedicated to the sacred memory of those connected with the parish who fell in the Great War"*

Robert Weir, Lieut. R.S.	*John S. Weir, Sgt. R.S.*
Robert Affleck, L/Cpl . Tank Corps.	*Thomas W. Bell, L/Cpl Cameronians.*
Adam P. Blake, L/Cpl. N.Z.F.	*Bateman W. Leeming, Cpl. G.H.*
Robert Anderson, Pte. Canadians.	*Adam F Burrell, Pte. G.H.*
Charles Chisholm, Pte. G.H.	*George Crawford, Pte. G.H.*
Walter Douglas, Pte. K.O.S.B.	*William Hunter, Pte. S.H.*
David Hope, Pte. R.S.F	*Thomas Hume, Pte. K.O.S.B.*
Charles Mathewson,Pte.Canadians.	*William W. Ovens, Pte. M.T.A.S.C.*
Adam D. Renwick, Pte. R.S.F.	*John Scott, Pte. R.S.F.*

1939 - 1945

Andrew A.Anderson, Commandos. Robert Allan, Royal Corps of Signals.

'Greater love hath no man than this that he laid down his life for his friends.

This stone was laid by Mrs. W. Sleigh, wife of Lord Provost of Edinburgh 1924"

The first War Memorial Hall Committee meeting was held on 14th April 1926, and consisted of twelve members, they were;

Chairman & Treasurer	R. W. Mathewson
Secretary	J. P. Cree
Members:	J. Fleming, A. Young, A. Reid, R.Oliver, W. Hopson, J. C. Walker, J. Black, A. Munro, A. Brown and J.Cowan.

The Committee met every month for the first year. The Carpet Bowling started in September 1927. The prices for hiring the hall were: - Dance £1, Concert £1, Ordinary meetings 4 shillings, Sale of Work £2, use of the piano for a dance 5 shillings, other occasions 1 shilling. The Hallkeeper was paid £17. per year.

A memorial clock was donated to the hall by Mrs. Logan of Birkenside in memory of her brother Robert Dickinson of Longcroft, in July 1928, it is still in the hall.

The Badminton Club started in 1932. The first mention of electricity to the district was in 1935.

Major Munro, Harryburn, Lauder requisitioned the War Memorial Hall for Home Guard training from 1st. November 1940 until 2nd. May 1945.

When the war ended the new Committee decided to raise the hall rates: Dance 30 shillings, Whist and Dance £2, ordinary meetings to remain at 4 shillings.

The Carpet Bowling Club bought the bowling boards from the Hall Committee for £12. in 1947. In 1948 the Hall was re-roofed at a cost of £267.10.9. The Hallkeepers salary was raised to £35.

Electricity was installed in 1951. A new floor was laid in 1952 at a cost of £230. In 1958 eighty chairs were bought through a grant from the Carnegie United Kingdom Trust Scheme.

The Post Office had the use of the kitchen for Christmas mail from 19th. - 25th. December 1958. Repairs to the Hall, including the roof, were undertaken in 1977, a fund raising occasion was held in the field adjoining the Hall, over £1,200. was raised. A separate Committee was formed to organise events to celebrate the Queen's Silver Jubilee in 1977.

A Barn Dance held at Midburn in 1980 raised £960. for Hall funds.

During the 1980's and 90's the Hall was in use almost every night of the week, Badminton on Mondays, Carpet Bowling on Tuesdays, the W.R.I. met once a month on Wednesdays, the Guild once a month on Thursdays and Scottish Country Dancing every Friday. The Hall was also hired for private functions and different Committee meetings, it was one of the most used halls in the Ettrick and Lauderdale area.

In 1994 a new kitchen was built, new toilets were installed including a disabled facility, at a total cost of £10,000. grants being obtained from various sources and including a donation from the Church, as the Church use the Hall for services during the period from January to March each year.

In 1997 a bus shelter was erected in a corner of the Hall grounds. New infra-red heaters were installed in 1999 at cost of £2,820.

The remembrance service each year commences with the villagers gathering outside the Memorial Hall to remember the dead of the World Wars, and to observe a two minutes silence, this is then followed by a service in the Hall.

Oxton Stories
Mrs Anna Hunter (née Sutherland)

Prior to the construction of a railway between Fountainhall, Oxton, and Lauder, a shopping trip to Edinburgh must have been quite an occasion. Starting from home with a driver and a pony and trap, the journey was made by Threeburnford then over by Eastertown to Fountainhall. The return journey by pony and trap could well have been in the dark apart from the oil lamps on either side of the trap.

Schools

There had been an early school in the vicinity of the church. Later, probably earlier than 1850, the public school was held in the lower flat of the Old Schoolhouse which is now known as Clorabank. The schoolmaster resided in the upper floor. The school was known as 'Nicol Dodd's School'. The church school was held where the post office was in the Loan. My grandmother, Mary Blaikie, attended the church school. My grandfather, Andrew Sharp, was a pupil of Nicol Dodd's. Great rivalry existed between the two schools as to whose handwriting was the neatest. The present Channelkirk School was built in 1865. In 1866 Mr. Liddell came as headmaster he and Mrs Liddell must have been a great asset to the village. Mrs Liddell taught violin and piano in the Schoolhouse. Her pupils were quite advanced on the piano. Also she taught art (watercolours and oils).

Then the 'Christmas tree' when the school pupils provided a programme of recitations, songs, and dances. Miss Cowan was the infant teacher while Mr. Cree was headmaster. After an evening children's party in the winter, they would be collected by horse and cart. The carts were lined with dry straw and blankets were taken to wrap the children up cosily for the journey home.

The school garden, now no more either, had a splendid array of apple trees, which was a great temptation to the local boys. The schoolmaster used to watch from the upstairs window of the schoolhouse for the apple raiders to appear.

Halls

The hall was in the upper room of a building in the Loan which still exists. Scottish country dances were taught. After the 1914-18 war a war memorial was considered and so it was decided that a War Memorial Hall incorporating a memorial plaque would be appropriate. After a big local effort in raising funds through dances and whist drives the War Memorial Hall was complete. Edinburgh's Lord Provost at that time was Sir William Sleigh [an uncle of the Reid family formerly of Oxton Mains and later Carfrae] He had been an enthusiastic supporter and he and Lady Sleigh were present at the opening of the Hall. Very soon there was a bowling club and a W.R.I.

The Church of Scotland Women's Guild

Channelkirk Guild was instituted in 1917. Its 21st Birthday was celebrated on October 24, 1938. The Guild Social was an annual event The Guild ladies each headed a table bringing their own china and eatables. A number of visiting clergy were present. Then the Burns Supper organised by the Hall Committee, was another occasion.

In the 1920/30s accommodation for a cinema projector was built into the wall of the War Memorial Hall opposite the door. This was taken down after 4 or 5 years as attendances diminished.

Children's Poems

Anna lost her money; she was very much upset,

She had put it in her hanky, and hadn't found it yet

The collection box was coming round, a bit before its time,

I was so very sorry for her; I went and gave her mine.

Ian Sutherland aged 8 years to his sister Anna.

Seven sheep were standing by the pasture wall,

'Tell me' said the teacher to her children small

'One poor sheep was frightened, jumped and ran away,

One from seven, how many woolly sheep would stay?'

Up went Kitty's fingers, a farmer's daughter she,

Not so good at figures as she ought to be,

'Tell me then, Kitty, tell me if you know!'

'Please, if one jumped over, all the rest would go!'

By Ian Sutherland, recited at the 'Christmas tree' party.

Oxton Clubs and Societies

Oxton Badminton Club

The building of the War Memorial Hall in Oxton served a double purpose. In the first place, it was intended to remind future generations of the sacrifices made on their behalf and in the second it provided the village with a pleasant venue for clubs and other social activities.

In the early 1930s a Badminton Club was established with help from Mr Hogarth, Hartside and Mr. Mitchell, Collielaw. The exact date of its foundation has unfortunately been lost but it was originally called the 'Young Peoples Guild, Oxton Badminton Club'. There can be few if any of the original members left, but George Bell recalls taking a keen interest in 1944 at the age of fourteen. Youngsters were encouraged to watch and then in 1953 a junior section was formed for those between the ages of 12 -15 years. Another of the early members was Dorothy Bennett, a lady who liked to keep abreast of the times. One can imagine the raised eyebrows and comments when Dorothy appeared for a match wearing white shorts! Had she set a new trend?

When the one and only Minute Book was begun in 1949, thirty-three members were enrolled. A Committee had been in existence from the outset and had continued throughout the war. The Committee met regularly, mainly to discuss match fixtures and to pick the teams. In 1949, the membership fee was 10/-; in 1996 it was £5.50 for adults.

Enthusiasm for the game was never lacking in the early years but funds were a problem as they were for many other village organisations. However, with skill and ingenuity the club was able to keep its head above water. Dances and whist drives were the main fund-raisers. Dance tickets were sold for 3/-, lemonade for 6d a bottle and crisps for 4d a packet. Jim Johnston's Band was a favourite with the dancers.

The Badminton Club, like other clubs in the village was not self-centred and contributed as generously as possible to the Children's Picnic Fund, Channelkirk Church Fabric Fund and the Queen's Coronation Fund in 1953. Monthly dances were helping to swell the coffers when in 1965 Bill Kellett became President. A generous donation of £10.00 was made to the old Peel Hospital Fund. Following the tragedy at Aberfan in Wales, when many pupils in the village school lost their lives in a gigantic mudslide, the Badminton Club subscribed the sum of £5.00.

As with so many team sports the opportunity to travel and meet fellow players from a wide area was a big bonus. Very soon the Club got well established and matches were arranged both at home and away with teams from Edinburgh, Dalkeith, Pathhead, Fala and Blackshiels, Stow, Heriot, Dingleton Hospital, Earlston, Greenlaw, Gordon and Lauder. Private transport was mainly used, at least in the early stages. For home matches the ladies provided an excellent tea and 'a good time was had by all' as frequently stated in the local press. Dorothy Bennett always brought a big pot for the tea. With so many matches to be played, at least two nights a week were necessary for practice. An extra charge per night helped with the cost of hiring the hall. A very thoughtful entry in the Minute Book for March 1951 states *the Committee agreed to make a donation of 10/- to the hall keeper for all his goodness throughout the session'.*

It was always necessary to bring on young players. Talented older players were always on hand to give coaching advice. Such was the enthusiasm for the game that it was not unknown for Christmas dances and parties to be held. In 1963 over a hundred tickets were sold for a Christmas Day dance. In 1968 a league was organised with winners receiving cups at the end of the session. Players who had made the most progress were presented with a racquet.

There were set rules for the Badminton Club that were adhered to most closely. The cost of replacing a suspended light if damaged by a racquet was the responsibility of the player whereas if a shuttlecock had caused the damage the club met the cost of replacement

The decimalisation of the currency in the early 1970s caused costs to soar everywhere. Even the cost of hiring the War Memorial Hall was affected, but the village clubs and activities rose to the challenge and all managed to survive.

Discotheques began to replace dances to live music and this appealed to younger members. A sponsored walk in 1984 was well supported, especially as dogs were allowed to accompany the walkers. The first leg of the walk was from the village to Carfraemill, up to Carfrae Farm and Sparrow Castle and then on to Headshaw Farm and down to the A68. Once safely across the road the second leg began with the ascent to the church, then down to the quarry near Hartside and back to the village by way of the railway line. The walk was claimed to have been a great success and raised £60.50 for the Badminton Club. Another fundraiser in 1985 was the 'sponsored play'. There is, alas, no record of how long it lasted but it attracted a substantial number of players. The sum raised was £227.55, which was donated to the Lauder and District Health Centre Equipment Fund. This was well reported in the local press.

In 1995, Bill Kellett decided that it was time, after thirty years, to relinquish the position of President of the Oxton Badminton Club, which he had successfully steered through some financially difficult times. With the completion of the sports facilities at the Leader Leisure Centre in Lauder, the membership of the Oxton Badminton Club began to decline, and the Club decided to wind up its affairs.

Several players still get together for a game during the season just to keep their hand in. However, with the development of Oxton as a dormitory suburb it may well be possible to resuscitate the club should the time prove right in the future. The floor of the War Memorial Hall is still marked out for play and may serve to remind the new generation of villagers that once upon a time Oxton once boasted a flourishing Oxton Badminton Club.

Oxton Dramatic Society

Oxton, along with many other rural communities, was still recovering from the effect of the Second World War when, in 1950, some stalwart villagers decided to form their own dramatic society. In October of each year, when the bulk of farm work had finished, the selection of the next plays to be performed was made. Light comedies were the most popular and they always attracted good audiences when they were performed the following March. Costumes were kept simple and easy to make or adapt. Fortunately the stage at the War Memorial Hall could accommodate a large number of performers. Off stage however, it was very cramped. Oxton Dramatic Society's productions were always very popular. They ran for two consecutive nights with a packed house at each performance. As time went on, new leisure areas became available and this, together with the coming of television caused interest in the dramatic society to fall. The curtain was pulled down on the society in 1961. It had provided a great deal of fun and gave much pleasure while it lasted. Its passing is greatly to be regretted.

Oxton Drama Club. "Cobbler's Luck" 1952.

Scottish Country Dancing Club

There had been a country Dancing Club in the 1930s. The new club was formed in 1983 after a notice was put in the window of the local Post Office asking if people were interested, it attracted twenty names.

Country dancing has roots deep in our past. Kirns and harvest balls kept country dancing alive in the Borders. After the hard work in the fields, dancing was at once sociable and relaxing. It is little wonder that news of a dance spread from village to village and people walked many miles to attend it. There is a photograph in the

War Memorial Hall showing those members who gained a 1st Class Certificate in 1932. In 1984 the new club danced at Torsonce House as part of the Stow Centenary celebrations. The main dance of their performance was the Oxton Reel, a dance, which dates back to 1792. Di Henderson was the tutor and she had taught army dancers to perform in the Edinburgh Tattoo. Many of the practices in 1984 took place in the square opposite the hall and provided much entertainment for the villagers. When Di left, the dancers were coached by Wilma Miller. Wilma eventually became the President of the Royal Scottish Country Dancing Society, so Oxton had really the best possible tuition for such a small village.

A few of the original members are still dancing. Numbers vary greatly as people come and go in the village. For a few years there was a very strong primary class, sometimes twenty-six at a time, but once children reach their teens most find other attractions. However, once learnt, dancing is seldom forgotten and who knows these youngsters may become tutors of others in the future.

Cleekhimin School after closure.

Agnes Cockburn Remembers Oxton in the 1920s

I had occasion to be back in Oxton recently. I got out of the car and looked around. Immediately I was struck by how quiet it was. It had never been a busy, bustling place but with the various small shops and businesses, there were always people around.

Along the Loan there was a nice double storey house where Mrs. Swan had her baby linen and millinery shop. It had been well patronised but with modern transport and people travelling further afield to shop, its trade gradually dwindled. Then there was the Post Office, run for many years by the Mathewson family and finally by Miss Jean Mathewson who was the last member of the family in Oxton. She lived in Argyle Cottage at the top of the Row.

Also there, opposite the War Memorial Hall, was John Cowan, the bootmaker's shop. Clusters of children would peer in at the window watching him cobbling away. He was considered a very fine bootmaker and some who had left for distant parts of the world continued to wear John Cowan's boots.

The Lammermuir shepherds would only wear his boots and swore they had the *"heather loup"* - made for ease of walking in the hills. His daughter, Agnes, was the local teacher and May looked after the house. A few doors down were the premises of Walter Walkinshaw the tailor. He could be seen, stitching away, by a large window overlooking, the main road. A suit of the real Border Tweed made by Walter Walkinshaw lasted for many a year. Walter was also a faithful singer in the choir.

We come next to Cockburn's Provision and Meal Merchants. In these days all the shepherds kept poultry as well as two cows and two pigs. Cockburns was their only source of feed for their animals. A horse and cart were used for delivery on the hill track roads. This was also the outlet for selling their butter, eggs and ham which was cured and hung from the ceiling. It was a kind of barter system, which worked well. Early on a Saturday morning, this produce was taken into Edinburgh and sold at a stand in the High Street.

Dave Fairbairn lived in Lauder and cycled in all weathers to play 'the organ at Channelkirk. He also came to the monthly meetings in the hall. In earlier days he produced a *"kinderspiel"*, *"The Flowers of the Forest"* and every child in the parish had a part in it, Mrs Weir of Roselea had the huge task of designing and making the costumes for this. Her son, the well-loved schoolmaster, was tragically killed in WW1 and a plaque to his memory hangs in the school.

A happy bonus in the school year was when Sir William I. Sleigh became Lord Provost of Edinburgh. During his term of office each child in the schools of Oxton, Cleikhimin and Lauder received a gift of a tuck box. Sir William, who was a native of Lauder, was founder of the Rossleigh Motor Co. and was a brother of Mrs Reid of Oxton Mains. His niece, Miss Alice Reid, always came to the school to present the boxes. As well as farming Oxton Mains, her brother Peter was the blacksmith.

Oxton showing a thatched cottage where the Tower Hotel now stands.

Channelkirk and Oxton

The name "Channelkirk" seems to have come into general use about the beginning of the eighteenth century. It first appeared in the Presbytery Records in the year 1716.

The origin of the name is difficult to determine, but like all very old place names it has seen many derivations. On the Kirk bell it apparently says "For Channonkirk 1702", although the names "Ginglekirk" and "Jinglekirk" were often used throughout the Kirk records, and "Chinekirk" was used frequently in the records of the Earlston Presbytery from 1696. The earliest Kirk record of 1650 spells the name "Chinghilkirk", or perhaps "Chinghelkirk", as the second "i" is not dotted and may have been an "e". In about 1634 the spelling used is "Cheinilkirk": about 1630 "Chingelkirk": 1620 "Chingilkirk". In 1586 it is spelled once as "Chingclek". In 1580 it is "Cheilgill Kyrk". In 1567 it is "Chynkilkirk" along with "Chingilkirk". In 1560 it is "Cheindilkirk" or "Chenidilkirk" and in 1535 "Chyndylkirk". The Monks of Dryburgh Abbey used "Child" in most of their spellings: "Childinchirch", "Childenchirch", "Chyldinchirch" or "Childenenchirche". These spellings were used in Charters granted to the Abbey between 1153 - 1318, and between 1268 and 1318 "Childenkirk" was sometimes used instead of "Childinchirch"

Most of the information in this article comes from the book "History of Channelkirk" by the Rev. Archibald Allan. Late Minister of the Parish of Channelkirk, and printed in 1900, and he suggests that as Channelkirk Church is the mother Church of Lauderdale, with its connection with the young Cuthbert, afterwards St. Cuthbert, the original spelling of the name may have been "Childeschirche". Who are we to argue?

So much for the name and the various spellings, but what of the Church and the Village of Channelkirk? There is no record of when the first habitation was constructed at Channelkirk, but we do know that Dere Street passed very close to where the present Church stands and that a number of Roman fortifications were in the vicinity. So what came first, the Village or the Church? We must assume surely that the village came first. If that was the case then, it has been suggested that St. Cuthbert may have founded the first Church, or that it was founded shortly after he started his ministry, in his name. St.Cuthbert as we know died on 20th March 687. The first written evidence we have is a Register of Dryburgh Abbey marked "No 6", and the earliest one found which opens with a Charter dealing with the church of Channelkirk. The title of the Charter runs: *"The confirmation regarding the donation of Hugo and Robert de Morville concerning the Churches of Childinchirch and Saltone".* This Charter is by Malcolm, King of the Scots, and it confirms the bequest of Hugo and Robert de Morville, the Church of Childinchirch with the land adjacent. As this was from Malcolm IV., grandson of David I., it must have been granted between 1153-1165 AD.

Another point in history for the Village came when it is thought that General Sir John Cope wrote his battle report, after the battle of Prestonpans in a room in the old Channelkirk Inn, before riding down to Lauder to spend the night in the house that is now known as Cope's House. All that is left of the village, apart from the Church and the old Manse is Channelkirk Cottage thought to be part of the old Inn.

The name "Oxton" would appear to have come into general use about the middle of the 19th century, although "Ugston" was still occasionally used for a time. "Uxton" was sometimes used, but in the Exchequer Rolls, the Great Seal, the Retours, the Sasines and other similar sources, the name appears as "Ugstoun", "Ugstone", "Uggistoune", and such like names. The Rev. Henry Cockburn, Minister from 1625 - 1650 spelled it "Huxtoun" or "Huxstoun". In 1464 it is referred to as "Lilestoun" and "Ugistoune". Like Channelkirk, in the ecclesiastical domain the spelling changes greatly. The Monks of Dryburgh spelled it "Wlkeston", "Ulkeston" and "Ulkylyston". While the Monks of Kelso, change it again to "Vlfkelyston", "Vlfkeli Ston", "Vlfkiliston", "Hulfkeliston" and "Ulkilleston". It has been suggested that the source of the name is from the Norse "Ulfkill", from the great Danish hero "Ulfcytel". From the Rev. Archibald Allan we have: "The name Ulfcytel was in this country as early as the ninth century. Therefore the Norse influence was very strong from then until the 1100's". From this then we can perhaps fix the original settlement of Oxton sometime between the 9th. and 11th. century's.

It has been suggested that there were at one time two villages Ugstone Over and Ugstone Nether, it has also been suggested that in early times it was not just a village, but an estate or territory, encompassed in a rough circle starting at Mountmill Haugh and following the Leader down to it's junction with Kelphope Water at Carfraemill, from there up to where the road crosses the Over Howden burn, then up to Over Howden, from there to the burn which passes Inchkeith Farm and Threeburnford Farm, and from Threeburnford down the burn to Mountmill.

In the early days all the lands were the gift of the Crown or whoever was strong enough to hold them, but by the beginning of the 17th. century the lands of Oxton or Ugston were being broken up into smaller properties, with some intriguing names: "Pickleraw", "Luckenhaugh", "Ugston Mains", "Temple Lands", the "Two Husband Lands", and "Forty-Shilling Lands".

One area of land which is worthy of special mention is "Wideopen Common", which like Lauder Common must have been in the ownership of the community for many, many years but, unlike Lauder a proper management of it must never have been exercised.

It seems that on Wideopen Common, individual ownership developed which became heritable, whereas on Lauder Common it was never heritable, a Burgess could only pass his rights on to his widow but not to his sons or daughters. So it would seem that on Wideopen a "Right" became ownership, and that there was no controlling authority. The result was that individual owners were greedily putting on so many sheep and cattle that the land could not cope. The result was that there were many quarrels leading to an ever increasing number of lawsuits. The thirty-eighth Act of the Scottish Parliament of 1695 dealt with these "Commons" and power was given whereby these commonties may be divided at the insistence of those whose properties and rights were involved.

This facility was taken advantage of in the case of "Wideopen", by Robert Scott, Esq. of Trabrown, who started the legal process in 1762. An indication of how complicated the whole business was is evident in that the case didn't close until 1769. Mr. Scott raised the case to have the commonty divided out among the various people who had the right to pasture animals on it. These were: -

1.   The Earl of Lauderdale, for Whitelaw.

2.   Adam Fairholm, banker, Edinburgh, for Pilmuir barony, which included Upper Shielfield, Pilmuir, Blackchester, Midburn, Haverlaw or Halkeslaw, Wiselaw-mill, etc.

3.   Sir John Paterson, of Eccles, for Kittyflat.

4.   Miss Christian Hunter, for Nether Howden.

5.   Robert Scott of Trabrown, for part of Trabrown barony, with the New Mill.

6.   John Christie of Baberton, for Meikie Catpair.

7.   James Justice of Justicehall, for the lands of Ugston, Over Howden, and Upper and Nether Carsemyres.

8.   James Murray of Uplaw, for Heriotshall in Ugston.

9.   John Thomson, for Nether Bowerhouse.

10.   James Somervell, for Arras (Airhouse) and Ugston Mains.

11.   James Watherston, for the Lands of Haugh.

12.   Alison Watherston, widow of Wm. Cuthbertson, portion of Trabrown.

13.   Janet, Isabel, and Margaret Watherston, children of James Watherston, deceased, and Janet Watherston, his widow, for part of Trabrown Lands.

14.   John Watherston, for acres in Trabrown belonging to his father, Simon Watherston of Netherfield, deceased.

15.   James Watherston, for Netherfield or House-in-the-Muir.

16.   Thomas Murray, baxter in Edinburgh, for Mitchelson and Gilmerton.

17.   John Cuming-Ramsay, for Threeburnford.

18.   George Thomson, Lasswade, for Burnhouse.

19.   George Addiston of Carcant, for Collielaw.

20.   James Hogg, for Longmuir Lands.

When we see the number of people involved and the area of land covered by the Common it is hardly surprising that it took seven years for the courts to arrive at a settlement that apparently failed to please everyone. What does seem surprising is that the people of Oxton Village would appear to have lost out completely, as one would assume that at one time they would have been beneficiaries of the Common.

It is interesting to note in the Rev. Archibald Allan's book he says *"Oxton is a village freer from cases of inebriation than any the writer has ever known. This does not mean however, that it is totally free from vice. It has a bad reputation for certain forms of sin."* Whatever could he have meant?

The Rev. Allan also lists for us the Merchants and Tradesmen of 1825:

John Bell, shoemaker, Ugston.
Malcolm McBean, shoemaker, Ugston.
George Mitchell, shoemaker, Ugston.
David Scott, shoemaker, Ugston.
Andrew Campbell, draper, Ugston.
William Dalgleish, tailor, Ugston.
John Murray, tailor, Ugston.
Robert Glendenning, flesher, Ugston.
John McDougal, master of the Parochial School, Ugston.
Nicol Dodds, assistant master, Parochial School, Ugston.
Thomas Donaldson, baker, Ugston.
James Howden, cartwright, Ugston.
George Mitchell, innkeeper and grocer, Ugston.
James Lyall, innkeeper and grocer, Ugston.
James Turnbull, innkeeper, Carfraemill.
James Wood, senr., grocer, Ugston.
James Wood, grocer, Ugston.
William Lindsay, grocer, Ugston.
Andrew Reid, blacksmith, Ugston.

In 1866 he lists only the trades this time in Oxton.

Bootmakers	John Bell.
	David Scott.
	Thomas Scott.
Cartwrights	William Bell.
	Robert Watson.
	John Campbell.
Grocers	James Mathewson.
	Robert Macintosh.
	Andrew Campbell.
	Robert Walkinshaw (also spirit dealer).
Milliner	Mary Ann Forrest.
Blacksmiths	John Murray.
	Alexander Reid.
	James N. Reid.

Tailors and clothiers	William Waddell.
	Adam Richardson.
	John Waddell.
Drapers	James Swan.
	Adam Watson.
Baker	John Scott.

Looking at those two lists one must assume that Oxton was quite a thriving community during the nineteenth century and with the advent of the railway at the start of the twentieth that prosperity must have continued. The coming of the Lauder Light Railway must have provided quite a few welcome new jobs to the village. However any prosperity brought by the railway was fairly short lived, with the cessation of passenger traffic in 1932 and the complete closure of the line in 1956.

As with the country as a whole the twentieth century did not really start well for Oxton despite the building of the railway. With the First World War starting in 1914 and devastating many families with the loss of so many young lives. Then into the twenties and thirties with the depression and the collapse of confidence, and then along came world war two. Coupled with the mechanisation of farming, rural areas like Oxton and Lauder were losing people fast, particularly young people, also with the advent of shopping malls and supermarkets in the towns and cities most small country shops were closing down, now Oxton has only one shop left. However all is not doom and gloom, since the early eighties Oxton has slowly been recovering, small businesses have started up, and the population has been expanding once again. We know that not everyone is happy with the number of new houses being built, but new houses mean new people and that must be good for any community, unless you want that community to die. New houses also mean that there is more work for the local painters, joiners, plumbers and electricians etc, we believe that the future is bright for Oxton.

The Tower Hotel, Oxton, built after the opening of the Lauder Light Railway

Oxton showing the house known as The Castle, eventually burned down then demolished.

Carfraemill Hotel pre-second world war.

Channelkirk Church

Channelkirk Church, the Mother Church of Lauderdale, serves the village of Oxton and the parish of Channelkirk. It is believed the Church was founded between the 7th & 9th Centuries, however, it was not until 1242 that the site was formally consecrated by Bishop David de Bernam. In 1992 the 750th Anniversary of the dedication of the Church was celebrated with an Ecumenical Service.

The Minister at the beginning of the 1900's was the Rev. Archibald Allan, the author of 'The History of Channelkirk'. In 1925 the Rev. Henry McKinley was Minister for two years, followed by the Rev. John Gordon in 1927. In 1932 Rev. Ernest Lawson ministered with 3 elders until 1945 when 5 new elders were ordained, he retired in 1949. Rev. J.N. Macpherson was inducted in 1950 and died in 1951. The Rev. R.P. Mackenzie was inducted in 1952. During his time in office Lauder West Church donated 2 Silver Communion Cups, a Baptismal Bowl and Brass Vase in 1955. Rev. G.K. Wood was inducted in October 1957. In 1958 the Kirk Session accepted the offer of Individual Communion Cups from St. Andrews Church, Stow. Mr. Wood was the last Minister of Channelkirk, he retired in 1966. A congregational Meeting was held in the Oxton War Memorial Hall on 15th February 1967 to discuss the 'Calling' of a Minister, this was opposed by 20 votes to 2. It was decided to have a prolonged vacancy. During the vacancy the Rev. C.H. Duncan was Interim Moderator and the Services were mostly conducted by Divinity Students from Edinburgh.

A congregational meeting was held on 24th January 1973 when it was decided to Link with Lauder Old, the vote was 29 for and 3 against. Rev. R.F. James was inducted as first Minister of the Linked Charge on 1st July 1973. The Channelkirk Manse was sold.

Electric lights and heaters were installed in the Church in 1974. Rev. R.F. James retired in August 1982. Rev. D.J. McGregor was inducted on 19th September 1982.

To commemorate the 750th Anniversary of the Church the ladies of the parish made a Wall Hanging which is on display in Channelkirk Church.

Rev. D.J. McGregor retired due to ill health in September 1996.

A portrait of the Rev. J. Rutherford, Minister 1828-1862 was found in the Bell Tower of St. Mary of Wedale Church, Stow, and given back to Channelkirk in 1997, it was cleaned and is now hanging in the vestry.

The bell in the bell tower is of an Edinburgh casting dated 1704, this bell was repaired locally by the blacksmith sometime around 1930 and again in 1993 at Whitechapel Bell Foundry, London.

Rev. J.M. Shields was inducted in 1997.

Channelkirk Church

Channelkirk Church of Scotland Women's Guild

The Church of Scotland Women's Guild was started in 1887 by Dr. Archibald Charteris. The Channelkirk Guild was formed in 1917, with the aims of enriching the spiritual life and organising the charitable work of women members.

No records exist as to where meetings were originally held but since 1923 meetings and social events have been in the War Memorial Hall. In 1987 a fund raising was started to prepare for the centennial celebrations of the Guild. The Church at Channelkirk got much needed shelves for the storage of bibles and handbooks. A tablecloth was made for use at Sunday worship and for Guild meetings. One of the highlights of the year was the Women's Guild Social. Each member headed a table and provided the food and china for her own invited guests. The ladies of the Guild were renowned for their baking

In 1996 radical change swept through the Guild. The name was changed to The Church of Scotland Guild. Men were encouraged to join but, as yet, no man has become a member of the Channelkirk Guild. Delegates from the various branches no longer attend the General Assembly of the Church of Scotland. The Guild Presbytery Council now lays out the agenda of activities for the year. The agenda consists of a topic, a discussion theme and a choice of five or six projects and also the opportunity for personal education. Charities, both at home and overseas, are well supported. Channelkirk Guild is now organised like a club. Office bearers are chosen from the membership, who all belong to the church. The AGM is held in April when the syllabus for the year is drawn up, diary dates are fixed and ever more ingenious methods of fund raising are discussed. These have included exhibitions, teas, quizes, competitions, sales tables and Songs of Praise evenings, although the present Guild membership is down compared with years past, it continues to raise exceptional amounts of money.

The Guild has raised between £500 and £700 each year towards the congregation's Mission and Service commitments. Each year there are social meetings with other Guilds. Those in the Melrose area meet together five times in the year. These rallies have different emphases such as Annual Communion and business with a speaker, an ecumenical Christmas Carol service and a workshop style rally. A joint rally with Guilds from Peebles is hosted alternately between Melrose and Peebles. At the beginning of a new session the rededication of the Guild takes place at the morning service. For many years the annual World Day of Prayer, held on the first Friday of March, has been of great significance to Guild members and non-members alike. It brings together, in thought and prayer, churches of every denomination throughout the world. The theme and programme are set by a different country each year and highlights the needs and concerns of that country. The venue for this service, which is conducted entirely by members of the Guild, rotates between Lauder, Oxton and Stow.

Although the work of the Guild concentrates on serious worldly issues, the members are not a lot of sanctimonious fuddy-duddies! Oxton Horticultural Society's annual flower show in September would not be the same if it was not for the excellent cups of tea and plates of delicious home baking provided by the ladies of the Guild.

Oxton School - 2000.

Oxton School - 1938.

Channelkirk School

Channelkirk School lies tucked away in the village of Oxton situated west of the A68 five miles north of Lauder. The fact that it is not called 'Oxton School' causes perplexity to first time visitors. The school takes its name from the ancient parish of Channelkirk, formerly Childeskirche or Chinglekirk Only the church, the Mother Church of Lauderdale dedicated to St. Cuthbert, who was reared as a child close by, and the school still retain the old parochial name.

According to the various copies of old HMI reports, the school has been a good source of learning throughout its long history, a reputation it has maintained. The present building is a refurbishment of a typical stone built two class-roomed village school dating from the second half of the 19th century. From what can be gleaned from the logbooks the first school was a single roomed building, possibly sub-divided by a partition. A second room was added in 1874. The number on roll at that time was 90! An older schoolroom with an earth floor situated somewhere in the village had served as a temporary accommodation.

The school as it is today is the result of a complete refurbishment of the earlier building in 1991/92. Lack of space had always caused difficulties. This reached a crisis point in the 1970s when itinerant families with young children arrived to work in the parish. To overcome the immediate problem, two demountable classrooms were erected on the land that had earlier been the site of the much cherished school garden. One was later removed to make way for a level play area. By the year 2000, the second demountable classroom was in an advanced state of disrepair, and was replaced by a modern and well equipped building which now houses the middle school, and the recently formed nursery school which has its own teachers. A playgroup for toddlers also shares the nursery facilities.

The school now consists of two spacious classrooms, a general purpose room, a library/resources area, a staff room, kitchen, toilets, and store cupboards. To mark the opening of the new-look school an exhibition of old artefacts was laid out in the library/resource area. Intruders broke into the building on the night before the opening of the exhibition. Fortunately, these irreplaceable objects were of no use to the intruders, who might have been expecting to find money, and nothing was broken – a lucky escape!

School and Staff

HMIs frequently visited the school and the children were examined at regular intervals to determine the quality of the teaching In the early days of the 20th century, three teachers instructed the pupils: the Head Teacher or Principal Teacher as he was known, an Assistant Teacher, and a Pupil Teacher. The Head, always in those days a man, was a certificated teacher. The Assistant was a lady, also certificated or well on her way to becoming so, while the Pupil Teacher, often have been a bright young teenager, would have received four or five hours instruction from the certificated teachers per week. On July 1st 1900, Mary Jane Wilson Leeming began her Pupil Teacher training. The County of Berwickshire offered bursaries for competition among the children. Several of the Channelkirk entrants were successful and went on to secondary education.

Down through the years the amenities of the school were improved; flush toilets, hot water, the change from solid fuel stoves to centrally heated radiators, the building of a kitchen to provide hot meals, to name but a few. In 1913 the school bought its first piano from the proceeds of a sale of work and a 'kinderspiel', a play performed by the children called, 'The Happy Family' which ran for two nights. A sewing machine was acquired for use by the girls of the day and evening schools.

A large school garden where the new classroom is now situated proved a great success. It had been suggested by a member of Edinburgh Agricultural College. The layout had to follow a standard plan, which included plots for vegetables, flowers, and fruit bushes. Careful instruction was given for pruning the fruit bushes so that the older pupils could look after them. The garden was begun in 1912, and by 1914 was in full production. An entry in the log book for that year states '*On October 23rd a hamper of flowers from the school garden and the children's own homes was sent to Edinburgh for the Belgian Relief Fund Sale*'.

Evening Classes

At the beginning of the 20th century such was the desire for the improvement of knowledge, and of agricultural, domestic, and craft skills that an evening school was set up to run parallel with the day school. After their day's work as many as fifty-four young adults made their way, through fair weather and foul, to attend classes from 7-9 p.m. The men studied arithmetic, measurement and simple surveying of land, while the girls did needlework, essential for patching clothes and darning socks. Both were taught writing and composition, and book keeping as well as vocal music and geography of the British Isles. The evening school came under the same close scrutiny of the HMIs as the day school. The general expense of a child's education was 12/- per annum.

Wind and Weather

From its beginnings the weather has had a strong impact on the day to day running of Channelkirk School. The earliest records show that severe snowstorms and low temperatures of the winter months have constantly caused disruption to school work. Only the children who lived near the school were able to attend. The narrow winding roads from the farms, farm cottages, and other dwellings became impassable, often for weeks on end. Snowstorms could begin in October and continue well into April or even May, preventing spring sowing and causing late harvests. The first mention of a snowplough in the school logbook is in 1929. Snow was not the only hazard. Heavy rain and strong winds also affected school attendance.

Before the side roads were metalled the loose surfaces became watercourses. Three burns had to be forded on the Tollishill and Kelphope roads before the bridges were built The same applied to the Threeburnford road, as the name implies. By 1950 the winters were becoming less severe but periodically the conditions of old returned. 1947 and 1963 were exceptionally bad. Even as late as 1978/79 a severe blizzard struck the Lammermuirs with little warning. As always the safety of the children was paramount. The Head Teacher telephoned the Education Department in St. Boswells for permission to close the school. The voice from the Department replied *'But it isn't snowing here!'* However, permission was granted. The children from the village had to be escorted home by a teacher or parent. Those from further out were taken home by tractors, the only vehicles capable of getting through the drifts. Even then the tractors had to make their way over the fields rather than along the roads. Such requests for permission to close the school were not made lightly, nor was permission readily given – a change from the days when the Head Teacher had a much freer hand with regard to school closures. But the telephone changed all that!

Child Labour

Channelkirk is an upland parish at the north end of Lauderdale. The outlying farms lie at anything between 750 – 1500 feet above sea level. The area of the parish is about 14,202 acres. It is evident that travel by young and old could be long and arduous in adverse conditions. The long winter months put great pressure on the farming communities to complete the seasonable work as early as possible. Child labour was important for two reasons, to provide additional help and to earn money. Towards the end of the 19th century cheaper imports of grain and meat forced down the price of products of the smaller farms. Using the labour of the farm servants' children could reduce running costs but only with consequent disruption of their education. Seasonal work included lambing, clipping, speening, potato planting and lifting, singling turnips, hay making, and stooking at harvest time. There was also money to be made by beating for shooting parties from Edinburgh. The girls sorted potatoes and worked in the farm kitchen preparing and carrying out meals to the men and boys working in the fields. Raspberry picking also took place during the summer. Other distractions were farm sales and the Hiring Fairs at Lauder and Earlston.

The Scottish Education Act of 1872 laid down that attendance at school from the age of 5 until 13 was compulsory. The School Board and the Compulsory Officer found it difficult to convince parents that their children had to attend school when their labour was so essential, but the increasing mechanisation of farm work eventually brought the exploitation of child labour to an end. In 'A Century of the Scottish People' T. S. Smout states *'In Scotland in 1840 it took 22 man-days to tend an acre of barley. By 1914 it was 12 days, and by 1958 only 3 days'*. Farming wasn't the only occupation of Channelkirk inhabitants. In 1925 there was a blacksmith, a cobbler, a draper, two grocers, a haulage contractor, a joiner, a spirit dealer, and two tailors. However, none of these trades was reliant on child labour. Once a child had reached his or her 14th birthday, he/she was allowed to leave school.

Health and Disease

Prior to the use of vaccines and the comparatively recent introduction of antibiotics, serious outbreaks of childhood diseases occurred every year. Whooping cough, measles, scarlet fever, mumps and chickenpox were the scourges of the winter months. Children and adults alike were vulnerable to colds, sore throats and influenza. Naturally, such outbreaks affected the attendance and thus the day to day running of the school timetable. Parents were really concerned when a fever was reported it meant a quarantine period of six weeks for whole families. Scarlet fever cases were taken to the isolation hospital at Gordon. Following the end of the Great War in 1918, a particularly virulent form of influenza swept through the whole world, killing more people than died in the war. By order of the Medical Officer for Berwickshire, the school remained closed for four weeks. An outbreak of measles closed the school for five weeks. Cases of impetigo, scabies and ringworm from cattle occurred from time to time. However, in spite of the foregoing, children in Channelkirk and the country generally were taller, heavier and healthier then those in the towns.

Wee Treats

At the beginning of the 20th century the holiday at Christmas was very short, from December 25th to January 3rd was all that was allowed. Life at school wasn't always 'doom and gloom'. In 1900, during the Boer War in South Africa, the Relief of Mafeking, a town in the north-west of Cape Colony besieged by the Boers, was celebrated by two holidays on the 25th and 28th of May. On July 1st, 1901, scholars from Channelkirk were given a free ride to Lauder, and back on the Lauder Light Railway, which opened officially on July 2nd. This was a new experience for most of the children. But on November 21st 1902, the School Board threatened to begin legal proceedings against some parents for their children's persistent absenteeism. In 1923, Lord Provost Sleigh of Edinburgh (whose wife had opened the War Memorial Hall) sent boxes of fruitcake to the headmaster, Mr. Cree, with the instruction that every child was to receive part of the contents.

1935 was the year of King George the Fifth's Jubilee. To mark the occasion, a picnic and sports were held on Justicehall Haugh on May 6th. Pupils received boxes of chocolate and candy, and a commemoration mug. Older children received a copy of 'The King's Grace' by John Buchan. King George the Fifth died in 1935. In May 1937 King George the Sixth and Queen Elizabeth were crowned. The school celebrated with a week's holiday and no doubt more picnics and sports. In 1938, the Empire Exhibition was held in Glasgow, and Mr. William Anderson, the Headmaster took fourteen children to visit it. Empire Day on May 12th was as usual celebrated with a holiday, and the Hiring Fairs at Lauder and Earlston gave the children another few days off school.

The outbreak of World War II, in September 1939, brought travel restrictions as well as food rationing. People had to make their own entertainment. A real treat was when the film show visited the village. People didn't mind if there was the occasional 'hiccup' in the running of the film it all added to the entertainment. In 1944, Jenny Stewart received her first pen pal letter in New Jersey USA through a school correspondence scheme. A memorable holiday was that for VE Day – Victory in Europe – on the 8th and 9th of May 1945. Once the troops had been brought home after VJ Day - Victory over Japan - a grand Victory Parade took place on 8th June 1946. Schools throughout the land celebrated with a holiday and each child received a copy of a letter from King George VI.

Christmas has always been celebrated with a drama performance in the War Memorial Hall put on by the school children. A party organised by the people of the community and known as the Christmas Treat was the highlight at the end of term. All of these facts have been taken from the logbooks of Channelkirk School. No logbook was kept after the date when it was deemed that log books were no longer a necessity. If one had the time to question the more senior members of the community no doubt tales of more 'wee treats' would be revealed.

What treats do the children have today? There are occasional holidays apart from the 'Inservice Days', but the opportunities for enjoyment of children nowadays would have been classed as 'Huge Treats'; trips abroad, camping holidays in the summer term, the opportunities to learn about and take part in the major outdoor and indoor games plus athletics and the chance to meet foreign children from similar schools, visits to exhibitions, are all part of school life in this day and age.

Fluctuations of the School Roll

The children of the 'hinds' (shepherds) and other farm servants were those whose schooling was most likely to be disrupted through no fault of their own or their parents. Where the labourers could find work depended on the Hiring Fairs at Martinmas and Michaelmas. Families readily moved from district to district and this was reflected in the changes within the school roll. The last Hiring fair recorded in the school logbook was in 1941.

Before World War II children from Edinburgh began to be evacuated to the safer areas of the country villages. Over thirty arrived in Channelkirk with their own teacher. The school roll jumped from forty-eight in July 1939 to seventy-nine in September of the same year. Not all of the evacuated families could cope with the 'culture shock' of life in such an isolated area – as Channelkirk was in their eyes. During the following weeks and months many found their way back to the city environment with which they were most familiar, happy to take a chance on what the enemy might throw at them. In the event, Edinburgh was never attacked. Not all found Channelkirk such a backward place. The sole remaining evacuee left on October 1943. This movement of people was again reflected in the school roll.

The last significant change was the arrival of families from Ireland who came to work on the potato fields at Midburn. At first, the children of these families stayed on the farm but once their presence came to the notice of the education authority they were ordered to attend school. Such was their number that a third teacher was employed at the school for three years. The attendance of this latest influx of family was very erratic. Families would return to Ireland and be replaced by different ones. No warning would be given. Faces would simply come and go. This seasonal employment eventually came to an end and the school roll gradually declined until only the two original teachers were left.

Over the last three years the number on roll has steadily increased as the village of Oxton has been developed and once again Channelkirk has three teachers. The school year now begins and ends on the same date and compiling the register is much simpler.

Dominies

The role of the Head Teacher has changed significantly over the years. Since the introduction of devolved management he or she is responsible for the school budget as well as being a class teacher in an ever-widening curriculum. The staff now has to work as a team. The pace of modern teaching far outstrips that of a hundred years ago. The old Head Teachers were meticulous in recording events in the life of the school.

Mr. Henry Marshal Liddell F.E.I.S. was the first Parochial Head or Principal Teacher to be appointed to Channelkirk. He joined the school in 1866, aged thirty-four years, retiring in 1912 after forty-six years of dedicated work, aged 80. Mr. Dickinson, Chairman of The School Board wrote the following tribute.

'*The Head Teacher is about to retire after a period of service in this school for longer than falls to the lot of all but a very few. For more than forty years he has served faithfully and well as The Parochial Teacher and has well gained the affection of his pupils, the confidence of their parents and the respect of all. Now that the time of his retirement has come, it is hoped that he may be granted many years in which to enjoy his well-earned leisure*'. A plaque commemorating Mr. Liddell's long service still hangs in his beloved Channelkirk School to this day.

The man to follow the well-trodden footsteps of Mr. Liddell was Robert Weir. He came in October 1912 from the Assistant Supplementary Department Burgh School Dalkeith. It was Mr. Weir who was strongly urged to begin the popular evening school and the school garden. When the Great War broke out in August 1914 Mr. Weir left Channelkirk School to join the 8th Royal Scots. He was killed, as an officer of the battalion, on 16th November 1916, during the closing stages of the Battle of the Somme. His brother had been killed in the previous July. A plaque In memory of Lieutenant Robert Weir also hangs in Channelkirk School.

Two interim Head Teachers followed. Firstly came Mr. Angus Mackay from September 1914 to February 1915. Then came Mr. Thomas Dickie from February 1915 - February 1918. From March 1918 Mr. Joseph P. Cree took up the appointment as Head Teacher and continued until July 1931, a noble service of nineteen years. It was during Mr. Cree's time that the end of the school year was changed from February to July. From the logbook for this period it appears that the annual Religious Instruction Examination, set by the incumbent minister of Channelkirk church, ceased to be held. The last report of this exam was in June 1937, having continued for at least forty years. Mr. William Anderson took up the post in September 1937, and successfully steered the school through the difficult years of World War II. He resigned in December 1945 to become Head Teacher of Ballinluig in Perthshire. Mr. Anderson was well remembered for his musical interests and abilities. Mr. Alfred Angus Mackay commenced his appointment in January 1946. Unfortunately he was forced to retire in March 1950 because of illness. At the beginning of the new session in September 1950 Mr. Ernest Tolson succeeded Mr. Mackay. He had previously taught at Earlston Junior Secondary School. The school roll at this time was only thirty-nine but it increased steadily until it reached fifty-two.

On 17th January 1958, Mr. Harvey. Head Teacher at Lauder Primary School became indisposed and for the remainder of that spring term Mr. Tolson acted as Head Teacher at Lauder, returning to Channelkirk at the end of March. During Mr. Tolson's tenure an unusual incident occurred. One morning in May 1965 the infant teacher 'failed to report for duty'. The police were informed as her absence was causing concern. She was traced two days later but did not resume her duties until 11th June.

An entry in the logbook by the acting lady Head Teacher reports that Mr. Tolson had died suddenly. Although there had been three ladies who had acted as Head Teacher in Mr. Tolson's time no lady had ever been appointed Head Teacher at Channelkirk. That changed in 1968 when Mrs. Jesse McEwen, an experienced teacher, was confirmed in the appointment. It was during Mrs. McEwen's time that the two demountable classrooms were erected. She was also involved with the plans for the more recent enlargement and improvement to the old building. Mrs. McEwen retired in 1991 after twenty-three years of dedicated and wholehearted service to Channelkirk School. Until the arrival of Mrs. Jeanette Fox, Miss Edith Brown, herself a former pupil of Channelkirk, acted as Head Teacher. As Assistant Teacher, she had for many years ably taught the younger children of many of the families in the parish.

Mrs. Jeanette Fox took up the reins in 1991, in her first appointment as Head Teacher, in the refurbished school. By now the age of computers had come to stay and Scottish education was in a distinct period of change. In 1997, however, Mrs. Fox accepted the post of Head Teacher at Lauder Primary School, which meant that she remained in Lauderdale and in touch with Channelkirk. The present Head Teacher is Mrs. Kay Livingston, a senior teacher of much experience. Each new head teacher brings a fresh approach and an individual style of management that prevents the school from becoming too introspective, or too immersed in its own affairs.

Today, Channelkirk School continues to flourish as new families move into Oxton village. While it seems that the workload, with which every teacher has to contend, grows greater with each term that passes, it is all the same regrettable that the school logbook is no longer maintained in written form. The events and occurrences recorded in a school logbook are not only interesting from the point of view of the school but can also provide an invaluable source of information regarding the life and times of the community it serves. The computer screen is no substitute.

Oxton School - 2002.

Patricia Mitchell Remembers

When I came to Oxton in 1943 it was a quiet, grey village. Many of the men were away in the forces and their work was done by the Polish Forces. Miss Mathieson reigned supreme in the Post Office where, always keen to keep up with the news, she was a regular fount of information. She was a keen attender at Kirk and always had a clean handkerchief with two pan drops in it. One was for a Kirk cough and the other was for anyone else similarly afflicted.

When I first arrived, I was fascinated by the mortsafes - those iron grids clamped on coffins to defeat body snatchers. I did not know then that Edinburgh University's reputation for brilliant surgeons was founded on body snatching. Since then I have learned that the custom was rife in Lothians and Berwickshire.

There was only a footpath outside the Hall, the other side of the road was rough ground and rubble. My husband, known locally by his farm name, Collielaw, arranged for the present path to be built after I had a bad fall there. Later he was active in getting street lights for the village.

The War Memorial Hall always featured high in the social activities of the village. I remember many happy events there. The S.W.R.I. members won the Federation cup and the men of Oxton gave the victorious ladies a party to celebrate. The men did everything; the tables were beautifully set, an elegant meal was served and greatly enjoyed. When it came to taking the large linen tablecloths off however, chaos prevailed! I don't think any of them had ever folded a large tablecloth before. The ladies watched the shambles with much hilarity. At a Burns Supper, a speaker looked round at our homely faces at the start of his talk. *"Ladies,"* he said. *"if Rabbie Burns was alive now, not one of you would be safe"* He literally raised the roof, for the next morning it was found that the hall roof was leaking in six places.

The Poles delivered their work squads to farms in their lorries, which they drove like bulldozers. There were Italian, Hungarian, Yugoslav and German P.O.W. squads working on local farms. The drivers were quite irresponsible and you always had to be ready to jump out of their way. After six cats had been run over we made them stop the lorries at Bowerhouse corner and the squads made their way on foot up to the steading. They brought their own pieces with them but had soup provided at lunch-time.

I must have made hundreds of gallons of soup, as well as feeding my family, on my three-burner oil stove. During the war cookers were not available. You had to apply for an allocation of iron for an Esse cooker; and my allocation did not arrive until after the birth of my son in 1945. Sometimes I would look at the cauldron of soup boiling for the POWs and then at the babies nappies boiling on the other, and I would think to myself, *"That might not be the thing to do, but I've still got lunch to cook"*. No prisoners ever tried to escape, they just seemed to be thankful to be out of the war.

The Coronation was a great event. Sports and games had been organised for the youngsters. Television sets, which few people had ever seen, were hired for the OAPs to watch in the hall. In the event it was a very wet day, so the sports were cancelled and everyone packed into the hall. We were all thrilled to see the Queen of Tonga drive in an open carriage. Despite the heavy rain, she seemed to be having a great time. Later there were fireworks and a dance at Collielaw and I took our children for a drive round the district to see all the bonfires that had been lit in the hills by villages. I remember with pride being asked to open the new gates at Channelkirk, which had been beautifully made by Willie Riddell, the blacksmith. Also the many times I have been asked to open the Oxton and District Horticultural Society's annual show. The vegetables are always fantastic and the flowers exquisite, the children's entries are invariably interesting and imaginative and there are mouth-watering entries in the Industrial Section. It is always a great place for meeting old friends. Oxton is indeed blessed with a community that enjoys competitions. Then there was the WRVS work party which was held twice a year at Collielaw. One room had up to six sewing machines on the solid oak dining table, which I had always disliked as I prefer mahogany, but I learned to appreciate it as it was as steady as a rock with all the sewing machines going full toot. I think that I am now able to tell you about our secret members. Some laddies had come up to me and said that if I gave them the wool they would knit it up for me, but I had not to tell anyone. They produced perfectly knitted garments, and no one ever found out.

In the terrible winter of 1947 we were snowed in for six weeks. Collielaw rode his horse over the frozen fields for supplies. He had two panniers on his horse and brought bread for all the cottages as well as ourselves.

When we were ploughed out we went down to the village and then over Soutra through snow passages as high as the car. Later that year a speaker from America came to the Womens' Guild. During his talk he said, *"and now we will show you slides of real snow."* He and his wife were quite mystified when his entire audience burst out laughing. When they had recovered the members gently explained that he was showing us slides of three feet drifts, whereas we had just got used to drifts of seven feet deep.

I can remember the station and the Sheep Sale Special. On sale day at St Boswells, the shepherds of the district walked their sheep down to the station, loaded them into wagons and then sat in state in the single passenger carriage attached to the wagons. The train was affectionately known as "Midside Maggie" and it played an important role in our lives. It brought in coal fertilisers and many other supplies for the district, and stock for the Food Store in Lauder. I was happy at Collielaw and enjoyed all the local activities.

Everything I did had the full support of my husband, who was always glad to help the community. Our children grew up there and they have happy memories of Oxton.

Local Government

For the first time in Scotland, reforms during the nineteenth century introduced popularly elected councils. First to Royal Burghs and later smaller towns, counties and parishes, and progressively wider responsibilities and powers were entrusted to them. For example in 1872 the parish and burgh became the principal units of administration for the new educational system and in 1894 for poor-law administration. By the end of the 19th Century a complex apparatus of local government had grown up consisting of 200 Burgh Councils, 33 County Councils and 869 Parish Councils, together with a network of committees, boards and similar bodies appointed to carry out particular functions such as maintenance of roads and bridges and the provision of public health services. Although a systematic attempt had been made in 1889 to rationalise local government services this did not result in simplifying the structure. The first general measure of simplification was the Education (Scotland) Act of 1918 which, replaced about 1000 school boards with education authorities elected triennially for each of the counties and for a few of the larger burghs.

A more comprehensive reform was brought about by the Local Government (Scotland) Act of 1929 which abolished many of the smaller units of administration and introduced the structure that remained in place until the introduction of the Local Government (Scotland) Act of 1973.

On the 15th May 1975 Lauder Town Council ceased to exist. For all of the 20th Century until that date it had shared the duties of local government with Berwickshire County Council. During that time the County Council had been responsible for roads, health, social work, police, planning and education and from 1918, rural housing, water and sewerage etc. Lauder Town Council was responsible for housing, water and sewerage, cleansing, refuse collection, Lauder Common, The Common Good Fund, collection of rates and rents and Lauder Burgh Court. In Berwickshire there were also East, Middle and West district councils whose powers were very limited.

One of the few functions that they performed was looking after cemeteries and they shared this function with Lauder Town Council as far as Lauder Cemetery was concerned. The West District Council took in Oxton, Lauder, Earlston, Nenthorn and Gordon.

The District Councils were made up of directly elected members and the Burgh Councillors and County Councillors in their areas.

The Burghs also had representatives on the County Council. All of these councillors were elected for a three year period. Lauder Town Council had nine councillors with three retiring each year. The Council had a Provost, Senior Baillie, Junior Baillie and a Dean of Guild. The Clerk and the Chamberlain were both paid officials. The Burgh Police (Scotland) Act 1892 provided that in a Burgh with a population of less than 10,000, a Chief Magistrate to be called Provost should be elected and two other Magistrates to be called Baillies.

On 9th November 1894 the Lauder Town Council resolved to elect a Provost and two Baillies in terms of the Act.

Lauder of course is the only Royal Burgh in Berwickshire, a title granted on 21st December 1502 by King James IV.

The last meeting of Lauder Town Council took place on 15th. May 1975.

Present were:

William Y. Walker	Provost
William Hardie	Senior Baillie
John Rhind	Junior Baillie
William T. F. Brown	Treasurer
Christina Morgan	Dean Of Guild

Councillors

William Miller

Anthony W.Baxter

Margot Douglas

Ian K. McLaren

Also Present Were

Andrew Y. Henry	Town Clerk
Stewart Harcus	Burgh Chamberlain
John H. G. Scott	Master Of Works

The structure in Scotland, which replaced the 430 existing local Authorities in May 1975, comprised 9 Regional Councils and 53 District Councils.

The Borders Region, which encompassed Lauderdale, covered the areas of the old County Councils of Berwickshire, Peeblesshire, Roxburghshire and Selkirkshire. The four new District Councils were Berwick, Roxburgh, Tweeddale, Ettrick & Lauderdale, the latter encompassing Lauderdale and Earlston from the old Berwickshire County and the area around St. Boswells from the old Roxburgh County, plus all of Selkirkshire.

The people of Lauder fought long and hard to keep alive the name Lauderdale in the name of the new District and finally succeeded, with the help of the Earl of Lauderdale, as the legislation passed through the House of Lords.

Part of the 1973 legislation directed that all District Councils were required after consultation with local people to submit to the Secretary of State before 16th. May 1976 schemes for the setting up of Community Councils in their areas. These bodies, which were seen mainly as consultative and deliberative associations representing the interests of the inhabitants of their areas, were expected to form a principal channel of communication between district and regional authorities and the community.

They were to be free to take such action as they thought appropriate and practicable in the interests of their areas and could receive assistance both financial and otherwise from local authorities Central Government or any other appropriate source.

The new structure was not a resounding success. We still had too many tiers of local government that were not really local, which meant that there was still confusion as to which authority was responsible for providing which service. So once again it was decided that change was needed and this led to the Local Government Scotland Act 1994. The new act created 29 all purpose mainland councils. This means that in the Borders, the four district Councils of Berwick, Roxburgh, Tweeddale and Ettrick & Lauderdale ceased to exist and that the Borders Regional Council became Scottish Borders Council, a multi-purpose authority. The Councillors for these new authorities were elected on the same day in May 1999 on which the first MSP's were elected to the new Scottish Parliament. They, like their predecessors in the old district and regional councils would serve for four years and elections would be held every four years.

The complaints have already started. The units of local government are becoming larger and larger and therefore becoming more and more distant from the people that they are supposed to serve. The councillors are becoming fewer in number and not of the necessary calibre any more to be able to cope with the changes in size and complexity in 21st. century local government. However, the consultation documents are already out from the new Scottish Parliament on how to change local government once again.

The changes in Scottish local government gathered apace during the later part of the 20th. century. It seems that the pace is not slackening for the 21st.

Thirlestane Castle as it looks today.

The North Lodge to the castle near Greenside – No longer there.

The Maitland Family and
Thirlstane Castle

The first known Maitland came to Britain from Normandy as a companion of William the Conqueror in 1066, and a descendant was given land in Northumberland by King David I.

In approximately 1250, Sir Richard Maitland married Avicia, the daughter and sole heiress of Thomas de Thirlestane, and it was through this marriage that the lands of Thirlestane, Hedderwick and Blyth came into the Maitland family.

Through military service and contributions to law and to the arts in Scotland, the Maitlands gained increasing influence and power. By the 16th century Sir William Maitland, son of the poet Sir Richard Maitland, was Secretary to Mary, Queen of Scots. His brother John built the old tower house that forms the central part of the present Thirlestane Castle. He was Lord Chancellor of Scotland and was created Baron Maitland of Thirlestane in 1590 by King James VI. Chancellor Maitland's grandson, the 2nd Earl of Lauderdale undertook major improvements to Thirlestane. He was one of the most important figures in the second half of the 17th century and was known as the uncrowned King of Scotland. On the death of his first wife in 1672, the Earl married a 45 year-old widow, Elizabeth Tollemache, generally known as Elizabeth Murray, she was Countess of Dysart in her own right. He was granted the title Duke of Lauderdale and began transforming Thirlestane Castle into a palace from which to direct the affairs of Scotland. The most remarkable feature of the interior is the rich plasterwork found in the State-Rooms. The Duke died in 1682 having fallen out of favour with King Charles II. Having no male heir all the titles conferred on him became extinct, while the other honours and property passed to his brother Charles, who became the 3rd Earl of Lauderdale.

By the 19th century, Thirlestane's role had evolved in more peaceful times to that of Scottish country mansion for the Earls of Lauderdale. During the 1840's David Bryce and William Burn were commissioned to add two large wings flanking the central tower, thus forming the Castle as it is today.

On the death of his father in 1924, Frederick Colin Maitland became the 14th Earl of Lauderdale. He was born on 12 April 1868 and on 16 April 1890 married Gwendoline Lucy, daughter of the late Judge Vaughan Williams of Bodlonfa, Flintshire. He became a Brigadier in the Royal Company of Archers and served with several regiments, including the Scots Guards and the Royal Scots Greys as well as being an honorary Colonel in the County of London Yeomen. He was a Justice of the Peace and Deputy Lieutenant of the County of Berwickshire. Countess Gwendoline was much loved in Lauder and Lauderdale. Delicate of health she spent winters at her home in Palm Beach, Florida.

Fort Lauderdale, Florida, built by a Maitland ancestor, was re-built and re-named in her honour. Countess Gwendoline died in Florida and her embalmed body was returned to Thirlestane Castle, lying in state in the castle hall. She is buried in the family vaults on the estate, her body having been carried to its last resting-place by her favourite horse Tommy.

Origin of the name of Fort Lauderdale, Florida

Fort Lauderdale was named in Special Order No. 74, dated 16 March 1838, General Jessup, commanding *"The new post established on New River by the Tennessee Battalion of Volunteers and Company "D" 3rd Artillery, will be called Fort Lauderdale."*

It was named after Major William Lauderdale, commanding officer of the Tennessee Battalion of Volunteers in 1838.

Lauderdale commanded the Volunteers in the Seminole Wars in 1838. During the campaign he built a 30ft. square, two-tiered blockhouse with a 60-foot stockade. This was completed in April 1838, a few days after Lauderdale had departed with his troops, and in accordance with US army custom at the time, the fort was named after the officer charged with its construction

The City of Fort Lauderdale was named after the Fort.

Major William Lauderdale was a descendant of James Lauderdale who settled in Pennsylvania in 1714, and who stated that he was a Maitland by descent. James Lauderdale is thought to have migrated from Galloway to Ulster and thence to North America. The family moved from Pennsylvania to Virginia, where they built Lauderdale House in 1760, and then moved to Tennessee around 1794.

15th Earl of Lauderdale

Ian Colin, only son of Frederick Colin was born on 30 January 1891. He married on 11 November 1912 Ethel Mary (Ivy), daughter of James Jardine Bell Irvine of Makerstoun, Kelso by whom he had a son and a daughter. His son, Viscount Ivor Colin born 1915, married Helena Ruth Perrot by whom he had three daughters. The Viscount predeceased his father being tragically killed in action in North Africa in 1943. His youngest daughter was born after his death and his widow died in 1999. His daughter Lady Sylvia born 1913 married the 6th Baron Carew of Castleton in Ireland. She was the mother of the Hon. Gerald Edward Ian Maitland-Carew the present Maitland at Thirlestane Castle. The 15th Earl died at sea in 1953

16th Earl of Lauderdale

As the 15th Earl had no surviving male heir, on his death the title passed to The Rev. Alfred Sydney Frederick Maitland, son of his great uncle. He married first in 1938 Nora Mary La Touche and secondly in 1940 Irene Alice Mary Shipton, daughter of the Rev. CP Shipton. The Earl died in 1968 at Angmering, West Sussex.

17th Earl of Lauderdale

Patrick Francis, 17th Earl of Lauderdale succeeded his brother on 27 November 1968. Born 17 March 1911 he is married to Stanka, eldest daughter of Professor

Milivoye Losanitch of Belgrade, Yugoslavia. He has two daughters and two sons. His eldest son Ian born 1937 is Master of Lauderdale, Viscount Maitland. He is married to Ann Paule Clark, by whom he has a daughter, The Hon. Sarah Caroline Maitland born 1964 and a son, The Hon. John Douglas Maitland, also known as the Master of Lauderdale, a title the Maitlands have used since the early 17th century. The Hon. John Maitland married Rosamund Bennet in April 2001. The Earl's other children are Lady Olga Helen Maitland born 1944, Lady Caroline Charlotte Militsa Maitland born 1946 and The Hon. Sydney Milivoye Maitland, born 1951. The Earl was a war correspondent during the Second World War. His wife and son escaped from Yugoslavia before the German invasion of that country and made their way to New York. In the 1960's the Earl restored the Lauderdale Aisle, the private chapel of the Earls of Lauderdale at St. Mary's Church, Haddington, where many of the Earls of Lauderdale are buried. The Aisle is the focus of an annual ecumenical pilgrimage, brainchild of the Earl of Lauderdale, and takes place on the second Saturday in May.

Thirlestane Castle

The 20th century has seen many changes at the castle. Used as a hospital during The Great War there is a commemorative plaque in the hall *"To record the use of this building as an auxiliary hospital during The Great War and the thanks of the Scottish Branch of the British Red Cross Society to the generous donor April 1919"*.

St Hilary's School, Edinburgh (now a house of St Margaret's) was evacuated to Thirlestane in 1939 for the duration of the second World War. Many pupils still return and a 50th anniversary reunion was held at the castle in 1999.

In 1952 on the death of 15th Earl of Lauderdale, the castle and Estate passed to his widow, whose father in 1912 had bought off the considerable mortgage over the Estate: their only son Viscount Maitland was killed in action in North Africa in 1942. The Earldom of Lauderdale was inheritited by the 15th Earl's cousin, the Reverend Alfred Maitland.

The Hon. Gerald Maitland-Carew inherited Thirlestane from his maternal grandmother, the 15th Countess of Lauderdale, on her death in 1970. The castle was a virtual ruin with forty outbreaks of dry rot and the central tower in danger of collapse. The ogee tower had to be realigned with new steel beams and tension cables being inserted. Much of the stonework also had to be replaced. Chimneys, leadwork, roofs, sandstone all had to be either repaired or renewed. The ornate ceilings had suffered considerable damage, in particular The Drawing Room where one of the eagles was completely destroyed with rot. It was re-made by Mr. Grandison a specialist plasterer from Peebles. The ceiling in what is now the Chinese Room came down during the second war and was not replaced. Many of the main rooms in the castle were completely redecorated using specialist painters.

Gerald undertook the huge task of restoration of the castle, and after initial rescue operation by him, he persuaded the Historic Buildings Council of Scotland to grant aid much of the main restoration work. In 1980 the castle, for the first time opened on a regular basis to visitors. The same year the Country Life exhibitions were created in the South Wing by an enthusiastic team from the Youth Opportunity

Scheme. These exhibitions are much admired by visitors. In 1982, a friend of the family, Mrs. Fawdry who owned the Pollock Toy Museum in London gave to Gerald, on a long term loan, a magnificent collection of children's toys for exhibition. In 1984 in order to secure the future of the castle, Gerald, jointly with the National Heritage Memorial Fund, created Thirlstane Castle Charitable Trust. He gifted the main part of the castle including the valuable contents and the important family papers to the Trust, in return the Memorial Fund endowed the Trust with £1million, the income from which pays towards the upkeep of the castle The Family own and live in the North Wing. They nominate half of the Trustees of the Heritable Trust and the National Heritage Memorial Fund nominate the other half. This Trust was the first ever of its kind and has now been copied by a few other historic homes.

A great National Treasure has been saved for the foreseeable future and Thirlestane can now enjoy its new role as a living link with the past. That it can do so is a tribute to the many people who have loyally devoted their time and skills, not least the voluntary 'Friends of Thirlestane' who give their time and knowledge to interpreting the castle and its history for its visitors. Today, Thirlestane is one of the seven Great Houses of Scotland and welcomes visitors from all over the world.

An early picture of Thirlestane Castle 1794.

Thirlestane Castle Horse Trials

The parks at Thirlestane Castle were identified in the late 1970s as being a good place for a cross country course and, subsequently, a 'Hunt Team Chase' course was created, but owing to wintry weather it was never used. However, the successful Horse Trial at Whitehill, Lockerbie decided to close down and it was a natural move to create a new Horse Trial at Thirlestane. With willing hosts in Captain and Mrs Maitland-Carew, and the nucleus of the team that organised the Lauderdale Point-to-Point at Mosshouses, the first trial took place on 8th August 1982. Despite many teething problems, the event was a great success - it formed part of the Clydesdale Bank sponsored series run throughout Scotland at that time. The following year, the blanket sponsorship was taken over by national housebuilders, Barratt, from Aberdeen. Barratts wanted to sponsor all horse trials in Scotland with a Championship and it was Thirlestane they chose for this.

The two cross country courses were re-built to Championship standard and a feature event with a much higher class of presentation was held on 28th August 1983. Over the next 20 years the event progressed - the classes got bigger - there were more divisions of classes, other horse competitions were introduced, the trade stands mushroomed, corporate entertaining was introduced and the horse driving championships joined in 1999.

High profile sponsorship has been the lifeline of the Trials over the years;- Barratt the Builder passed their involvement onto the more local Edinburgh Woollen Mill who also supported Olympic rider Ian Stark. Later, Kimberley Clark sponsored us from their Kent headquarters and it was they who encouraged Thirlestane to run over two days. Finally we were delighted to have Pedigree Pet Foods, based in Leicestershire and part of the Mars Group. Their 'Fun Dog Agility' became a special favourite at Thirlestane and helped sell their dog food, the Pedigree Chum brand, all over Scotland.

The whole event with the Castle backdrop became a very high profile Scottish equestrian feature and is probably in the top three of Borders tourist attractions. Thirlestane has been used on four occasions as the final trial for the British team taking part in Olympic, World, or European Championships. Other nations have also used Thirlestane as a final trial and we have had, over the years, the top event horses and riders competing.

Thirlestane is held in great respect within the sport of Horse Trials and has enormous potential in this discipline as well as horse-driving, endurance riding and show classes. Bad weather has been a regular nuisance but has not dampened the enthusiasm of the organisers and competitors.

Painting of the Old Manse presented as a prize at the Bowling Club in the 1890s.

The Medical Profession in Lauderdale

Doctors

The Doctor in Lauder at the start of the twentieth century was Dr. Skinner who originally lived and practised at the Lodge in East High Street.

In 1898 he built a house in East High Street to serve as both a dwelling and Doctors house. It was built on what we believe was the site of the Manse for the old church, which had originally stood near to Thirlestane Castle. This new house was named the Red House obviously because of the predominance in the use of red sandstone in the building. Dr. Skinner lived and practised here until his death in 1911.

Prior to his death Dr. Skinner had engaged as his assistant Dr. Georgeson who was also his son-in-law. When Dr. Skinner died Dr. Georgeson took over the practice.

In the 1930s Dr. Georgeson's health began to fail and he began to make use of a number of different locums and by 1938 he was spending most of his time on his motor yacht moored at Kirkaldy. People became very unhappy with the situation and an approach was made to the practice in Pathhead to have a Doctor regularly in attendance in Lauder. The result was that Dr. Alston came to Lauder and stayed initially in West High Street, then after a time he bought the house in Stow Road known as The Bield, from which he carried on his practice until sometime in the early 1940s when the practice was taken over, by Dr. Jack. Dr. Jack had two daughters, Annette and Ailsa.

Meanwhile by the summer of 1938 Dr. Georgeson required a locum urgently and Dr. Smith was found in Edinburgh and available. However while still in Edinburgh preparing to go to Lauder, Dr. Smith received a telephone call informing him that Dr. Georgeson had died, and could he go to Lauder immediately and run the practice. Dr. Smith began in practice in Lauder on Monday 1st August 1938. (just in time for the first of his many Common Ridings).

A year later on the 3rd September 1939 the Second World War broke out. On the 28th September 1942 Dr. Harry Smith married Dr. Joan Campsie. In the same year he was called up for military service and embarked for India, and Burma, where he spent the next four years, returning to the UK in 1946 for demobilisation. During Dr. Smith's absence on military service his wife Dr. Campsie ran the practice. She later became Medical Officer of Health for Roxburghshire and Selkirkshire. Sadly Mrs. Smith died in 1976 leaving two sons John and Crawford.

Dr. Jack died in the late 1950s and his list of patients was moved to Dr. Smith's practice by the Executive Council B.R.S.P.. We had now reverted once again to one medical practice in Lauderdale.

Dr. John Smith joined his father in the practice in 1982 and he bought as his dwelling house a house in Stow Road named The Bield.

In 1985 the practice bought The Loanside and converted the ground floor for use as a surgery with examination rooms, dispensary, records office, waiting room, etc. much larger than the Red House. Dr. Harry Smith however continued to use the Red House as his home. The Loanside had previously been used as a hotel and before that a private house.

Dr. Harry Smith retired from the practice on 1st September 1988 exactly fifty years and one month after he took over in 1938. He died in August 2001. In 1988 Dr. John, as he is known locally, formed a partnership with Drs McKenzie and Lowles who were in practice in Stow, and when Dr. McKenzie left, Dr. Cormie became a partner in January 1990.

The partnership lasted for six years and when it split up Dr. John remained at The Loanside, Dr. Lowles and Dr. Cormie took over what had been the district nurses house in Factors Park. So now we are back to two medical practices in Lauderdale. How long will it last this time? The premises at Factors Park are barely adequate, but we understand that moves are afoot to extend them in the short term.

We are happy to report that the Smith family association with the Red House carries on as Dr. John has moved back home, in January 2003, and that Crawford is carrying out alterations to an outbuilding to provide himself and family with a holiday home.

Dentist

During the twentieth century only one dentist seems to have operated in Lauderdale, and that was a James Eunson. We understand that he previously lived in Musselburgh and came one day a week, on the Thursday, to Lauder to see his patients, eventually moving to 43 East High Street. We have no definite date for this move but it seems to have been sometime in the mid 1920s. From there he moved to Market Place, to the property between the Black Bull Hotel, and Rutherford's shop. No one seems to be able to remember exactly when Jim Eunson, as he was known locally, retired from practice, but it must have been sometime in the later 1950s as some people do remember attending his surgery in 1955. After his retirement he would be able to enjoy fully his two hobbies of marquetry and bee keeping until his death in the 1970s.

Chemists

The shop in Lauder used by a dispensing chemist from the start of the twentieth century until it ceased to dispense was the Post Office in Market Place. The owner and chemist in the early years was John Scroggie, a keen golfer, who in fact was a founder member of the Golf Club and was Secretary and Treasurer form 1897 to 1928. He eventually became Club President. Mr. Scroggie was obviously an enterprising man as not only did he run a post office and chemist's, but also produced illustrated guides to Lauder and Lauderdale. Diversification before its time. In the shop itself, as you entered the door the chemist's counter was on the right and the post office on the left.

Mr. Scroggie retired to Edinburgh sometime in the 1930s, and Mr. James Smith bought the shop. He also did the dispensing himself and carried on producing the illustrated guides.

In the late 1940s Mr. Smith sold the premises to the Galashiels Co-operative Society, and the first chemist they employed was Alex Holmes. He eventually left to open up his own chemist shop in Greenlaw. From then on there were a series of chemists who stayed for differing periods of time interspersed with the odd locum, until in 1969 or 1970 the dispensary was finally closed.

The dispensing of medicine was then taken on by Dr. Smith's surgery, and when the partnership between Dr. John Smith and Drs. Lowles and Cormie split up they each dispensed at their own surgeries.

On the 20th September 1971 Galashiels Co-operative Society sold the premises to Arch and Jean Anderson.

District Nurses

The first District Nurses were established in Lauderdale in the late 1940s, and the first two, who were here together were, Nurse Foster and Nurse McInnes, and they lived at 35 East High Street. During the later part of their time in Lauder, the authorities decided to build a new house for their use, however by the time that it was completed in the early part of 1953, they had both left and the first nurse to occupy it was Nurse McDonald. The new house being the bungalow built in Factors Park, now occupied by Drs. Lowles and Cormie.

Nurse McDonald only stayed for a short time and was followed by Nurse Shedden. We feel sure that we reflect the feelings of the vast majority of the people of Lauderdale when we say that Cathy Shedden was the most dedicated and highly respected of our nurses during the time she served us. She became so much part of the community that when she retired in 1973 she bought a house in Lauder and stayed there until her death in 2002. Cathy Shedden was followed by Nurse Robertson, and she in turn was followed by Nurse Hunter, who was the last District Nurse to live in the bungalow and in Lauder to date.

Loanside Hotel Fire in 1983 – now the Memorial Medical Centre.

Lectern made by J Middlemiss for Wilson College, Bombay and carved by Col. Fleming.

Songs and Poems of Lauderdale

The two songs associated with the Common Riding, are 'Bonnie Lauderdale' and 'Jeannie's Black E'e'.

> 'Mid the splendour and the beauty, o' the bonnie woods and glens,
>   Where Leader rins sae cheerie as it winds roon' ilka bend,
> Ye may boast o' Tweed or Ettrick, the Teviot or the Ale,
>   But gie tae me the Leader, and my ain dear Lauderdale.

> Chorus: Lauderdale!. Bonnie Lauderdale,
>   Sae dear tae me,
>   I will sing in praise where'er I go,
>   O' Bonnie Lauderdale.

> We hae bonnie lads and lassies and we fear nae ither toons,
>   Although we're kind o' wild a wee we're seldom oot o' boonds,
> We're a jolly lot o' fellows, aye heartie, true an' hale,
>   And proud we are tae be the sons o' Bonnie Lauderdale.

> Chorus:

> When the Cornet is presented on the Common Riding morn,
>   Wi' the flag his predecessors have safe and proudly borne,
> Let us all unite and cheer him, half-hearted nae but hale,
>   And let the laddie see he is the pride o' Lauderdale.

> Chorus:

Composed by the late John Riddell.

> The sun rose sae rosy, the grey hills adorning
>   Light sprang the lav'rock and mounted sae hie
> When true to the tryst o' blythe May's dewy morning
>   Jeanie cam' linking out ow'r the green lea
> Tae mark her impatience, I crep amang the brackens aft,
>   Aft tae the kent gate she turn'd her black e'e,
> Then lying doon sae dowielie, sigh'd by the willow tree
>   I am asleep, dinna waken me.

Saft thro' the green birks I stole to my jewel,
Strek'd on sprin's carpet aneath the saugh tree,
"Think na dear lassie that Willie's been cruel"
"I am asleep, dinna waken me".
"Wi love's warm sensations I've marked your impatience
Lang hid midst the brackens I watch'd your black e'e
You're no sleepin pawkie Jean, open that lovely e'e"
"I am asleep, dinna waken me".

The following is part of a poem describing Sir Douglas Archibald, one of the Nobles involved in the alleged hanging of the Kings favourites over Lauder bridge in 1482.

'I mean the Douglas, fifth of yore,
Who coronet of Angus bore,
And when his blood and heart were high,
Did the third James in Court defy,
And all his minions led to die
On Lauder's dreary flat.'

The next two poems are about Sir Richard Maitland, sometimes referred to as Auld Maitland, who was born sometime before 1250.

Wha does not know the Maitland bluid,
Tha best in a' the land?
In whilk sometime the honour stood
And worship of Scotland.
Of auld Sir Richard of that name,
We have heard sing and say:
Of his triumphant, noble fame,
And of his auld beard grey;
And of his noble sonnis three,
Whilk that time had no maik,
Whilk made Scotland renouned be
And all England to quake;
Whose loving praises, made truly
After that simple time,
Are sung in mony a far countrie
Albeit in rural rhyme.

The next poem was given by Margaret Laidlaw, the mother of the Ettrick Shepherd, to Sir Walter Scott. The Castle referred to is the old ruined one opposite Thirlestane Farm.

There lived a king in southern land,
    King Edward hight his name:
Unwordily he wore the crown
    Till fifty years were gane.

He had a sister's son o's ain,
    Was large of blood and bane;
And afterwards, when he came up,
    Young Edward hight his name.

King Edward rade, King Edward ran-
    I wish him dool and pyne!
Till he had fifteen hundred men
    Assembled on the Tyne.

And thrice as many at Berwicke
    Were all for battle bound,
Who, marching forth with false Dunbar,
    A ready welcome found.

They lighted on the banks of Tweed,
    And blew their coals sae het,
And fired the merse and Teviotdale,
    All in an evening late.

As they fared up o'er Lammermore,
    They burn'd baith up and down,
Until they came to a darksome house,
    Some call it Leader-Town.

"Wha hauds this house?" young Edward cry'd,
    "Or wha geis't ower to me?"
A grey-hair'd knight set up his head,
    And crakit right crousely.

"of Scotland's king I haud my house;
    He pays me meat and fee;
And I will keep my guid auld house,
    While my house will keep me"-

They laid their sowies to the wall,
    Wi' mony a heavy peal;
But he threw owre to them agen
    Baith pitch and tar barrel.

With springalds, stanes, and gadsof airn,
    Amang them fast he threw;
Till mony of the Englishmen
    About the wall he slew.

Full fifteen days that braid host lay,
    Sieging Auld Maitland keen;
Syne they hae left him, hale and feir,
    Within his strength of stane.

The next poem was written by Sir Richard Maitland 1496-1566, after the despoiling, in 1570, of Sir Richard's house and lands of Blythe, possibly by Border Reivers. We include here only the first verse.

Blind man be blyth, althoch that thou be wrangit;
    Thoch Blythe be herreit, tac no melancholie,
Thow shalt be blyth, when that they shall be hangit
    That Blythe has spulyeit sa maliciouslie.
Be blyth and glad; that nane perceive in thee
    That thy blythness consists in riches;
But that thow art blyth that eternalie
    Shall reign with God in eternal blythness.

The next is by Minstrel Burne, who is supposed to have been a native of St Leonard's in Lauderdale, and he probably lived about the end of the seventeenth century.

A house there stands on Leader side,
    Surmounting my descriving,
With rooms sae rare, and windows fair,
    Like Daedalus' contriving;
Men passing by do often cry,
    In sooth it hath no marrow;
It stands as fair on Leader side
    As Newark does on Yarrow.

A mile below, who lists to ride,
    Will hear the mavis singing;
Into St Leonards banks she bides,
    Sweet birks her head overhinging.
The lint-white loud, and Progne proud,
    With tuneful throats and narrow,
Into St Leonards banks they sing
    As sweetly as in Yarrow.

Park, Wanton-wa's, and Wooden cleuch,
    The East and West Mainses,
The wood of Lauder's fair eneuch,
    The corns are good in the Blainslies;
There aits are fine, and sald by kind,
    That if ye search all through
Mearns, Buchan, Marr, nane better are
    Than Leader Haughs and Yarrow.

In Boon-mill-bog and Whitslaid shaws,
    The fearful hare she haunteth;
Brig-haugh and Broadwoodshiel she knaws,
    And Chapel wood frequenteth:
Yet, when she irks, to Kaidslie Birks,
    She rins and sighs for sorrow,
That she should leave sweet Leader Haughs,
    And cannot win to Yarrow.

What sweeter music wad ye hear
    Than hounds and beagles crying?
The started hare rins hard with fear,
    Upon her speed relying;
But yet her strength it fails at length;
    Nae beilding can she borrow,
In Sorrowlessfield, Clackmae, or Hags,
    And sighs to be in Yarrow.

Sing Erslington and Cowdenknows,
    Where Humes had ance commanding;
And Drygrange, with the milk white yowes,'
    Twixt Tweed and Leader standing.
The bird that flees through Redpath trees
    And Gladswoad banks ilk morrow
May chant and sing sweet Leader Haughs
    And bonnie howms of Yarrow.

But Minstrel Burne can not assuage
    His grief? while life endureth,
To see the changes of this age,
    Which fleeting time procureth:
For mony a place stands in hard case
    Where blythe folk ken'd nae sorrow,
With Humes that dwelt on Leader side
    And Scotts that dwelt on Yarrow.

Next we have a poem by William Brockie (1811-90) who was the son of the tenant at East Mains farm. He was educated at the Parish Schools of Lauder, Smailholm, Mertoun, and Melrose. After having been Schoolmaster at Kailzie, he, in 1842, established the Galashiels Weekly Journal. Thereafter he was involved with various newspapers, until becoming Editor of the Sunderland Times, from 1862 to 1872. Mr. Brockie had a good knowledge of Botany and Geology, and had several European languages.

LAWTHER EAST MAINS

I wadna gie the braes of Boondreich,
That I used to speel langsyne,
For the olive groves of Lombardie,
Or the vineyards o' the Rhine.

I wadna gie the auld toor perk,
Wi' its ruin bald an' grim,
For the ducal palace o' Dalkeith,
Wi' its lawns and gairdens trim.

I wadna gie the witches' thimmles,
That grew near Howmeadows well,
For the fairest floors that florists prize,
Or the royal rose itsel'.

I wadna gie the laich herd's hoose,
Where I suppit nettle kail,
For the biggest and the bonniest ha',
I' the Merse and Tibbidale.

There's nae place like ane's native place,
Nae hame like ane's first hame:
It mattersna hoo puir an' cauld,
Oor love is a' the same.

We're drawn by some mysterious tie,
That nae man e'er defined,
To the sacred spot, hooe'er remote,
Where licht first on us shined.

An' sae of a' the wide, wide world,
Scotland I loe the best,
An' dearest to me o' Scottish streams
Leader dings a' the rest.

An' frae a' the ferms upon its banks
I'd turn to Lawther East Mains,
Tho' nane that kens or cares for me
For miles aroon' remains.

It's no that it's sae bonny a bit
That nane wi't can compare;
I ken there's nae great beauty in't,
But then it has what's mair:

A loving mother's gentle e'e
There first waked luv i' mine;
A gallant feyther's form first there
To me appeared divine.

There first I heard the name o' him
That made the bonnie floors;
There first I saw the virgin snaw,
An' the sparklin siller shoors.

Gae wa! gae wa! I pity ye a'
That's been brocht up in toons;
Nae wonder that ye're timmer tuned,
Preekt, pauchty, pudgel loons!

Yer bairntime amang styfe and reek
In clarty closes spent,
Ye scarce e'er saw the green, green gerse,
Or the clear blue firmament;

Ye never heard the bumbee's drone,
Nor the hurcheon's waesome cheep;
Ye never gumpt in a burn for troot,
Or fand a young peasweep;

Ye never gat a drink o' milk,
Sweet as it cam frae the coo;
Ye never built a rabbit hoose,
Or fed a rookety doo;

Ye never watcht the fleeing ether
Abune the mossy stank,
Or saw the hueront catching eels
Amang the reeds sae rank;

Ye never climbed a high hill tap
To see what ye could see;
Ye never played hael simmer days
On the bloomin' clover lea;

Ye never saw the Will o' the Wisp,
Nor the flickerin' Northern Lichts;
Ye ne'er crap roan the kitchen fire
I' the lang, wild, winter nights;

Ye never made a string o' beads
O' the rountree berries ripe;
Ye never blew a plane-tree whussel
Or a green yit-stalk pipe.

A grown-up man may thrive in a toon,
An' gather goud an' lair,
But ilka young thing sud enjoy
The caller country air.

Better than schuls and colleges
Are hills and valleys green;
For maist o' yer pedantic lore
I wadna gie a preen.

Ye learn the Greek and Roman names
O' things ye never saw.
While about real existences
Ye ken maist nocht ava.

For me, I had experience,
Ere I was three year auld,
O' things that at the present keep
My heart frae turnin' cauld.

An' hoo can I forget the place
Where that experience grew?
I wadna gie the memory o't
For a' that Newton knew.

The next is by Lady John Scott-Spottiswoode (1810-1900) she was the daughter of John Spottiswoode, of Spottiswoode. Lady John as she was commonly called, was we are told a true gentlewoman. Her affection for old times, old ways, and old folk was legendary, as was her charity to the poor and lonely. Her best known love-song was of course Annie Laurie.

LAMMERMOOR

> O, wild and stormy Lammermoor!
>   Would I could feel once more
> The cold north wind, the wintry blast
>   That sweeps thy mountain o'er.
> Would I could see thy drifted snow,
>   Deep, deep in cleuch and glen,
> And hear the scream of the wild birds,
>   And was free on thy hills again!
>
> I hate this dreary southern land,
>   I weary day by day
> For the music of thy many streams
>   In the birch woods far away!
> From all I love they banish me,
>   But my thoughts they cannot chain:
> And they bear me back, wild Lammermoor,
>   To thy distant hills again.

Next we have a poem by "Effie" Williamson who was born in Galashiels. She appears to have been born somewhere in the mid 1800's and seems to have moved backwards and forwards between Galashiels and other border towns, but never it would seem to Lauder, although she twice lived in Ireland. However by the tone of this poem she obviously knew Lauderdale well.

LAUDERDALE

> O bonnie braes and whimpling burns,
>   How oft to thee my fancy turns
> I seem to hear bright Leader's stream
>   Flow murmuring the wooded vale
> And see beneath the sunset's gleam
>   The fair round hills of Lauderdale.
>
> The springing sward beneath our feet,
>   The heather blossom, honey-sweet,
> With dewy fragrance fill the air;
>   O summer glories, waning pale,
> Still dost thou robe in garments fair
>   The breezy hills of Lauderdale

How fair 'neath western sunlight stood
Butterdean Braes, old Airhouse Wood,
Where oft at gloaming lovers met,
And whisper low the old, old tale,
Vowed to be true while suns should set
Above the hills of Lauderdale

The Watercleuch, the Holy Well,
Where saints of old, as legends tell,
Came oft by faith to kneel and pray.
Sweet prayer, thy virtues could not fail
To send rejoicing on their way
The faithful saints of Lauderdale.

On yon green hillsides softly tread:
There sleeps the dust of loved ones dead.
Here had they lived, and loved, and died –
The young and fair, the old and frail –
Now calmly rest they side by side
Among the hills of Lauderdale.

Now fades the sunset's ruddy glow,
We linger still, half loath to go;
And e'er we bid our last good-night,
The harvest moonbeams, clear and pale,
And shining stars, with silver light,
Fleck all the hills of Lauderdale.

The following is from a cutting taken from a newspaper printed at the start of the 20th. century.

LAUDER

Original poem rendered at band of hope social.

"Lauder Light Railway"

Cheer up, my lads, a mighty change
Has swept across our dale;
The old stage coach has yielded thus
To carriage, steam, and rail.

Old order giveth place to new,
The new old ways displace,

And now our good old town
  Should wear a brighter face.

For forty years in wilderness
  The Israelites did stray,
At length they reached the promised land,
  Though rough and long their way.
And so for forty years and more
  Our railway's been but talk,
But now that talk has issued forth
  A bright and certain fact.

The puff of "Billy" in the dale,
  The noise of whistle's scream,
Remind us of an enterprise
  Which once was but a dream
It's not exactly what we hoped,
  It's pace is rather slow;
It taketh "Billy" all his time
  From Fountain Hall to go.

Up through the moor to Hartside farm,
  Then by the Quarry round,
And past the Kirk upon the hill,
  Right on to Oxton town.
Of course when nearing Lauder town
  It runs a quicker pace-
A tribute this to Royalty.
  Whose mark is on this place.

And then although its pace is slow,
  There is some compensation,
It giveth time to minds inclined
  To serious meditation.

On hills, and fields, and crops, and farms,
  On bird, and flower, and weed,
Which surely you'll allow is good
  For such as live at speed.

Arid then there are some other things
  Not quite up to our mind,
We'd like a better run of trains,
  Some lamps our way to find.

Unwise it is that Light Railway.
A harbinger of light,
Should land us down in darkness gross,
And put us in a plight.

We'd like to see two goodly lamps,
Like those at head of town,
Which would ensure our safety
And discourage many a frown.

I pity those poor country folks
Who are on travel bent,
Their doubts, their horrid fears,
Their nights so sleepless spent.

Lest they should miss the early train,
And so their plans destroy;
And I believe, I'm sure I'm right,
There ought to be some change.

I hope this rhyme will reach in time
The three directors' ears
That at the council round the board
They may dispel our fears;

And grant us better light, and trains
At other times of day.
And we will wish success and speed
To Lauder Light Railway.

D.T.

LAUDER RAILWAY LAMENT

This was written by David Harvey. David was the much loved headmaster of Lauder school for 33 years. He travelled on the railway from Lauder, to Edinburgh, every day in his youth to secondary school and university.

15th November, 1958

'Tis six and twenty years, I ween,
Since passengers last graced the scene;
Now respite gained by freight is o'er,
Our Railway's passing we deplore.

As we all pleasant ties dissever,
  Our line has truly gone for ever!
And so we answer one last call
  To join the train for Fountainhall.
As our coaches smoothly glide along
  The verdant fields and hills among,
Shadows from the past appear-
  Visions of boon companions dear
Who spoke a kindly word of cheer;
  And railwaymen who strove to ensure
A journey happy and secure..
  Three leagues and a half from Lauder Station
We soon have reached our destination.
  Alas! there's no "Glenvarragill"
To pull us over Falahill!
  To Fountainhall a last good-day.
And we are on our homeward way.
  We duly round the final bend-
Dear Lauder Branch, it's journey's end.
  No rail chief joined our civic head
Beside the train, a tear to shed,
  No solemn march or peroration
Resounded over Lauder Station;
  No parson raised a hand to bless;
A brief valedictory address,
  Where once bright hopes ascended high-
An aubade for the century-
  Was ending meeting for this sad day.
As we retrace our homeward way,
  Along the Station Woodland ride
A blackbird sang for eventide
  Dear Maggie!* Now your race is run
We thank you for a task well done;
  Your faithful work let none deride-
Gently you lived and gently died.
  So let us all pay tribute due
With warmest thanks and blessings too!
  And, as I quit this final rally,
Dear Maggie, "AVE ATQUE VALE".

* The 4-4-0 tank engine which pulled the Lauder train was affectionately called "Maggie Lauder."

The next poem was written we believe by a girl who came on holiday each year to Dod Mill or Cambridge.

Near Leader burn stands Lauder toun
    Brawly dressed in summer goon
A bonnie sicht 'neath harvest moon
    It's hills and streams
Ma second hame - ah'l be back soon
    Place o' ma dreams.

Tae ramble 'mang its quiet ways
    Tae dream away the hours an' days
In raptured bliss an' peace to laze
    In woods I ken
Honest toun - yer worth mair praise
    Than I could pen

Sic happy folk - They're freends tae me
    Their smilin' faces noo ah see
The saddler smiles and winks his e'e
    When ah relate
Hoo much a've missed each causerie
    Ower gairden gate

The poaliss sergeant kens me weal
    He's Lauder's much respected chiel
Tae keep young imps far frae the deil
    Such is his task
A kindly man who works with zeal
    Nae praise he'l ask

Oh Lauder had I now the chance
    Thro' your braw woods an' glens tae prance
For aye sic mem'ries will enhance
    My future days
My heart yearns noo for but a glance
    O' thy fair braes.

Peryl Dodds - 6th March 1946

The following collection of poems were written by the late Walter Dykes, and are just a small sample of the many poems that he wrote during his lifetime. Wattie as he was affectionately known by his many friends, was born at Mountmill, Oxton on 5th. April 1906. His parents Robert and Margaret moved to Lauder Barns in 1907 when Walter was one year old. He lived at Lauder Barns for 72 years eventually taking over the farm from his father, his speciality was fattening good lambs and cattle for the sale at Gorgie Market, Edinburgh, every Tuesday. He was a dedicated Elder of Lauder Old Parish Church for over forty years. In 1979 he retired to New Channelkirk, near Oxton and lived there until his death in 1986 at the age of 80 years.

Walter Dykes reading his letter from the Queen for his poem on her 25th Jubilee.

WUDHEIDS KIRN (WOODHEADS KIRN)

The frost was keen the grund was firm
That nicht we gaed tee Wudheids Kirn
Youth that nicht was pleasure bent
A happy time indeed was spent.

Folk cam baith near and far awa
Dod Young the herd cam frae Carfrae,
Some even cam fraa Teviotside
Fine Queens appeared frae Gattonside.

By ten o'clock the loft was fou
We thocht na o' the wind that blew
Upon the cauld bleak Twin-law-Cairns
We had sic fine stuff in oor airms.

The Laird "Oor Host" he did his best
Tae entertain each honoured guest,
He made the barn rafters ring
His music box went oot and in.

In fact he over taxed his strength
For Ned his son fell a' his length
A shout got up "Ned's through the flair
The boards are a' beyond repair",

But Ned jumped up no much the waur
Unless he got some unseen scaur.
The dance gaed on wi' licht'nin pace
Just like the modern human race.

Next Agnes danced the Heighland Fling
A sicht for ony Laird of King
In Heighland garb she looked sae neat
Her steps were perfec' firm and fleet.

But pleasures ae come tae an end
Oor daily wark we must attend,
We a' stood up in circled line
And sung three verse of Auld Lang Syne.

As we stood there I thocht in vain
Wad we be spared tae meet again.
We a' gaed hame tae seek repose
*The **Woodheids Kirn** was at a close.*

The next is a poem written to celebrate Her Majesties Silver Jubilee, which Walter sent to the Palace, and duly received a letter of thanks.

Twenty-five years hath quickly sped
Since our most Gracious Queen
Ascended on the throne to reign
And she has reigned supreme.

Her life is full of goodness.
In her devotion to her nation.
With the sense of public duties
Her life is a dedication.

To hear her speak on Christmas day
In her lovely cultured voice
Her message is sincere and true
It makes our hearts rejoice.

Though difficult times may lie ahead
Our future is secure.
May God grant to our Gracious Queen
A faith both strong and sure.

That She may reign in right
Aye, wisdom love and peace
And by her good example
May crime and hatred cease.

Long reign our lovely noble Queen
May she be spared to see
Another twenty five years to reign
And her Golden Jubilee.

The next poem was written by Walter for, and recited at, Lauder Church Social to celebrate the Ter-Centenary of the present Church building on 4th. October 1973.

Well Ladies and Gentlemen we are all gathered here
*   And the Town Hall tonight is resounding wi' cheer.*
We have not just come here for a speech or a song
*   Its our Church Celebration that has brought us along.*

It is three hundred years since her foundation was laid
*   And the word has been preached throughout every decade.*
Now her walls are restored and a new lease began
*   May our Church be kept Sacred for generations to come.*

May each faithful member be spared to attend
*   And worship sincerely our Savour and Friend*
As weeks roll on and the years pan at length
*   May our Church ever prosper and go forth in strength.*

Each member has worked hard our objective to gain
*   And I am sure all our labours have not been in vain*
So this is the year of great celebration
*   But also a time for re-dedication.*

This next poem Walter entitled. **Noble Creatures.**

A Fermer stood upon the brae
*   And looked around Wi' pride*
He had a hamely feeling
*   For the Border countryside*
And far across towards the east
*   he thrilled at what he saw*
A little herd o' Kylies
*   in the field at Pyatshaw.*

He'd worked and toiled tae sow his seed
*   and hoe his turnips clean*
Had watched the tractor ploughing
*   and saw the reapers glean*
Yet aye the greatest pleasure
*   That reached abin them aw*
Was tae wander rooned the Kylies
*   In the field at Pyatshaw.*

He saw the shepherd gether sheep
*   High on the grassy hill*

He watched the Boondriech water
as it flowed towards the mill
A nature lay afore him
Frae Boon tae Lammerlaw
But aye heed mind his Kylies
in the field at Pyatshaw.

When a the crops has ripened
and a the fields are bare
And a the winters feedin
is stacked up wi care
There's aye a thocht ahint his mind
amid the sleet and snaw
God keep and watch the Kylies
in the field at Pyatshaw.

Finally a poem that Walter wrote and recited at a Burns Supper.

Yince mair weve met tae honour Burns
His memory tae reca
Twas 1759 when winds gie snell did blaw
Upon his humble thacket cot
Where dear auld Rab was born
The walls o' Allway did rejoice
That cauld bleak winters morn

He littleknew the talent great
That lay at his command
And how his name would be reveered
Throughout our Borderland.

He wrote o' Tammie Shanter
And about the mercland bairn
The twa Brigs and the Collie Dugs
And James, Earl o' Glencairn

He wrote aboot the humble moose
And the Daisy fresh and green
His charming Highland Mary
And his bonnie lovely Jean.

I'll now lay down my humble pen
And leave this wish sincere
That the memory of our Scottish bard
Grows brighter every year.

The next two poems come from an old book of poem entitled "Lammermoor Leaves" with the initials A.T.G. on the cover. On a page at the beginning of the book we find.

NOTE

This little Book is a Collection of "Leaves", gathered for the most part on the lower slopes of the Lammermoor Hills, during Autumn holidays.

In the folds of the Berwickshire News, the Border Advertiser, or the Border Magazine, they have been already pressed.

They are here stitched together for the sake of those who desire to preserve for a few days longer some simple thoughts they were pleased to value.

These "Leaves" shall fade, as all leaves do. Till then, they may have a memory of
"The Waters Trinklin Doun Amang The Fern."

September, 1898.

Old Airhouse Wood.

Around Old Airhouse Wood
    There breaks the morning sheen,
The golden light appears
    Above the Kirktown dean.
Here Cuthbert roamed of yore
    With shepherd plaid and rod,
And here in heav'nly dream
    He tarried with his God.

Above Old Airhouse Wood
    Full moon its blaze doth shed;
The holy waters clear
    Seek Leader's pebbly bed.
And Channelkirk stands fair,
    To Cuthbert's mem'ry reared;
And grassy mounds are seen,
    With grave-stones wond'rous weird.

Along Old Airhouse Wood
    The length'ning shadows fall,
The days bright beams have sped
    From saintly Cuthbert's hall.
Yet hallow'd is the scene,
    And mystic thoughts crowd fast,

As, wand'ring through the wood,
　　We muse, and mourn the past.

Farewell! Old Airhouse Wood;
　　Thy mantle green inspires
To link the passing hour
　　With mem'ries of our sires.
Saint Cuthbert! thou thy work
　　Did'st well and fearlessly:
We follow in thy steps,
　　And holy visions see.

Carfrae Tower.

All mantled o'er with trailing-ivy wreath-
　　The massive mould'ring walls scarce seen beneath-
The olden keep, with greensward all around,
　　Marks ancient landmarks on the Baron's Mound.

O'er Hillhouse glen, in days of feud and raid,
　　It held full sway. The Baron law down laid
That none should pass to Yester's lordly hall
　　But first must homage pay at bugle call.

Around its walls the rough-clad troopers lay
　　With sword or bow in hand, till break of day;
Or wander far afield to drive the kine,
　　Until they rested in the Baron's line.

All o'er from Fairnilees to Wha'plaw Pool
　　The war-horn sounded from Hansel to Yule;
This good old rule enforced-the simple plan-
　　"Tak'ye who have power, and keep ye who can."

Now peaceful the scene at midsummer noon.
　　No foray wild by the light of the moon:
The hirsel now browsing on heath'ry hill,
　　And corn waving ripe on holms by the rill.

Romantic and lone stands the old dark tower,
　　Keeping guard-haunted by some magic power;
And nestling beneath its green ivy gown,
　　Whispers a story of former renown.

Lauderdale Agriculture
In The 20th Century

Introduction

It is recorded in the minutes of the Oxton Bovial Society in 1898 that the first "horseless carriage" had passed through Lauderdale that year and it is also recorded in the minutes of 1900 that members of the committee were of the opinion that such things would not last! Oh that those gentlemen could be around one hundred years later to witness the effect that the power unit of the "horseless carriage" has had on the lives of people all over the world. They might think they were on another planet.

It is almost certainly the harnessing of power that has led to the dramatic changes which have taken place in agriculture over the past century. In 1900 horsepower in the form of the Clydesdale and other breeds for the heavy work, with lighter horses for transport and riding, were the order of the day. Water power was also harnessed to drive the threshing mills and to mill the grain, but the greatest power source was man himself. The ploughing and tilling of the land may have been done by horse but a great many of the harvesting tasks and the moving of the crop was done by hand. Farm labourers spent a great deal of time with a pitchfork, graip, scythe, shawing hook or hoe in their hands.

Today the single horsepower of the 1900's has been replaced by the diesel engine and the massive horsepower of the modern day tractor with the sophisticated equipment to match. Electricity has also provided a dramatic change in the lives of those who work on the farms as well as in their homes with power at the flick of a switch. Transport changes have also been completely dramatic – moving from the ridden horse or horse and carriage to today's luxurious saloon cars, from the horse and cart to the massive articulated wagons capable of carrying over 30 tonnes, travelling at over 50mph and from non existent air travel to aircraft carrying hundreds of passengers around the world at over 500mph.

Communication systems have also been developed which mean it is now possible to speak to people almost anywhere in the world or to send messages which will be received instantly. In 1900 communication was overland by the postal service and could take days or even weeks.

For agriculture the 20th century has been a period of transition and development to embrace and utilise the new and developing technology.

General Agriculture Situation and Weather

Looking back to the agricultural section of A Thomson's book on "Lauder and Lauderdale", written a century ago, makes one realise that some things may not change that much. Apparently the 19th century ended with agriculture very much in depression — so what's new? There is no doubt, however, that agricultural profitability has its ups and downs and that these variations are, more often than not, a result of influences affecting the industry over which agriculture has absolutely no control. The weather can pose its own problems but generally agriculture can cope with that. The interference of politicians is another matter altogether.

Perhaps the worst period for farming was in the 1930's. Prices collapsed completely and for some products there was little or no market. It is said that some farmers hung on to their wool rather than give it away. For some the dire financial situation obviously became too much and as a result more farms changed hands at this time than in any other period of the century.

The two World Wars increased the necessity for home food production and on these occasions it was all hands on deck to produce as much food as possible and grants were made available to encourage farmers to plough up and crop more land. In the aftermath of war, with food rationing still in place and a growing world population, few would have thought that, just over the horizon by the end of the century, food surpluses would become a problem. Even in 1980 the then Labour government produced a booklet entitled "Food from our own Resources", encouraging farmers to increase production and supported this with the "Farm and Horticultural Development Scheme" with grants available to achieve the aim of a greater output per labour unit.

Improved husbandry techniques, along with major technological improvements and increased mechanisation resulted in agriculture becoming vastly more efficient with the result of over production in most commodities and a subsequent collapse in prices.

In the 1930's the national economy was in trouble and no one could afford to buy food whereas today there is not a national depression and it is only isolated industries like agriculture which are suffering.

There is no doubt that in the course of a century consumer attitudes have changed significantly. During the first half of the century, and particularly during and after the wars, consumer concern was much more about whether there was enough food to go around. At present, when food is plentiful in Britain, concern is about food quality and how it has been produced. As a result food health scares can have an extremely damaging effect on market prices such as happened to the beef market as a result of the BSE scare in 1996.

Isn't it amazing that, on reflection, it is always so much easier to remember the bad times rather than the good, but there were periods when agriculture was buoyant with different commodities taking turns to be the profitable areas.

Whilst politicians have had a major effect on agriculture, it is often the weather that can provide some of the ups and downs, although of course only in localised areas. Weather patterns certainly seem to be changing as a result of global warming and the long cold winters of the past seem to be giving way to a much milder, but often wetter, climate - particularly in winter. Many villages in the Borders used to have curling ponds and there are many pictures of local people enjoying a day on the ice. Nowadays there are very few days when such ponds would be hard enough to play on. Again, it is usually the bad that sticks in the memory and the two winters that anyone alive at the time seems to remember were those of 1947 and 1962/3. The former was a storm of great ferocity which occurred late in the winter during February and brought great depths of snow which lasted well into the spring, resulting in very difficult and poor lambings. The 1962/3 winter was a much more prolonged affair with snow starting in early December and continuing right through until late March with the postman wishing some people a "Happy New Year" on the 20th March. Sheep, particularly those on the hills, became very lean and again lambings were very poor.

The winters of 1916, 1936, 1937 and 1968 are also remembered as some of the worst of the century. Severe snowstorms can result in some of the more outlying farms becoming isolated for long periods, although these days modern equipment can help to clear roads fairly quickly. However snowstorms can still result in out wintered hill sheep becoming buried when there is a severe drift. The 26th February 2001 will last long in the memory as the worst day the writer can remember for the ferocity of the storm. Even though, thankfully, the snow cleared after ten days, many sheep had been buried and whilst a large number were dug out alive, many farms in the district suffered losses to a greater or lesser extent.

Perhaps one is more carefree as a child or maybe life seemed more idyllic, but recollections of summers in the 1950's were that the sun shone for days on end and summer weather was certainly something to look forward to. Nowadays summer weather seems to be much more variable and good long warm dry spells occur only infrequently. 1975 and 1976 are well remembered as the long hot summers with long hot sunny days resulting in very little grass growth and by the end of the summer Lauderdale was looking extremely brown and parched. Stock, particularly lambs, generally thrive well under such conditions but winter keep was in distinct short supply although the quality was superb.

Because Lauderdale does not have very much flat land, floods do not cause damage by covering large areas or land, but it is the rate at which the water leaves that can cause the problem. River banks and roads can be eroded and bridges, fences and water gates all swept away leaving a great trail of damage. The flood of August 1948 is the one which appears to be the most frequently recalled, with a great number of bridges and roads being taken out and access to some farms being cut off.

The Land

It is hardly surprising that in the course of a century there should have been a significant change in the land ownership and occupancy in Lauderdale. Perhaps the most significant change is that in 1900 nearly all of the farmland was owned by estates and occupied by tenants whereas one hundred years later the majority, but not all, of the land is owner occupied.

The major landowner was undoubtedly the Earl of Lauderdale with the Lauderdale Estates owning at least two thirds of the land in the district. The land stretched from Airhouse and took in nearly all of the land on the south side of the valley whilst on the north side all of the farms from Lylestane along to Blythe were included - a huge and significant parcel of land. Yester Estate, belonging to the Marquis of Tweeddale, owned the land in the north west corner of the district from Longcroft round to Hartside with the exception of Kirktonhill and Glengelt which were owned by the Borthwick family of Crookston. Interestingly the Marquis of Tweeddale also owned Boon.

The start of the change in land ownership came in the 1920's when the majority of the Lauderdale Estate was put on the market at the one time. The reason for this was that the estate had become heavily mortgaged and the sale of a significant portion was required to clear the debts.

Although not all of the farms found buyers immediately, most were sold and in many cases to the sitting tenants. During the 1980's some of the remaining farms on the estate were sold, Whitlaw and Newmills to the tenants and Pilmuir to the Morris family. Now all that remains of this once great estate are the castle policies along with the farms of Wyndhead and Wanton Walls.

The Yester Estate was all sold in 1951 with, once again, nearly all of the sitting tenants purchasing the land.

Since the demise of the major estates several of these farms have been sold again and in a few cases on more than one occasion. In the first half of the century farms which were sold tended to be purchased by farmers from the southern half of Scotland but as transport links improved, purchasers have come from further afield. As the property boom of the late 20th century gathered pace, particularly in the south east of England, land in Scotland began to look very competitively priced and many farms, including some in Lauderdale, were bought by people from these areas who became affectionately known as "white settlers". The farms of Carfrae, Threeburnford, Airhouse, Lauder Barns, Collielaw and Nether Howden are currently all owned and farmed by families from south of the border, some of whom have moved a very long way to farm here, whilst the current owner occupier of Woodheads is a family from Ireland.

It is also worth mentioning in this section that Lylestane has an interesting history in that it was owned and farmed by the Dobson family from 1932 until 1957 and, in 1994 when the farm came back on the market, it was bought back by Mr Harry Dobson.

The heather clad hill farms of Lauderdale are part of the Lammermuir range of hills and are renowned for being some of the best grouse moors in the country. Although formal grouse shooting has taken place since the 18th century it was not until the late 19th century that sporting values significantly affected the value of property and currently grouse moor valuations are in excess of the agricultural value. Tollishill and Burncastle (including Braidshawrig) have both been sold in the recent past primarily as sporting properties with the Duke of Northumberland making a huge investment in Burncastle with the building of the new lodge.

In the interest of agricultural efficiency over the years there has been a tendency, which no doubt will continue, for farms to get larger with small units being swallowed up by their larger neighbours. This, however, has not happened in Lauderdale over the course of the last century, with most of the farms as we know them today still of a similar size. Glengelt is one farm which has been divided up with the land to the south of the A68 now on Kirktonhill, the remainder of the fields being the small farm of Channelkirk and the hill land on the top of Soutra being run as a separate unit, windmills and all!

The only other exceptions to this would be the smaller farms around Oxton and Lauder where current development is taking land from the likes of Loanend, Wyndhead, Heriotshall and Nether Howden for private housing. A lot of this housing is not being bought by local residents but more by people who commute to Edinburgh and its surrounds on a daily basis - something that would or could not have been contemplated a century ago.

Just as much of the ownership of the land has changed hands, so has most of the occupancy. In 1900 most of the farmers only had the tenancy of one farm, the notable exceptions to this being the Dickinson brothers, Robert and William, who lived at Longcroft but also tenanted Tollishill, Hillhouse and Lauder Haugh and John Bertram who farmed Addinston and Hartside. Today there are several cases where a family farms more than one unit as can be seen from the list of farms and their occupants.

Several families have been farming in the district for all of the past one hundred years but not necessarily in the same farm. The only family to achieve this distinction is the McDougal family of Blythe who took on the tenancy in 1852 and still farm there now as the owner occupiers. Runciman is a name synonymous with Lauderdale and the family has a history of farming in the district which dates back to 1793 when they took the tenancy of Wanton Walls, a tenancy which lasted for an amazing 198 years until 1991. Currently various branches of the family farm at West Mains, East Mains, Under Boon, St Leonard's, Muircleuch and Huntington as well as the farms of Allanshaws and Upper Blainslie immediately adjacent to the parish.

1900 saw the Waldie family in Muircleuch and one hundred years on they are owner occupiers of Newmills as well as tenant in part of Trabrown. Similarly the Sharp family were farming Over Howden and currently farm Longcroft, Lylestane, Newbigging Walls and Shielfield. St Leonard's has been occupied by the Torrie family throughout the 1900's until the death of Forest Torrie in 1994. The Middlemass family of Bowerhouse purchased their farm from the Lauderdale Estate in 1920 but remained as the landlord, letting the farm to Mr Purves until 1968 and only then taking the occupancy into their own hands. There are of course several farms which have been farmed by the same family for the greater part of the last century and these include:

Stevenson	Blackburn
Forrest	Boon and Whitlaw
McKerrow	Addinston
Middlemiss	Wiselawmill
Sutherland	Hillhouse
Anderson	Headshaw
Dagg	Woodheads, Lylestane and Pilmuir
Dykes	Lauder Barns and Kirktonhill

Bennet	Nether Howden and Hartside
Finlayson	Wyndhead and Trabrown
Gilchrist	Justicehall and Threeburnford

Farms and Farmers in Lauderdale, 2002

Blackburn	I Stevenson
Lauder Haugh	D Morison
Newmills	D Waldie
Trabrown (part)	"
Trabrown (part)	R McPherson
Whitlaw	J Forrest
Lauderhill	Lauderhill Sheep Company
Loanend	M Landells
Muircleuch	J P Runciman
Woodheads	I & G Davison
Lauder Barns	R Damerell
West Mains	W Runciman
East Mains	"
St Leonards	J E Runciman
Boon (Under)	R Runciman
Blythe	J McDougal
Thirlestane	T Barr
Wanton Walls	J Connell
Burncastle	Duke of Northumberland
Braidshawrig	"
Huntington	D Runciman
Newbigging Walls	J Sharp
Lylestane	"
Longcroft	"
Shielfield	"
Addinston	M McKerrow
Tollishill	Faccombe Estates
Kelphope	"
Hillhouse	J Sutherland
Carfrae	J Bartlett
Headshaw	R Anderson
Channelkirk	A Sutherland
Hunter's Hall	J Hunt
Kirktonhill	J Patterson
Hartside	A & D Kay
Threeburnford	A Glennie

Airhouse	M Houghton
Heriotshall	D Smith
Oxton Mains	J Greenwell
Justicehall	H Reid
Nether Howden	M Ridgway
Over Howden	J Home Robertson
Collielaw	I Parker
Burnfoot	H Sloan
Bowerhouse	J Middlemass
Inchkeith	D Wilkinson
Pilmuir	R Morris
Midburn	A Fair
Wiselawmill	W Middlemiss
Thirlestane Castle Policy Land	The Hon Capt Maitland Carew
Glenburnie	"
Wyndhead	"

Husbandry

They say that life goes in cycles and it is fascinating to note that in recent years there has been a movement to encourage farmers towards organic production when, of course, a century ago agricultural output was totally organic. The advent of inorganic fertilisers, herbicides, fungicides, insecticides, anthelmintics, vaccines and so on has allowed agriculture to become much more intensive with a huge increase in output and with much less reliance on balanced farming systems.

Crop rotations used to be extremely important to reduce the risk of disease spreading from crop to crop. A grass break in the rotation was also deemed advisable to help maintain the soil structure and the utilisation of the grass break by livestock helped soil fertility. Livestock production on the farm also ensured that organic manure was available and returned to the land. With the exception of the few entirely hill farms, most of Lauderdale was farmed in a balanced system using sheep, cattle and a short crop rotation based on oats, barley and turnips. Even the higher of the upland farms had to ensure that there was plenty winter keep by growing sufficient oats and turnips.

Turnips were undoubtedly the mainstay of the winter feeding systems for both cattle and sheep and huge acreages of the crop were grown. The particulars of Thirlestane farm, for sale in 1927, show that 100 acres of turnips were grown, along with 175 acres of oats and 25 acres of barley - the cropping rotation being, oats, turnips and oats undersown. Records show that Boon farm at the turn of the century was growing 400 acres of cereals along with 160 acres of turnips.

It can be seen why the crop rotation was so important in those days because with such a dependence on the turnip crop, finger and toe was a major problem if turnips were grown too frequently. Nowadays the overwintering of livestock is based on other fodder and turnips have rather fallen out of favour. It is unlikely that in the whole of Lauderdale today there are as many turnips as were grown at Boon a century ago.

The pattern of cereal growing has changed over the years with many of the higher, steeper upland farms having stopped, whilst some of the lower farms in Lauderdale have increased their acreage.

There are several reasons for these changes:-

- To grow a hectare of cereals on poor land costs just as much as on good land but for a much lower yield.

- Steep land does not lend itself to large equipment, particularly the modern combine harvesters.

- Feeding compounds for livestock can be purchased ready to be fed thus avoiding the labour required for processing home grown cereals.

- The making of grass into silage provides fodder for both cattle and sheep and big bale silage making can be conducted even on steeper land, providing care is taken.

As a result of the reduced cropping areas cattle and sheep numbers have tended to increase on these farms.

On the farms in the district with a higher percentage of better land, farmers have a greater choice of enterprises open to them. This has resulted in a greater cereal cropping programme, an increased cattle population on some farms and the disappearance of breeding sheep flocks altogether in some instances. The necessity to maintain rotations has gone and many fields in the centre of Lauderdale grow cereals year after year with the only break being oilseed rape or set aside (set aside is a European scheme whereby farmers are paid to keep land out of cereal production in order to reduce surpluses and is currently set at a minimum of 10% of the cropping area). Barley is now the main cereal grown, both for malting and feeding but winter wheat is also grown on some of the best land. There is a small acreage of oats but this crop is now generally out of favour.

Although dairy farming was never a major activity in the area, dairies were found around the villages of Oxton and Lauder but now Wyndhead, Loanend and Justicehall no longer continue to milk. Dairying was also practised by Mr Bartlett at Carfrae for around twenty years.

Admiring crooks made by shepherds, at Oxton Collie Trials.

Livestock and Sheep

Sheep production has probably always been regarded as the backbone of agricultural production in Lauderdale as the topography of the land tends to lend itself to this. The land produces good quality stock and breeding sheep from the district have always had a good reputation.

A century ago most of the inbye sheep were either Cheviot or halfbred ewes with the bigger halfbred ewes running on the best of the land. The popular terminal sire of the turn of the century was the Oxford Down ram on the halfbred ewes, producing big sheep. At about this time the Suffolk breed was introduced and eventually took over from the Oxford until nowadays there are very few Oxford Down rams used at all.

Unlike today when most lambs are produced for the prime lamb market at three to nine months of age, a century ago keeping sheep until they were 16 to 18 months old was a common practice, overwintering on turnips on inbye farms. On some hill farms wedders were often kept on the hill until they were three to four years old before slaughter. The young sheep or dinmonts as they were known have gone out of favour and have given way to fat lambs. However overfat lambs were not wanted by the consumer and when in the 1970's subsidy support was not available to the fattest lambs, the production of slightly leaner prime lamb was demanded. This shift in demand meant that lambs fit for the prime market could be produced off the farms in Lauderdale whereas before thousands had been sold in the autumn sales for further fattening in the lowlands. Very few lambs are sold store from the district nowadays, mostly being finished on the farm of birth.

Lauderdale is perhaps better known however for producing top quality breeding stock. The North Country Cheviot ewe crossed with the Border Leicester gives the half bred which was a popular ewe on low ground farms for crossing with a terminal sire. Many farms in the area specialised in producing half bred ewe lambs for sale at St Boswells market in August. Whitlaw, Woodheads, Boon, Thirlestane, Headshaw, Kirktonhill, Threeburnford and Airhouse were some of the flocks which produced significant numbers of these top quality ewe lambs.

Mr Ker, auctioneer, conducts "snowballing" of black lamb at Oxton, in aid of the Red Cross Agriculture Fund.

The half bred ewe has however currently fallen out of favour, giving way to the smaller Scotch mule (a Blackface cross Bluefaced Leicester) which has excellent maternal traits. The result is that many of the Cheviot ewes have been replaced by the Scotch mule and half bred ewe lamb production has become very limited. Mule ewe lambs from the district have featured prominently at the breeding sales in the 1980's and 1990's with top quality lambs from Bowerhouse, Hillhouse, Woodheads and Longcroft to name a few. There is a growing practice for farms to breed their own flock replacements by running blackface ewes to breed mule ewe lambs to be kept on the farm. Many people find this more financially rewarding than buying in breeding stock and this practice also helps to reduce disease risk.

In the 1970's there was a great influx of various breed of sheep from the continent as farmers struggled to produce sheep which met consumer demand. Many of these breeds enjoyed a brief fame as shortage of numbers kept pedigree prices high but unfortunately some were found wanting and to be no better than our native breeds when put to the commercial test. The exception to this would be the Texel and possibly the Beltex, both breeds which provided something that our native breeds lacked - big hindquarters. The result is that nowadays the Texel breed has taken over a significant portion of the terminal sire market and is a serious contender to the Suffolk breed.

In the 19th century many of the sheep were sold at the annual fairs where farmers set up their own pens and negotiated a price for the sheep with the buyers. The auction system, which appeared to be a much more open method of valuation, did not come into vogue until the latter part of the 19th century. Most of the store stock and the prime stock were marketed this way during the 20th century but in the second half there has been a growing number of farmers who consign their stock directly to the abattoirs and bypass the auction system altogether. With improved transport facilities allowing large numbers of stock to be moved quickly over longer distances and a decreased throughput at the markets, the auction companies have been rationalised until today only John Swan & Sons at St Boswells have facilities in the Borders Area.

The economies of today have dictated that the modern day shepherd must look after larger numbers of sheep and most shepherds will have at least double the number of sheep in their care than their predecessors. Production systems have also changed. The turnip is no longer the basis of the winter rations, being replaced by hay and silage (particularly big bale silage). Many ewes on the lower farms in the district are now wintered indoors in order to facilitate easier mechanical feeding, save the land from poaching in winter and to allow indoor lambing to take place. Shepherds now tend to inspect grazing sheep by four wheel drive vehicle or quad bike rather than horse or Shanks' Pony. Contract shepherds are now used to help with major tasks such as shearing, and sheep scanning which started around 1983 has now become normal practice on many farms and leads to more accurate feeding of the pregnant ewe.

Hill flocks have similarly been affected by economic forces and the number of shepherds has declined dramatically over the past thirty years. Traditional shepherding, whereby the sheep are "raked up" the hill at night and down in the morning has gone (although hill sheep do still tend to move up and down naturally) and been replaced by inspection via quad bike. Until the advent of the quad bike, increasing the number of sheep for a shepherd proved difficult as there was a limit to the amount of ground a man could cover on foot but this problem has now been resolved.

Feeding practices have also changed. Few hill flocks were fed regularly at all in the first half of the century - only being given hay in storms, but the advent of the 20kg self help feed block allowed sheep to be fed on the hill without the shepherd having to go there every day. Nowadays most hill sheep are fed regularly and many use the practice of scanning to identify twin bearing ewes and feed these separately by mechanical feeders towed behind the quad bike. Lambing very often takes place in enclosures and not on the open hill as in the past, again reducing labour requirements.

As far back as anyone can remember, the hill flocks in Lauderdale have been blackfaces. That the type has changed over the generations is without question and with wool being of such low value these days a much shorter wooled sheep, capable of producing a bigger crop of lambs is now in fashion compared to the pre 1950 days. Many of the hill flocks regularly produce 115 - 135% lambing percentages. From this district the blackface lambs, draft ewes and rams are now mostly sold through the markets at Lanark and Stirling, although, as with the upland farms, there is a growing tendency for lambs to be finished at home. Breeding stock from Lauderdale regularly feature in the top prices at the sales.

Andrew Sharp of Tollishill held the Blackface breed record with a shearling sold at Lanark in 1961 for £4100. The Kay family at Burncastle in the 1970's to mid 1990's often secured the top prices at Lanark with their ewes, shearlings and ram lambs and before them the Arnotts in the same farm. The Longcroft flock is also well renowned.

Pedigree flocks of other breeds have not been great in number in Lauderdale, which has been more noted for its commercial sheep production. However James

Walter Dykes with sheep beside the Eagle Bridge.

Dun ran a very successful flock of pedigree Suffolks at Burnfoot under the Lauderdale prefix before he moved it back to his home farm at Colmslie. Dr Sutherland of Channelkirk annually produces a pen of top quality registered Suffolk shearling rams at Kelso, whilst Mr Connell, Wanton Walls and Mrs Sharp, Newbigging Walls have successful flocks of Bluefaced Leicesters which feature regularly at the same venue.

Livestock - Cattle

As with the sheep, the cattle bred and reared in Lauderdale have changed both in the breeds used and their management. Breeding cattle nearly all used to be outwintered and calved in the spring so cattle that could stand the rigours of winter and be fit enough to produce a calf were what was required. The traditional blue grey cow (Galloway crossed with White Shorthorn) fitted the bill admirably as it had sufficient coat for protection and ample milk to produce a good suckled calf. The Galloway was an even hardier cow and, being required to produce the blue grey, herds were to be found on some of the hill farms – the McDougals at Blythe having a large Galloway herd of note at one time. The blue grey cow was then traditionally crossed with an Aberdeen Angus bull to produce quality beef cattle through which Scotland gained it worldwide reputation for "Scotch Quality Beef".

However in the 1950's and 60's the wind of change began to affect the beef cattle sector. In wintering of cows in modern portal framed buildings became the norm on many farms and so the necessity for a hardy cow disappeared. Good quality dairy bred heifer calves were available in large quantities, particularly from south of the border and, being milkier than the blue grey, were able to produce a faster growing calf. Hereford and Angus cross Friesian cows were excellent mothers and produced good quality calves, especially if the cows were bred from good shaped Friesians. However at the same time the Aberdeen Angus breed was fast becoming too small in size for commercial Scottish farmers, as the pedigree breeders chased the high priced South American market. Some farmers began to use the Hereford as an alternative terminal sire, being slightly bigger than the Aberdeen Angus, but the real change came with the impact in the 1970's of several new breeds of cattle from the continent. These cattle were much bigger, grew faster and tended not to become as fat as the native breeds and so Charolais, Simmental and Limousin, to name but a few of the imports, came into common use as terminal sires. They were, of course, not without their problems, the most common one being the calving difficulties associated with bigger calves.

The Aberdeen Angus breed has thankfully not stood still and has risen to the challenge of the continentals by producing much bigger cattle and, as a consequence of good promotional work cashing in on the breeds long standing reputation, premium prices are being paid for Aberdeen Angus crosses. Currently farmers are faced with a choice of using Aberdeen Angus bulls and producing for a premium market or using continental sires, achieving faster growth rates and producing a heavier carcass.

On the dam side there have been problems as well. The supply of top quality heifer calves from the dairy herd has become limited as most milk producers have been using Holstein cows in the dairy to replace the Friesian. The Holstein is far too narrow and angular an animal for beef production and so beef farmers are looking to the beef herd to supply the breeding females, perhaps losing out on some of the milking qualities. Aberdeen Angus, Limousin and Simmental crosses are now being used as beef cows along with the specialist female breeds such as the Luing and the Salers.

Husbandry practices have also changed. Once again the turnip along with oat straw was the mainstay of winter rations a century ago but this has changed to silage based rations in many cases. Cattle numbers in Lauderdale have most definitely increased with some farms carrying very large herds. Suckled calf production was the norm for most Lauderdale farms earlier in the century, the calves being sold at the autumn sales at St Boswells, but nowadays, rather like sheep, more farms are taking the cattle right through to slaughter. Many of these cattle are now being intensively finished on ad lib barley based rations with the continental cross cattle being particularly suited to such treatment. Whilst some cattle are still sold live at auction at the weekly St Boswells prime stock sale, an ever increasing number are being consigned directly to the abattoir.

As a result of the changes which have taken place in both the breeding and the management of the cattle, primestock are sold at a much higher weight these days. Before the importation of continental breeds 450 - 500 kgs liveweight was the normal weight range for steers whereas today 500 - 600 kg would be considered suitable for market requirements.

Pedigree herds of cattle have been thin on the ground in Lauderdale although Aberdeen Angus herds were established on both Addinston and Thirlestane in the 1920's and 1930's and Major Lascelles ran a herd of Aberdeen Angus cattle at Newbigging Walls in the 1940's to 1960's. Mr Patterson at Kirktonhill currently owns a fine Galloway herd and, amongst many show ring successes, includes a recent Royal Highland Show Championship.

Cropping

Arable cropping in Lauderdale has always taken second place to livestock production in the agricultural scene but some of the farms in the centre of the Leader valley, with a larger proportion of the land being arable, are well able to grow some very good cereal crops.

Over the century the oat acreage has fallen into major decline and this has been replaced mostly by barley grown both for malting and feeding. Very little wheat used to be grown in the district but now improved varieties and earlier autumn sowing practices have resulted in an expanding wheat area, grown mostly for feeding. Oilseed rape is grown as a break crop for cereals on a limited acreage. Virtually no commercial crops of potatoes are grown as this has become a very specialised and capital intensive crop to grow and is mostly confined to the best arable areas, although Mr Rowe had a large potato growing business based at Midburn in the 1970's, contracting potato growing land in and around the district.

As has been detailed before turnips and swedes are a declining acreage with those that are grown being mostly for feeding to lambing ewes and ewe hoggs. Fodder rape and kale are grown on some of the more upland and hill farms as a means of breaking up old pasture before reseeding and are, of course, excellent crops for finishing hill lambs. The rest of the land and certainly the biggest area is grass.

Whilst livestock production has changed considerably over a century it is the cropping areas which have been revolutionised by mechanisation. Out has gone the horse and hard physical labour and in their place has come an ever increasing size of tractor as the power unit on the land.

A 1923 International Junior 8/16 used on Whitslaid Farm from 1923 to 1939.

The little grey Fergies of the 1940's and 1950's with a horsepower of 35 have been replaced by ever bigger, more sophisticated tractors with a hundred horsepower more and in some cases even bigger. The horse drawn binder for harvesting has likewise been revolutionised to the massive self propelled combine harvester of today. Dr Shirra Gibb's book - A Farmers 50 Years in Lauderdale (1872 - 1922) - makes reference to the fact that a harvest of 400 acres at Boon in 1872 required 63 people to secure it, whereas nowadays a medium sized combine harvester would complete the job comfortably with perhaps only two people involved.

The large power units can handle much larger equipment. Conventional two and three furrow ploughs have been superseded by four and five furrow reversible ploughs and in most cases the cultivation of the soil and the sowing of the seed are carried out as a one pass operation. The result of all these changes mean more capital investment in machinery and less people on the land. Due to the high capital investment required, many farmers in the district are contracting some of the cultivating and harvesting operations from neighbours or using the relatively recently formed machinery ring.

Winter fodder production has also changed dramatically. Out has gone the turnip crop and the substantial areas of hay that used to be made and in their place has come grass silage. Whilst hay is still very suitable for sheep, especially hill flocks where it can be stored in hill hay sheds, it is of notoriously variable quality being very weather dependent for its production. Grass silage making is now a very quick, highly mechanised operation, often carried out by contractors but does require a considerable capital investment in the pit for storage, with its associated effluent tanks. The development of the big round bale in the 1970's and the subsequent polythene wrapping of grass to make the silage bale has been a major step forward. It has enabled small farms to be in a position to make silage without a huge capital investment and, for those on steeper ground, to have a system which is much safer than conventional silage making. Of course, silage making is also much less dependent on the weather than hay making.

Whilst mentioning the big round bale it is worthy of note that Ian Sutherland of Hillhouse was probably the first person to consider the concept of the big bale and, being of an inventive mind, did consider how it could be achieved. It was about ten years after his original idea that round balers began to come on to the market.

Crop husbandry has also made huge strides during the past 50 years or so. As a result the sprayer, which started life more or less as a source of weed control, now passes through the cereal crops several times in the season to put on herbicides, fungicides, insecticides and growth controllers. Inorganic fertiliser usage has become more of an exact science with increased quantities being used as the century progressed and new, more productive varieties of cereals are continually being brought forward by plant breeders. All this has meant that yields have increased significantly over the century with production being about double what it was at the end of World War II. Expected yields are currently around 2.5 tonnes/acre for spring barley, 3 tonnes/acre for winter barley and 3.5 tonnes/acre for winter wheat.

Winter cereals never used to be grown in Lauderdale but now a significant area is sown in the autumn. Amongst other reasons this does help to spread the workload.

Labour

From all that has been written before about farm mechanisation over the past century it can only be obvious that there has been a dramatic fall in the number of people employed on the land. Many of the farms were significant communities in themselves and one only has to look at the number of farm cottages on some of the bigger farms to appreciate this. Farms such as Blythe, Thirlestane and Lylestane are all typical examples. Nowadays where farm cottages have been maintained they are mostly occupied by people who do not work on the farm. Some of these houses have been sold off and some are rented out, thereby providing an additional source of income to the farm business.

In the early part of the century there was no doubt that labour was relatively cheap and plentiful. At the "Hiring Markets" in the early 1900's, where farmers and farm workers met to arrange their terms for employment, 25 shillings advancing to 30 shillings per week (£1.25 to £1.50) appears to have been the going rate. Over and above this the worker had what was known as his "Gains" which were a rent free house with a vegetable garden, an allowance of meal for bread making, potatoes and permission to keep a cow and one or two pigs. The cow provided milk and butter for the family and a calf to sell whilst the pigs consumed all the swill and were slaughtered on the farm for home cured bacon. So whilst cash was limited there was quite a degree of self sufficiency. It's funny how life goes round in circles; today this would be described as the "Good Life".

Shepherds had a similar deal on the "Gains" system but, over and above, had a small flock of their own "pack" sheep, the number of which was determined by agreement with the employer.

Farmworkers used to work long and hard with very little time off and it was only in the early 1900's that any regular holidays began to be allowed. By the 1920's however a regular working day of 9 hours for 6 days a week had come into being with an annual holiday allowance.

On many farms more than one employee might come from a cottage with sons often following father on to the land. In many instances workers wives would help with the labour intensive jobs such as singling turnips, hay making and harvest. To augment the seasonal labour supply, a significant number of Irishmen used to come across annually to help with the summer's work. Dr Shirra Gibb at Boon quotes that for his 1872 harvest, out of 63 people employed that year, around half were Irish. The number of Irishmen coming each year dwindled as the century wore on until, by the 1960's, there were very few, as the turnip crop had gone into decline with singling no longer being necessary and hay making and harvest had become much more mechanised.

One of the advantages of the larger labour force was that there was always an opportunity for a young lad to get started and to learn his job. The youngster could start with the "odd" horse and do a variety of tasks before advancing to the more skilled jobs on the farm and there was always an experienced man to teach them how. Similarly shepherds often had a laddie to assist them and the opportunity was there for the youngster to learn. Nowadays, with labour much more expensive, farmers are looking for men with instant skill and ability and these people are becoming much harder to find with fewer young people coming in to the industry.

The decline in the labour force really began to gather pace from the middle of the century as mechanisation began to take over and, at the same time, the cost of labour was rising much faster than the value of what that labour was producing. Many farms which in the 1950's employed five or six full time workers may now only have the farmer and one other, if that, and use contractors to do some of the major cultivation and harvesting jobs.

With the passing of the time when many people were employed in agriculture perhaps the biggest miss these days is the community spirit. In the days when all those who lived on a farm were employed there, there was a great sense of camaraderie and, in the days before television, people used to provide their own entertainment at the social gatherings. Many of the bigger farms used to hold their own "kirn" or dance in the grain loft to celebrate the end of the harvest. Although most of the houses on the farms are currently occupied, many of the inhabitants leave each day to work elsewhere. Working on a farm has now become a lonely life with people spending long hours working without seeing anyone.

For those left on the land, conditions have changed and mostly for the better. Housing has improved enormously from the cramped conditions of a century ago, with most cottages now being about three bedroom size and usually with central heating and double glazing. The "Gains" or "Perk" system has mostly been replaced by cash payment with milk, bacon, meal and potatoes being purchased from local supermarkets. Most people these days have their own form of transport and, with refrigeration and deep freezing, are able to go to the shops and buy and store their requirements. Today's farm worker can earn between £16,000 and £18,000 per annum including overtime and over and above has a free dwelling for which a rent of some £2,500 to £3,000 per annum would be payable if he lived away from the farm.

Many of the families who have lived and worked on the farms in Lauderdale have either been on the same farm or in the district for generations and have given much loyal and dedicated service. Over the century Blythe never seems to have been without members of the Brotherston and Lothian families. Several members of the Nisbet family have been at Addinston and Hillhouse, with Sandy Nisbet spending his entire life as shepherd at Addinston. Three members of the Lothian family worked as shepherds at Longcroft over the second half of the century but perhaps the most amazing and loyal record of service was that of the Clark family at Lylestane. Between 1860 and 1979 three successive generations of Alexander Clarks were shepherd there and enjoyed a wonderful reputation of being top class men. The second Alec Clark was a renowned shearer of sheep and was nicknamed the "Lauderdale Express" after his feat of clipping 17 half bred ewes (by hand, of course), in one hour.

The Thomson family has also been at Lylestane for most of the second half of the century and the Walker family served Carfrae for a long time. Similarly Thirlestane was served by the Young and Falconer families.

Many of the men who lived and worked in Lauderdale have been totally committed to the their jobs and treated the livestock that they tended as their own. As Jimmy Lothian (39 years at Longcroft) used to say "I only live for two things - blackface sheep and collie dogs" and nothing that he ever did would make one disbelieve that statement.

Many of the shepherds in Lauderdale were expert collie dog breeders and handlers with several top dog trialists. Tom Watson, who finished his shepherding days at Longcroft, had a wonderful way with his dogs and, as well as winning the Scottish National Championship, also went on to win the British International Championship. Jimmy Gilchrist of Justicehall and his brother, John, were renowned the length and breadth of the country with both winning the Scottish Championship. Again, brothers Andrew and George Brown from Longcroft were famous for their dog trialling abilities in the early part of the century. The story is told of one of them, that whilst on his way to a dog trial at Duns from Earlston by train, time had been spent in a local hostelry while awaiting the arrival of the train. On coming out of the pub the collie dog was nowhere to be seen, but undaunted the train was boarded and the dog whistled on. By the time the train arrived at Duns the dog had caught up and went on to run in the trial.

The employment of people on farms was not totally confined to those who did farm work. Lauderdale boasts a number of very substantial farm houses and these in themselves provided a significant number of jobs. Pre electricity and household gadget days, there were always jobs available in the farm house for the girls and wives from the farms. These days, with motorised transport, many farm workers wives and families seek jobs in the towns and villages. The farmhouse garden used to provide the major part of a job for an employee who would have to help on the farm at busy times such as hay and harvest. Many farms also employed their own full time rabbit trapper. In the immediate post war period when food was scarce, rabbits were plentiful and were relatively dear so a farmer could make a profit by employing a full time trapper and selling the rabbits. Nowadays this is no longer a profitable exercise but the rabbits are still there and reducing their numbers is a cost which must be borne. The advent of myximatosis in the mid 1950's almost wiped out the rabbit population as well as eliminating the jobs of the trappers.

Over the century the agricultural labour force in Lauderdale has declined dramatically and, whilst some families will have disappeared from the district altogether, there are many who live in Oxton and Lauder who have connections and are descended from families who were previously employed on the land. Many people who live in the district have fond memories of childhood or family visits to relatives and friends on farms in Lauderdale.

Young Farmers Club

On 18th January 1944 a public meeting was held in Lauder to consider forming an Agricultural Discussion Society or a Junior Agricultural Club for the district. As a result of that meeting Lauderdale Agricultural Discussion Society was formed under the chairmanship of Andrew Sharp. Before the year was out however, at the AGM of the aforementioned society on 23rd October, it was agreed that a Young Farmers Club should come in to being and so Lauderdale JAC was formed under the chairmanship of Ian Sutherland.

The immediate post war period, when everyone was desperate to get life back to normal, was an ideal time to get the club up and running and for a long time Lauderdale JAC was a healthy, thriving club.

Although not one of the biggest clubs in the country, its members were generally fired with enthusiasm and gave a good account of themselves both in competition and social activities. The major competition was the annual East Area Rally for clubs form the East of Scotland and Lauderdale JAC won the Scott Watson trophy several times for being the best small club and in 1965 had the distinction of winning the Bibby Shield for the best overall club in the area - no mean feat when it was actually the second smallest club in the competition.

As well as the rather more serious tasks of stock judging, valuations and the "ladies competitions", the social side of the club has always been well to the fore.

One of the highlights was the annual social when club members entertained those who had hosted them throughout the year and generally poked fun at all and sundry.

In 1994 the club celebrated its 50th anniversary by printing a book covering its history. It makes fascinating reading and is to be recommended to anyone who has not yet come across it. The list of Chairmen and Secretaries is most definitely a "Who's Who" of agriculture in Lauderdale in the second half of the twentieth century.

Unfortunately the ills which are currently affecting agriculture have also afflicted the younger members of our community with fewer young people wanting to be involved in agriculture these days. As a result membership of the Club fell in the 1990's to dangerously low levels and with similar problems in other clubs it was deemed that a merger with the Selkirk Club should take place, with the resultant club taking the name of Ettrick and Lauderdale JAC.

This fledgling club, formed in 1998, now appears to thriving and we would all wish it well for the future.

Blacksmiths

One vocation which has almost disappeared over the past century is that of the local blacksmith. Not surprisingly with the demise of the farm horse the requirement for horse shoeing has declined dramatically and implement repairs now require a visit to a more sophisticated engineering works.

Lauderdale boasted six smiddy's during the last century, being situated at Oxton, Boghall, Newbigging Walls, High Cross, Cambridge and Lauder. Today all of them have disappeared with the exception of Cambridge from where John Threadgall operates a farrier business. Today's blacksmith has a different job from that of the past with much of his horse shoeing work taking place at the stables rather than the horse being brought to the smiddy. Whether the recently introduced fox hunting ban will reduce the demand for a farrier in country areas even further only remains to be seen.

Whilst most of the blacksmith's businesses have disappeared altogether the one in Lauder has changed course and developed to meet current demand. The old forge has disappeared and been replaced by more modern engineering equipment and the Turnbull family ventured in to a shed building operation as well. On the death of William Turnbull the business was taken over by James Sutherland of Hillhouse and moved from what is now the Leisure Centre to its present site on the Industrial Estate.

Looking back over the records it appears that the blacksmith business was very much a family affair with many of the same names appearing at more than one smiddy. Rutherford, Riddell, Reid, Robertson, Halliday and Turnbull are the names of the families who have shod the majority of horses and effected implement repairs in the district over the past century.

There is no doubt that the blacksmith's shops as well as carrying out their primary function were also a social centre with many a caller getting the chance to catch up on the local gossip. Most of the smiddies, with the exception of the one at the High Cross, were still in existence until the second half of the century but as the tractor took over from the horse so the blacksmiths have gradually disappeared.

Oxton Friendly Bovial Society

Oxton Friendly Bovial Society, or as it is more commonly known, the Cow Club, came into existence on 11th May 1839. At that time, many of the farm workers had their own milk cow which was extremely important to them and, in many cases, represented their wealth. To lose a cow was a financial disaster to a working man and his family.

It was one Andrew Campbell who was the instigator of the society, persuading shepherds and herds of the benefits. Basically, for an annual subscription to the society, a member's vet bill was paid if the cow became ill and a fixed lump sum payment was made if a cow died, the only proviso being that to qualify a cow had to be less than twelve years of age.

The benefits of the society were obviously much appreciated because membership grew rapidly and by 1889 the total number of members was 244. Interestingly, in that year the total income of the society was £1727 whilst expenditure was £1577, leaving a balance of £150, so they seem to have got things about right. Although it was called the Oxton Society, the boundaries for membership extended beyond the parish, but boundaries there were and no member was admitted outwith a circle which included Westruther, Corsbie, Kedslie, Glendearg, Buckholm, Tynehead, Upper Keith, Longyester, Johnscleuch and Cranshaws.

However by the early 1900's numbers had started to decline and in the centenary year of 1939 membership had dropped to 125 despite the boundaries being extended to include Dunbar and Northumberland.

Two meetings have been held annually since the inauguration of the society, originally on the first Wednesdays in June and December, being changed to the first Saturdays of the same months in 1933 to encourage greater attendance. There is no doubt that after the business of the evening had been conducted these meetings would become very sociable affairs!

As far as can be traced, the first annual subscription was 5 shillings but it has been impossible to ascertain the level of compensation at that time. In 1940 £20 was paid out for a dead cow which was raised to £30 in 1953 and, with inflation, has steadily increased to the current level of £300 with an annual subscription of £15.

Financially the society has had its ups and downs like most other organisations but mostly it has been on a sound footing. The biggest financial shock came at the June meeting in 1940 when, following the death of local vet Tom Connachie, large accounts for vet fees were presented going back several years. Although it was proposed that selling War Loan stock should be considered this did not take place as funds apparently showed signs of recovery.

As well as paying veterinary fees and compensation for dead cows, the society has, within its constitution, the power to pay out money to any needy and deserving cases. In the recent past payment has been made to two widows of young agricultural workers who have lost their husbands in tragic circumstances and to a tractorman who became paralysed.

The two main positions of office are the President/Chairman and the combined post of Secretary and Treasurer. It appears from the records that the society has been well served over the years by men who have held office for long periods. A Mr Denholm was Secretary/Treasurer for 31 and a half years from 1896 and Mr Alec Clark completed 20 years prior to the current incumbent, Mr Alastair Fallas, who has occupied the post for 25 years. Similarly Chairmen have served the society for long periods with Mr Robert Dickinson achieving 26 years from 1897 and the current chairman, Mr Leslie Coltherd, a mere 28 years. All these people and many more have given loyal service and dedication to the society in order to achieve its aims.

It is sad in a way to report that it is likely that the society will be wound up this year (2002). This is in no way a reflection of failure, indeed quite the opposite, simply the reason for which it was formed no longer exists. Today a shepherd who keeps his own cow has become a rarity as the farmworkers lot has improved over the years. With literally only a handful of members left, and some of them not even owning a cow, it seems likely that the society will cease to exist after the June meeting. As the society still has funds the committee has decided to make a

TOLLIS KING from Andrew Sharp Farmers,
which made £4600 at Lanark mart in 1961.
Also in the picture are the seller, the buyer
and some of the local shepherds.

donation to Oxton Hall where most of the society's meetings have been held and also to Channelkirk Church for gates at the new car park. It will be at these gates that the Oxton Friendly Bovial Society will be remembered with a suitable plaque.

And finally

Having completed the last century, what will happen in the next? No doubt most of us will think that it would be impossible for as much progress and change to be made in the 21st century as there was in the 20th. Those men who sat in Carfraemill Hotel 100 years ago and predicted that the horseless carriage would not last would be absolutely astounded at what they would see today and those of us present today would probably have difficulty in appreciating what Lauderdale could be like in the year 2100. One thing is certain, agriculture in Lauderdale will again show huge changes in the next century. Who can predict what they will be?

Smiddies

The Smiddy was an everyday part of life in rural Lauderdale at the start of the twentieth century, yet today we are reduced to one, and even that only for the purpose of shoeing horses. For at least half of the century they were essential for the day to day operation of every farm, large or small, from the shoeing of the large number of horses used on the farms, to the making and repairing of all manner of tools and equipment, not necessarily farm equipment.

Perhaps It would be appropriate to record here the Smiddies and Blacksmiths that were working in Lauderdale, before they closed in the twentieth century, and before the information is lost forever. At Oxton and Newbigging Walls we had Jock Riddell and his son Willie. At Boghall there was Willie Rutherford. At the Highcross there was Watt Brotherston. In Lauder there was Willie Tumbull and his son Bill. At Cambridge there was Tommy Halliday, where today we have the one and only Blacksmith left In Lauderdale in Jock Threadgall. In Blainslie there were two Smiddies until the 1930's, when Jim Park retired. The other Smiddy in Blainslie ceased to operate In 1952 when Willie Turnbull stopped coming from Lauder one day per week

Oxton Smiddy – 1940s picture.

Oxton Dance – 1950's.

The Hill Herds Houses

Today there are hidden in the hill valleys looking down into Lauderdale the remains of old dwellings. Some have been renovated, others are slowly sinking into the ground. What are they and when were they in use? The answer is a story told over many centuries. Wherever there is an isolated house in the hills it is probably not the first or even the second on the site. It was a good place to live but often for differing reasons over time.

In early times people moved up the hill as populations grew and the climate improved. They lived off the land as hunters, then as farmers, but left little trace of their passing. A house of three or four high dry stone walls with a Birch or Alder branch roof covered with turf may sound harsh, but was doubtless warm and comfortable to the people of the times. The only traces to be seen are in some lights and shadows on the ground.

Then the climate got worse and they were deserted, only to be redeveloped again later, sometimes as refuges for outlaws or for people looking for peace in disturbed times, later again came the sheep.

At first the Monks and Estates, sending flocks to summer grazing, needed some sort of housing for the shepherds and probably for the young women to milk the ewes and make cheese for the winter, and for clipping and shearing. Then of course some would stay on keeping a small flock of their own all year round, and looking after the big flocks from the low country in the summer. By the 17th. and 18th. centuries there were regular flocks in the hills looked after by full time shepherds, and now having housing up to the same standard as lowland farm cottages, but always with the extras - byres for the cows and kennels for the dogs.

It is interesting to follow a few of these from the nineteenth through the twentieth century and Sebastapol is a name familiar to many who have walked on Burncastle and Braidshawrigg. This house was built on the site of an older house called Blythe Rigg; the "new" name was given when the news of the Battle of Sebastapol came as the house was being finished. That was in 1855. The house was occupied by a gamekeeper up to the 1940's; then became a hay store and is now a shooting lunch hut. The shepherd now comes from Burncastle on a quad bike and looks after the next Hirsel of Braidshawrigg as well!

Two miles down stream is Braidshawrigg, where it looks as though a 19th. century house replaced the older house which became byres for the new. This was a bigger house made for a double herding and possibly a "boy" as well; but has now been reduced and modernised as a Lodge for the shootings. The last shepherd left in the 1960's and all the work is done from Burncastle. Even the byres have gone to make room for a large shed for clipping and other handlings of the sheep.

A further quarter mile down the burn, but still really part of the same very pleasant but isolated area of land, are the ruins of a house which was last occupied in 1917. This is the site of Howebog, a name now virtually lost. The last house on the site had the usual two rooms and a small room with a byre at one end, and at the other end are the remains of a much older building, built without mortar. This was similar to "Black Houses" found in the Highlands and of any age - up to several hundred years, perhaps back to the Monks from the Abbeys or large landowners from the Borders or Lothians such as the Thirlestanes who owned this, the lands of Thirlestane and Blythe, in the 12th. century.

The shepherd from Howebog moved to a new house at Gairmuir but still looked after the same flock on Gairmuir hill. This was a similar house but with larger rooms and a kitchenette and bathroom at one end, complete with hay shed byre and kennels. This has now been modernised and enlarged considerably for a gamekeeper. The last shepherd to live here left in 1972 and the flock was managed from Blythe by landrover or tractor, and then the ubiquitous quad bike.

These changes have been driven by the changing values of wool - once the purpose and point of hill flocks - which is now being a very minor by product. In 1900 the wool would have more than paid the year's wages of the shepherd; in 2000 it might pay about two weeks wages. This article is a personal snapshot of one small area of the Lauderdale Hills but is repeated up each burn and glen and sadly reflects the decline in importance of the hill sheep farm in Border economies. Change goes on and the 21st century may see all the houses empty or perhaps needs may change and more new hill herds and houses may be required. Who can tell? The same sort of story occurs in each hill valley - sometimes with a period of new building in some and complete modernising in others taking place immediately after the 1939 - 45 war. This was caused by the demand for greater production from the hills and a belief that it might be paid for. As always in rural history this belief proved false and hence there are many hill houses empty or used as weekend or holiday homes.

We thought the reader might be interested in a short history of some of the houses, and their use in the twentieth century. It has not been particularly easy to collect accurate information, but it has been enjoyable, the majority of people only too willing to help, and to talk and reminisce about times past. However, due to time and memory lapse there are a few gaps. We start in the north west corner of Lauderdale and travel in a clockwise direction to the eastern end, all in the Lammermoor hills.

Little Hartside

Adam and Phemie Steele –
the last shepherd at Little Hartside.

Little Hartside

This house is reached by a track from Hartside Farm, and was at one time two houses. The last shepherd to live there was Adam Steele, who left in 1972. It is now a private residence.

Hunters Hall (Lourie's Den)

Is on top of Soutra Hill and was formerly an Inn with a very unsavoury reputation. It had become a shepherd's house by the beginning of the twentieth century and would probably be on Glengelt farm, as in those days New Channelkirk was an Inn.

In its days as an Inn the sign had a painting of a huntsman blowing his horn, while surrounded by his hounds. The following lines were also on the sign.

> *"Humpty, Dumpty, peerie, peerie,*
> *Step in here and ye'll be cheerie;*
> *Try our spirits and our porter,*
> *They'll make the road the shorter.*
> *Your horse can get guid corn and hay.*
> *Good entertainment for man and horse."*

From the 1940's onwards the shepherds were Davey Lees, Jimmy Laing and Harry Luke, the last shepherd was thought to have been a Ewan McQueen, who left in the late seventies, early eighties. The present owner of the farm lives in Lincolnshire, and the house is becoming something of a ruin.

Old Fairnielees

Old Fairnielees.

Built right on top of the hill, catching the wind from all directions. It is accessible by track from the road between Hillhouse Farm and Carfrae Farm. It ceased to be used as a shepherd's house in 1950, then was used for a few years as a holiday cottage and is now a ruin. The last shepherd to live in the house was John Scott. It is now part of Hillhouse Farm.

New Fairnielees

Built down in the valley below the old house in 1960. The first shepherd to live in this new house was Bob Young. It is still used as a shepherd's house today. (Also on Hillhouse Farm.)

Friarsknowes (The Nose).

Friarsknowes

The local name for this house is "The Nose". Part of the hirsel, that the shepherd who lived in this house was responsible for, is in East Lothian. The house is reached by a track from Kelphope Farm. There is a tarmac road from the farm down to Carfraemill and the A697, approximately four miles. The last shepherd to live here, Bob Smith left in 1953. It is now a private residence. The hirsel is now part of Fackham Estate, prior to which it was part of Tollishill Farm.

Kelphope

A new house, a bungalow was built here in 1954, and the new shepherd then was Selby Wilson. This house did not last long as a residence for a shepherd as the last one, Andrew Bell left in the mid 1990's. The house is now used by a gamekeeper. The farm is also now part of Fackham Estates, having previously been a farm in its own right.

Tollishill

In the time of the Duke of Lauderdale, "John 2nd Earl" 1616-1682, this place was known as Midside Farm, this was where the famous "Midside Maggie" or Maggie Hardie lived, if you know anything at all of Lauder history you will have heard the tale. A new house was built here in 1974 again a bungalow, the only shepherd to live in both the old house and the new was Allister Fallas. All that is left of the old house is a gable end that is part of an outbuilding. This house is still occupied by a shepherd, Steve Patterson. It is now also part of Fackham Estates, and is accessible by tarmac road from Carfraemill, the road to Kelphope farm branches off at the foot of the hill.

The Howe.

Dod Cleugh

This house is again a bungalow, built in 1954 to replace a house farther out in the hills called The Howe. When the new house was built here the shepherd was transferred from The Howe, his name was Jock Little. The last shepherd to occupy this house, until 1967, was Alick Little, who we understand was no relation to Jock Little. The house is now occupied by a gamekeeper, it is also now part of Fackham Estates. It was previously part of Tollishill. It is reached by a short track from the Carfraemill to Tollishill/Kelphope road.

The Howe

This is probably one of the most remote houses in the Lammermoors, in Lauderdale, and was last used as a shepherds house in 1954 when Jock Little moved to the Dod Cleugh. It is now used as a summer residence. Now also part of Fackham Estates, previously part of Tollishill. It can be reached by track from Tollishill, Dod Cleugh, or Longcroft Farm.

The Dod or The Dod House

This house should probably not be included here as it was quite possibly never used as a shepherds house, and was never occupied in the twentieth century. However it was an isolated house in the Lammermoors, on top of the hills and there is still a gable end and other walls still standing with the outline of other habitation visible. It was apparently a small croft with its own land which ceased to be occupied in approximately 1855, when we assume it became part of Longcroft farm, which it still is to this day. It is reached by track from Longcroft farm, or by a track from the Kelphope/Tollishill road, this track is locally known as the Swape Road, and was possibly the original road to the croft. There is no trace left of anyone who lived there.

Soonhope

Soonhope which is over a bridge and up the burn a short distance from Longcroft farm, has two houses. The old house was last occupied in the early 1960's by a farm worker John Doohan. The newer house built in 1937 was last occupied by a shepherd Jimmy Glasgow, who left in 2001. The house is now occupied by a gamekeeper. A shepherd who was there for many years and well known in the district was Jim Lothian. The hirsel covered by Soonhope is part of Longcroft farm.

Glenburnie

This house is almost two miles up the right hand burn behind Longcroft farm, and is reached by a track that follows the burn. We understand that only two families have lived in this house. The first we believe must have been Andrew Brown, whose daughter Elsie, was born there in 1909. She eventually married James Gilchrist who became the farmer of Justicehall at Oxton. We understand that Andrew Brown left in the early 1900's to take over the farm of Carfraemill, and eventually built the house near Oxton road junction called Riggside. The next and last shepherd to live here was Tom Hunter who left in either 1936 or 37. The house is now a complete ruin with most of the roof caved in. The hirsel was part of Longcroft farm, but is now a part of Thirlestane Castle Estate, no doubt used in part for Grouse shooting.

A painting of Earnscleugh.

Earnscleugh

At one time there were two houses here both occupied by shepherds, the two, at one time were John Skeldon and Bob Falconer. The last shepherd to live here was Jock Little, who left sometime in the early 1960's . After that it was occupied by gamekeepers until the early 1990's when it was knocked down to build a large shooting lodge for the Duke of Northumberland, with a Keepers house, a bothy and various other buildings. The hirsel was on Burncastle farm and is now part of Burncastle Estate. It is reached by a tarmac road from the A697 at Newbigging Walls farm.

Bermuda

The local spelling for this house is Bermoudie, and unfortunately there is very little information available on previous residents. Although it has been suggested on more than one occasion that a shepherd by the name of Dinwoodie, may have lived here in the early 1900's. We understand that the last person to live there was a drainer called Jimmy Sandilands who moved down to Earnscleugh in 1946. The building is accessible and the roof is still secure, it is about a mile and a half up stream by track from Earnscleugh. It was part of Burncastle farm and is now part of Burncastle Estate.

Braidshawrigg

The present house was replaced by a larger one sometime in the later part of the 19th. century. The last shepherd to live here, Sandie Jolly, left in the early 1980's. The house is now occupied by a gamekeeper and is reached by a track from Blythe farm, some two miles. It was at one time part of Thirlestane farm, then Burncastle farm and is now part of Burncastle Estate.

Howbog

Located a quarter of a mile downstream from Braidshawrigg, but is now a complete ruin. The last shepherd, Tom Brown, left in 1917 when he moved to a new house at Gairmuir. The site is still on Blythe farm, and is reached by the track to Braidshawrigg.

Sebastapol.

Sebastapol

This house was at one time known as Blythe Rigg, but was changed when, as a new house was being built in 1855 news came through of the battle of Sebastopol. Situated about a mile and a half up stream from Braidshawrigg with only access by track from there this must be possibly the most remote of all the herds' houses in Lauderdale. Shepherds here at some time in the early part of the century were Jimmy Skeldon and Andrew Anderson. The last time this house was occupied was by a gamekeeper, who left sometime in the 1940's. It has now been converted for use as a lunch hut for shooting parties. At one time the hirsel was on Thirlestane farm, then Burncastle farm and is now part of Burncastle Estate.

Gairmuir

This house, as has already been mentioned, was built in 1917 when the shepherd, Tom Brown moved here from Howbog. The last shepherd to live here was Andrew Patterson who left in the early 1980's. It has just been modernised to be used by a gamekeeper. This hirsel is also now part of Burncastle Estate, having previously been part of Blythe farm.

Snawdon.

Snawdon
This house was a farm in its own right at one time probably in the 19th century. The last shepherd to live here was John Young who moved to a new bungalow at Thirlestane farm in 1984. The house is now used as a holiday cottage and is accessible via a track from Thirlestane farm, probably half a mile.

Game Shooting

Shooting in Lauderdale at the beginning of the century was mainly on the large estates of the day. Yester, Thirlstane and the like, employed a large number of men to look after grouse, partridge and pheasant. This continued until the First World War when these large estates started to decline and until the end of the Second World War there were virtually no game keepers left. During this time only friends of the owner, or the shooting tenant would have been allowed to kill game. For anyone breaking these rules the consequences were severe.

With the break up of the large estates, small syndicates or farmer shoots, with part time or no keepering took over. This continued until the early sixties, when Lord Biddulph started to keeper the grouse moors again, with a local syndicate of friends to help with the costs. Starting with his son's estate at Burncastle he talked three of his neighbours into renting their moors to him. He then employed two more keepers. This system continued until he finished with the syndicates and went on to letting the shooting by the week to sporting group's from Britian and the U.S.A.

At the beginning of the eighties Eskdale Shooting Services started by renting the pheasant shooting from Lauderdale Estates and employed keepers, and let out the shooting. As they acquired more shooting rights from the farmers, they began employing more and more keepers until they now have some eight full time men and several part time men.

At the start of the nineties the Burncastle moors were sold, quickly followed by Tollishill. The new owners increased the keepering staff by three. Where Lord Biddulph had three keepers, there were now six. So that by the end of the century Lauderdale had more game keepers working in it than it had ever had before.

The work that a keeper does today is quite different to what it was at the start of the century. Then all the game would have been wild, with just a few pheasants reared under broody hens, and all vermin ruthlessly killed by fair means or foul. Each under keeper would have had a small beat that he would walk round, or if lucky he would have a push bike, the head keeper would have had a pony and trap. Today the modern keeper has a four-wheel drive car or quad bike.

Modern farming methods have been disastrous for wild game, so that now the birds have to be reared artificially then released back into the wild, which takes a lot of time and means attendance seven days a week while rearing the birds. Another big change is game crops, strips of kale and cereal grown to provide food and cover to fly the birds from. This is usually on the highest ground to make the shooting more sporting. The shooters themselves have changed, now they come from all over Britain, Europe and America, taking two or three days at a time, paying by the day, and staying in hotels. Much different from being a guest of the Laird and staying in his home or shooting lodge, as would have been the case at the start of the century.

The work that a grouse keeper in particular has to do is much the same as his predecessor, except that today he has Land Rovers and Agro Cats to make life easier. When it comes to vermin life is more difficult, at the start of the century the keeper had a free hand to do as he wished. Today the law is much more stringent on what you can and cannot do to control vermin, and of course raptors are completely off the menu.

Is this what happens when the tractor breaks down ?

Three Horse Power

Lauderdale Ploughing Match

After attending church on a Sunday morning, farm workers would talk about their work on the way home with neighbours from other farms. After the harvest thanksgiving was past, the conversation would get round to ploughing the fields for the following year. If someone said there was a well ploughed field at Birkenside, ploughmen for the Oxton and Channelkirk farms would meet later than afternoon and walk down to Birkenside and inspect the 'so-called' well furrowed field. On the way home the ploughmen from Addinston or Nether Howden would say, *"It nae better ploughed than ours at hame"*.

Some time in the 1870's a local farmer proposed a ploughing contest to find the best ploughing in Lauderdale. He asked ploughmen to compete against each other at a particular farm. Word soon spread about this challenge and it was called the "Lauderdale Ploughing Match". In those days ploughs were made in local blacksmiths shops. They made everything with socks and feathers to suit different soils; long mouldboards for lea (grassland) ploughing and short mouldboards for stubble ploughing for root crops, turnips of tatties in the following spring.

A class for lea ploughing and a class for stubble ploughing would take place at the match. The lea ploughing would have to be straight with well closed furrows so that oats or barley sown by hand would lie between the furrows. The stubble ploughing class had to have a firm top on each furrow so that the frost in the winter split up the knots of clay to break down in springtime for a good tilth for turnips or tattie crop.

Each competitor was given a rig to plough measuring 100yds long by 20yds wide where he made a feering on the number allocated to him in the morning. Gathering eight furrows on each side of his start, he cast off to his higher number to complete his plot making a reaper finish in the middle.

The judges were usually a farmer and his steward from outwith the area. The overall winner would be presented with a medal for his outstanding work. When the Lauderdale Ploughing Match was held at Upper Blainslie, the champion ploughman on that day was William Cowan, the grandfather of Wullie Cowan and Bob Anderson who stay in Lauder at the present day.

Ploughing matches became so popular that competitors would travel from Duns, Kelso and St. Boswells with their teams of horses; Clydesdales, Shires, and many other breeds. There would be extra prizes for the best kept harness; best dressed harness, best working pair, best mare and best gelding.

The prize money wasn't much, but the sheer delight of winning was much more important than the money. A dance was held on the night of the match in the barn of the farm.

As the years went by the ploughing match remained an important annual event in the Lauderdale area. It was held in the fourth Saturday of November at a different farm. They would draw lots of people on the day supporting the ploughmen from the farm where they worked, often a father and son would compete against each other or two brothers would plough against one another. You talk about 'rivalry!', that was it.

No ploughing matches were held during the two World Wars. In 1946 a tractor ploughing class was introduced. Most were Fordson's with Ransomes trailing ploughs or Caterpillars using 3-furrow of 4-furrow trailing ploughs. When the match was at Burnfoot near Oxton, the Tractor Class was won by Eckie Nisbet from Addinston using a crawler with a trailing plough. What an achievement by a young man!

By the late forties, more and more tractors had appeared. By this time some, like the 'Wee Grey Fergie', had a lift plough attached. This was operated from the tractor seat by a lever that lifted the arms attached to the plough from the ground, it was a great invention. By this time wheels with engines had taken over from horse power.

At least when you ploughed with horses you walked between the stilts of the plough watching the furrow turn over to the right position. In the tractor, as one spectator said, *"Ploughmen now need extra een in the back o' their heid"*, one set to look where he was going, the other set to watch the plough movements. Yes those were the days.

When the match was at Collielaw in the late 40's the Champion was Dod Hardie from Carfrae. Dod was using a Bennet No2 plough which had been hand made at Danskin smiddy near Garvald. By this time Thomas Bennet, the plough maker, had moved to farm at Nether Howden. He also had a blacksmiths workshop there. This same plough today stands by the Lauder Police Station grass verge on the A68 as you enter Lauder from the south. Leading ploughmen in the early 50's were Jim Anderson from Headshaw; Jimmy Dickson, Howlets Ha', Westruther; Bob Ainslie, Broomiebank, Houndslow, also Jim Burrell, Kirktonhill. Jackie Thomson, Lylestane and John Gilchrist, Justice Hall, were both young up and coming ploughmen, as was Doddie Wilson, Newbigging Walls. All were keen to play their part. In the mid-1950's ploughmen from Maxton and Kelso began to take part, like Bill Nairn, Ploughlands; Jim Romanis, Frogden; and Sandy Palmer, also from Frogden trying to take top awards.

In 1947 the running of the Lauderdale Ploughing Match had been taken over by the Lauderdale Agricultural Discussion Society, whose secretary was Mr Buckpitt from Greycrook, St. Boswells. A ploughing match committee was formed. The Discussion Society kept the committee informed about what was happening around the country, which was interesting for competitors.

In the year 1952, the British Ploughing Association was formed. Many ploughmen travelled to watch the 1952 British Ploughing Association, which entitled the winner and runner up to go forward to compete at the 1st World Ploughing contest to be held in Canada the following year. Lauderdale soon became a member of the B.P.A. so that their champion and runner up could qualify to plough at the B.P.A. match the following year. Winners Jim Borthwick Sen. and Jim Borthwick Jnr, West Printonan, Duns, and Bill Nairn, Ploughlands; Jim Romanis, Frogden all qualified to plough at national level.

The first trophy was presented to the Lauderdale Ploughing Match in 1964, when it was held at Nether Howden, by Mrs Bennet, the Host Farmer's wife. The trophy was for the 'Best Ploughed Rig' at the match – the winner being Bob Anderson, Hangingshaw Farm, Heriot, who had ploughed a superb rig on the day in the semi-digger class. The same year Mungo Riddell, Highchester, Roberton, presented a shield which was to be given to the runner-up – who was Tom Brotherston, Flass, Westruther, winner of the digger class.

Ploughing, tractors and engineering in general had moved forward a long way by this time. 1963 was the year the Scottish Championship Ploughing Association was formed. Their first match was held at Tibbermore, near Perth which drew a large number of competitors from all over Scotland. Bob Anderson from Hangingshaw, Heriot represented Lauderdale and won 4th place in the 11-inch class.

Three years later at the Scottish National, Bob took 2nd place which entitled him to go forward the following year to plough in the British Championships at Stoneleigh, Warwickshire. It was quite a challenge to take on the best ploughmen in Great Britain. Bob ploughed 2nd in his class on the first day, which meant he ploughed the second day in the 'Plough Off Finals'. The winner of the Plough Off would represent Great Britain at the World Ploughing Contest, to be held in Rhodesia in April 1968. Well, Bob ploughed his heart out and won the British Ploughing Championship. A great achievement for a ploughman who ploughed at the Lauderdale match every year.

At the World contest the ploughman from Lauderdale won first equal place in the stubble ploughing on the first day and 7th place in the grassland ploughing the second day, finishing 5th place overall.

In 1968 the Lauderdale match was being held at Fans, Earlston. The host farmer being Tom Stewart, who insisted that there be a class for reversible or turn over ploughs which were now replacing the trailing and lift ploughs. This was a class introduced at Lauderdale for the first time in its history, and turned out to be very successful. The winner was Bill Henderson, Fans, Earlston.

1971 Bob Anderson, who by this time had moved to Nether Howden, Oxton with his family, was asked if he would take over the ploughing match secretary's job as Mr Buckpitt was retiring, Bob accepted and is still secretary 30 years further on.

Lauderdale has always been an leading name in ploughing, Bob Bennet, Nether Howden was Vice-Chairman, then Chairman of the Scottish National in the late 60's. They also had in 1970 John Gilchrist, Threeburnford, winning the Scottish National at Lockerbie.

After the 1971 World contest, which was held at Taunton, Somerset, the British Ploughing Association ended and a new organisation known as the 'Society of Ploughmen' was formed. Bob Anderson representing Lauderdale at this open meeting was appointed a member director for the Society, in which he served for 18 years.

In 1973 Bob Anderson won the Scottish Championships at Culbeuchly, Banff. 1974 both John and Bob ploughed in the same class at the British National held near Ross-on-Wye, Herefordshire. John came 1st and Bob 3rd so both qualified for the 'Plough Off' Finals on the second day when Bob came 2nd place and Reserve Champion which meant he would represent Great Britain again in the world contest in Canada in 1975, Bob being placed 16th over the two days.

As years went on, reversible ploughing became more popular which meant that more competitors took part. In the Silver Jubilee year of 1977 a trophy was presented by Prentice Grain Merchants, Berwick-upon-Tweed.

In 1984 the Scottish National was held at Adinston Farm, Tranent, East Lothian. Many ploughmen from the Lauderdale area took part. One of them was George Black from Earlston who won the overall Championship that day using a 4-furrow reversible plough, the first competitor to achieve this using a multi-furrow plough, a great honour for George and Lauderdale Ploughing Match.

In 1993 the Ploughing Match Committee split from the Discussion Society and a special meeting was held in the Lauderdale Hotel and a new committee appointed:–

Lauderdale Ploughing Society

Chairman	Jim Cruikshank, Laidlawstiel, Clovenfords
Vice-Chairman	Graham A. Stewart, Fans, Earlston
Secretary	Bob Anderson, Lauder
Treasurer	John Gilchrist, Helmsdale, Oxton

A Committee of fifteen people of which five will retire each year.
Venue for match Blackburn Farm, Lauder.

Due to adverse weather the match was postponed on original date of 27th November, but was held two weeks later on Saturday 11th December.

1994 – The Scottish National was held at Fogorig Farm, Greenlaw. This is the first two-day event of the Scottish, there being a 'Plough Off' on the second day – the prize winners of the first day competing against each other. The outcome was that Douglas Stewart, Fans was placed second in the reversible section, this qualified him to plough in the European Reversible Championships the following year at Taunton, Somerset – again a great honour to our Society. The other ploughman at this event was Robert McDairmat from Annan, Dumfriesshire. The ploughing coach appointed was Bob Anderson from Lauder; both ploughmen ploughed in the British National Match on the second day.

In 1997 our match was held at Legerwood, Earlston, where we had a record entry of 114 competitors plus ten demonstration plots by local trade companies.

We are always supported by the trade and other companies each year at our ploughing match wherever it may be held.

We now cover all types of ploughing:

Reversible Multi-Furrow Ploughs
Rerversible 2- and 3-Furrow Ploughs
Class for Junior Competitors under 21 years old
Class for Competitors under 26 years of age

Class for Semi-Digger Work Conventional
Classes for Vintage Trailing Ploughs
Classes for Hydraulic Tractor Ploughs

Our match is very popular because we cater for all types of ploughing.

Bob Anderson was elected to judge at the world ploughing contest in Germany 1998, the following year he was appointed to be a board member representing Scotland at future World Ploughing Contests. A great honour for the Lauderdale Ploughing Society.

The Millennium year was something special for the Society. Bob, as a W.P.O. board member. The British Championships and the World Ploughing Contest being held near Lincoln, England. John Gilchrist, Helmsdale, Oxton was appointed to judge at the W.P.O. event.

Bill Steele, 16 Smithy Croft, Lauder and George Gilchrist, Smithy House, Oxton were elected to judge classes at the British National Match, and Bobby Douglas, Scara, Ancrum, Jedburgh qualified to plough in the British National Vintage Ploughing Finals, where Bobby ploughed a superb rig and won first prize to become British Vintage Ploughing Champion. For our society what a great achievement for everyone concerned, and maintained the superb record of the Lauderdale Ploughing Society.

We are proud that our ploughing match is probably the largest held in the world, attracting more competitors than any other match, we have a very hard working committee who put a lot of thought and work into running the event. There is a good atmosphere amongst the ploughmen on match day and leg-pulling after the event is over.

Our judges are selected from a wide area as well, and have a large task judging their prospective classes. Our ambition is to produce a ploughman to win the Scottish National and qualify to plough in the World Contest in the near future.

A Fordson Major tractor at the Ploughing Match.

An early Fordson tractor.

Eckie Nisbet ploughing at Burnfoot, Lauderdale Ploughing Match 1948.

St. Leonards Mill

The earliest records of a mill at this spot, below St. Leonards Farm on the road to Boon by the banks of the River Leader, can be traced to 1758, the records describing *"The Spittal known as St. Leonards and the mill thereof"*. It is also shown on an Ordnance Survey map dated 1771. Built around 1750 as a corn mill driven by water brought down the mill lade from the River Leader, it is described as 3-storeys high in The Name Book in the 1850's. In "A Farmer's Fifty Years in Lauderdale" dated 1935, we are told that every two or three farms were 'thirled" to their own mill. St. Leonards Mill had five or six farms "thirled" to it, therefore it must have been a mill of some consequence.

St Leonards, sometimes referred to as a hamlet, originally consisted of a chapel and hospital, one of nine around the Lauder district, and was named after a French nobleman called Saint Leonard who lived as a hermit near Limoges and whose particular care was prisoners. The name was first given to the area by the De Morvilles (circa 1170).

St Leonards is also mentioned in "Leader Haughs and Yarrow", a poem on which Robert Burns commented - *"probably written by an itinerant minstrel calling himself Minstrel Burn."*

> *A mile below wha lists to ride*
> *They'll hear the mavis singing;*
> *Into St Leonards banks she'll hide*
> *Sweet birks her head o'erhinging;*
> *The lintwhite loud and Progne proud*
> *With tuneful throats and narrow*

The official census forms show the following information about the occupancy of St Leonards Mill:

1851 - William Waldie, 54 years, (miller), born at Roxburgh in 1797

1861 - James Kirkwood, 45 years, miller, born at Gordon in 1816

1871 - George Wilson, 40 years, miller, born at Haddington in 1831

1881 - Andrew Halliday, 31 years, miller, born at Legerwood in 1850 (Andrew was the son of Francis Halliday who lived at Bridgehaugh Mill in 1871).

1891 - James Kinghorn, 42 years, miller, born at Chirnside in 1849

1901 census was a disappointment as the information given was not clear. It would seem that Isabella Halliday, 23 years, unmarried and with no employment details, lived at a cottage at St Leonards which could have been the miller's cottage since it had only one room, with her sister, Robina, 11 years. This would suggest that the mill was no longer a working mill as there is no record of a miller being in residence. However, the County Directory of Scotland 1902 records Alexander Craw as resident at St Leonards Mill, but whether it was still a working mill is still uncertain.

However in "A Farmer's Fifty Years in Lauderdale" we read that it is around 35 years since St Leonards Mill closed, which would be around the turn of the century. What is certain is that by 1908, according to the Ordnance Survey map of that date, St Leonards Mill was disused.

"The Spittal called St Leonards and The Mill thereof" had remained in the ownership of the Maitlands of Thirlstane until 1921.

In 1921 St Leonards Farm (including The Mill), was sold out of the Maitland Estate by public auction and bought by Douglas Crichton Torrie, who was the tenant farmer at that time. The roof was removed from the mill, as a result of which the stonework slowly disintegrated until only the derelict ruins of The Mill and collapsed kilnhouse, as found in 1997, remained. A smaller ruin lies at right angles to the back wall, and was probably where the engine was housed, and there appears to be a run-off for the lade running under it. It is unlikely that water will ever be diverted to the lade again.

St. Leonard's Mill, Lauder – before conversion.

In August 1997 the ruined mill was bought by Sandie Boa from Edinburgh, and the slow and painstaking restoration process began. After some research of mill buildings and detailed studies of the ruins, architect, William Smalley from Oxfordshire, and Sandie Boa decided that the mill would have been a two and a half storey building with pantiled roof, divided into the main mill containing all the machinery and grinding stones driven by a water-wheel, and a kilnhouse of smaller proportions. The kitchen of the now restored building was built on the foundations of the kiln house to one storey.

After 21 months of excavation work to clear the site and reclaim all the stone, Dave and Andrew Bunyan from Selkirk were engaged to rebuild the shell in May 1999.

By September 2000, the stonework was completed, and after a further 4 months of work involving the other trades, St Leonards Mill was once more inhabited - approximately 100 years after it was closed down and had ceased to work as a mill.

St. Leonard's Mill, Lauder – after conversion.

Other tradesmen involved were,

Eck Prentice from Selkirk, Joiner:

Eric Nicholson from Galashiels, Electrician:

Bill and Gary Watson from Lauder, Plumbers.

Bill Matthews of WRM Joinery Tweedmouth made all the windows and staircase.

Underfloor Heating Scotland were responsible for the heating system.

In the spring of 2002, stonemasons Dave and Andrew Bunyan were awarded the Master Builder of The Year Award for Scotland for their restoration of St Leonards Mill, a just reward for their efforts.

So The Mill stands proud again amidst the green fields and by the banks of the River Leader in a timeless way, where the old stone stands endless as forever in its contribution to beauty and life. Let us hope that those craftsmen who built it - and craftsmen they were for it to have stood firm for hundreds of years - would be proud of its restoration.

Lauder Town Hall.

Memories of the Sweetie Shop

Mary Scott was a much loved long-time resident of Oxton. She and her husband, George (Dod), lived in the Row and Mary ran the sweetie shop from her house. Her son, Jim Archibald, recalls that some of his earliest memories included, the constant ringing of the doorbell and of his mum rushing to the shop to answer and how important it was, during the war years, to make sure that the windows were fully blacked out. Although generations of children remembered it as the sweetie shop, it sold everything from boot-laces to hanks of wool, black lead, Brasso and soap. He remembers how Mary explained to the children about war-time rationing and why they could only get 4ozs a week. She would wait patiently while a child made the all-important decision on what sweeties an old penny would get. They usually got a bargain. Though Mary often managed to get something that didn't need coupons and which she divided up among her bairns. On Saturdays she made ice cream. Jim remembers the hard work involved in this. His job was to turn the handle - with stops for tasting sessions of course! When children were parked in their prams outside Mary's shop, out she would come with a luckpenny. These same bairns were tottering down to her shop as soon as they were able to walk.

Years later as adults they still remembered Mary and her shop with great affection. Friendships were formed which were to last through Mary's entire life.   Her son remembers a small boy showing her his holiday photographs. He pointed proudly to a picture and said, *"That's the donkey Mary, and that's me."* Every night, at 8.00 p.m, curfew was called. Mary stood in the shop door and blew loudly on her whistle. This was the signal for children to go home. After serving the village for thirty years the shop was finally closed.

The Sweetie Shop by John Mackay

The wee shop by' the village Row,
Although it had, alas to go,
Will aye bring back a memory
When Oxton bairns around today
Have grown up - for then they'll say
When I was wee - och, just a tot,
I'd aye buy sweets from Mary Scott.
Now supermarkets are the thing -
(And my! - the prices fairly sting) -
Which makes me all the more, you know,
Think of the wee shop by the Row.

Gwendoline Lucy, wife of Frederick Colin, 14th Earl of Lauderdale,
shortly after their marriage in 1890.

The Loan, Lauder, at the start of the century.

Elizabeth Rae Remembers her Father, Andrew the AA man.

I belong to Oxton and have lived in the village all my life. I am the fourth generation of my family to stay in my home, my son Geoffrey being the fifth. Walking has long been a favourite pastime of mine. There are a few roads leading out of Oxton. The old railway line was a field's width away from the road, so I used to hurry along to see the train carrying goods to Lauder, Oxton and Fountainhall. I remember seeing groups of haystacks on the various farms outside Oxton, they were always very well made.

My father, Andrew Swan, had been an AA patrolman before the war and after he came back he returned to his old job. Working in the open air, in all kinds of weather, really appealed to him. Today AA patrolmen cover great distances in their distinctive yellow cars but before 1963 my father travelled about on a motorbike and sidecar. The sidecar was painted yellow and had an AA badge on it. Fitted into the sidecar was a box of tools and maps for use in helping motorists unfortunate enough to break down. In those days petrol and electrical systems were not as reliable as they are now. Once a month an inspector would examine all tools and replacements were made if necessary.

Each day, when my father was on duty, he drove from his base garage in Edinburgh Road, Lauder to the main base at Cameron Toll. Soutra Hill could be very tricky then, as it is now in thick fog and wintry conditions. Fellow patrolmen said they wouldn't care to work, on such a bad section of the road.

Before AA vehicles were fitted with radios, requests for help had to be passed by word of mouth by fellow travellers. The patrolman wore distinctive khaki coloured breeches, tunic and overcoat, and black leather knee high leggings. He was issued with a crash helmet, and a peaked hat with white cover and white gloves. If, on occasions the police needed extra help with parking, the AA man was called in to assist. When this happened my father covered his peaked cap with the white cover and wore his white gloves. In inclement weather he was well protected with a large yellow oilskin coat.

His normal working day was from 8am to 5pm. There were two AA call boxes on his route, one at Fordel and one at Carfraemill. From there he was able to contact the garages and the headquarters in Edinburgh to give and receive information. These two boxes were visited each day. Sometime in the 1950s the patrolmen were given radios which helped to speed up the breakdown service. In 1963 the change over to small vans helped even more. About this time the custom of saluting all members displaying an AA badge on their vehicle was discontinued. My father worked an irregular shift system during the week but was allowed Sunday off duty once every eight weeks.

Being a generous hearted man, he would oblige any of the locals even on his rest days. He would help pull out vehicles stuck in ditches or start up those with flat batteries. Another part of his work was to enrol new members for the AA and collect lapsed subscriptions. This was always done outside the patrolman's own area and was known as 'Canvassing Day'. But with the rapid growth of the AA and the major organisational changes the local services of men such as my father are no longer relevant.

Roads in Lauderdale

In early times, and at least up until the beginning of the agricultural revolution in the 18th century there was no real need for roads in Lauderdale, people did not travel any great distances and the few that did either walked or travelled by horseback. The routes through the Dale were mainly just tracks that had to keep to the higher ground to avoid the valley floor which was predominantly undrained bog and of course the river Leader and its tributaries were unpredictable at that time. With the great improvement in drainage that came with the agricultural changes it became much easier to construct roads on the lower, more level ground. With the improved farming methods it was necessary to use roads to transport more goods by using wheeled carts. By this time more people wanted to travel farther afield by carriage.

We must not forget the Roman Road, Dere Street, which ran from Corbridge in Northumberland, in the south, to Edinburgh, in the north, passing along the west side of Lauderdale. Dere Street, would no doubt be the route taken by many of the invading, and retreating armies from both Scotland, and England, during the many years of conflict between the two countries.

Attempts were made in the 17th century by various Acts of the Scottish Parliament to improve the roads, without a great deal of success. An Act of 1669 was introduced so that labour could be used for the first time to repair roads and bridges. The roads were to be twenty feet wide and suitable for horses and carts, the local heritors were empowered to use their servants and tenants to work on the roads, for six days each per year, unpaid, these were known as "parish road days". The Act really came into force in 1730 when the care of roads was put into the jurisdiction of the sheriff of the county, and the heritors were taxed by commissioners appointed locally.

Eventually, in 1770 proper workmen were employed, under supervision, in the summer months, to repair and maintain the roads. This meant of course that all moneys used to repair the roads was raised locally and any strangers using them did so without charge, a situation that could not continue. So it was that the idea of charging tolls became necessary. It was not a new idea, it had been in use on the continent, and in England, for some considerable time, but the traffic using our roads so far had not justified the cost. An Act was passed by the Westminster Parliament in 1751 enabling turnpikes to be set up in Scotland. A turnpike road was a road over which you had to a pay toll to pass, usually you had to be riding a horse, travelling with a cart or carriage or droving cattle or sheep, the exception being a toll at a bridge, at which, even on foot you had to pay. It was usually the owner of the estate through which a road ran who applied to parliament to manage the turnpike trust or trusts in his area, the trust was usually granted for 21 years, and the right to collect tolls was let on an annual basis. The person granted that right was able to set his own charges, and was known as a tackman.

In the early days road construction was very basic, consisting of small stones laid, approximately twenty feet wide with much larger stones on the edges to stop the smaller ones scattering.

By the 1850s, it had become obvious that it was not economic to have a large number of small trusts, so the result in the Borders was the formation of six:

Berwickshire Roads Trust - divided into three divisions: Lauder, Middle based on Duns, and Eastern based on Ayton.

Kelso Union Turnpike Trust - divided into three, West, North, and South. Covering the northern part of Roxburghshire.

Selkirk and St. Boswells Turnpike Trust - most of whose roads were in southern Roxburghshire and based on Hawick.

Roxburgh Turnpike Trust - covering the rest of Roxburghshire and based on Jedburgh.

Selkirkshire and Ettrick Turnpike Trust - covering the County of Selkirk.

Peeblesshire Turnpike Trust - covering the County of Peebles.

These Turnpike roads had to have a specific point where the toll was paid, so at the Turnpike there needed to be a house to accommodate the toll keeper. The expression Turnpike comes from an army description of a defensive weapon used to defend infantry against a charge by cavalry, the turnpike was considerably changed for its use, to stop people and animals as a toll barrier, usually just a simple pole across the road that either swung up, or across the road. As far as we know there were three toll houses in Lauderdale, alas all gone now unfortunately, but remembered by some of our older inhabitants.

We had Cleekhimin Toll just south of Lylestane on the A697, not to be confused with Cleekhimin School which is north of Lylestane, Trabroun Toll at the junction to Trabroun Farm on the A68 north of Lauder, and Stonyford Toll at the north junction to Blainslie on the A68 just south of Lauder. The Local Government Scotland Act of 1895 which created the new County Councils finally saw the end of many ad hoc arrangements to raise money to provide for local services, with the introduction of a proper rating system.

Sketch drawing of Cleekhimin Toll.

Sketch drawing of Trabroun Toll.

Before that however, the Roads and Bridges Act of 1883 saw the official end of the turnpike system in Scotland, from then on all roads in the country would be under the jurisdiction of the County Councils and Burgh Councils, until the 15th of May 1975, when they became the responsibility of first the Borders Regional Council, and then in 1999, the Scottish Borders Council.

Since the middle of the eighteenth century and the two early Turnpike Acts the road from Carfraemill down through Lauder to Stonyford Toll has changed little, except for the odd realignment. However in those early days from Stonyford Toll the road south took the line of the present road through Blainslie, passing Clackmae and joining what is now the A68 South of Earlston. It was not until the middle of the nineteenth century that the present route from Stonyford Toll via Galadean, and Birkenside, to Earlston, was established. This part of the A68 has had quite a few realignments in the later part of the twentieth century, and at the crossing of the river Leader at Galadean there are no fewer than three bridges, with two still in use. There are three other roads south of Lauder that are worth a mention, some of which have partly disappeared. One from the High Cross to Boon, then Ledgerwood, joining the B6397 south of Purvishall on the Earlston to Kelso road, the part from the High Cross to Boon has virtually disappeared, though it is still visible today as it leaves the High Cross within an avenue of trees. One from Birkenside to the B6397 south of Purvishall, that is still used by farm vehicles, and one from Stonyford Toll that crossed the river Leader somewhere near Lauder Barns farm and on to Galadean, there is no sign of this one.

As mentioned earlier, the early way to make a road was to lay large stones along the edge and fill in the centre with smaller ones. The main problem with this principle was that as stones are mainly round they tended to move around a lot under the wheels of any vehicles that passed over them, very soon the road would develop deep ruts. Help was at hand however in the person of John Loudon McAdam, born at Ayr in 1756, who became a famous road engineer, his theory was that if you broke stones into small pieces and added something to bind them you would then have a much more stable and firmer surface for your road. After McAdams death and with the introduction of gas lighting in towns, the by product of gas being tar, people started experimenting with this new product, the rest as they say is history. It was not until well into the twentieth century that all the roads in Lauderdale were treated with tarmacadam.

In the early part of the eighteenth century, due to the tremendous changes taking place in agriculture it became increasingly necessary to move away from the old method of transporting goods, namely by pack-horse. The new system was a fairly primitive unsprung vehicle, pulled by bullocks, horses or mules. These were owned by a licensed carrier who operated a fairly regular service between towns and, for Lauder in particular, between Lauder and Edinburgh. Some of these carriers would also take the odd passenger for a small charge, it could not have been a very comfortable journey. This form of transport for all kind of goods, both into and out of the Borders would last until the advent of the railway in the middle of the nineteenth century.

It is only natural that with advent of the wheeled cart then there must follow the coach and carriages to transport people, and these appeared shortly after the former.

Sketch Drawing of Stonyford Toll.

As was mentioned earlier, Dere Street was the main thoroughfare that passed through Lauderdale for hundreds of years, used by all kinds of travellers, it has been suggested that as many as seventy armies at least have passed along its route. As mentioned before it tended to stay on the higher ground, which of course meant that some of the gradients were fairly steep, and this in turn created problems for the horses when more, and larger horse drawn vehicles were introduced. In the middle of the eighteenth century it was agreed that Dere Street needed to be replaced. It was agreed by the Trustees on both sides of the boundary between Berwickshire and Midlothian after the Turnpike Act of 1760, that the new route should go round the north side of Soutra Hill from Soutra Mains farm, and on to Huntershall then follow the valley of the Headshaw Burn down past New Channelkirk, on the east side of the burn, and then on to Carfraemill. This was an important junction, where the road divided, the road to the east went to Duns, Greenlaw and Coldstream, and to the south Lauder, Kelso and Jedburgh. At New Channelkirk an Inn was built to accommodate travellers. Some difficulties must have persisted in the deep valleys north of New Channelkirk, as a short section was re-routed at the end of the eighteenth century.

By the early part of the nineteenth century the increase in traffic meant that there was a demand for even better roads. The Trustees, after being pressurised by the GPO, appointed the famous Thomas Telford, to survey the route, his proposals were accepted and work started in 1835 and the end result was virtually the line of the road that we have today the A68. The new route meant that this was the end of New Channelkirk Inn, and the birth of Carfraemill Inn, now known as The Lodge. What was New Channelkirk Inn can still be seen today as a private house, lying in the valley to your right as you climb Soutra Hill from the south.

The A697 from Carfraemill to Coldstream has changed very little as it passes through Lauderdale. The short stretch that did change, probably at the start of the nineteenth century, is best described by taking you south from Carfraemill to Huntington farm, as you pass the farm you are on a straight piece of road with a wood on your left. As you travel on slightly downhill you will have a fence and hedge on your right hand, now look ahead and you will see that the hedge on your right will carry on in a virtually straight line for some distance, but at the end of the wood the road will turn left.

After you are round the corner you will see that on your right is a fairly long field with the previously mentioned hedge at the far side of it, that hedge marks the line of the old road, and you will see that it disappears down into a wooded valley. In the field close to the far hedge you will see an very old building that still has a roof on it, this was Norton Inn that must have served the travellers on that road. At the bottom of the wooded valley the old road crosses the Easter Burn or East Waters at the side of which stands Drummonds Hall Lodge a small house that is still occupied, Drummonds Hall itself however has long since disappeared. The old road then climbs up a very steep hill and crosses the new road on its old route up to Wanton Walls farm, from there it would have carried on to a junction above the Highcross, the right hand fork would have then gone straight down to the Highcross to become part of the road to Boon (Mentioned later).

At the junction above the Highcross the old road carried on to Thirlestane Farm passing between the farm and the farm house and then on down to a small bridge over Snawdon Burn, after which it passed The Heugh now known as Braefield Cottage and then on to another small bridge at the Boondriech Burn at Dod Mill where it carried on to Whiteburn and eventually Coldstream.

This route from Coldstream to Carfraemill was a alternative road in the old days for travellers and armies.

Returning to the High Cross, the road from there carried on into the valley over the Boondreigh Water and then up to just below Boon Farm, and from there to Whitlaid Farm, eventually joining the Blainslie to Birkenside road at Galadean.

There were quite a number of old roads in Lauderdale, but we will content ourselves by showing them on the map.

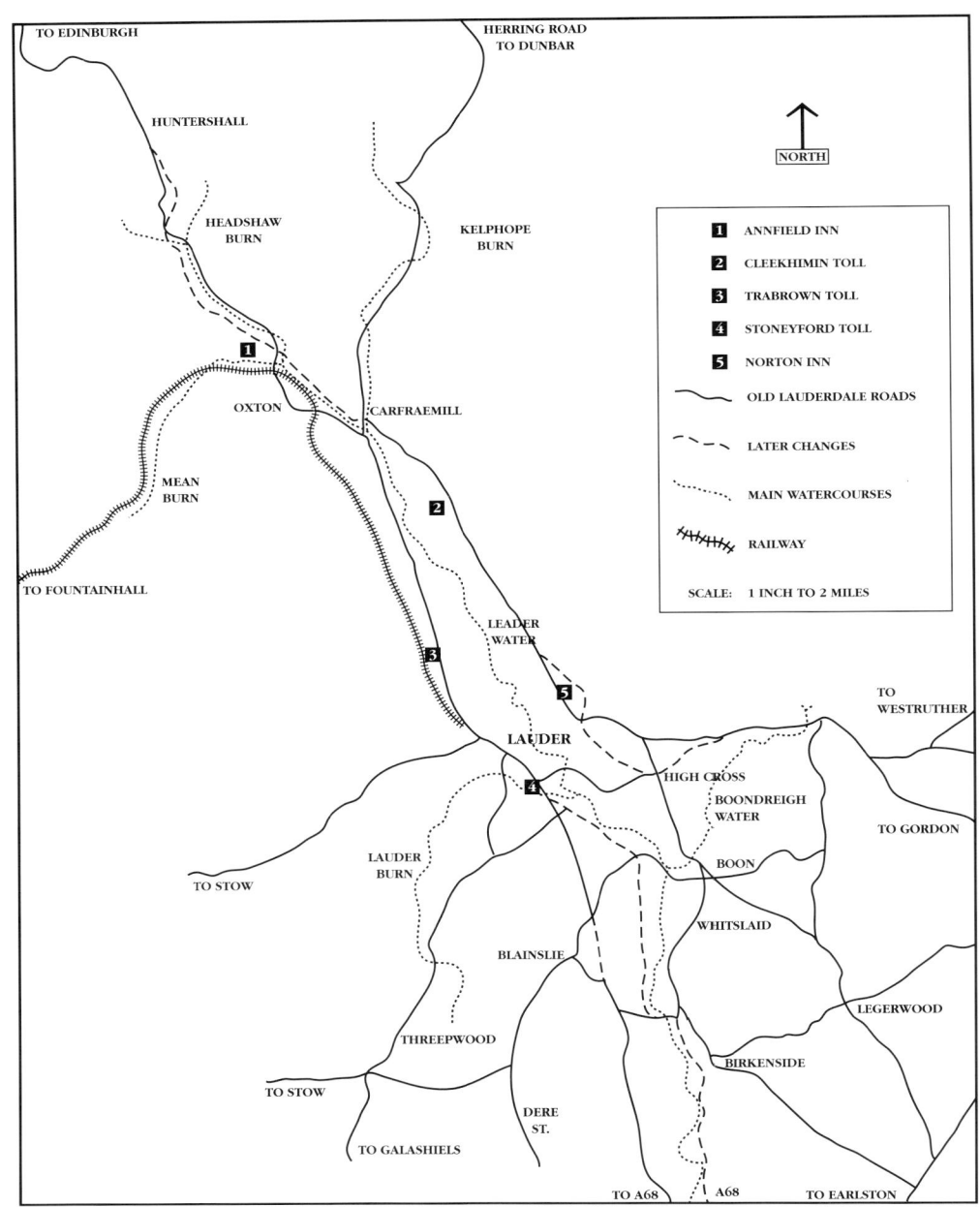

Roads of Lauderdale

The Lauder Light Railway

Although the Edinburgh & Hawick line opened as far as St. Boswells In November 1849 under the auspices of the North British Railway Co., it was not for another 52 years that the Lauder to Fountainhall line was opened in July 1901. Much hot air was expended over those 52 years and by the time that the line was built, the writing was already on the wall for the small branch line. The advent of the internal combustion engine, propelling motor cars, buses and lorries, that were much more versatile, spelled the doom of most branch lines.

During those wasted years various schemes were suggested that included Lauder in their plans. In 1864, a line to be called the Berwickshire Central Railway was proposed to run from near Fountainhall, to Oxton, then Lauder, from Lauder to Earlston, then Smailholm, terminating at Kelso, where it would join a proposed line to Tweedmouth. By 1863 a branch line owned by the Berwickshire Railway had reached Earlston from Duns and two years later the line was extended to St. Boswells, to join the Edinburgh & Hawick line. In 1889 there was a proposal for a new Border Railway network, this was to consist of a main line from Berwick to Lockerbie, passing through, Mindrum, Yetholm, Morebattle, Cessford, Jedburgh, Denholm, Hawick, Branxholm, Teviothead and Glendinning; and from Edinburgh, to Mindrum, passing through, Pencaitland, Humbie, Lauder, Mellerstain and Kelso; joined by a branch line from Hawick, passing through, Lilliesleaf, Selkirk, Galashiels to Lauder. All of these schemes and others came to nought, and there things might have remained, without a railway ever coming to Lauder were it not for the advent of the Light Railways Act 1896.

The idea behind the Act was to allow Railway Companies to build the infrastructure and the vehicles using the railways to a lighter specification and in so doing be able to build and run railways at greatly reduced cost. This would particularly benefit rural areas.

An interesting statistic that came out at the time when consideration was being given to the building of a line to Lauder was that in the year 1882-3, a total of 6,450 passengers were transported between Lauder and Stow by horse-drawn bus. Officialdom takes time however, and it took until the 30th. June, 1898 before an order made by the Light Railway Commissioners authorising the construction of a Light Railway between Fountainhall and Lauder was passed. The Lauder Light Railway Company was authorised to build a standard gauge line 10 miles 1 furlong or thereabouts in length. The Company was authorised to enter into an agreement with the North British Railway as to the operation of the line. A contract was entered into with Messrs Dick, Kerr & Company, Kilmarnock, who agreed to construct the line for £34,151, and the permanent way for £5,660.The estimated value of the land required was £4,845. The seal of the Company was an adaptation of the Lauder Burgh Seal, and on Saturday 3rd. June 1899 Ada, Countess of Lauderdale, cut the first sod at the site of the Lauder Railway Station.

After quite a few problems during the construction of the line, the Lauder Light Railway opened for traffic on Tuesday, 2nd. July 1901.

Mr. Rogers, the booking clerk at Peebles, became the first Station Master at Lauder Station, and Mr Lockhead, spare signalman at Galashiels, became the first Station Master at Oxton Station.

> *The puff of "Billy" in the dale,*
> *The noise of whistle scream,*
> *Reminds us of an enterprise,*
> *Which once was but a dream.*

Here are a few technical details for the enthusiast:

The track was single throughout except for a passing place at Oxton.

No engine or carriage putting a greater weight than 12 tons on the rails by one pair of wheels was permitted to be employed. Speed was curtailed to 25 m.p.h. and to 10 m.p.h. on curves.

The engine used on the passenger train in 1930 was: 4-4-OT type, coupled wheels, 5ft. diameter; bogie wheels (solid centres) 2ft. 6ins.in diameter. Heating surface 700 sq. ft; tank capacity 655 gallons. This type was introduced by Drummond on the old N.B.R. in 1880.

Traffic on the line seems to have been better than expected, in the first three months of operation the LLR traffic receipts were £383.18s. In September of the first year 750 tons of goods were dealt with at Lauder and 299 tons at Oxton, while a total of 11,300 passengers ha been carried, and 2,046 sheep had been sent from Oxton.

In the beginning a total of eight passenger trains per day ran, two each way in the morning and two each way in the afternoon. Due to strikes , and the first World War, virtually from 1912 until after the war only two trains each way per day were allowed to run.

The Railways Act of 1921 changed everything, both the North British Railway and the Lauder Light Railway became part of the London & North Eastern Railway Company, and this company would have a monopoly on railway transport in the east of Britain, a forerunner if you like to British Rail.

The advent of George Deans buying a Char-a-banc in 1924, was the first warning that the days of a passenger service on the railway were numbered. Eventually the rapidly expanding Scottish Motor Traction Company bought out George Deans, and started daily services through Lauder to Jedburgh. The result was that by 1931 Oxton Station was handling an average of only 23 passengers a week, and Lauders' total was little better.

The inevitable result was that the General manager of the Scottish Area LNER, made an application to the Traffic, Locomotive and Works Committee of the Company to close the passenger service on the 12th. July 1932. Authority was given, and intimation was made that on or after Monday , September 12 1932, passengers will no longer be conveyed to and from Lauder and Oxton stations on the Fountainhall-Lauder branch railway.

From that time onwards Lauder Light Railway, carried out a "goods only" operation until its final closure. There were however a few twists before that happened. On the 1st. January, 1948 the line became part of British Railways, Scottish Region and that same year in August an event occurred that could have seen the immediate closure of the line. During the early part of August, torrential rain fell in the Borders, and many road and rail bridges were either, swept away or badly damaged, including the one that carried the branch line over the Galawater just outside Fountainhall Station. Over two years passed before the line was reopened on Monday, 20th. November, 1950, and the resumption of the pre-flood service, which consisted of a single daily trip, which left Galashiels at 9.26 am arriving at Lauder at 11.43 am and returning from there at 12.15 pm. The only reason why the line had not been permanently closed at this time was the presence of the Food Depot at Lauder. This Depot was built during the War, adjacent to the Station, and was used to store vast amounts of non perishable food. It was retained after the end of the War, into the early years of the so-called 'Cold War" as it was seen to be strategically important.

By 1956, rumours started to circulate that the line was about to close, to no great surprise, with mechanisation on the farms going on apace, with farmers even, owning their own lorries, and the Food Depot being taken over by the Scottish Co-operative Wholesale Society, and using their own lorries to transport its goods in and out of the Depot, the end was clearly in sight.

On Tuesday 30th. September, 1958 the last goods train was run over the Lauder Light Railway and as from the following day Lauder and Oxton stations were closed. On Saturday 15th. November, 1958 the Branch Line Society, organised what was the last train on the Lauder Light Railway to carry passengers. Many older people in Lauderdale have many happy memories of "Maggie Lauder" as the engine was affectionately called, and still regret her passing.

To some people it does seem rather strange that 100 years after she was introduced to this area, we are once again involved in discussions on introducing trains to the Borders. There seems to be no debate this time as to the route of this new line, it seems it must pass through Galashiels, despite the obvious horrendous costs involved. Reading the history of railway building proposals in the beginning, it would appear that quite a number of those proposals favoured using Lauderdale as a route. With the Scottish Borders preference to have new housing concentrated around St. Boswells, surely this route would be much cheaper and more sensible.

For any one wishing to read a more detailed account of the Lauder Light Railway we recommend the book by Andrew M. Hajducki and Alan Simpson, published by The Oakwood Press.

*14th Countess of Lauderdale cutting the first sod at the
construction of the Lauder Light Railway.*

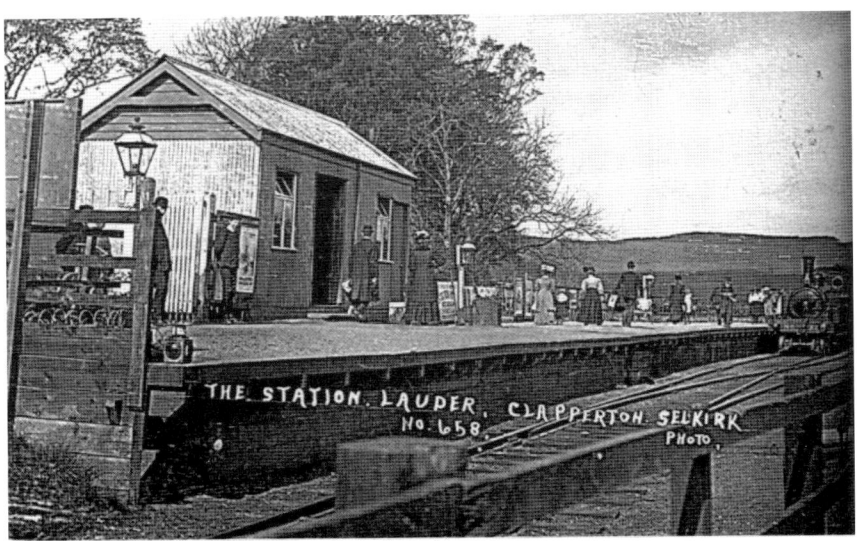

Lauder Station just after opening. By courtesy of Robert D. Clapperton Photographic Trust.

Other Schools in Lauderdale

Although articles have been written for this book on Channelkirk and Lauder Schools, it must not be forgotten that there were three other schools in Lauderdale for the greater part of the twentieth century. They were Cleekhimin, on the A697 a mile south of Carfraemill, Pyatshaw, which is just past Cambridge on the way to Blythe farm, and of course Blainslie.

Cleekhimin

Cleekhimin at one time would provide all of the formal education for the children on the farms and in the hill herd's houses on this area. It was a single teacher school. There is some doubt locally as to when the school actually closed. However, the following extract from the Schools Log Book may help to clarify the confusion.

"27 May (1960) The public meeting on the future of the school was held on Tuesday. Mr. Birch the Director and Capt. Home the Chairman of Education Committee were in attendance. On Wednesday the final notice of the closure was given."

"1st July. A normal week. Attendance 94%. One girl on holiday." (This is the last entry)

The last teacher of the school was Mrs. Anne H. Thomson. The school house is now a private residence and the school a double garage.

Pyatshaw

Pyatshaw was a similar type of school to Cleekhimin, again catering for the children from the farms and hill herds' houses in its area. It burnt down in the 1950's and rebuilt, then closed as a school on 8th July 1966, but used by Berwickshire County Council as an outdoor centre for a number of years before being sold. A new house was eventually built on the site. The last teacher at the school was Mrs. Vera A. M. Mortimer, who, on the closure of Pyatshaw moved to Westruther School.

Blainslie

Blainslie was different in that it served the village of Blainslie and the farms around, and it was a two-teacher school at one time. Although by the time it closed, it had been reduced to a one-teacher school. Again, as with Cleekhimin there is a local confusion as to when this school actually closed and who the last Head Teacher was. The following information from the Scottish Borders Education Archive Department should clarify the situation.

The final entry in the Blainslie School Log Book is date 20th October 1961 and states that *"The new Head Teacher Mr. Izatt is here and I now leave Blainslie school after doing three weeks supply work. J. F. S. Vert."*

The admission register continued until 1968.

The following appears in the County of Roxburgh Education Committee Minute Book 1968-1973.

Blainslie Primary School

The Director of Education reported that the roll of Blainslie School is at present 15 and he estimated that the roll would be 13 in 1969 and would fall considerably in future years. He also reported that the Headmaster had resigned and that temporary teachers had been holding the position in the meantime. He suggested that this might be an appropriate opportunity to consider the closure of the school and he reported that there had been a public meeting with parents and members of the public at the school.... The Director of Education reported that he had arranged that the school be closed temporarily after the Christmas vacation. The Sub-Committee agreed to recommend that the school be closed permanently....
(Minute dated 20 December 1968)

It was reported that the intimation has been received from the Scottish Education Department that the Secretary of State has approved the permanent closure of Blainslie Primary School.
(Minute dated 14 march 1969)

Mr. A. L. Izatt, Head Teacher, Blainslie Primary School resigned with effect from 20th October 1968
(Minute dated 20 December 1968 Staffing Sub-Committee)

The school and school house were both sold off and are now two private residences.

Blainslie School and Schoolhouse very early in the 1900s.

Matthew McKerrow

Matthew McKerrow of Addinston Farm served with the Home Guard during World War II.

"We were originally known as the Local Defence Volunteers. There were about a hundred members under the command of Major Graham Munro from Harryburn who was a dentist in Edinburgh. I was a lieutenant in charge of the Oxton platoon and Ian Sutherland was in charge of the Lauder one. Alan Cunningham was over us but Mr Munro was in overall command. There were lots of farmers and men from different trades in the platoon. We had our regular drills and meetings in the local public halls. Sometimes we would go out on exercises going round the district to try and work out the best places to stop an invasion coming in. A lot of the men who were from villages themselves probably didn't know all the places in the county. These exercises let them see just what their area was like.

At first we just had armbands with 'LDF' on them. We got uniforms eventually. Not for quite a while though. You would get sort of one bit of a uniform, then you would get other bits coming in the next batch of stuff. You didn't manage to get things to fit everybody but gradually we built up to having our full kit. We didn't have any weapons either to begin with. Some people brought along their own weapons you know, rifles, shotguns and even some revolvers. Eventually we were fully equipped.

We were issued with spigot mortars and we used to go to Coldingham beach and fire at rocks with them. Some of them did have an explosive head but most of them didn't. They just had a dummy head that was full of cement or something like that, but they went off with a crack when the fuse hit the other end. There was a rifle range up at the Burn Mill. It had been a territorial one from the First World War or whatever. I mean it's a proper range with targets and machines for putting the targets up and down. That's where we would go when we actually had some ammunition that we were allowed to use for target shooting. One time we were issued with sten guns, just sort of little sub-machine guns. One of the men couldn't hit the target at all and we heard afterwards that his shots were all landing in the farm behind the range.

It was a serious business most of the time. I remember when we were on an exercise and Willie Coulthard was the dispatch rider because he had a motorcycle. While he was out, he stopped in to see Mrs Leeming and discovered she was in the middle of having a baby all by herself. That was quite an experience for him.

It could be dangerous though, if you weren't careful. When you were firing grenades you had to be careful and check that the sheer wire wasn't broken. The sheer wire stopped the grenade from exploding when you were training. It happened one time that a man hadn't checked the sheer wire and it exploded in the face of a man at the other end. The man who was doing the firing was practically unhurt. About a month or two later I was doing a course at the Scottish Command Arms School. It was a demolition course, you know, about things that hadn't gone off.

Well, we were shown this rifle grenade the same kind as before. A man was loading it for me and I said, "Just check on that before you put the grenade in." He checked and there was no sheer wire; it had fallen out,

I remember George Dobson, he was away on a course where they were under fire with live ammunition, They were lying down coming forward, but the people that were doing the firing were not firing high enough and the man next to George was shot in the head and killed.

There was a shepherd who lived at Tollis Hill. It was noticed that he had a light in the house and the Air Raid Warden was informed, When he was visited he said that he didn't bother blacking out the back windows because nobody could see them."

Mrs May Anderson – Oxton Castle

The "Castle" was an old building which stood on the south side of what is now Campbell's Yard where the lorries are kept. I remember some of the residents: downstairs there were the original J & G Campbell. Jock and Dod. On the other side lived Davy Purves. He kept a few cows, which he took out every day to graze on the roadsides. As they were grazing he made hay for them by cutting the roadside grass with a scythe. He was a kenspeckle character, his hair white and flowing, his trousers and underwear equally spectacular and with his boots unlaced. He kept a few ducks that made their home on the Clora Burn. Sadly the castle burned down.

In the Annfield inn the family I remember best was the Grahams. He was a rabbit catcher and was a great lad when he was dressed! He wore a Black Watch tie, that having been his regiment in the Great War. He was fond of a dram so it was battles drawn between him and his wife. They had four sons and a daughter who joined in the fights. Mrs Graham was very house proud; everything was spotless, with a spittoon provided for her husband and woe betide him if he missed. There were no "mod cons" and the cold tap was at the byre door.

Sketch Drawing of Annfield Inn.

Watson Brothers 1914-18.
Duncan   Robert   James

Lauder Common Riding Threepwood Ceremony 1938.

Lauderdale at War and Peace

The 20th Century opened with the nation already at war! Indeed, The South African War, or The Boer War as it was more popularly known, would continue until 31st May 1902, when the Treaty of Vereeniging finally brought it to a close.

For Lauderdale, this conflict was of only passing significance, except, of course, to those who had husbands, fathers and sons serving in that war. Actually 22,000 British soldiers died in The Boer War and at that time this seemed a terrible price to pay.

But Lauderdale also contributed in its own small way.

One of the Regiments which carries South Africa as a Battle Honour on its Colours is the Local Regiment, The King's Own Scottish Borderers, and recruited as they were and are from every part of the Borders including Berwickshire, we can be sure that Lauderdale played its part.

However, scarcely had The Boer War ended; scarcely had the lessons learned from that conflict been absorbed, than another war erupted. This time it wasn't centred in some far-flung post of empire, but in Europe - almost on our own doorstep. Only 12 years had elapsed before "The War to End All Wars" broke out and devastated most of Western Europe; not to mention the Dardanelles and the Middle East. "The Great War" of 1914-18 left no community in the land unscathed, but that statement is only made with the benefit of hindsight. Initially there was a great rush to join the colours, with young men leaving the farms, the mills, the schools and colleges all over the Borders, and Lauderdale was no exception. They enlisted from every social background, determined to see action before it was all over, little understanding how the nature of war had changed in the years since the end of the South African War.

Far from ending quickly, this war dragged on. By March 1916 conscription had been introduced in order to fill the gaps being left by the ever mounting numbers of casualties. The Scottish Borders, like every part of the nation, suffered and Lauderdale was part of that suffering. One example was the fate of the 4th Battalion of The Kings Own Scottish Borderers, (heavily recruited from Lauderdale) which on the 12th July 1915, went into action on the Gallipoli Peninsula and in the course of a morning lost 362 all ranks. Indeed, when the 4th battalion was withdrawn there were only 70 unwounded left. Among these 70 was one young Lauderdale man, **John Walker**. John had joined the KOSB in 1914, aged nineteen, and both his brothers Robert and George also served with "The Borderers', but only John took part in the Dardanelles campaign. He continued to serve, seeing service in France, but seldom could he be drawn to talk about his experiences, especially Gallipoli.

Not only individuals like John Walker suffered as a result of actions like this and the long drawn out trench warfare in Europe; whole communities were badly effected. The casualty rates continued to climb. By early 1916 it had been necessary to impose the Universal Military Service Act, which meant that all men between 18 and 41 were eligible for conscription, and to ensure the flow of men for military service, the 'Exemption Tribunals' were established. The exemption tribunals became a fact of life as the older generation tried to keep enough young men at home to ensure that life would go on! But this new kind of warfare proved insatiable, and still the numbers of the fallen rose. Not just human beings; the farms had to give up many of their horses and farmers, who were struggling to keep their farms alive and producing badly needed food for the table, found that not only had they to survive without the men to work the land, they had to do it with far fewer horses.

For four years the war dragged on. When it was over, Lauderdale like every other part of the country had to come to terms with the price that had been paid. Locally it was decided that memorials should be set up in homage to those young men who had died, and so in the parishes of Lauderdale decisions were taken as to what form these memorials would take. In Lauder the War Memorial took the form of a column with the names of the dead engraved for every passer-by to stop and note; whereas in Oxton the decision was made to build a community hall in memory of their lost ones - again the names were inscribed.

In both parishes these memorials still play an important part in the life of the community with Lauder's Memorial having a small but significant role in the events of the Common Riding and Oxton's War Memorial Hall still acting as the centre for all social life within the village. In addition, both parish churches erected plaques with the names of the fallen inscribed where they can be read by worshippers and visitors alike.

The Great War was the impetus for much social change which was to be reflected in Lauderdale over the next few generations. For example, agriculture whilst still being a most important part of the society employed an ever reducing number of men. Suddenly, boys and youths could no longer assume that they would follow their fathers into an established way of life which their families had been engaged in for many generations.

But the real impact of this change was not to be felt immediately, although the signs were clearly there. Before, this new agricultural revolution could take effect, yet another devastating war erupted, and once more the young men of Lauderdale were sent off to fight. The nature of this "Second World War" was very different from that of The Great War. This war was also fought on many fronts and the casualty lists were immense, even larger than the "Great War", but now these lists were swollen by the numbers of civilian casualties in those places where the fighting was taking place, not to mention the horror of "Death Camps" where whole peoples were systematically destroyed. Fortunately Lauderdale was away from all of that and even the destruction of air raids which did so much damage to the cities by-passed the Dale.

Actually, to say that 'Lauderdale' was far from the hostilities is only true in part! HMS Lauderdale, played an honourable role from the date of her commissioning in December 1941. Having been briefly attached to Western Approaches Command the 'Lauderdale' left Londonderry and crossed the Atlantic to serve with the Royal Canadian Navy from February 1942. However this attachment only lasted one month

...very many thanks for all your help
and the encouragement which you have often
given me frequently.

May God's perfect blessing

Continue with you and your wife and family

Yours very sincerely

Richard Harris

to him that your resignation would be taken and the Congregation.

I just wanted to inform my own disappointment and at the same time my very warmest thanks to you for all your important help in the past years. You have always been most conscientious in carrying your district and carrying out the duties there. Your contacts with the Sunday School have been very greatly

The Manse,
Fowlis,
17th Sept. 1976

Dear Mr. Stewart,

The Kirk Session at its meeting on Tuesday
received your resignation with the very greatest
regret and you will be keenly [missed?] especially from the
Session Clerk, knowing that you would not come
to such a decision lightly to [remain?] felt bound

appreciated. You took your share in the government of the Church as a Presbytery Elder and your contributions to the discussions in Kirk Session have been most valuable. You have shared very fully in the life and fellowship and worship of the Congregation and in all these ways you have played your part most faithfully.

and was spent on convoy duty, before returning to Londonderry.

The rest of the war saw the Lauderdale flitting from role to role: Patrol and escort duties; the 60th Destroyer Division, based in Malta, during which she participated in the invasions of Sicily and the South of France. By the time of this latter action, the ship had been transferred to the 5th Destroyer Flotilla at Alexandria, under which command she saw out the end of the War. In 1946 this 'proud vessel which bore the name of our Dale with honour, was transferred to the Greek navy, and continued to give service under a new name.

But it was not left to a ship, no matter how 'proud she be' to represent Lauderdale in the hostilities of the 2nd World War. The following brief accounts simply represent a few of the contributions of sons and daughters of this dale, as well as men and women for whom Lauderdale has been home these many years.

James Stewart: Like many another young man, perhaps because he felt that war was inevitable, Jim joined the supplementary reserve in February 1939 and, as a result was called up immediately on 1 September 1939. Jim reported to the RASC at York but as an example of just how fast things can move in war, he found himself in France by 19th September. All that Jim says about France is that he left via Dunkirk. Perhaps no more has to be said!

Rest, recuperation and training followed and by August 1940 Jim was on his way to South Africa (Freetown), from where In June 1941 he sailed north through the Suez Canal to Port Said in Egypt. Once kitted out Jim was sent into the desert (Mersa Maruh), and from there he took part in the retreat into Egypt. After a short spell in Cyprus, he was back in Egypt (1942). The Lebanon (Beirut) followed and also Syria (Damascus).

Jim then joined the 156 Battalion 1st Airborne Division and saw action with them in Italy. Returning to Britain, Jim was stationed at Melton Mowbray awaiting the landings in Europe, from where Jim reached Arnhem! He was demobbed October 1945.

James Shaw: Between 1932 and 1935 Jimmy had spent three years in the Royal Artillery, so it could have come as no surprise that soon after the outbreak of war, he found himself conscripted. Following initial training at Maryhill Barracks, Jimmy was transferred from the RAOC into the REME. As a driver mechanic, he was attached to the 71st Infantry Brigade; part of the 53rd Welsh Division, and in the fullness of time, Jimmy landed on Arromanches beach on D Day + 4. (Jimmy describes as an unforgettable sight, an evening spent on a hillside watching allied bombers attacking Caen.)

His unit was part of the drive through Northern Europe and it was during 'The Battle of the Bulge' that Jimmy came into contact with our American allies. Cut off at Arnhem, during the taking of the Nijmegen Bridge, Jimmy and his comrades were eventually able to resume their advance into Germany in time to endure the 24 hours artillery bombardment during the Battle at Reichwald Forest.

Among his other war-time memories, Jimmy remembers crossing the Rhine in a glider; entering Hamburg (or what was left of it) on VE Day, and from Hamburg, Staff Sergeant Shaw was posted to Wuppertal, from where he was involved in forming a Divisional Workshop employing German civilians. (One of the early attempts at rehabilitation?).

Finally Jimmy spent three months at Gottingen University, in the beautiful Hartz mountains, courtesy of the British Army, from where he returned to Britain for demob.

John Manson: John is one of those unsung heroes who served throughout the war in the Merchant Navy, where of course, boys of sixteen were appreniced on ships in the front line of the naval battle, thus facing the enemy at an age not legally allowed in the Royal Navy, Army or Air Force. John signed his indentures for a four year apprenticeship in December 1939, and as a result he arrived in the River Plate to find the Pocket Battleship 'Graf Spee' had been scuttled with three Royal Naval Vessel awaiting her attempt to break clear. By 1942, John still only 19, but now a veteran with three years experience behind him, found himself in a 63 ship convoy from Norfolk, Virginia en route to Greenock. On one night an attack by German Submarines cost 16 ships from the convoy. On yet another occasion in 1942, sailing from Durban to Liverpool, they were overtaken by the Helenus, a ship of the Blue Funnel Line. As she disappeared over the horizon she was torpedoed. Calling for cover from shore bases of the RAF, they went to rescue the survivors. The RAF attacked the submarine whilst they saved 86 passengers and crew-of the Helenus. In 1943 John joined a newly commissioned ship, 'Greenwich', and sailing in it he circled the globe two and a half times, taking part in the landings at Berbera, North Africa, Aden, and, in Italy at Naples and Salerno. They were twice in Calcutta and Bombay and eventually Rangoon and Burma, escaping from Singapore just before it finally fell to the Japanese.

Harry Crombie-Smith: Early in the war, Lauder 'lost' one of its doctors, when Dr Harry enlisted, leaving his practice in the most capable hands of his wife. Given the Rank of Captain, Harry spent nearly all his time in Field Ambulances. These were, and indeed are, the medical units (small hospitals) which provide the immediate care to casualties after the initial attention of the regimental Aid Post. Harry found himself east of the Irrawaddy River in Burma, serving in that unforgiving campaign until it ended; thereafter being sent with the 2nd British Field Ambulance to Singapore and Malaya. Harry arrived back in Britain in Jan 1946, before being demobbed in September 1946.

Nora Munro: It wasn't just men who found themselves being summoned away from home. June 1942 saw Nora pack her bags, saying farewell to her nearest and dearest, and, having been enlisted in the ATS, and after training as a Radar operator, attached to an Ack-Ack Battery. She spent most of the next three years savouring the 'delights' available during war-time of such places as Falmouth, Plymouth, Yarmouth, Bude, Oswestry, Hornsea, Whitby, Leeds, Leicester, Nottingham (twice) and Didcot. Nora's 'war' finally ended when she was demobbed in May 1946 - a year after the war in Europe had ended.

Isabella Nisbet: Early 1943 saw yet another young lass leave Lauderdale to serve. Bella MacIvor, as she was then was conscripted into the Wrens, and having left Carfraemill where she had been working, she travelled to Rosyth for six weeks training.

Bella and Willie Nisbet.
W.R.E.N.S. and R.A.S.C.

Like most service men and women, Bella soon found that war often produces the unexpected - in her case she was posted home; Stornoway on the Isle of Lewis, only a hop, step and jump from her family in North Tolsta. Bella was on Lewis for a year until the Navy sent her to yet another Island - The Isle-of-Man. Finally, she was sent to Chester where she was attached to the Naval College until the end of the war, and then it was back to Carfraemill, from whence it had all begun. Circle complete!

William Anderson or soon to be A/B Anderson W AJX849360: It was in 1941 that Bill joined the Royal Navy and after 10 weeks training at HMS Raleigh, Devonport, he was posted back north to Aultbea in Wester Ross. After 8 months he was back in Devonport, but a few weeks there was enough for Bill and he volunteered for a change in role. After further training he joined 15 Flotilla LCA (Landing Craft Assault) and was posted to the Med where they trained with the troops who they would be landing on hostile shores. That certainly was the case, as the first landing Bill was involved in was Sicily where they landed The Royal Engineers. Next was Salerno where Bill helped to put the Scots Guards ashore, and then Anzio where his passengers were American Rangers. After about two years in the Mediterranean, Bill was involved in the landings on Southern France, but that was to be his last.

In 1944 it was back to the U.K, and Devonport once more. However not for long! After about four weeks he joined HMS Lagos which was going to the Far East. Bill spent a further nine months in the area of Singapore but was then sent home to be demobbed in April 1946.

James Fulton: A native of Helensburgh, Jim served with the Royal Corps of Signals between 1942 and 1943. In 1943 he transferred into the Airborne Forces and was eventually posted to the 4th Parachute Brigade Signal Section. In September 1944 Jim dropped with his brigade into Northern Europe, but wounded and unable to walk, he was captured and spent seven months as a POW in Stalag XI B at Fallingbostel in Germany. Jim was demobbed in 1945.

Flt/Sgt James Mercer R.A.F.

James Mercer: A name from the Lauder War Memorial. James was brought up on Whitslaid Farm and joined the RAF in 1943. He was selected for aircrew as rear gunner and following battle school he was eventually sent to 624 Squadron in Algeria from where they flew several missions over southern France. On the night of 26th June, they took off for a supply drop to the French Resistance, but before they could complete their task they crashed. James' remains, together with his comrades was found by the Resistance and taken to the local Protestant church where, guarded by the resistance and the townspeople they lay in state until being buried in the Protestant cemetery; a funeral to which the whole countryside came. It was not until June 1947 that the War Graves Commission found the grave and registered it. James was 19.

1766 Tweed – August 1944.

Tweed: Also from Whitslaid farm was sent Tweed the dog. Serial Number 1776, he served as a guard dog from November 1943 until the end of the war, whereupon he was 'demobbed' and returned to Whitslaid farm.

Robert Thomson: 1943 saw Bob Thomson, serving as a gunner aboard the aircraft carrier 'Premier', indeed Bob served on board this enormous vessel until December 1946 (with one small interlude to be mentioned later) when he was finally demobbed. Based at Scapa Flow, the Premier was used to escort convoys on the north Atlantic and when back in Orkney, her planes were often flying sorties against German bases in the Norwegian fjords. Bob also sailed into even more northerly waters reaching Murmansk and Archangel. Bob's other claim to fame was that whilst still serving with his Aircraft carrier he took part on the D Day landings. As an experienced bulldozer and caterpillar driver, he volunteered to man one of these machines aboard the landing craft, so that in the event of a tank or other armoured vehicle failing to start or breaking down, it could be pushed over the side and not block the other invasion vehicles or hinder the Landing Craft getting back to collect more troops. During the course of the landings Bob made three crossings without ever having to use his bulldozer.

David Murray: One of the Scotland's truly distinguished soldiers (not to mention Pipers) is Lt Col David Murray. David is not a native of Lauderdale, but he has lived in Oxton so long that he should soon be considered a native. In June 1940 David (18 years old) enlisted in the Royal Scots (Private 3058694). Three months later, as a potential officer (PO) he was transferred to the Black Watch in Perth, and eventually he was Commissioned into his family regiment the Cameron Highlanders, in which various members of his immediate kin had served.

David arrived with his battalion in India in the Spring of 1942, which was at that time preparing itself for the expected Japanese invasion. For two years they trained and waited for the action which seemed as though it would never come, but when it did, it did with a vengeance at Kohima. One of the truly decisive battles of World War Two - the Japanese who had suffered defeat for the first time, called it 'that great, bitter battle'. The battalion advanced through the jungle reaching the Irrawaddy and the bitter fighting that was involved before it could be crossed.

At the end of the war David and the Cameron Highlanders were part of the occupation force that was sent to Japan. A professional soldier whose career continued for many years, the war remains for David, in his own words: 'the supreme experience of my life'.

Helen Cranston: Helen is another incomer to Lauderdale. Her husband Bill, a Lauder man, was in the KOSB when they met in 1941, but Helen joined the ATS in 1942. After training at Newbattle Abbey and Arborfield, Berkshire, she was posted to Heavy Anti-Aircraft Artillery and spent the rest of the war helping to defend cities such as Liverpool, Southampton and then London from the V1s and V2s. She married Bill in 1944 and while in Southampton watched the convoys drive past to join their ships for the invasion of Europe. Knowing that somewhere among them was Bill, she waved to them all. After the war, once Bill was demobbed, they settled in Lauder, and it has been home ever since.

Catherine Forsyth: Yet another young woman called up in that period in the middle of the war, when the powers that be were realising that women were capable of so much more than simply 'keeping the home fires burning'. Catherine was called up in March 1942 and enlisted in the ATS. Following her six months training at Newbattle, she was posted to York where she worked in the Stores. Her work so impressed her superiors that Catherine received a Commendation for the work she had done. Eventually she returned to Scotland in 1945 (Stirling) from where she was demobbed, returning to her husband and married life up the Ettrick Valley. Catherine had been married in 1943.

Edward Fraser: A naval officer, Eddie Fraser packed a wealth of experience into a few short years; but of course that is the nature of war. Following a lengthy period of training he was appointed to HMS Lynx, based at Dover for Radar and RCM (Radio Counter Measures) duties. Operating from tunnels under Dover Castle they had command of the 12 Coastal Stations at Dungeness. The stations monitored the reception of German Radar signals which were jammed by the transmitters on site, thus preventing the enemy tracking our Channel traffic which included convoys. In June 1944, whilst on secondment to the French Navy Eddie carried out RCM duties in support of the D Day landings. In August 1944 Eddie was appointed as an RCM instructor at Funtington, near Chichester. January 1945 saw Eddie again on the move, having been appointed to the HQ of the C in C Pacific Fleet It was whilst in this appointment that the war against Japan was brought to an end with the dropping of the Atomic Bombs on Hiroshima and Nagasaki. Eddie continued serving for several more years until ill-health ended his career, but it was during this time he met his future wife, Beatrice, who was herself a nursing Officer.

John Walker: John, a veteran of The Great War (14-18) - see above, found that in 1940, the nation still had use for men like him who were now deemed too old for enlistment. So was formed the Home Guard in which John served for four years. The Home Guard, gave a home defence roll to men in reserved occupations as well as others like John, many of whom had previous war service.

Bob Aitchison – Royal Scots.

Robert Dodds Aitchison - 2nd Battalion Royal Scots. Robert was taken prisoner on Christmas Day 1941 and was a Japanese prisoner of war for three years and 11 months. He was first taken along with other prisoners, to Shinagawa prison in Hong Kong. Next two ships, the SS Lisbon Maru and the SS Kuku Maru took the prisoners to a prison of war camp in North Japan. However, disaster struck on route, the ship in front, the SS Lison Maru was torpedoed by the U.S. as it was not known to them that they were full of POWs. The prisoners in both ships were in the hold, with all escape hatches welded down, the SS Lisbon Maru was sunk with great loss of life. R. Aitchison was in the second ship the Kuku Maru and had a lucky escape.

When they eventually arrived in the prison camp in North Japan, they were forced to work in iron foundries and railways until their release. When he was liberated he was only allowed one biscuit per day for two weeks, as his stomach had shrunk so much. After two months of being looked after on an island off Hong Kong, he and the rest of the survivors of his regiment were taken to Vancouver in Canada to recover and build up their strength. They were there for six months before being taken by train across Canada, a journey that took six days and six nights, to Halifax in Canada. Then back home by ship.

Of course, there were many others who served, but those listed here simply provide us with examples of the variety of experience which has helped to shape the life of our community here in Lauderdale in the years since the end of the second major war in the 20th century.

But don't think for one moment, that the need for military service ended in 1945/46. Far from it, and whilst people like David Murray and Eddie Fraser served on, it was clear immediately that the nation's military needs required forces larger than our regular Navy, Army and Air Force could provide. So, National Service was introduced and together with the remaining regulars the nation continued to be served faithfully and well by conscripts. (The following is just another small sample):

Beatrice Fraser: (1945 -47) - Beatrice joined the Queen Alexandra's Imperial Military Nursing Service just after the end of the war, but still at a time when war-time restrictions were in place and the casualties of war still required to be cared for. As a nursing sister with the rank of Lieutenant, Beatrice was posted to Woolwich and then soon after to a hospital ship, but suffering a bout of jaundice that posting was cut short. On recovery she was posted to Naples, travelling out on a ship with four other women and five hundred men - a good time was had by all. From Naples Beatrice was sent to Venice, where she served in the British Military Hospital. There was still a great deal of suffering - and much bravery.

The next posting was Trieste, on the border between Italy and Yugoslavia, and since there was an ongoing dispute between these two countries the British military community was continually on the alert guarded by the Royal Scots. From Trieste, Beatrice was given seven days leave and it was during this leave, spent in Rome, that she met Eddie her future husband. Beatrice's service career gives a good indication of just how scattered were our servicemen. From Trieste she was posted to Udine, (still in the Italian Theatre), and from there she went to Malta. In Malta she was married and shortly afterwards returned home to be demobbed.

William Walker (1948 -50) - Bill, son of John Walker whom we met as we looked at 'The Great War' did his National Service with the Royal Air Force. With the service number 2386612 Bill did his training between West Kirby and Cosford, before being posted for the remainder of his time to RAF Cranwell. However, this clearly did not put Bill off the military life, as he enlisted in the Army Emergency

Father and Son John Walker 1914-18 K.O.S.B.
and Bill Walker 1948-50, R.A.F.

Reserve in 1954. In both 1954 and 1955 all that was required of him was that he attend two weeks at training camp, but 1956 brought a new dimension to Bill's military life - Suez! He was called up and sent to Woking for training before moving to Aldershot to await posting which eventually was earmarked for the Canal Zone. Bill remembers the mixed feelings when, as a result of a an injury sustained on the football field, he was unable to accompany his unit when they deployed.

Ian Forest (1950-1952) – Ian's National Service proved to be among the more dramatic. Having completed his apprenticeship as a motor mechanic, he was called up for 18 months (soon to be extended to 2 years) which he served with the 1st Battalion, King's Own Scottish Borderers. The Borderers were in Hong Kong, and Ian an athlete and rugby player found life quite congenial. However that was to come to an end, when the Battalion was sent into Korea. The war in Korea was relatively short, but it was vicious. Having gone ashore by landing craft at Inchon, the Borderers were faced with a major Chinese offensive which forced a withdrawal to the Imgim River, where these young conscripts held the line in the face of intense Chinese pressure. As part of the Motor Transport section responsible for moving troops and ammunition forward to the front along extremely difficult hill tracks and mined roads, Ian and his comrades also had the harrowing task of moving the wounded back to the Field Hospital. In the extremes of weather, typical of Korea - very warm in the Summer, 30 degrees below in the winter - the problems of coping were many and varied, but as usual, in war, two things happened: boys became men quickly, and friendships were established that continue to last even now, long after the war has become a distant memory.

Robert Landels (1950-52) - Rob served with the KOSB and the CAMERONIANS and as a Medic saw service in Malaya alongside the Gurkhas.

George Gilchrist (1951-1954) Whilst registering in 1951 for National Service, George volunteered to serve for an extra year, which he spent with the Royal Artillery. As a trained signaller, and later a driving instructor, George spent nearly all his time in Hong Kong, experiencing the 'joys' of a cruise for 28 days on a troopship carrying 14000 men.

George Megahy (1950s) - Serving in the Royal Air Force as a regular, provided George with a variety of interesting experiences, but, as he says, they were not always pleasant. Living in '24 man' huts with cold water for washing and shaving can be character forming, but it was hard to believe it at the time. Serving in the RAF meant that it was difficult to take weapon training and handling seriously, but as experience was to prove, in the 50s it was an essential element in service life. Having completed his training, George was sent to the Middle East, where for the next two and a half years, he was seldom without his personal weapon. From his early days in the Suez Canal Zone, George then had a number of postings in the Middle East, and the daily round of guards and duties was interspersed with more interesting assignments, including a spell on Special Duties involving working alongside Staff from the Foreign Office. At that time leave in Cyprus was a great escape from the restrictions of the Canal Zone and other areas, but, sadly, when George was finally posted to Cyprus, the EOKA troubles had broken out - the personal weapon was still his constant companion. Then it was back home. There life was duller, and you had to pay your own train fares, but at least you didn't need that constant companion!

Jim Middlemiss in Berlin – Dispatch Rider.

James Middlemiss (1952-1954) - National Servicemen had little or no say in the units to which they were attached; so perhaps Jim was not too surprised to become a Royal Scots Fusilier. The Fusiliers being the Ayrshire Regiment, would in normal times expect to recruit locally, but National Servicemen would come from all over. After his initial training at Ayr, Jim was sent to Germany (Wuppertal) where he passed his driving test. The battalion then moved to Berlin as part of the allied occupation of that city, and Jim was promoted L/Corporal and then Corporal. In the summer of 1953 Jim's ability on a motor cycle saw him qualify as an instructor, which meant that he was now in charge of the Motor Cycle Section, an appointment to which he brought the battalion some success; they were 2nd in the BAOR and 2nd in the Army championships. Then it was back to Scotland and demob.

Jim immediately joined the T.A. and rose to the rank of sergeant, and after leaving the T.A. he joined the Berwickshire Civil Defence Rescue Section, where again he experienced success, being part of the team (largely from Lauder) which won the Scottish Championship in 1959.

Stuart Allister (1952 - 1954) Stuart's naval service was essentially spent in Scotland, but during it he was able to become familiar with many of the ships which had given such sterling service during the war.

James A. M. Bell (1954-58) - Another old serviceman who remembers his number, Martin (4152391) volunteered for the Royal Air Force at the age of 17, and left Oxton in June 1954, reporting to RAF Wilmslow for 8 weeks basic training. In September 1954 he was posted to RAF Weeton to train as a Safety Equipment Worker on Parachutes. Having completed the course he was posted to Northern Ireland where he remained for 10 months. Martin was then sent to do an advanced course and following the successful completion, he was promoted and sent to RAF Kinloss where he was on standby for Suez. He remained at Kinloss until demob.

William Kellett (1956-1958) - National Service provided men with an incredible range of experiences. For 5033241 ACI Kellett W.J. it was about being constantly in the public eye! After his training Bill was posted to Uxbridge, from where he spent the next two years as part of a drill squad travelling the length and breadth of the country giving displays. This was interspersed with more serious moments like providing bearer parties for funerals - not that being part of the drill squad was anything but serious. Appearing in the Festival of Remembrance on T.V. with memories of war-time still so fresh in the public mind, must have brought a lump to the throat as the poppies were falling. For Bill, National Service was slightly different from the normal, but it introduced him to a world away from Lauderdale and the loyalty which grows among comrades.

James Falconer (1957-60) - Another of Lauder's sons who chose to serve the extra year, Jim, who had served his time as a mason, volunteered to sign up for 3 years. Enlisting in the Royal Signals, and learning to drive, Jim was sent to Germany, where so much of the army was stationed at this time. Posted to Oldenburg he was attached to the Royal Artillery and spent much of his time laying communication lines between mobile radar stations and Headquarters. Jim then had a couple of months on the fairly tedious task of water-proofing vehicles, but then was posted to HQ Baor Rheindalen, and from there just down the road to Munchengladbach. The nature of this posting provided Jim and his colleagues with a wonderful social life, between the many exercises and further educational courses in Belgium, Holland, and Germany.

As his time was coming to a close, Jim was posted back to the U.K (Chester) and there he was demobbed at the end of three happy years after which, as with so many, the comradeship of friends proved hard to replace.

Lawrence Halliday (1957 - 1959) - Another, who having completed an apprenticeship in the motor trade, found that in spite of the reputation of the military for putting square pegs in round holes, he spent two years with the Royal Air Force in various postings working within his own trade. Following his square bashing, which Lawrence admits he enjoyed, after the initial shock to the system, he was posted to RAF Boulmer in Northumberland, the largest radar station in the U.K. at that time. Working within the Motor transport section, he admits that he had a most enjoyable time. Six months at Boulmer brought a posting down to RAF Sandwich in Kent where there was constant turnover of men from RAF Auxiliary units coming through on refresher courses. At this time Lawrence was put on stand-by for Cyprus which was in the throes of the EOKA terrorist campaign, but, one could say that in typical fashion when his move did come, although it was an island to which he moved, there is a difference between Cyprus and Saxa-Vord right in the far north of Shetland. From Shetland he moved to Northern Ireland (Ballykinler) and finally back to Boulmer for demob. Like several others, Lawrence's memories of his military service are positive.

John Murray (1958-1961) - It is always interesting to wonder why certain things stay in the mind. National Service for John began the day that George Wilson, the postman, brought his call-up papers all the way up to Soutra Hill where he was working. The next memory was being dropped at the Barrack gates in Berwick to begin his spell in the KOSB. Being a dancer, he found himself performing at the Edinburgh Military Tattoo, which involved a daily journey by train to and from the city, but after only eleven weeks in Berwick John found himself in Brooke Barracks Berlin. Again his civilian interests came into play, because as soon as it was discovered that John was a motor bike enthusiast he was appointed dispatch rider. Berlin has always been a fascinating place and it was so for the young Private Murray. Travelling round the city, the Queen's Birthday Parade, Minden Day, Spandau Prison with its famous prisoner Rudolph Hess; these are all among his recollections.

Andrew Mercer (1959 - 1961) - It is amazing what a range of talents and experiences a relatively small place like Lauderdale can hide. Andrew was enlisted into the Royal Engineers and after training in the use of explosives, bridge building and demolition, he then was posted to Gibralter where for almost the remainder of his service he helped to maintain and run the diesel alternators at the back-up power station. This work was based on a shift system, so Andrew had a more organised existence than many other servicemen. Eventually, he found himself training all the new hands who were recruited to work on the engines, until ill health forced his return to the U.K. and finally a medical discharge. A premature end to a fascinating interlude in his life.

Walter Brotherston - (1960 - 1972) From Lauderdale Walter travelled, via RAF Cardington to RAF Bridgenorth for basic training. (The name Bridgenorth must conjure up a host of memories for many people, based on the number whose first military experiences were there.) Further training prepared Walter as an operations clerk in the Air Traffic Control world. His first posting after he qualified was to RAF Silloth, but only for three months, as that station was about to close, and from there he returned to Scotland - RAF Kinloss - for the remainder of his service.

Gerald Maitland-Carew (1960-1972) - A regular Army Officer, Gerald was commissioned into the 15th/19th Hussars in 1960. There he followed the life of a young Cavalry Officer working within an armoured regiment. By 1964, he had been promoted Captain, which allowed him to move into the world of Command as the ADC to the GOC 44 Division based in Dover Castle. A demanding job, Gerald honed his administrative skills to the extent that he survived in the post for three years, before returning to Regimental duties. In 1969, Gerald found that his military masters had a whole new world for him to explore; that of the Army Cadet Force, and to this end he was appointed as Officer Commanding the Cadet Training Team covering Northumberland, Cumberland and Westmoreland. In1972, Gerald got married and that coincided with a change in his family circumstances which necessitated that he resign his commission and come to live in Lauderdale.

Alistair Smith (1974 - 1998) - A member of a military family. Alistair's father Andrew, served with the TA in Lauder, in two spells between 1947 and 1963 and following this he became an instructor with the Army Cadet Force for a further 13 years, before he retired. Alistair's sister Irene, served in the Royal Military Police for 13 years, rising to Staff Sergeant, before leaving to get married to another soldier, Warrant Officer Larry Furlong of the Coldstream Guards. From that environment, it could have come as no surprise when Alistair (aged 16) decided on a military career, but perhaps his choice of service raised a few eyebrows - The Royal Navy - not the army of his father or sister. However Alistair proceeded to serve his country for 24 years reaching the rank of Chief Petty Officer, having served in a large number of ships and military theatres. His service took him in his early days from The West Indies, USA, and Canada, to the Mediterranean via Norway, all this aboard HMS Hermes. Then followed fishery protection around British waters aboard HMS Bickington. This lasted for two and a half years, but his next appointment involved very little sea time, as after an initial voyage to the West Indies, his ship (HMS Ambuscade) went in for a ten month refit.

Perhaps this was just as well as Alastair got married to Eileen at this time, and a spell ashore in Plymouth would have allowed them to get settled. Soon after the birth of his daughter Joanne, Alastair sailed for the Indian Ocean and the Persian Gulf, to be on stand by as a result of the Iran/Iraq war.

Alastair was now posted to a shore based training establishment, and so missed the Falklands War, although his comrades on the Ambuscade sailed for the South Atlantic. Alastair's next Ship (HMS Liverpool) a destroyer took him to the Falklands where they spent four months and it was during this time that his family moved back to Scotland.

Then another visit to the West Indies, before returning to Rosyth and a whole year in home waters.

January 1986 brought another six months in the South Atlantic, with a visit to Gibralter, and than was when he got news of the birth of his son Craig. On the way home they travelled via South America and the Panama Canal, arriving in Rosyth June 1986; there to meet his son for the first time.

Then followed: two and a half years in Rosyth, a trip to the United Arab Emirates to join RFA Diligence, Rosyth until August 1990, rejoin Diligence in the Gulf at the start of the Gulf War, most of two years in Northern Ireland, Rosyth until 1994, HMS Guernsey and more Fishery Protection, 1996, final eighteen months at HMS Caledonia, then discharge.

Alastair's daughter Joanne, has now joined the Royal Navy and is in her first posting as a Wren Writer in Portsmouth. So the family tradition continues.

Fraser Carmichael (1977-97) - Fraser really started his service with the Air Training Corps in 1976, when he enrolled as a civilian instructor, but it was only a year before he was commissioned into the Royal Air Force with the rank of Pilot Officer. The following years saw him work with young people with various courses and promotions in between until he was appointed Commander of 2496 ATC squadron, Glasgow and Western Wing, in 1986; followed by his appointment as Wing Staff Officer in 1992 at Wing Headquarters, Glasgow. Fraser retired from this most rewarding service in 1997, before coming to live in Lauderdale.

Stuart Thomson (1979-1983) - We have already met Stuart's father Bob, and perhaps it was his father's wartime experience that persuaded Stuart to join the Merchant Navy in 1979. His first ship was the cruise ship Oriana, working in the South Pacific out of Sydney. After eight months the Oriana came home to Southampton and the cruising continued in the Mediterranean. After that Stuart served in various tankers, cargo ships, etc. He joined the Royal Fleet Auxiliary, whose ships tended to be crewed by merchant navy personnel. So it was that the RFA called him up in March 1982 at the beginning of the Falklands crisis. Stuart joined RFA Fort Grange - a supply ship.

In mid April they sailed for the South Atlantic, and on arrival off the Falklands supplied the Naval ships anchored it San Carlos Bay. During this time they were subject to constant air attacks during daylight hours, but because the bombers were avoiding the Rapier Missile Batteries the bombs did not always have time to get primed before they hit the ships; hence no ships were actually sunk while Stuart was there.

A week before the final push, they left San Carlos in order to supply the ships in the open sea, although by this time their holds were nearly empty. Luckily, the Argentineans surrendered on the 15th June. Stuart was involved in the rescue of a helicopter crew which had to ditch in the sea, and during this operation he suffered a neck injury, which eventually meant that he was flown home. Stuart left the Merchant Navy in January 1983.

Much of the preceding illustrates that the end of hostilities in 1945 did not bring the longed for peace to the world. From 1945 until the end of the century, in only one year were British troops not involved in operations in one place or another. Our servicemen and women have been involved in a whole catalogue of conflicts and just to illustrate the point, in so-called "peace time", The Kings Own Scottish Borderers, to name but one regiment have been involved in Palestine, Korea, Egypt, Malaya, Borneo, Aden, Northern Ireland and the Gulf War.

The 20th century is over! It opened with war and continued in war! Let us pray that the 21st century will truly herald a period of "peace in our time" and thus allow each generation to enjoy the tranquillity of Lauderdale which is their heritage.

A list of the Fallen

The Great War 1914 - 1918

MAJOR	The Hon A. H. Maitland	Camerons
2nd LIEUT	Robert Logan	K.O.S.B.
L/SGT.	John Joyce	Royal Scots
CPL.	William Allan	Gordons
CPL.	James D. Bruce	A.S.C.
CPL.	Alexander P. Kelly	Royal Scots
CPL.	Robert Oliver	Scottish Rifles
L/CPL	William Halliday	H.L.I.
L/CPL.	William Lockie	Camerons
L/CPL.	William Todd	K.O.S.B.
PTE.	George Anderson	Gordons
PTE.	Andrew Anderson	K.O.S.B.
PTE.	Robert F. Anderson	Dragoon Guards
PTE.	James Anderson.	K.O.S.B.
PTE.	William Bell	K.O.S.B.
PTE.	John Brodie	Australians
PTE.	William Brown	K.O.S.B.
SAP.	Andrew Bruce	Royal Engineers
PYE.	George Bruce	Scots Guards
PTE.	Thomas Bruce	Scots Guards
PTE.	John Coultherd	Camerons
PTE.	Thomas R. Dickson	Scots Guards
PTE.	Adam Fleming	KO.S.B.
PTE.	Andrew Guthrie	K.O.S.B.
PTE.	John Galbraith	KO.S.B.
SAP.	George Halliday	Royal Engineers
PTE.	David Hardie	A.&.S.H.
PTE.	John Hopkirk	K.O.S.B.
PTE.	Alexander Hunter	Canadians
PTE.	William Hunter	K.O.S.B.
PTE.	Andrew Kelly	Royal Scots Fusiliers
PTE.	John Kinnon	K.O.S.B.
PTE.	James Laidlaw	H.L.l.
PTE.	William Mauchline	K.O.S B.
PTE.	William Middlemiss	Royal Scots
PTE.	Thomas Moore	Canadians
PTE.	Thomas Nisbet	R.A.M.C.

PTE.	William Noble	Rifle Brigade
PTE.	Robert H. Robertson	Lancashire Fusiliers
PTE.	Alexander Rutherford	K.O.S.B.
PTE.	Adam Scott	K.O.S.B.
SAP.	Armour Scott	Royal Engineers
PTE.	Adam Skeldon	A.&.S.H.
PTE.	James Stevenson	KO.S.B.
PTE.	John Stuart	Seaforths
PTE.	John James Todd	Canadians
PTE.	William Torrie	Australians
PTE.	George White	K.O.S.B.
PTE.	John White	K.O.S.B.
PTE.	James Welsh	K.O.S.B.

World War II 1939 - 1945

LIEUT.	Donald A. Bird	R.A.M.B.
CAPT.	David Colville	K.O.S.B.
MAJOR	John Elliot MC	KO.S.B.
A.B. SEAMAN	Thomas Norman Elliot	R.N.
SGT.	Gordon Hodge	R.A.F.
LIEUT.	Viscount Ivor C. Maitland	Lothian & Borders Horse
FLT/SGT.	James Mercer	R.A.F.
PTE.	Ian Mercer	Cameronians
CAPT.	George N McDougal	Royal Engineers
Chief Petty Officer	Hector McDonald	R.N.
L/CPL.	Thomas Redpath	Royal Scots
L/CPL.	George B. Redpath	Royal Scots
Piper	Leslie Ross	K.O.S.B.
Pilot Officer	Robert Watson	R.A.F.

H.M.S. Lauderdale.

HMS Lauderdale, seen on the day of her commissioning Decemder 24th 1941, was the only Hunt to cross the Atlantic for trials with the Royal Canadian Navy during February 1942.

HMS Lauderdale joined the Western Approaches Command and the 20th Escort group briefly in early 1942, but on February 16th, 1942 she sailed from Londonderry accompanied by the destroyer Caldwell on being allocated to the Western Local Escort Force at St. Johns, Newfoundland. She arrived at St. Johns on February 21st, 1942, and Halifax three days later. HMS Lauderdale then acted as a local escort between Halifax and St. Johns for the next month, escorting convoys SC72, ON70 and SC75 during that period. It is assumed that Lauderdale was under trial by the Royal Canadian Navy as an alternative to the pre-war destroyers and Town Class vessels then on loan to the RCN. Nothing came of this trial; the Hunts were probably rejected becaue of their lack of endurance.

She returned to Londonderry on March 30th, 1942 and after a further period with the Western Approaches Command she transferred on patrol and escort duties to the Rosyth Escort Force until February 1943. After refitting between February and March 1943, HMS Lauderdale made passage to the Mediterranean where she was allocated to the 60th destroyer division at Malta until mid 1944. She participated in the blockade of Cape Bon in May 1943, the invasion of Sicily and the invasion of the South of France in August 1944. By this time HMS Lauderdale had joined the 5th Destroyer Flotilla at Alexandria with which she served until the war's end.

After briefly returning to the UK to give leave, HMS Lauderdale was on passage to refit at Simonstown when the Japanese War ended. However, the refit proceeded and on its completion in January 1946, she returned to the Mediterranean.

HMS Lauderdale was surveyed during March 1946 and was transferred on loan to the Royal Hellenic Navy on May 5th 1946 as the "Aigaion". She was to serve with the Greeks until September 1959 when approval was given to dispose of her locally and she was finally discarded by the Greeks on December 12th 1959.

Officers and N.C.O.'s of Lauder and Oxton Home Guard – 1939-40.

Members of the Lauderdale A.R.P.

Oxton Memorial Hall – built 1924.

Blainslie in the 20th Century

The beginning of the 20th. century was a bad time weatherwise and also for epidemics. Entries in the Blainslie School Log Books state that in 1901 the weather was so severe that all roads to the village were blocked by snow, and that very few pupils were able to reach the school. In 1907 influenza, which was a very serious disease in those days, struck the Blainslie area. It was followed by a period of intense cold, during which the Blainslie school inside thermometer registered below freezing point, and at Chapel some thirty degrees of frost was recorded. Also in 1911 there was a serious outbreak of whooping cough in the district which seriously affected school attendance.

Throughout World War I, the tempo of life in the area hardly altered except for official pressure to grow more food. The main incident locally was that in 1915, the rather cumbersome village well arrangement of windlass and bucket was replaced by a hand operated pump, the handle of which was forged by Jim Park, the blacksmith, with his name on it.

Some two years later, severe weather was again experienced with heavy falls of snow, and intensely cold temperatures were registered with ten degrees of frost inside Blainslie school, and thirty degrees of frost outside. Then in 1918, the Roxburghshire Medical Officer of Health, Dr. Oliver, closed Blainslie school for a fortnight because of another severe outbreak of influenza.

Following the Depression some two years after the end of World War l, the population in the Blainslie area decreased sharply; with many families leaving to seek work elsewhere, or to emigrate overseas. This situation is reflected in the schoolmaster's comments in the Blainslie School Log Book for 1900 that *"large numbers of children have left the district"*. Whereas in 1900, there had been 80 enrolled pupils, by 1922, the Blainslie school population had fallen to 38.

1922 was also notable for the retirement of Mr. Bennett, the schoolmaster. According to a report in the Southern Reporter newspaper, Mr. Bennett's teaching career at Blainslie school had spanned some thirty-eight years. At his retirement ceremony, he was presented by the Rev. W. McConnachie of Lauder with a smoking cabinet on behalf of the Church congregation, and at Blainslie, Mr. and Mrs. Bennett were presented with easy chairs. It is evident that Mr. Bennett must have been something of an institution, as he was also the Registrar of Births, Marriages and Deaths, and his advice, which was always sound, was much sought after on a wide variety of subjects.

Undoubtedly he was a very good schoolmaster, who supplemented the usual school curriculum with vocational subjects such as carpentry for the boys and cooking and knitting for the girls, as he realised that these subjects would be useful to them in later life. Some of his teaching methods might not be looked upon with favour today, but they did produce results. At least one pupil's memory of Mr.

Bennett is a painful one, since Mr. J. S. Riddell still remembers the "ruler hammering" he got for not answering a question quickly enough.

Prior to 1925, the young Blainslie folk used to foregather at the "roadend" to talk among themselves, or to dance to a melodeon. Dances were also held in the old barn now demolished, and the older residents took part in amateur theatricals.

The year 1925 was notable In the Blainslie area because of the provision of a Village Hall. The ground on which it stands was obtained on feu from the Earl of Lauderdale, and was vested in five Life Trustees who at that time were Thomas Lambie, John Lambie, George Hume, James Little, and George Halliday. Mr. Fairholme of Chapel gifted a wooden galvanised iron clad Hall which was constructed on the site, and a Committee working to a Village Hall Constitution administered its use. The Blainslie Village Hall Constitution is an interesting document in that it, like some of the Smithy House Title Deeds, refers to Blainslie not as a township but as Blainslie village.

From then on the Village Hall became a popular venue for public meetings, weddings, carpet bowling matches in which a Blainslie team participated in a Bowling League, whist drives, and many other local activities.

Miss Elizabeth Park, then residing in Blainslie Village took an active part in the running of the Village Hall, and remembered three Presidents of the Blainslie Branch of the W.R.I., viz. Mrs. Cowan and Mrs. Gibb both of the Roan, and Mrs. Hume of Blainslie, after which the branch ceased to function.

It should be mentioned that Mrs. Gibb's husband, Mr. Shirra Gibb of the Roan used to ride along the various rights of way in the Blainslie area each year to ensure that they were kept open. Lieut. Col. F.R.C. Stewart of Middle Blainslie followed a similar practice.

The cottages down the lane, continued to be uninhabited, and eventually became ruinous. Miss Betty Riddell of Blainslie recalls that the first cottage was known as "The Washhouse" as it was used for that purpose by the ladies of the village, and that as a child she played at "Houses" in it. By 1935 the cottages had become dangerous to life, and they and the adjoining barn, were demolished by the District Council. Mr. J. Halliday of the Borders Regional Council's Road Works Department remembers as a child being driven by his father in the cab of a Foden Steam Engine which hauled a trailer filled with rubble from the demolished cottages and barn to a site on the present A68 trunk road at Red Tile cottage where the debris was used in a road widening scheme. The Fodon Steam Engine must have been in great demand by the children since both Miss Betty Riddell and Mrs. W. Brotherston of Blainslie remember being given a "hurl" on it.

By 1950, only some twenty pupils were attending Blainslie School, a sign that the Blainslie community was beginning to decay, and by 1966, the school had closed, the remaining pupils being taken by special bus to Melrose and Galashiels schools. The following list of school teachers at Blainslie school during the 20th. century may not be complete as numerous changes occurred in teaching personnel during the last years of the school's life;

Mr. Alex. W. Bennett 1884-1922

Miss J. N. McKinnon 1922-1928

Miss M. I. Watt 1929-1938

Miss G. M. Erskine 1938~1938*

Miss J. Roup 1939-1951

Mr. W.H.P. Ramage 1951-1965

* This teacher died suddenly after 16 years service with the Roxburghshire Education Department.

In the early 20th. century, the basis of the Blainslie economy was still an agricultural one, with the farmers depending either on family help, or itinerant local labour or at harvest time particularly on Irish workers. Miss Elizabeth Park remembered that many of the Irish workers came to Blainslie year after year, and that they were very honest and hard working. Most of them were illiterate and she used to help them by writing letters home to their families in Ireland; she could recollect many of the names of the Irish Post Offices to which she addressed the letters. She also wrote to other farmers in Scotland and England for whom they tied contracted to do harvest work. Miss Park also made them small leather purses to hold the gold coin in which their wages were paid. They told her that without this money their families would have starved to death the following winter.

The farming communities consisted of Upper Blainslie (800 acres), Sunnybrae (87 acres), Old Blainslie (19 acres), Nether Blainslie (200 acres), New Blainslie (312 acres), Middle Blainslie (97 acres), South Blainslie (42 acres), Bluecairn (300 acres), Jeaniefield (250 acres), and Chapel Mains (300 acres). The actual acreages of the farms varied from time to time as the smallholdings were absorbed into the larger farms, or were split up. These farms continued under various owners, and to meet the economic conditions of the times, they gradually became highly mechanised. One effect of this was to cause the water and horse mills to fall into disuse. These were first replaced for a period by mobile threshing machines or combine harvesters which went round the various farms on contract, until such equipment was bought by the farmers for their own use. The horse mill at Nether Blainslie was in situ although not working, until 1972 when it was demolished. The lintel stone dated 1763 has been incorporated in an external wall at "Blain". Mr. J.S. Riddell remembers as a child being given a ride on one of the two horses that worked inside supplying the motive power for the mill.

In general the various Blainslie farmers now concentrate on raising sheep and cattle, and growing their own cattle and sheep feed and bedding straw, all of which are harvested by modern farming machinery to cut down labour costs. Barley and oats, and sometimes potatoes are grown as cash crops. In addition ponies are bred and exhibited by Lady Daphne Stewart (Middle Blainslie), and Mrs. R.E. Chaplin (Netherfield), and police dogs by Mrs. C.P. Fairbairn (Fordswell).

As regards the two blacksmith businesses in Blainslie village at the turn into the 20th. century, time was beginning to run out for them because adaption to new conditions was more difficult than in other trades. One factor which must have affected the amount of their work was the steady decline in the number of horses used on farms in the district, and this is reflected in the Agricultural Returns for Melrose parish which may be taken as typical for the Blainslie area. These returns show that over a long period, the number of farm horses in work had been steadily decreasing, viz. 410 horses in 1894, 365 in 1905, 297 in 1926, and 261 in 1933. This situation worsened as mass produced tractors and trailers came onto the market, together with new farming implements and machinery from new factories, and backed by a spare part replacement service. By the 1930s, the smithy run by Jim Park "down the lane" had ceased to operate. Finally the other smithy at the Smithy House, closed down in 1952 when the last horse to be shoed there was led away by Mr. Turnbull, the blacksmith. One can speculate that if the blacksmiths could have held on until the current revival in horse riding associated with the Lauder Common Riding and hunting activities had occurred, and oxyacetylene welding had been adopted for certain aspects of their work, then these highly skilled businesses would still be operating in Blainslie village today. Undoubtedly other factors contributed to their demise, the main one being that the blacksmiths themselves were elderly and reluctant to change their techniques, and that there were no young men sufficiently interested in the art to come forward and take over from them.

In contrast the joinery and sawmill business in the village has managed to cope with the changing economic conditions and has survived. Following the death of William Scott, the business passed to his relations, the Riddell family who have carried on the business until the present day. According to some of the Cash Books of the business that have survived, the firm concentrated in the early part of the present century in the manufacture of gigs and carts, the wheels being tyred by the local blacksmiths. According to Miss Elizabeth Park, she remembered helping the smiths by pouring water onto the heated iron tyres so that on cooling they would contract onto the wooden wheel rims. The gigs, carts and wheels were then gaily decorated by a painter, a Mr. Wilkinson, in the Paint Workshop. Apparently the Blainslie gigs were noted for the soundness of their construction, and orders were received for them from as far away as London. Also it is understood that a small amount of simple kitchen furniture was made, and a few examples have survived.

With the advent of the motor cycle, motor car, lorries, tractors and trailers, gigs and carts went out of fashion, and as a consequence the Blainslie joinery business changed over to the production of farm gates, feeding troughs and general jobbing work. After World War II, Mr. J. S. Riddell mechanised the sawmill and joinery workshop. The sawmill had previously been powered by a marine engine, the chimney for the boiler of which still stands, then by a tractor, and finally by an electric motor. Similarly electrical power was used to operate the workshop machinery such as band saws, planers, mortise jointers, etc. The farm gates and other products continue to be in great demand, and are sold as far away as Wooler in Northumberland. This joinery business is an excellent example of a small family business which through skill and foresight has been able to meet the challenge of changing social and economic conditions in the 20th. century.

This the commercial enterprises in the village were unable to do for any length of time, and the business which survived the longest was the grocery shop run first by Robina Park (1838-1918), and then by her niece Elizabeth Park. The fact that it was able to survive until the 1940s was due to the high standard of personal service given, and by the wide range of stock that was carried. Mr. J. S. Riddell has stated that the shop was very popular, and he remembers the patient queues that formed from time to time outside the shop. Miss Elizabeth Park stressed in conversation that an external seat was provided for the convenience of waiting customers.

Apparently the shop catered for a great deal of passing traffic, and it was quite usual for flocks of sheep to be halted at the road, whilst the drovers went into the shop to buy a pint of ale to be consumed off the premises; the shop operated on an Off Licence basis for the selling of beer. Similarly the shop was patronised by the local blacksmiths and joiners who found their trades thirsty work. With the advent of motorised grocery vans coming into the village from Lauder and elsewhere for custom, the village grocery business was unable to meet the competition, and with the declining population in the Blainslie area, the shop closed down.

By the 1920s, most of the old Blainslie families had moved away. Fortunately we are able to know something about the Blainslie residents in the first part of the 20th. century because of the existence of a booklet entitled "Gala and its Tributaries", written by a Mr. Eckford, in which he gives very brief but colourful comments about the village worthies, and from which the following extracts are taken;

"Jock Carruthers, the blacksmith, was ever forthright in his speech, his verbal thrusts straight from the shoulder, whereas the other blacksmith, Jim Park, was more cautious, quieter, and more discreet. Wullie Scott and his nephews the Riddells were a feature of the workshop, the outside of which was strewn with wheels and carts. "Wullie" was quiet and reflective, and carefully weighed up the pros and cons on any subject before expressing an opinion. He kept aloof from the debating scene, but all agreed that he was the unofficial "Provost" of the hamlet. An Elder and a staunch Free churchman with unshakable religious convictions, "Wullie" Scott always struck one as being of the same stuff of which the Covenanting Martyrs were made". (Unless Mr. Eckford knew about "Willie" Scott's ancestor, Alexander Scott who featured in the Covenanting troubles at Blainslie, this surely must have been an inspired comment on his part). *"Only illness kept him away from his place of worship. I could always picture him and his relatives in the gig making for Lauder Free Church on a Sunday morning".*

Mr. J.S. Riddell of Blainslie states that "Wullie" Scott was of a very large physique, with the largest feet of anyone in the district, and he was also reputed to be the richest man in the immediate countryside around Blainslie. Miss Elizabeth Park was able to add to the foregoing in that the Riddells and Scotts were United Presbyterian Church members in contrast to herself who was Free Church, commenting that she walked to and from Lauder every Sunday to attend religious worship, and that baptisms were usually performed in the houses in Blainslie.

Continuing Mr. Eckford's comments which are unfortunately too brief, *"There were the Lambies, the village farmers, quiet and unassuming, and George Pringle with his smallholding, always rearing a calf or two. He had a sort of reflected fame for was he not the uncle of the stalwart M.P., W.M.R. Pringle, the famous Parliamentary critic during the last war. Jack Little was always so polite and genial".*

Mr. Eckford also mentions Miss Robina Park, and Miss Elizabeth Park and their grocery store, and the "Schulemaister", Mr. Bennett. How delightful are these word pictures, recapturing for posterity, the attitudes and personalities of those Blainslie folk in the past.

Over the years a number of environmental improvements have taken place in the Blainslie area. Possibly the most important was the provision of sewers for Blainslie village round about 1961, the cost being borne by the Scottish Home and Health Department. This involved the laying of 1,930 lineal yards of 6" fireclay sewers, and the building of sedimentation tanks of 2,000 gallons capacity in the Kitty Burn gulley, designed for a population of 40 people. This improvement did away with outside "privies", and must have improved greatly health and amenity in the village. The surrounding Blainslie farms still continue to operate cesspits. At much the same time running water was provided from the Berwickshire Water Mains. According to a 1936 Valuation Roll for the area, a refuse dump was operated in the vicinity of the Blainslie School playground, but in 1961, a direct refuse disposal service was instituted with a weekly collection of refuse using the Langlee Incinerator Unit.

In 1976. the Standing Library in the Village Hall was replaced by a Mobile Library carrying some 3,000 books which visits the Blainslie area every fortnight. With the provision of new road signs, it was decided to formalise the name of the village as "Blainslie"; the additional posting on the A68 Trunk Road is particularly good, although improvements on other main roads are needed. The street through the village is swept mechanically at intervals. and street lighting may be introduced in the near future, when more local government money becomes available. Supplementing the school buses is a Minibus Courier service which has been introduced linking Lauder with Galashiels via Blainslie village at very reasonable fares, and has proved very useful for those folk without transport of their own. The service joins up with other routes throughout the Borders Region.

As regards local government electoral representation, Lieut. Col. F.R.C. Stewart of Middle Blainslie served on the old Roxburgh County Council for many years. In 1975, prior to Regionalisation, at a Public Meeting in Blainslie Hall, it was decided that the Blainslie community should be served by the Lauder Provisional Community Council, the first of its kind to be set up in Scotland, voluntarily in advance of the new legislation. Following a local election, Mr. R.D. Runciman and Col. W.H. Oliver were elected to the new council. When the Lauderdale Community Council was inaugurated on the introduction of Regionalisation, Col. W.H. Oliver served on it, and also as Editor of its "News Sheet". Mr. W. Hall represented the Blainslie area as a co-opted member. In 1979, the Blainslie area was incorporated into the Lauder electoral constituency for District Council purposes as a result of various electoral boundary changes. At this time the Ettrick and Lauderdale District Councillor for the Blainslie area was Mr. W. Hardie of Lauder, and its Borders Regional Councillor was Mr. J. Logan McDougal, Blythe, Lauder.

Returning now to the local population, during the latter part of the 19th. century onwards, many Blainslie folk were buried in the Lauder new cemetery, and the following gravestone inscriptions for past Blainslie residents have been noted;

"George Noble died Blainslie, 4.7.1930, aged 79 years, and his wife…died 13.2.1920, aged 64 years".

"Adam Dagg, farmer, Upper Blainslie, died 31.11.1969, aged 64, and his wife Agnes Young who died 14.10.1972"

"George Fairbairn who died at Sunnybrae, Upper Blainslie on 15.7.1954, aged 6…".

"Erected by James Park, grocer of Blainslie in memory of his wife, Jessie Haig, who died at Blainslie, 18.12.1820 aged 84, James Park died at Blainslie 12…18…aged 87, and third daughter Robina Park who died at Blainslie, 7.3.1918, in her 85th. year"

"Ralph Broomfield sometime of Nether Blainslie who died at Leith, 13.6.1882".

"James Dick who died at Wineburgh, Blainslie on 20.2.1922 aged 82, and third daughter Mary Dick who died a Wineburgh on 14.8.1941, aged 78".

"Margaret Fairgrieve, wife of William Scott, joiner, Blainslie who died 19.10.1895, aged 57, and his second wife Elizabeth Hume who died 24.5.1912, aged 57".

"James Hall of New Blainslie, farmer, died on 15.12.1928 aged 63, and his wife Mary Aitchison who died 30.10.1949, aged 85"

"Andrew Weir Hume of Jeaniefield died 2.5.1970, aged 49".

"David S. Hume, farmer, Nether Blainslie, who died 21.3.1929 aged 71. George Lothian Hume, farmer, died 1.11.1946, aged 56, and Mary…Weir died 20.7.1965, aged 71".

"Mary Smith wife of Thomas Hume who died at Jeaniefield on 24.1.1924 aged 53. Thomas Hume, farmer, died 31.10.1939, aged 72. John Hume died at Jeaniefield…aged 65".

"John Little, died Wineburgh, 24.2.1930 aged 68".

"Richard Park who died at Wineburgh, Blainslie on 12.9.1885 aged 45 years".

"William Scott Riddell born Blainslie 30.3.1891, died 30.7.1969 at Maxton, aged 78"

Some of the Blainslie inhabitants are buried well away from their old homes, viz.

At Jedburgh, a gravestone indicates that James Lunn of Upper Blainslie died at Otterburn on 30.8.1908, aged 59, and his wife Janet Linton died 19.2.1933, aged 79. Also Agnes eldest daughter of James Lunn died 4.8.1944, and Ellen Hall Ord wife of R.G. Lunn died 7.3.1938, aged 62.

At Ednam a gravestone is inscribed to the effect that Thomas Brown of South Blainslie died 13.9.1809 aged 75, and Isabel Cairns his wife died 6.4.1814, aged 74.

In the case of one Martin of Blainslie descendant buried in the North of Scotland, Blainslie earth was scattered over the grave.

As regards the old burying ground at Upper Blainslie, apparently the old gravestones were taken up by a former owner of Upper Blainslie, and used as foundation material for a steading at Woodheads farm. Whether any of the inscriptions were still legible is not known, but if they were then some of the information about Blainslie people in the past has been lost for ever since the Melrose registers are deficient in burial data, and civil registration of deaths did not commence until 1855.

Sometime prior to 1960, the Blainslie area was transferred from the ecclesiastical parish of Melrose to that of Lauder, and in consequence its residents came under the pastoral care of Lauder Old Parish Church, and its Minister and Kirk Session.

The Village hall continues to serve the Blainslie community as a venue for Coffee Mornings, Xmas and other Children's parties, Public Meetings, and for meetings of the Young Farmers Club Langshaw when the hall there was demolished.

Despite the many difficulties under which the Blainslie farmers are labouring, they continue to manage efficiently and to improve their farms, and together with the other Blainslie businesses, contribute to the prosperity of the Blainslie area. An upturn in population with the arrival of new families and new babies, the Blainslie community is taking on a new lease of life in the closing quarter of the 20th. century.

Blainslie Reel Club

The Club was started 17 years ago at the request of several people who wanted to learn of re-learn the popular Scottish Country Dances for Balls, Dances and Weddings. Robert and Marjory Hamilton were known to do a lot of Scottish Country Dancing and Robert was persuaded to tackle the job.

This quickly attracted those who wanted to learn much more that the basics and is as popular as ever. There are seldom less than two sets and unusually, a good proportion of men.

After a year or two John Bowie Dickson, a famous dance deviser, presented the Club with *The Blainslie Reel* and one of the members composed an appropriately named tune *The Winding Road to Blanslie*.

Tim Stead

Tim Stead was born in 1952 in Cheshire. As a student he studied sculpture at Trent Polytechnic and Glasgow School of Art, where he developed his life-long passion for creating sculpture and furniture using natural materials.

While studying for a post-graduate diploma at Glasgow School of art in 1976 he met his wife Maggy Lenert, a language graduate who was working as a language assistant in Langside College.

In 1979 Tim fitted out the visionary Café Gandolfi in Glasgow, Tim's first large-scale commission.

After living in Glasgow for 2 years, Tim and Maggy moved to the Borders, first to Monteviot Estates near Jedburgh. In 1980 Tim bought the old farmhouse from Weir Hume and they moved in with their children Sam and Emma. The house and workshop lay at the heart of Tim's family life and work. After 20 years the house has developed into an enormous and constantly evolving artwork. Tim loved Blainslie and its surroundings; he was a very popular member of the community.

After a decade of using hardwoods to create sculpture and furniture, Tim began to feel increasingly strongly about trying to put something back, and conceived the 'Axes for Trees' project in 1986. Tim made a sculptured wooden axe head for each day in 1986, raising money to contribute towards the purchase of Scotland's first community woodland at Wooplaw. These woods are now well established, and function as a role model for other community woodlands, as well as creating a natural backdrop for wide range of community activities. The success of the Borders Community Woodlands led to the creation of the Borders Forest Trust and Woodschool, based on Monteviot Estate. Tim was a director of the Woodschool and a Trustee of Borders Forest Trust, and in 1999 was awarded an MBE for his contribution to national woodland restoration and community participation.

Internationally famed for his sculpture and furniture, Tim made a throne for the visit of Pope John II to Scotland in 1982; the lectern, communion table and chairs for the North Sea Oil Memorial Chapel in Aberdeen in 1989; a reconstruction in wood of Skara Brae house for the McLellan Gallery in 1990. In 1993 Tim exhibited the Botanic Ash at Edinburgh Botanic Garden, a celebration of a 200-year old ash tree.

The Botanic Ash exhibition was a follow-up in a big scale of a similar local project, the Blainslie Ash, that Tim had realized from an ash tree belonging to Mr Runciman, from Upper Blainslie.

His last project was the creation of the Millennium Clock for the Royal Museum in Edinburgh, a collaborative project with Russian artist Eduard Bersudsky (who lived in Blainslie in Scott Riddell's cottage from 95-97), Jürgen Tübbecke, a clock maker who lived in Galashiels at the time and now has a shop in Peebles, Annica Sandström, from Lindean Mill Glass.

Tim died on 21 April 2000 and is buried in his beloved Wooplaw wood.

The village blacksmith at Blainslie shoes a horse in 1909.

A History of Whitslaid Tower

Having lived nearly all my life on Whitslaid farm, the Tower, overlooking the River Leader, has always been an important part of my life. I often played in it as a child, which was possibly dangerous, but didn't seem so at the time. Immediately after the war ended in 1945 the late H.H. Cowan of The Roan expressed an interest in the tower's history. He was a very keen member of the Berwickshire Naturalist's. Club, and so was ideally placed to do research. Some of the material in the following pages comes from letters and conversations, which he exchanged with members of our family over the years.

Letters between H.H. Cowan and R.F. Mercer.

To

Mr R F Mercer

Whitslaid Farm

Lauder

The Roan 28 Feb 1945

Dear Mr Mercer

I noticed the other day that a large part of the Whitslaid Peel Tower had fallen on the north side. Can you tell me on what date it happened and whether it was all at one time or has been going on for a while, and also the probable cause if you know it.

I am not sure if it is on the Office of Works list of Ancient Monuments, but I will have to report it to them. It has of course been in a ruinous state for many years, but as it has an ancient history way back to John Balliol it would be a pity if it were to disappear all together without some record of it being recorded. There is a long description of it in a volume of the 'Transactions of the Berwickshire Naturalist Club' when it was visited by the members in 1886.

Sincerely

H. Hargreaves Cowan

To

H.H. Cowan Whitslaid 1 March 1945

Dear Mr Cowan

Whitslaid peel tower fell down on the morning of 9th February, it all fell at once. I think the cause was rabbits undermining the gable as there had been a crack in it for many years, which was always getting wider, the ivy roots and dirt would also help to widen it, then of course the frost would make it worse. I enclose a plan, which one of our visitors got for me which I would like returned. I was also wondering if there would be any chance of reading the article on Whitslaid Tower in the Transactions of the Club.

Yours sincerely

R.F. Mercer.

To

R.F. Mercer

The Roan Friday 2 March 1945

Dear Mr Mercer

Many thanks for the document you sent which I now return. I have made a copy of it and also of the plan. The reports of the tower are contained in three volumes of the 'Transactions' so I thought the best way would be to copy them out (and I enclose them also) as the books themselves are a bit bulky. The late James Craw made an index of all the interesting things in the volumes, but these three are the only references I can find. I hope they will be of interest.

The reference to the space of ground or 'platform for a landowner's garden in the warlike times' remind me that at one period of time when my wife and I were searching for a place to lay our heads. That platform came into the picture as a possible site to build upon, but the delay by the lawyer in coming to a decision about repairing the old wooden bridge knocked our plans on the head. I think it would have made an ideal site all the same. Kind regards and best thanks for telling me about the collapse of the wall.

Sincerely

H.H. Cowan

Whitslaid Tower was reputed to have been built by William Lawder, who came to Scotland with Malcolm Canmore in the twelfth century. Many of the same name held high office in the golden age of the medieval times which lasted from David I, to Alexander III. it is also stated that Robert Lawder joined with William Wallace at Musselburgh, and fought with distinction at the battle of Stirling Bridge in 1297.

When the Commissioners of peace met at Newcastle in 1325, Sir Robert de Layered appeared for Robert the Bruce, as Elder, Justiciaire of Lothian and Sheriff of Berwick. A Justicaire acted as a viceroy in the absence of the King, with special authority in courts of law. He was also present at the battle of Halidon Hill in 1333, but as that battle was fought on foot it was unlikely that he would have taken an active part.

In Pre-reformation rolls the name appears variously as Lawedir, Loweder and Lawdir. Half of the fulling, or cloth making mill, at Lauder and half of the Mains of Lauder, formerly the property of Sir John Balliol (Toom Tabard) was granted to Alan de Layered in 1371. It included Lauder Tower, which remained in the family until 1633. By 1792 the tower at Lauder had disappeared, all that Sir Andrew Dick Lauder found then was a few stones, one of them bearing part of the family arms. This was a shield with a red background bearing a Griffin. This stone is now built into the attic of a house near Heriot in Gala Water, which belonged to the family at that time. Lauder Tower was situated to the southeast of the present Lauder church, which was built by the first, and only, Duke of Lauderdale in 1673, because he felt that the old church was too near to Thirlestane Castle It is more than probable that he used the stone from the tower for the construction of the church. Tower House, in Mill Wynd, is reputed to be built on its site.

Around 1438 William Lauder was Bishop of Glasgow and Chancellor of Scotland, and was a representative of Scotland to arrange a treaty with the English. At the same time his brother Alexander was Bishop of Dunkeld. In 1583 Whitslaid Tower appears as in the hands of Gilbert Lawder.

Whitslaid tower is built on a high point overlooking the River Leader, so that it could keep a lookout up or down stream. Built mainly of local stone it was three stories high with a stone arched ground floor. The walls, at ground level are seven feet thick, covering an area of thirty-two feet by forty feet. Two flights of stairs are contained inside the east and south walls. The north wall, which had a large fireplace and chimney on the first floor, collapsed on February 9th 1945, possibly after having been undermined by rabbits and pushed out by frost.

Around the start of the last century the then Laird, Lady Reay, put her own preservation order on the tower after finding men quarrying the walls for road making. The highest wall is now about twenty five feet. The last known resident of the tower, George Montgomerie died in 1689. He was buried in Legerwood churchyard and the tower was afterwards abandoned.

From about 1830 Whitslaid Tower was in the possession of Carolside Estate and, in the lettings, was listed, like the shootings and woods, as "the express property of the Landlord". In 1959 Sir John Gilmour sold Whitslaid farm, and Tower, to the then tenant, Robert F Mercer. In 1990 the farm was sold to Mr Douglas Younger of Chapel on Leader.

Maybe, some time in the future, someone with vision, and money, will restore Whitslaid Tower to something of its former glory.

Previous known Tenants over the years 1830? to present day.

Robert Lyle to 1850 went to Greenknowe, Gordon

James Harper 1850 to 1880 went to Fordel Mains, Dalkeith

Simon Hunter 1880 to 1900 emigrated to Canada

Inch 1900 to 1910 returned to Echline

James Mercer 1910 to 1927 succeeded by son Robert

Robert Mercer 1929 to 1959 bought farm from Carolside Estate

R. F. Mercer & Sons 1959 to 1973 Robert Mercer died succeeded by

Alex Mercer 1973 to 1990 farm sold November to

Douglas Younger 1990 to present day (October 2000)

Whitslaid Roads & Bridges

In the early eighteenth century the network of roads in the area was very different to that of today. The road from Kelso to the north through Lauderdale ran by Legerwood crossing the Boondreigh burn near its junction with the River Leader, thence to the High Cross and Norton House and beyond. From Purveshaugh a road branched off over Kelso Hill, and on by way of the stone arch bridge at Galadean to the Blainslies and Lauder. From Galadean a road branched off through Whitslaid Farm joining the former road at what is now Under Boon Farm another road left that one down hill to Whitslaid Tower just before the tower the road crossed the Glen burn which still exists today then carried on down hill to cross the River Leader then most probably went up by New Blainslie to join the Blainslie road thence on to the old Chapel at Sterniehall (there are still a few stones remaining there) another old road exists that came from Woodheads, Sterniehall, Upper Blainslie and down by the saw mill to the school and the side of the Kitty glen towards Bridge Haugh Mill then to Galadean. The original road into Blainslie village came off this road at the first junction up from the school where again there is evidence of old buildings. W. Park's blacksmith's shop was on this road. Most of these roads are still in use today as farm tracks or some other signs are visible.

The "New road" from Lauder to Earlston built about 1850 included a new wider bridge built 200 yds down stream from the old bridge at Galadean. That bridge has now been superseded by a new concrete bridge built in 1973 to carry the Birkenside bypass. Of the three bridges only the oldest and the newest still carry traffic, the 1850 bridge has been largely abandoned but still carries a water main along its side.

The first reference to a bridge at Whitslaid is found in a report by James Hardy of the Berwickshire Naturalist Club in 1886 on a visit to Whitslaid Tower when he says *"The river was crossed by a new footbridge"*. Prior to this the nearest bridge was Boon bridge which at this time was a three arch stone structure built in 1875 and washed away in 1888 as was the new footbridge at Whitslaid as were most of the other bridges of the Leader valley. The Boon bridge was replaced by a single arch steel suspension bridge. A year later expansion rollers were installed to protect the abutments. A hundred years of rust finally made it unsafe so it was replaced by a Bailey type bridge in 1989.

About a mile down stream from Whitsiaid Tower is the single stone arched Galadean bridge built about 1770 it is still sound today thanks to an excellent restoration by Borders Council.

At Whitslaid after 1850 a ford would have been put in to take all horse traffic and a new road was constructed from ground acquired from the farm of St. Leonards, this was by act of parliament, where Whitslaid has right of passage but the ground remains St.Leonards, this joined the "new road". A wooden bridge for traffic was built just before the turn of the century by the owner of Carolside Estate no doubt for their own use by 1924 the bridge had deteriorated and the tenant found it gradually unsafe to use. One of the workers on the farm asked *"how many black and white stamps would it take to build a new bridge?"*.

The estate was taken over by Col. Ferguson at this time. A flood on the 22nd of September 1927 washed away the wooden bridge and a new steel structure with a wooden deck was commissioned by Aimers McClean (engineers) of Galashiels. The structure measured 180 feet long with six spans of 30 feet each with four 14 inch by 7 inch R.S.J.s they were supported by latticed piers set in concrete cutwaters. The decking was originally 9 inch by 5 inch by 10 feet 6 inch pine battens giving a 9 foot roadway. It was immensely strong but the Estate was taking no chances so they erected a sign saying

"No weight exceeding 4 tons allowed on this bridge By order D.G. Stalker (factor)"

The ford was also repaired at this time with round timber and tree tops to act as feathers downstream. This was the access for heavy vehicles The bridge was opened by Mrs. Ferguson riding across on horseback.

The great flood of August 12th 1948 again damaged the bridge by washing out the foundations under two of the piers. On the centre span the cutwater broke up and was washed away leaving the steelwork suspended by its bolts; The pier nearest the east bank was undermined and dropped about six feet leaving the bridge vee shaped on that span.

The flood left a great amount of damage to river banks for the whole length of the Leader and a government initiative paid for putting it back in its original channel, over the next two or three years bulldozers and excavators worked to restore the banks giving much needed work to the area. Carolside Estate applied for cash aid to repair the bridge but failed on the grounds that the road was private and only led to one farm, this delayed the start of repairs for nearly eighteen months during this time light vans and cars started to use the bridge even in its damaged state to save longer and sometimes sticky journeys through fields. Livestock for market were walked to a temporary pen at Galadean to meet lorries.

The bridge was repaired by Struthers & Denny of Edinburgh by driving five reinforced concrete piles deep into the river bed at the damaged piers, jacking up the bridge and building reinforced concrete sills to support it. Steel pileing was put round the base of the undamaged piers to protect them from any future flood damage. Even though the engineers on the bridge said there was no need for any weight restriction the Estate insisted on retaining it.

When the wooden deck was put on it soon became apparent that it would eventually rot. Fortunately the battens rotted at different rates so replacing them was a steady continual process spare battens were usually kept for emergencies and the local saw mill could provide them at very short notice when needed from any softwood they had at hand. It was always the tenants responsibility to keep the decking in good repair, and when the farm was sold to the sitting tenant in1959 the bridge then belonged to him and the weight restriction was gradually ignored. Lorries got heavier and longer but there were no incidents as the load was spread over more than one pier, the approaches to the bridge were also realigned to take larger vehicles. After the farm was again sold in 1990 the new owner replaced the whole deck with Australian hardwood sleepers measuring 12ins by 6ins and 12ft. 6ins. long making a wider roadway lorries in the region of 40 tons now use the bridge regularly without any problems.

Betty Riddell Remembers

Betty Riddell, her parents and Grandfather were all born in Blainslie. She is one of a family of ten. She attended Blainslie School. Her Grandfather Riddell was the first pupil at Blainslie new school which was opened in 1867. The school prior to this having been called Wineburgh. Subjects taught: English, Arithmetic, Geography, History PE. Each school day started with hymn singing. There were two class rooms. Infants/older. At this time there were two teachers and 40 pupils. School leaving age was 14. If a child won a bursary they went on to attend school in Melrose. At present the children attend Lauder Primary School and then Earlston High School.

Infant teacher was Miss Carr. Others were Miss Banks & Miss Knox. Miss Waft was headmistress followed by Miss Erskine. Mr. Bennett was headmaster, Mr. Izatt in the 1960s. During the interval games of Beds (hopscotch), tig and ball games were played.

Shops/Trades

There were two blacksmiths in the village.

Park whose smithy was down the lane.

Scott at the bottom of the village in the early 20th century who was followed by Jim Little and later on Wullie Turnbull.

Mr. William Scott was a joiner in the 1800s making furniture, governors cars, pony traps etc. Today Blainslie has a sawmill run by Harry and Scott Riddell.

At one time there was thought to be an inn in the village The Black Bull (or Swan).

Lizzie Park had a grocery business.

There was also a drapers and a bootmaker.

There were many visiting vans -

Grocers A. J. Rutherford & A. B. Brown

Butchers: Shaw, Scott & Brodie

Bakers: Shaw & Brown

Draper: A. Thomson

Ice Cream: Bessie Pow

Ironmonger etc: Jimmy McLauchlin

all the above from Lauder

Ironmonger: Eckie Lindsay (Houndslow)

The Post came from Lauder

The Riddells attended the UF Church in Lauder. They travelled by pony trap and the pony was stabled at Lizzie Wood's in Lauder. Betty also remembers walking to church, which was a long way especially if you had new shoes.

Burials were to Lauder Churchyard and Cemetery.

Hall

The hall was built in 1923 by two brothers who were joiners in Lauder. The hall was used for dances, concerts, Burns suppers, WRI, Carpet Bowling, Whistdrives, Country Dancing etc.

Electricity arrived in the village in the early 1950s and mains water shortly after. Before this water came from the village pump which was still working until a few years ago.

Pump and Well in Blainslie.

A Natural History Of Lauderdale

Lauderdale is a varied and attractive area of the Borders, parts of which retain a semblance of remoteness. Almost entirely rural, the district remains good for wild things. Although there have been some changes in local biodiversity in the hundred years since Thomson published the only previous account in 1902, there is still an abundance of wildlife. Indeed, much of Lauderdale had been unexplored in relation to its natural history until recently, and a significant amount remains yet to be discovered, particularly in groups such as the fungi and invertebrates. The following chapter attempts to list some of the species that have been recorded in and around Lauderdale in the last hundred years. Records have largely been drawn from the database held by the Scottish Borders Biological Record Centre at Harestanes (SBBRC), including plant records from the Botanical Society of the British Isles (BSBI), to both of whom we are much indebted. The list has been supplemented with some local knowledge and conversations with local naturalists. The vast majority of records for Lauderdale have been made over the last two decades and therefore most of the species described can still be found - with a little careful searching and some good luck!

Thomson and Andrew Kelly, who compiled the original lists, were rather loose in their definition of Lauderdale, with mention of species from places as far away as the Bass Rock! Records have been taken from a rectangle of 224 km sq bounded by OS grid references NT480440 to the SW and NT620600 to the NE. This includes land bounded roughly by Soutra Hill to the North, Whitslaid to the South, the Stow edge of Lauder Common to the West and Spottiswoode to the East. This block of land includes the boundaries of Lauderdale Parish, as shown in Thomson's book. To this have been added records from Longmuir Moss and Threepwood Moss plus Wooplaw Woods, just to the West and SW of Lauderdale proper respectively, and Everett Moss to the SE, but all associated with Lauder and its environ.

Habitats within Lauderdale consist primarily of upland moorland and semi-improved pasture with improved farmland in the valley. Much of the Lammermuirs is still actively managed for grouse shooting, and retains good heather coverage. The height above sea level varies from around 150m to the south of Lauder to over 500m in the Lammermuirs. Seenes Law is the highest point at 513m. There are a number of important boggy areas, with Threepwood, Longmuir Moss, Corsbie Bog and Pickie Moss being the most significant of these locally. The Leader Water flows through Lauderdale and is supplied by a number of small burns draining the uplands. The Allan Water rises to the SW and flows directly into the Tweed near Galashiels. There is a distinct lack of still water bodies in the district. Spottiswoode Loch is the largest lake. There are also a number of artificial ponds and moss pools. Outwith the upland areas, there have been some changes over the last century.

There are a number of coniferous plantations, mostly around Lauder, of which Edgarhope is the largest. There is little broad-leaved woodland and almost no semi-natural woodland other than in upland cleuchs. Airhouse Wood is an exception, but is now in a very poor state. Although the tilled farmland remains mixed, with barley still the predominant crop, more and more arable land has been converted to permanent improved pasture. The area of policy land around Thirlestane Castle and elsewhere has probably been much reduced over the last century, but still remains an important habitat. The urban area of Lauderdale has expanded, mostly in the last 10 years, and there has been a general shift in population away from the outlying countryside and into Lauder itself.

There are no protected areas or wildlife reserves within Lauderdale itself, however local areas of interest included Sites of Special Scientific Interest at Threepwood Moss, Airhouse Wood and Colmsliehill Junipers. Wooplaw Community Woodlands are also well recorded and readily accessible.

Recording effort has varied greatly with the groups of organisms concerned. The lists for vascular plants and vertebrates are reasonably complete. Lichen records have been contributed mostly by Dr. Brian Coppins and are drawn from a limited number of sites. Bryophytes are covered in a separate section by David Long, and are taken almost entirely from his own records. Records for invertebrates are sparse, again covering very specific localities, with many groups of animals hardly being touched at all. Taxonomy is a dying art amongst the sciences, and there is a real concern that we will be unable to assess local biodiversity before unknown species are lost through events such as global warming. Records from any of the species groups listed below are most welcomed by the SBBRC, whose address is listed at the end of the chapter.

The lists are arranged in taxonomic order with Orders and Families shown for each group, following the nomenclature used by the National Biological Records Centre. Two status designations have been shown below, a national status, and a local status (where known). The first shows whether the species is of particular note and any designations attributed to the species, including whether it has been listed in either the UK Biodiversity Action Plan (UKBAP) or Local Biological Action Plan (LBAP) for the Borders. For groups that are poorly recorded in the Borders, such as invertebrates, the National Status also indicates whether the species is nationally common, local or uncommon. The Local Status is a subjective assessment of the abundance of well-recorded groups in Lauderdale, and gives an indication of the likelihood of encountering each species.

Other designations of National Status used are:

Notable/Na - Recorded in >15 but <30 10km grid squares or <8 Vice Counties nationally since 1970

Notable/Nb - Recorded in >30 but <100 10km grid squares or >7 but < 20 Vice Counties since 1970

Nr - Regionally Notable   RDB - IUCN Red Data Book species
pRDB - proposed Red Data Book species

References:

Scottish Borders Local Biodiversity Partnership (2001) Scottish Borders Local Biodiversity Action Plan. Scottish Borders Council (available from Department of Development and Economic Planning).

UK Biodiversity Steering Group (1995) Biodiversity: The UK Steering Group Report Volume II: Action Plans.

Contact:

Scottish Borders Biological Record Centre, Harestanes Countryside Visitor Centre, Nr. Ancrum, Jedburgh TD8 6UQ Tel 01835 830306 Fax 01835 830734 e-mail SBBRC@scotborders.gov.uk

PLANTS

The vascular plants of the area have been well surveyed since 1986, and the list is therefore largely complete. This is mainly thanks to the sterling efforts of the Botanical Society of the British Isles (BSBI) recorders for the vice counties of Berwickshire (VC81, Michael Braithwaite) and Roxburghshire (VC80, Dr. Roderick Corner) to whom hearty thanks are extended. In particular Michael Braithwaite has covered almost every moss and cleuch in the parish, but thanks are also extended to Dr. David Long and to Luke Gaskell.

In the list of vascular plants, all records date from 1986 onwards, unless a specific earlier date is given. Plants that have not been recorded in the last twenty years may well fall into the category of 'locally extinct , although diligent searching might lead to a few rediscoveries. Most of the records of plants rare to Lauderdale noted in 1960 are from a BSBI field visit led by Dr. Franklyn Perring and Dr. Albert Long. Letty Whiteside recorded other local rarities in 1982. A separate table is given of those plants that have not been recorded in Lauderdale since the publication of Lauder and Lauderdale in 1902. Species that are thought to be introductions to Lauderdale are marked with an asterisk. Nomenclature is that used by the JNCC in Recorder 2000 and follows that of Stace, 1997.

Local bryophyte specialist, Dr. David Long, has contributed a separate section on mosses and liverworts, with records from his own database, providing extensive cover of the area. Michael Braithwaite has kindly provided an introduction to the section on flowering plants. In contrast, the coverage of lichens is incomplete. A list compiled mainly from three sites has been kindly contributed by Dr. Brian Coppins, from the Royal Botanical Gardens Edinburgh. There are notably no records of fungi.

References:

Braithwaite, M.E. and Long, D.G. (1990) The Botanist in Berwickshire. The Berwickshire Naturalist Club.

Coppins, B.J. (2002) Checklist of Lichens of Great Britain and Ireland. London: British Lichen Society.

Corner, R.W.M (1985) Flowering Plants and Ferns of Selkirkshire and Roxburghshire (with additions made in 1992). BSBI.

Fitter, R., Fitter, A. and Farrer, A. (1984) Grasses, Sedges, Rushes and Ferns of Britain and Northern Europe. Collins.

Rose, F. (1981) The Wild Flower Key. British Isles - N.W. Europe. Warne.

Stace, C. (1997) New Flora of the British Isles. Cambridge.

Lichens of Lauderdale

Compiled by Dr. Brian J. Coppins

The list of 190 lichens (187 species) is compiled largely from three sets of records:

near Lauder Barns, 1975, B.J. Coppins

Kelphope Burn, 30 March 1991, B.J. & A.M. Coppins

Boondreigh Water, 36/56.45(–6), 10 April 1997, B.J. Coppins, with D.G. Long

Six species, marked with asterisks, have been added to Dr. Coppins' list that have mostly been recorded from Threepwood Moss by a number of different people including Chris Badenoch, Rod Corner and Alan Gray.

The list includes four species that are currently categorized as Nationally Scarce (NS), and one as Vulnerable. No Nationally Rare or Red-listed lichens have been recorded for Lauderdale. As few lichens have common names, these have not been shown for this group. Lichen nomenclature follows Coppins (2002).

Lichens Ascomycotina

Leotiales
Baeomyces rufus

Arthoniales
Arthonia cinnabarina, Arthonia didyma, Arthonia punctiformis, Arthonia radiata, Chrysothrix candelaris (Nationally Scarce)

Caliciales
Calicium glaucellum, Calicium salicinum, Calicium viride, Chaenotheca chrysocephala, Chaenotheca ferruginea,
Chaenotheca furfuracea, Chaenotheca trichialis, Cyphelium inquinans, Stenocybe pullulata

Graphidales
Diploschistes scruposus, Graphina anguina, Graphis scripta, Gyalideopsis anastomosans, Dimerella pineti

Lecanorales
Acarospora fuscata, Aspicilia caesiocinerea, Aspicilia grisea, Bacidia incompta *, Bacidia inundata, Bacidia rubella,
Bryoria fuscescens, Buellia aethalea, Buellia griseovirens, Candelariella reflexa, Candelariella vitellina, Candelariella xanthostigma, Carbonea vorticosa, Catillaria chalybeia, Cetraria aculeata, Cetraria islandica, Cetraria muricata, Cetraria sepincola *, Cladonia arbuscula, Cladonia bellidiflora, Cladonia cervicornis s.str., Cladonia cervicornis var. verticillata, Cladonia chlorophaea agg., Cladonia ciliata s.str., Cladonia ciliata var. tenuis, Cladonia coniocraea, Cladonia diversa, Cladonia fimbriata, Cladonia floerkeana *, Cladonia furcata, Cladonia gracilis, Cladonia humilis, Cladonia macilenta, Cladonia polydactyla, Cladonia portentosa, Cladonia pyxidata, Cladonia uncialis *, Cliostomum griffithii, Evernia prunastri, Hypocenomyce

caradocensis, Hypocenomyce scalaris, Hypogymnia physodes, Hypogymnia tubulosa, Immersaria athroocarpa, Ionaspis lacustris, Lecanactis abietina, Lecania cyrtella, Lecania cyrtellina, Lecania naegelii, Lecanora aitema, Lecanora campestris, Lecanora carpinea, Lecanora chlarotera, Lecanora conizaeoides, Lecanora dispersa, Lecanora expallens, Lecanora gangaleoides, Lecanora intricata (Nationally Scarce), *Lecanora muralis, Lecanora orosthea, Lecanora persimilis, Lecanora polytropa, Lecanora pulicaris, Lecanora rupicola, Lecanora saligna, Lecanora soralifera, Lecanora sulphurea, Lecanora symmicta, Lecanora varia, Lecidea fuscoatra, Lecidea lactea, Lecidea lapicida, Lecidea lithophila, Lecidella elaeochroma, Lecidella scabra, Lepraria incana, Lepraria lobificans,Lepraria rigidula, Leproloma membranaceum, Melanelia exasperata, Melanelia fuliginosa s.str., Melanelia fuliginosa subsp. glabratula, Melanelia subaurifera, Micarea leprosula, Micarea lithinella, Micarea micrococca, Micarea peliocarpa, Micarea sylvicola, Miriquidica leucophaea, Mycoblastus fucatus, Parmelia omphalodes, Parmelia saxatilis, Parmelia sulcata, Parmeliopsis ambigua, Phaeophyscia orbiculari, Physcia adscendens, Physcia aipolia, Physcia caesia. Physcia stellaris, Physcia tenella, Physconia distorta, Physconia enteroxantha, Physconia grisea, Placynthiella icmalea, Platismatia glauca, Porina aenea, Porpidia cinereoatra, Porpidia crustulata, Porpidia macrocarpa, Porpidia soredizodes, Porpidia tuberculosa, Protoparmelia badia, Pseudevernia furfuracea s.str., Pseudevernia furfuracea var. ceratea, Psilolechia lucida, Pycnothelia papillaria *, Pyrrhospora quernea, Ramalina farinacea, Ramalina fastigiata, Ramalina fraxinea, Rhizocarpon distinctum, Rhizocarpon geographicum, Rhizocarpon polycarpum, Rhizocarpon reductum, Rimularia furvella, Rinodina griseosoralifera , Rinodina sophodes, Scoliciosporum umbrinum, Tephromela atra, Tephromela grumosa, Trapelia coarctata, Trapelia involuta, Trapelia placodioides, Trapeliopsis flexuosa* (Nationally Scarce), *Trapeliopsis gelatinosa, Trapeliopsis granulosa, Trapeliopsis pseudogranulosa, Umbilicaria polyphylla, Usnea hirta, Usnea subfloridana*

Opegraphales
Lecanactis abietina, Opegrapha atra, Opegrapha herbarum, Opegrapha niveoatra, Opegrapha ochrocheila, Opegrapha sorediifera, Opegrapha varia, Opegrapha vermicellifera, Opegrapha vulgata

Peltigerales
Peltigera hymenina, Peltigera membranacea

Pertusariales
Ochrolechia androgyna, Ochrolechia microstictoides, Ochrolechia parella, Ochrolechia subviridis (Nationally Scarce), *Pertusaria amara, Pertusaria aspergilla, Pertusaria coccodes, Pertusaria corallina, Pertusaria hemisphaerica, Pertusaria lactea, Pertusaria leioplaca, Pertusaria pertusa, Pertusaria pseudocorallina, Pertusaria pupillaris, Schaereria cinereorufa*

Pyrenulales
Porina aenea

Teloschistales
Caloplaca cerina (Vulnerable) – Oxton, *Caloplaca cerinella, Caloplaca holocarpa, Caloplaca obscurella, Fuscidea cyathoides, Fuscidea lightfootii, Fuscidea recensa, Xanthoria parietina, Xanthoria polycarpa, Xanthoria ucrainica,*

Verrucariales
Verrucaria nigrescens, Amandinea punctata, Anisomeridium biforme, Anisomeridium polypori, Myxobilimbia sabuletorum, Phlyctis argena, Tuckermannopsis chlorophylla

Dothideales
Arthopyrenia analepta, Arthopyrenia punctiformis, Leptorhaphis epidermidis, Tomasellia gelatinosa

Lichenicolous fungi
Laeviomyces opegraphae on *Opegrapha niveoatra, Sclerococcum sphaerale* on *Pertusaria corallina, Stigmidium aggregatum* on *Pertusaria lacteal*

Mosses and Liverworts (Bryophytes) of Lauderdale

David G. Long

Lauderdale, as the westernmost part of Berwickshire, remained largely unrecorded for bryophytes until very recently and most recording has taken place since 1989. Early Berwickshire recorders such as James Hardy and J.B. Duncan scarcely visited the valley. Perhaps surprisingly, the bryophyte flora, with 273 species recorded (over one quarter the British total) is remarkably rich for a relatively small mostly upland valley. Many bryophytes occupy small microhabitats and even though habitats such as ancient woodland are now reduced to fragments in upland valleys such as the Brunta Burn and Blythe Water, these are still large enough to contain a rich diversity of mosses and liverworts.

Undoubtedly the most important habitats in the valley are the relict wetland habitats, which are a nationally important asset. These include valley mires such as Pickie Moss and Longmuir Moss, raised bogs such as Threepwood Moss, and calcareous flushes along the hill burns such as the Whalplaw Burn, Brunta Burn, Wheel Burn and on Lauder Common. These contain nationally scarce species such as *Tomentypnum nitens* and *Amblyodon dealbatus,* which are in national decline due to habitat loss. On the highest Lammermuir hilltops blanket peat is dominant but this too is important, for example for the rare moss *Hypnum imponens.* Seventeen species of Bog-moss (*Sphagnum*) are recorded, a remarkable total which is clear evidence of the richness and diversity of Lauderdale's wetland habitats.

The main reason for the richness of the mires and flushes is the underlying calcareous Old Red Sandstone rocks, which provide lime-rich water to feed the springs and streams. This bedrock has contributed to the fertility of Lauderdale as a whole and its rich grazing land, which unfortunately has led to widespread loss of unimproved grassland and 'wildflower meadows' which are now rare. Where these rocks outcrop, as along cleughs such as in the Blyth Water and along the Leader in places, a good representation of rock-loving species occurs. Other than the cleugh woodlands, more extensive woods occur along the Leader and at Spottiswoode, and these add greatly to the diversity with a several nationally scarce species such as *Pylaisia polyantha* and *Syntrichia virescens.* The clean air of the valley also means that the old roadside Ash and Sycamore trees support a rich flora of epiphytes such as *Syntrichia papillosa,* which is locally abundant.

However, many changes that affect the bryophyte flora are taking place. Recent invaders, such as *Campylopus introflexus* and *Orthodontium lineare,* have a good foothold. Important habitats are still being lost through forestry and intensification: notable are the loss of the raised mire Jordonlaw Moss (to forestry) and most of Flass Old Wood (to agriculture) in quite recent times. Along the roads many of the old trees rich in epiphytes are being lost in storms, but a very welcome trend is the establishment of many new areas of broadleaf woodland rather then the sterile blanket conifers of the recent past.

Mosses and liverworts are extremely good indicators of environmental quality, they reflect the cleanness of the air, they frequent hills, bogs, forests, riversides and wooded cleughs, all of which are places of great beauty and great assets for

Lauderdale's future for tourism and outdoor recreation. Many of the finest habitats in the valley in 1902 are still places of great diversity and beauty and our goal should be to protect and enhance these habitats for the next century and beyond.

Common Name *Species* (National Status) Local Status

Liverworts Marchantiopsida

Lepidoziaceae
Creeping Fingerwort *Lepidozia reptans* Common

Calypogeiaceae
Common Pouchwort *Calypogeia fissa* Common, Mueller's Pouchwort *Calypogeia muelleriana* Common, Nees' Pouchwort *Calypogeia neesiana* Rare

Cephaloziaceae
Two-horned Pincerwort *Cephalozia bicuspidate* Common, Forcipated Pincerwort *Cephalozia connivens* Local, Moon-leaved Pincerwort *Cephalozia lunulifolia* Local, Wood-rust *Nowellia curvifolia* Local, Bog Notchwort *Cladopodiella fluitans* Rare, Bog-moss Flapwort *Odontoschisma sphagni* Local

Cephaloziellaceae
Common Threadwort *Cephaloziella divaricata* Common

Lophoziaceae
Trunk Pawwort *Barbilophozia attenuata* Local, Bearded Pawwort *Barbilophozia barbata* Local, Common Pawwort *Barbilophozia floerkei* Common, Hatcher's Pawwort *Barbilophozia hatchery* Common, Lesser Notchwort *Lophozia bicrenata* Local, Capitate Notchwort *Lophozia excisa* Local, Jagged Notchwort *Lophozia incisa* Local, Tumid Notchwort *Lophozia ventricosa* Common, Bantry Notchwort *Leiocolea bantriensis* Rare, Inflated Notchwort *Gymnocolea inflata* Local, Larger Cut Notchwort *Tritomaria exsectiformis* Rare, Lyon's Notchwort *Tritomaria quinquedentata* Local

Jungermanniaceae
Anomalous Flapwort *Mylia anomala* Local, Dark-green Flapwort *Jungermannia atrovirens* Local, Cordate Flapwort *Jungermannia exsertifolia subsp. cordifolia* Local, Crenulated Flapwort *Jungermannia gracillima* Local, Shining Flapwort *Jungermannia paroica* Local, Ladder Flapwort *Nardia scalaris* Common

Gymnomitriaceae
Notched Rustwort *Marsupella emarginata* Local

Scapaniaceae
White Earwort *Diplophyllum albicans* Common, Blunt-leaved Earwort *Diplophyllum obtusifolium* Rare, Thick-set Earwort *Scapania compacta* Local, Heath Earwort *Scapania irrigua* Local, Tongue Earwort *Scapania lingulata* (Nationally scarce) Rare, Grove Earwort *Scapania nemorea* Local, Norwegian Earwort *Scapania scandica* Local, Water Earwort *Scapania undulata* Common

Geocalycaceae
Bifid Crestwort *Lophocolea bidentata* Common, Variable-leaved Crestwort *Lophocolea heterophylla* Common, St Winifrid's Other Moss *Chiloscyphus pallescens* Local, St Winifrid's Moss *Chiloscyphus polyanthos* Common

Plagiochilaceae
Greater Featherwort *Plagiochila asplenioides* Common, Lesser Featherwort *Plagiochila porelloides* Common

Radulaceae
Even Scalewort *Radula complanata* Common

Ptilidiaceae
Ciliated Fringewort *Ptilidium ciliare* Common, Tree Fringewort *Ptilidium pulcherrimum* Local

Frullaniaceae
Dilated Scalewort *Frullania dilatata* Common, Tamarisk Scalewort *Frullania tamarisci* Common

Lejeuneaceae
Micheli's Least Pouncewort *Lejeunea cavifolia* Local

Fossombroniaceae
Common Frillwort *Fossombronia pusilla* Local

Pelliaceae
Endive Pellia *Pellia endiviifolia* Common, Overleaf Pellia *Pellia epiphylla* Common, Nees' Pellia *Pellia neesiana* Local

Blasiaceae
Common Kettlewort *Blasia pusilla* Local

Aneuraceae
Greasewort *Aneura pinguis* Common, Jagged Germanderwort *Riccardia chamedryfolia* Local, Bog Germanderwort *Riccardia latifrons* Local

Metzgeriaceae
Blueish Veilwort *Metzgeria fruticulosa* Common, Forked Veilwort *Metzgeria furcata* Common

Lunulariaceae
Crescent-cup Liverwort *Lunularia cruciata* Common

Conocephalaceae
Great Scented Liverwort *Conocephalum conicum* Common

Marchantiaceae
Narrow Mushroom-headed Liverwort *Preissia quadrata* Rare, Mountain Liverwort *Marchantia polymorpha subsp. montivagans* Local, Star-headed Liverwort *Marchantia polymorpha subsp. polymorpha* Local, Common Liverwort *Marchantia polymorpha subsp. ruderalis* Common

Mosses Bryopsida

Sphagnaceae
Red Bog-moss *Sphagnum capillifolium subsp. rubellum* Common, Compact Bog-moss *Sphagnum compactum* Common, Feathery Bog-moss *Sphagnum cuspidatum* Local, Cow-horn Bog-moss *Sphagnum denticulatum* Local, Flat-topped Bog-moss *Sphagnum fallax subsp. fallax* Common, Fringed Bog-moss *Sphagnum fimbriatum* Common, Girgensohn's Bog-moss *Sphagnum girgensohnii* Common, Lesser Cow-horn Bog-moss *Sphagnum inundatum* Local, Magellanic Bog-moss *Sphagnum magellanicum* Local, Blunt-leaved Bog-moss *Sphagnum palustre var. palustre* Common, Papillose Bog-moss *Sphagnum papillosum* Common, Five-ranked Bog-moss *Sphagnum quinquefarium* Local, Russow's Bog-moss *Sphagnum russowii* Local, Spiky Bog-moss *Sphagnum squarrosum* Common, Lustrous Bog-moss *Sphagnum subnitens* Common, Rigid Bog-moss *Sphagnum teres* Rare, Warnstorf's Bog-moss *Sphagnum warnstorfii* Rare

Andreaeacaeae
Black Rock-moss *Andreaea rupestris var. rupestris* Local

Tetraphidaceae
Pellucid Four-tooth Moss *Tetraphis pellucida* Local

Polytrichaceae
Common Smoothcap *Atrichum undulatum var. undulatum* Common, Aloe Haircap *Pogonatum aloides* Common, Urn Haircap *Pogonatum urnigerum* Common, Alpine Haircap *Polytrichum alpinum* Local, Common Haircap *Polytrichum commune var. commune* Common, Bank Haircap *Polytrichum formosum* Common, Juniper Haircap *Polytrichum juniperinum* Common, Bristly Haircap *Polytrichum piliferum* Common, Strict Haircap *Polytrichum strictum* Local

Archidiaceae
Clay Earth-moss *Archidium alternifolium* Rare

Fissidentaceae
Maidenhair Pocket-moss *Fissidens adianthoides* Local, Lesser Pocket-moss *Fissidens bryoides*

Common, Rock Pocket-moss *Fissidens dubius* Local, Common Pocket-moss *Fissidens taxifolius var. taxifolius* Common, Green Pocket-moss *Fissidens viridulus* Local

Dicranaceae
Rusty Swan-neck Moss *Campylopus flexuosus* Local, Brittle Swan-neck Moss *Campylopus fragilis* Local, Heath Star Moss *Campylopus introflexus* Common, Dwarf Swan-neck Moss *Campylopus pyriformis var. pyriformis* Common, Redshank *Ceratodon purpureus* Common, Jenner's Dog-tooth *Cynodontium jenneri* Rare, Transparent Fork-moss *Dichodontium pellucidum* Common, Silky Forklet-moss *Dicranella heteromalla* Common, Marsh Forklet-moss *Dicranella palustris* Local, Rufous Forklet-moss *Dicranella rufescens* Local, Schreber's Forklet-moss *Dicranella schreberiana* Local, Awl-leaved Forklet-moss *Dicranella subulata* Rare, Variable Forklet-moss *Dicranella varia* Local, Beaked Bow-moss *Dicranodontium denudatum* Rare, Common Pincushion *Dicranoweisia cirrata* Common, Crisped Fork-moss *Dicranum bonjeanii* Rare, Dusky Fork-moss *Dicranum fuscescens* Local, Greater Fork-moss *Dicranum majus* Local, Mountain Fork-moss *Dicranum montanum* Rare, Broom Fork-moss *Dicranum scoparium* Common, Fragile Fork-moss *Dicranum tauricum* Local, Cylindric Ditrichum *Ditrichum cylindricum* Common, Curve-leaved Ditrichum *Ditrichum heteromallum* Local, Large White-moss *Leucobryum glaucum* Common, Taper-leaved Earth-moss *Pleuridium acuminatum* Local, Delicate Earth-moss *Pseudephemerum nitidum* Local

Encalyptaceae
Spiral Extinguisher-moss *Encalypta streptocarpa* Common

Pottiaceae
Rounded Pygmy-moss *Acaulon muticum* Rare, Lesser Bird's-claw Beard-moss *Barbula convoluta* Common, Bird's-claw Beard-moss *Barbula unguiculata* Common, Rufous Beard-moss *Bryoerythrophyllum ferruginascens* Rare, Red Beard-moss *Bryoerythrophyllum recurvirostrum* Local, Cylindric Beard-moss *Didymodon insulanus* Common, Rigid Beard-moss *Didymodon rigidulus* Common, Brown Beard-moss *Didymodon spadiceus* Local, Olive Beard-moss *Didymodon tophaceus* Local, Soft-tufted Beard-moss *Didymodon vinealis* Local, Hornschuch's Beard-moss *Pseudocrossidium hornschuchianum* Local, Small Hairy Screw-moss *Syntrichia laevipila var. laevipila* Common, Water Screw-moss *Syntrichia latifolia* Local, Marble Screw-moss *Syntrichia papillosa* Local, Great Hairy Screw-moss *Syntrichia ruralis* Local, Lesser Screw-moss *Syntrichia virescens* (Nationally scarce) Rare, Cuspidate Earth-moss *Tortula acaulon var. acaulon* Common, Wall Screw-moss *Tortula muralis* Common, Awl-leaved Screw-moss *Tortula subulata var. subulata* Local, Common Pottia *Tortula truncata* Common, Narrow-fruited Crisp-moss *Trichostomum tenuirostre var. tenuirostre* Rare, Green-tufted Stubble-moss *Weissia controversa var. controversa* Common

Grimmiaceae
Donn's Grimmia *Grimmia donniana* Rare, Grey-cushioned Grimmia *Grimmia pulvinata var. pulvinata* Common, Yellow Fringe-moss *Racomitrium aciculare* Common, Dense Fringe-moss *Racomitrium ericoides* Local, Green Mountain Fringe-moss *Racomitrium fasciculare* Common, Bristly Fringe-moss *Racomitrium heterostichum* Common, Woolly Fringe-moss *Racomitrium lanuginosum* Local, Thickpoint Grimmia *Schistidium crassipilum* Rare

Funariaceae
Common Cord-moss *Funaria hygrometrica* Common

Splachnaceae
Slender Cruet-moss *Tetraplodon mnioides* Rare

Bryaceae
Slender Silver-moss *Anomobryum julaceum var. julaceum* Local, Silver-moss *Bryum argenteum* Common, Bicoloured Bryum *Bryum bicolor* Common, Capillary Thread-moss *Bryum capillare var. capillare* Common, Pale Thread-moss *Bryum pallens* Common, Marsh Bryum *Bryum pseudotriquetrum var. pseudotriquetrum* Common, Wall Thread-moss *Bryum radiculosum* Local, Crimson-tuber Thread-moss *Bryum rubens* Common, Sauter's Thread-moss *Bryum sauteri* Local, Lesser Potato Bryum *Bryum subapiculatum* Local, Flabby Thread-moss *Bryum subelegans* Local, Golden Thread-moss *Leptobryum pyriforme* Local, Cape Thread-moss *Orthodontium lineare* Common, Pale-fruited Thread-moss *Pohlia annotina* Local, Crookneck Nodding-moss *Pohlia camptotrachela* Local, Opal Thread-moss *Pohlia cruda* Local, Pink-fruited Thread-moss *Pohlia melanodon* Local, Nodding Thread-moss *Pohlia nutans* Common, Pale Glaucous

Thread-moss *Pohlia wahlenbergii var. wahlenbergii* Local, Rose-moss *Rhodobryum roseum* Rare

Mniaceae
Swan's-neck Thyme-moss *Mnium hornum* Common, Woodsy Thyme-moss *Plagiomnium cuspidatum* Rare, Tall Thyme-moss *Plagiomnium elatum* Local, Marsh Thyme-moss *Plagiomnium ellipticum* Local, Long-beaked Thyme-moss *Plagiomnium rostratum* Common, Hart's-tongue Thyme-moss *Plagiomnium undulatum* Common, River Thyme-moss *Pseudobryum cinclidioides* Rare, Felted Thyme-moss *Rhizomnium pseudopunctatum* Rare, Dotted Thyme-moss *Rhizomnium punctatum* Common

Aulacomniaceae
Bud-headed Groove-moss *Aulacomnium androgynum* Local, Bog Groove-moss *Aulacomnium palustre* Common

Meesiaceae
Short-tooth Hump-moss *Amblyodon dealbatus* (Nationally scarce) Rare

Bartramiaceae
Straight-leaved Apple-moss *Bartramia ithyphylla* Local, Common Apple-moss *Bartramia pomiformis* Common, Thick-nerved Apple-moss *Philonotis calcarea* Rare, Fountain Apple-moss *Philonotis fontana* Common

Orthotrichaceae
Mougeot's Yoke-moss *Amphidium mougeotii* Local, Wood Bristle-moss *Orthotrichum affine* Common, Anomalous Bristle-moss *Orthotrichum anomalum* Common, Naked Bristle-moss *Orthotrichum cupulatum var. riparium* Local, White-tipped Bristle-moss *Orthotrichum diaphanum* Common, Lyell's Bristle-moss *Orthotrichum lyellii* Local, Elegant Bristle-moss *Orthotrichum pulchellum* Common, River Bristle-moss *Orthotrichum rivulare* Local, Straw Bristle-moss *Orthotrichum stramineum* Local, Bruch's Pincushion *Ulota bruchii* Common, Crisped Pincushion *Ulota crispa* Local, Frizzled Pincushion *Ulota phyllantha* Local, Lesser Yoke-moss *Zygodon conoideus* Local, Park Yoke-moss *Zygodon rupestris* Local, Stirton's Yoke-moss *Zygodon viridissimus var. stirtonii* Local, Green Yoke-moss *Zygodon viridissimus var. viridissimus* Common

Hedwigiaceae
Starry Hoar-moss *Hedwigia stellata* Common

Fontinalaceae
Greater Water-moss *Fontinalis antipyretica var. antipyretica* Common

Climaciaceae
Tree-moss *Climacium dendroides* Common

Neckeraceae
Blunt Feather-moss *Homalia trichomanoides* Local, Flat Neckera *Neckera complanata* Common

Hookeriaceae
Shining Hookeria *Hookeria lucens* Local

Thamnobryaceae
Fox-tail Feather-moss *Thamnobryum alopecurum* Common

Thuidiaceae
Rambling Tail-moss *Anomodon viticulosus* Local, Slender Tamarisk-moss *Heterocladium heteropterum var. flaccidum* Local, Common Tamarisk-moss *Thuidium tamariscinum* Common

Amblystegiaceae
Brook-side Feather-moss *Amblystegium fluviatile* Local, Creeping Feather-moss *Amblystegium serpens var. serpens* Common, Fountain Feather-moss *Amblystegium tenax* Local, Heart-leaved Spear-moss *Calliergon cordifolium* Local, Giant Spear-moss *Calliergon giganteum* Local, Straw Spear-moss *Calliergon stramineum* Local, Pointed Spear-moss *Calliergonella cuspidate* Common, Yellow Starry Feather-moss *Campylium stellatum var. stellatum* Local, Fern-leaved Hook-moss *Cratoneuron filicinum* Common, Intermediate Hook-moss *Drepanocladus cossonii* Local, Drab Brook-moss *Hygrohypnum luridum var. luridum* Common, Claw Brook-moss *Hygrohypnum ochraceum* Local, Curled Hook-moss *Palustriella commutata var. commutata* Local, Claw-leaved Hook-moss *Palustriella commutata var. falcate* Local, Sickle-leaved Hook-

moss *Sanionia uncinata* Local, Woolly Feather-moss *Tomentypnum nitens* (Nationally scarce) Rare, Floating Hook-moss *Warnstorfia fluitans* Local

Brachytheciaceae
Whitish Feather-moss *Brachythecium albicans* Common, Rusty Feather-moss *Brachythecium plumosum* Common, Matted Feather-moss *Brachythecium populeum* Local, River Feather-moss *Brachythecium rivulare* Local, Rough-stalked Feather-moss *Brachythecium rutabulum* Common, Velvet Feather-moss *Brachythecium velutinum* Local, Hair-pointed Feather-moss *Cirriphyllum piliferum* Common, Swartz's Feather-moss, *Eurhynchium hians* Common, Common Feather-moss *Eurhynchium praelongum* Common, Common Striated Feather-moss *Eurhynchium striatum* Common, Silky Wall Feather-moss *Homalothecium sericeum* Common, Larger Mouse-tail Moss *Isothecium alopecuroides* Common, Sender Mouse-tail Moss *Isothecium myosuroides var. myosuroides* Common, Tender Feather-moss *Rhynchostegiella tenella* Local, Wall Feather-moss *Rhynchostegium murale* Local, Long-beaked Water Feather-moss *Rhynchostegium riparioides* Common, Neat Feather-moss *Scleropodium purum* Common

Plagiotheciaceae
Curved Silk-moss *Plagiothecium curvifolium* Local, Dented Silk-moss *Plagiothecium denticulatum var. denticulatum* Common, Bright Silk-moss *Plagiothecium laetum* Rare, Juicy Silk-moss *Plagiothecium succulentum* Common, Waved Silk-moss *Plagiothecium undulatum* Common, Elegant Silk-moss *Pseudotaxiphyllum elegans* Common

Hypnaceae
Chalk Comb-moss *Ctenidium molluscum var. molluscum* Common, Glittering Wood-moss *Hylocomium splendens* Common, Mamillate Plait-moss *Hypnum andoi* Local, Cypress-leaved Plait-moss *Hypnum cupressiforme* Common, Pellucid Plait-moss *Hypnum imponens* (Nationally scarce) Rare, Heath Plait-moss *Hypnum jutlandicum* Common, Supine Plait-moss *Hypnum resupinatum* Common, Red-stemmed Feather-moss *Pleurozium schreberi* Common, Many-flowered Leskea *Pylaisia polyantha* (Nationally scarce) Rare, Little Shaggy-moss *Rhytidiadelphus loreus* Common, Springy Turf-moss *Rhytidiadelphus squarrosus* Common, Big Shaggy-moss *Rhytidiadelphus triquetrus* Common

The Flowering Plants and Ferns of Lauderdale

Lauderdale's fertile farmland lost almost all its native wodland long before 'Lauder and Lauderdale' was written. There have been later losses such as the lower part of Edgarhope Wood and, today, woodland remnants may be best enjoyed along the Boondreigh Water, Blythe Water and Brunta Burn and also at Airhouse Wood. These are also the sites for the best riverside and grassland communities. There has been a recent reversal of the post-war trend towards planting of coniferous trees, with more broadleaves being introduced at Wooplaw and Edgarhope. The formation of new Community Woodlands on Lauder Common as well as at Wooplaw is a welcome development. While native woodland may be scarce there are notable patches of juniper scrub by the Blythe Water, at Colmsliehill and in some of the hill cleughs. The Blythe Water junipers are particularly valuable as they are associated with a wide diversity of habitat, and here are superb colonies of wood crane's-bill.

There are several interesting mosses in the district. These include a rich valley mire and a good raised bog at Longmuir Moss, a large raised bog and a small adjacent fen at Threepwood Moss, a further small remnant of raised bog with a wet meadow at Corsbie Bog, and good mires at Pickie Moss and Everett Moss. At Longmuir Moss there is the only Berwickshire colony of lesser tussock-sedge, where it was first found by Andrew Kelly, and at Everett Moss the only Berwickshire colony of cowbane.

Extensive moorland yet remains in the Lammermuirs, but diverse communities are best looked for in the hill cleughs where there is a degree of protection from muirburn and over-grazing, especially up the Whalplaw and Soonhope burns and the Blythe Water. Here are colonies of a Borders speciality, hairy stonecrop.

There have been some major changes in the flora of other parts of Lauderdale over the last century, with some gains as well as losses in species diversity. Improved farming practice has much-reduced the abundance of the arable weed flora over the last century, and a poppy is now an unusual sight. Lauder itself has ruderal habitats that are quite species-rich. The flora of the tall old walls in the town is especially interesting and includes ferns and several species of toadflax. Many alien species have been introduced intentionally or by accident, and some of these have become a familiar part of the local flora, such as the monkeyflowers, pink purslane and few-flowered garlic. Changes in the environment have led to a marked increase in some native species, such as rosebay willowherb in woodland and reed canary-grass by the Leader.

Common Name Species (National Status) Local Status Distribution/Locality

Vascular Plants

Lycopodiopsida
Lycopodiaceae
Stag's-horn Clubmoss *Lycopodium clavatum* Scarce. Moorland. Earnscleuch Water, near Longmuir Moss

Equisetopsida
Equisetaceae
Water Horsetail *Equisetum fluviatile* Common. Grows in water margins
Field Horsetail *Equisetum arvense* Common. Drier grassland
Wood Horsetail *Equisetum sylvaticum* Uncommon. Woods and moorland. Whitlaw, Corsbie Bog
Marsh Horsetail *Equisetum palustre* Common. Marshes and damp grassland

Pteridopsida
Ophioglossaceae
Moonwort *Botrychium lunaria* Scarce. Grassland, moors. Corsbie Bog, near Longmuir Moss
Polypodiaceae
Polypody *Polypodium vulgare* Uncommon. Woods, burnsides in Lauderdale
Dennstaedtiaceae
Bracken *Pteridium aquilinum* Very Common. Moorland, woodland edge
Thelypteridaceae
Lemon-scented Fern *Oreopteris limbosperma* Uncommon. Upland, burn sides. Whalplaw and Soonhope Burns
Aspleniaceae
Hart's-tongue *Phyllitis scolopendrium* Scarce. Below Drummond's Hall
Black Spleenwort *Asplenium adiantum-nigrum* Uncommon. Old walls, Harryburn
Maidenhair Spleenwort *Asplenium trichomanes* Common. Old walls
Wall-rue *Asplenium ruta-muraria* Uncommon. Old walls, Harryburn

Woodsiaceae
Lady Fern *Athyrium filix-femina* Common. Damper woods, acid soils.
Oak Fern *Gymnocarpium dryopteris* Scarce. Rocks and scree in Lauderdale. Damp woods elsewhere. Airhouse, Whalplaw Burn, Lauder Burn
Brittle Bladder-fern *Cystopteris fragilis* Rare. Walls. Spottiswoode

Dryopteridaceae
Hard Shield-fern *Polystichum aculeatum* Uncommon. Woods, rocks. Brunta Burn, Below Drummond's Hall
Common Male Fern *Dryopteris filix-mas* Very Common. Woods, banks
Scaly Male Fern *Dryopteris affinis* Common. Woods, banks, acid soils
Narrow Buckler-fern *Dryopteris carthusiana* Uncommon Damp woods and bogs. Pickie Moss, Corsbie Bog, Houndslow, Longmuir Moss Broad
Buckler-fern *Dryopteris dilatata* Very Common. Woods, banks

Blechnaceae
Hard Fern *Blechnum spicant* Common. Woods, moors.

Pinopsida

Pinaceae
European Silver-fir *Abies alba* Uncommon. * Policy woodland
Giant Fir *Abies grandis* Uncommon. * Policy woodland
Douglas Fir *Pseudotsuga menziesii* Uncommon * Policy woodland
Western Hemlock *Tsuga heterophylla* Uncommon. * Policy woodland
Sitka Spruce *Picea sitchensis* Very Common. * Plantations
Norway Spruce *Picea abies* Very Common. * Plantations
Larch *Larix deciduas* Common. * Plantations
Hybrid Larch *Larix decidua x kaempferi (L. x marschlinsii)* Common. * Thirlestane, Carfrae.
Japanese Larch *Larix kaempferi* Uncommon. * Plantations
Scots Pine *Pinus sylvestris* Common. * Plantations (extinct as a native, which is nationally scarce)
Western Red Cedar *Thuja plicata* Scarce. * Policy woodland

Taxodiaceae
Wellingtonia *Sequoiadendron giganteum* Uncommon. * Policy woodland

Cupressaceae
Lawson's Cypress *Chamaecyparis lawsoniana* Uncommon. * Policy woodland
Juniper *Juniperus communis* (LBAP) Uncommon. Moorland. Blythe Water, Airhouse, Colmsliehill, Upland cleuchs

Taxaceae
Yew *Taxus baccata* Scarce. * Policy woodland

Magnoliidae

Nymphaeaceae
Spatter-dock *Nuphar advena* Rare. * Spottiswoode Loch

Ceratophyllaceae
Rigid Hornwort *Ceratophyllum demersum* Rare. * Spottiswoode Loch

Ranunculaceae
Marsh Marigold *Caltha palustris* Common. Burnsides, marsh
Globe-flower *Trollius europaeus* (LBAP) Rare. * Upland wet meadows.Washing Burn
Monk's-hood *Aconitum napellus* Uncommon. * Woodland. Thirlestane
Wood Anemone *Anemone nemorosa* Common. Old woodland and moorland
Meadow Buttercup *Ranunculus acris* Very Common. Pasture
Creeping Buttercup *Ranunculus repens* Very Common. Pasture, woods, wasteland
Bulbous Buttercup *Ranunculus bulbosus* Scarce. Old grassland. Lauder Common, Whitlaw, Boondreigh Water
Goldilocks Buttercup *Ranunculus auricomus* Scarce. Woods. Airhouse, Boondreigh, Old

Thirlestane Castle
Celery-leaved Buttercup *Ranunculus sceleratus* Rare. Mud at edge of ponds. Corsbie Bog
Lesser Spearwort *Ranunculus flammula* Common. Bogs and upland burnsides
Lesser Celandine *Ranunculus ficaria* Very Common. Woods, gardens, meadows
Ivy-leaved Crowfoot *Ranunculus hederaceus* Uncommon. Aquatic, mainly upland burns
Common Water-crowfoot *Ranunculus aquatilis* Uncommon. Leader, burns

Berberidaceae
Barberry *Berberis vulgaris* Rare. * Planted. Whiteburn, nr Lauder 1961
Hedge Barberry *Berberis darwinii x empetrifolia* Rare. * Planted. Boondreigh Water

Papaveraceae
Common Poppy *Papaver rhoeas* Scarce. Arable. Near Carfraemill
Long-headed Poppy *Papaver dubium* Uncommon. Wasteland. Lauder, old railway
Yellow-juiced Poppy *Papaver dubium ssp. Lecoqii* Scarce. Wasteland. Oxton
Welsh Poppy *Meconopsis cambrica* Uncommon. * Damp, rocky places. Lauder

Fumariaceae
Climbing Corydalis *Ceratocapnos claviculata* Uncommon. Dry woods, moorland. Spottiswoode,
Blythe Water, Boondreigh Water
Common Ramping-fumitory *Fumaria muralis ssp. boraei* Uncommon. Arable, waste. Oxton,
Carfraemill, Addinston
Purple Ramping-fumitory *Fumaria purpurea* (Nationally Scarce) Rare. Arable. Addinston 2000
Common Fumitory *Fumaria officinalis* Common. Arable, waste

Ulmaceae
Wych Elm *Ulmus glabra* Common. Woodland, deans, much reduced by Dutch Elm disease

Urticaceae
Common Nettle *Urtica dioica* Very Common. Woodland, waste
Small Nettle *Urtica urens* Rare. Woods, arable. Soonhope
Pellitory-of-the-Wall *Parietaria judaica* Rare. * Banks, rocks, walls. Spottiswoode

Myricaceae
Bog Myrtle *Myrica gale* Locally Extinct. * Upland marsh. Formerly at Spottiswoode to 1955

Fagaceae
Beech *Fagus sylvatica* Very Common. * Woods and hedgerows.
Sweet Chestnut *Castanea sativa* Uncommon. * Policies
Evergreen Oak *Quercus ilex* Scarce. * Planted, Hillhouse
Sessile Oak *Quercus petraea* Uncommon. Native, riverine woodland, and planted.
Pedunculate Oak *Quercus robur* Common. * Planted

Betulaceae
Silver Birch *Betula pendula* Uncommon. * Planted
Downy Birch *Betula pubescens* Common. Woods, moorland, bogs
Alder *Alnus glutinosa* Common. Wet and riverine woodlands
Hornbeam *Carpinus betulus* Scarce. * Planted. Hillhouse
Hazel *Corylus avellana* Uncommon. Woods and cleuchs

Chenopodiaceae
Good King Henry *Chenopodium bonus-henricus* Common. * Waste, river and burnsides
Fat-hen *Chenopodium album* Very Common. Arable, waste.
Spear-leaved Orache *Atriplex prostrata* Uncommon. * Roadsides
Grass-leaved Orache *Atriplex littoralis* Scarce. * Coastal species. A68, Channelkirk
Common Orache *Atriplex patula* Common. Waste and arable.

Portulacaceae
Pink Purslane *Claytonia sibirica* Common. * Woods, burnsides. Boondreigh Water, Harryburn
Blinks *Montia fontana ssp fontana* Common. Wet places
Blinks *Montia fontana ssp minor* Uncommon. Bare ground. Thirlestane

Caryophyllaceae
Thyme-leaved Sandwort *Arenaria serpyllifolia* Common. Waste, arable, burnsides
Three-nerved Sandwort *Moehringia trinervia* Common. Woods

Common Chickweed *Stellaria media* Very Common. Arable, waste
Greater Stitchwort *Stellaria holostea* Common. Dry woods banks
Lesser Stitchwort *Stellaria graminea* Common. Open woods, acid grassland
Bog Stitchwort *Stellaria uliginosa* Common. Marshes, wet woods
Snow-in-summer *Cerastium tomentosum* Rare. * Roadside-walls near gardens. Lauder
Common Mouse-ear *Cerastium fontanum* Very Common. Grassland, meadows, waste
Sticky Mouse-ear *Cerastium glomeratum* Common. Arable, waste
Knotted Pearlwort *Sagina nodosa* Uncommon. Base-rich flushes. Wheelburn
Procumbent Pearlwort *Sagina procumbens*Very Common. Wasteland, grassland
Annual Pearlwort *Sagina apetala* Uncommon. Bare ground, walls.
Annual Knawel *Scleranthus annuus* Rare/Extinct. Dry waste, arable, grassland. Oxton 1960
Corn Spurrey *Spergula arvensis* Uncommon. Arable and waste. Old railway line
Lesser Sea-spurrey *Spergularia marina* Uncommon. * Coastal, spreading along roadsides
Sand Spurrey *Spergularia rubra* Rare. Dry grassland. Boon
Ragged Robin *Lychnis flos-cuculi* (LBAP) Common. Wet pasture and bog
Bladder Campion *Silene vulgaris* Scarce. Arable, roadside. Hillhouse, Oxton 1960
White Campion *Silene latifolia* Uncommon. Arable, waste banks. Hillhouse
Red Campion *Silene dioica* Common. Woods, hedges

Polygonaceae
Amphibious Bistort *Persicaria amphibia* Common. Water. Leader and burns
Redshank *Persicaria maculosa* Very Common. Waste, arable, wet ground
Equal-leaved Knotgrass *Polygonum arenastrum* Common Waste, arable
Knotgrass *Polygonum aviculare* Common. Waste, arable
Black Bindweed *Fallopia convolvulus* Common. Arable
Sheep's Sorrel *Rumex acetosella* Common. Dry acid grassland, moorland
Common Sorrel *Rumex acetosa* Very Common. Grassland, open woods
Curled Dock *Rumex crispus* Common. Waste, arable, roadsides
Wood Dock *Rumex sanguineus* Uncommon. Woods, banks. Thirlestane, Boondreigh Water, Muircleuch
Broad-leaved Dock *Rumex obtusifolius* Very Common. Waste, arable, roadsides, hedges

Clusiaceae
Perforate St. John's-wort *Hypericum perforatum* Uncommon. Scrub, grassland. Blythe Water, Oxton 1960
Imperforate St. John's-wort *Hypericum maculatum* Scarce. Woodland edge. Carfraemill
Square-stalked St. John's-wort *Hypericum tetrapterum* Uncommon. Damp meadows, marshes. Whalplaw, Carfraemill
Slender St. John's-wort *Hypericum pulchrum* Uncommon. Grassland, scrub, dry woods. Uplands

Tiliaceae
Large-leaved Lime *Tilia platyphyllos* Rare. * Planted. Brunaburn Wood
Lime *Tilia cordata x platyphyllos (T. x vulgaris)* Uncommon. * Planted.
Small-leaved Lime *Tilia cordata* Scarce. * Planted. Bruntaburn Wood

Droseraceae
Round-leaved Sundew *Drosera rotundifolia* (LBAP) Uncommon. Acid bog. Jordonlaw Moss, Whalplaw Burn

Cistaceae
Common Rock-rose *Helianthemum nummularium* (LBAP) Uncommon. Basic grassland, moorland. By upland burns.

Violaceae
Sweet Violet *Viola odorata* Rare/Extinct. *Banks, woods, scrub. 1960.
Common Dog-violet *Viola riviniana* Very Common. Woods, banks, grassland
Marsh Violet *Viola palustris* Uncommon. Acid marshes and bogs.
Mountain Pansy *Viola lutea* Common. Upland grassland. A speciality of the area.
Field Pansy *Viola arvensis* Common. Arable, waste

Salicaceae
White Poplar *Populus alba* Uncommon. * Planted. West Mains Brae, Boondreigh Water
Aspen *Populus tremula* Uncommon. Damp woods. Flass Wood, Wheel Burn

Hybrid Black Poplar *Populus x canadensis (P. deltoides x nigra)* Scarce. * Washing Burn
Bay Willow *Salix pentandra* Scarce. Mosses. Threepwood, Longmuir Moss, planted by Whalplaw Burn
Crack Willow *Salix fragilis* Uncommon. * Burnsides, wet woodland. Leader
White Willow *Salix alba* Uncommon. * Burnsides, wet woodland. Lauder Burn. West Mains, Oxton
Purple Willow *Salix purpurea* Uncommon. * Marshes and fresh water. Planted Annfield
Osier *Salix viminalis* Common. * Marshes and fresh water
Goat Willow *Salix caprea* Common. Woods, hedges, scrub
Grey Willow *Salix cinerea* Common. Marshes, fresh water, wet woods
Eared Willow *Salix aurita* Common. Moorland, damp woods
Tea-Leaved Willow *Salix phylicifolia* Rare. Threepwood, Longmuir Moss
Creeping Willow *Salix repens* Rare. Mosses. Pickie Moss, Longmuir Moss, Everett Moss

Brassicaceae
Dame's-violet *Hesperis matronalis* Uncommon. * Woods near rivers. Wooplaw
Hedge Mustard *Sisymbrium officinale* Uncommon. Banks, waste. Railway cutting.
Garlic Mustard *Alliaria petiolata* Very Common. Banks, open woods.
Thale Cress *Arabidopsis thaliana* Uncommon. Gardens, waste ground, rocky ground. Lauder, Oxton
Winter-cress *Barbarea vulgaris* Common. Damper banks, waste ground, river shingle
Narrow-fruited Water-cress *Rorippa microphylla* Common. Most burns
Large Bitter-cress *Cardamine amara* Uncommon. Alderwoods, deans. Boondreigh Water, Corsbie Bog
Cuckoo-flower *Cardamine pratensis* Common. Damp pasture, unimproved grassland.
Wavy Bitter-cress *Cardamine flexuosa* Very Common. Burnsides, waste, gardens
Hairy Bitter-cress *Cardamine hirsute* Common. Gardens, waste
Aubretia *Aubrieta deltoidea* Rare. * Garden escape. Lauder
Honesty *Lunaria annua* Rare. * Garden escape. Lauder, Carfrae, Oxton
Common Whitlowgrass *Erophila verna* Uncommon. Walls, rocks, open sandy ground.
Glabrous Whitlowgrass *Erophila glabrescens* Uncommon. Thirlestane Castle, Old Thirlestane
Shepherd's-purse *Capsella bursa-pastoris* Very Common. Arable, waste
Field Penny-cress *Thlaspi arvense* Uncommon. Arable, waste
Smith's Pepperwort *Lepidium heterophyllum* Uncommon. A notable species of shingle by the Leader
Cabbage *Brassica oleracea* Rare. * Casual. Lauder
Rape *Brassica napus* Common. * Oilseed rape common along roads, and arable as 'weed'
Turnip *Brassica rapa* Scarce. * Riverbanks, waste. Lauder
Charlock *Sinapis arvensis* Common. Arable
Wild Radish *Raphanus raphanistrum* Uncommon. Arable, waste. Pyatshaw

Resedaceae
Weld *Reseda luteola* Scarce. * Disturbed ground. Wanton Walls, Below A697. Lauder

Empetraceae
Crowberry *Empetrum nigrum* Uncommon. Moors and bogs.

Ericaceae
Rhododendron *Rhododendron ponticum* Common. * Policy woodland
Heather *Calluna vulgaris* Very Common. Dominant on Lammermuir grouse moors.
Cross-leaved Heath *Erica tetralix* Common. Moors, peatland
Bell Heather *Erica cinerea* Common. Locally dominant in Lammermuirs
Cranberry *Vaccinium oxycoccos* Rare. Raised bogs. Corsbie. Threepwood.
Cowberry *Vaccinium vitis-idaea* Uncommon. Higher areas of moorland. Whalplaw and Boondreigh Burns
Bilberry *Vaccinium myrtillus* Common. Moorland, acid woodland

Pyrolaceae
Common Wintergreen *Pyrola minor* Scarce. Ancient woodland. Wooplaw, Longmuir Moss

Primulaceae
Primrose *Primula vulgaris* Very Common. Woods, grassy banks

Cowslip *Primula veris* Uncommon. * Grassland. Pyatshaw
Yellow Pimpernel *Lysimachia nemorum* Common. Acid woodland, upland burns
Bog Pimpernel *Anagallis tenella* Rare. Less-acid bogs. Wheel Burn

Grossulariaceae
Red Currant *Ribes rubrum* Uncommon. * Wetter and policy woodland. Thirlestane, Lauder.
Black Currant *Ribes nigrum* Uncommon. * Deans and mosses. Brunta Burn, Thirlestane
Gooseberry *Ribes uva-crispa* Common. * Wet woodlands, banks.
Flowering Currant *Ribes sanguineum* Scarce. * Policy woodlands. Thirlestane

Crassulaceae
Biting Stonecrop *Sedum acre* Scarce. Walls, dry grassland. Lauder, Carfraemill
White Stonecrop *Sedum album* Scarce. * Walls, rocks. Lauder
Hairy Stonecrop *Sedum villosum* (Nationally Scarce, BAP) Uncommon. Upland burnsides. Area speciality.

Saxifragaceae
Meadow Saxifrage *Saxifraga granulata* Uncommon. Dry grassland, meadows by water.Brunta Burn, Boondreigh
Opposite-leaved Golden-saxifrage *Chrysosplenium oppositifolium* Very Common. Wet areas, often in woods, uplands.
Alternate-leaved Golden-saxifrage *Chrysosplenium alternifolium* Scarce. Boggy woods, upland flushes. Earnscleuch. Old Thirlestane
Grass of Parnassus *Parnassia palustris* Uncommon. Marshes and flushes. Lauder Common. Wheel Burn, Boon, Longmuir, Earnscleuch Water

Rosaceae
Steeplebush *Spiraea douglasii* Rare. * Policy woodland. Thirlestane
Meadowsweet *Filipendula ulmaria* Very Common. Wet pasture and bog.
Raspberry *Rubus idaeus* Very Common. Wet woodland, moorland edge
Bramble *Rubus fruticosus agg.* Common. Woods, scrub, waste, hedges.
Marsh Cinquefoil *Potentilla palustris* Uncommon. Bogs, upland flushes and wet pasture.
Silverweed *Potentilla anserine* Common. Waste, roadsides, meadows.
Sulphur Cinquefoil *Potentilla recta* Rare/Extinct. * Waste, grassland. Nr Carfraemill 1960
Tormentil *Potentilla erecta* Very Common. Moorland, grassland
Creeping Cinquefoil *Potentilla reptans* Uncommon. Banks, grassland, waste.
Barren Strawberry *Potentilla sterilis* Common. Woodland, scrub
Wild Strawberry *Fragaria vesca* Common. Woodland scrub, basic grassland
Water Avens *Geum rivale* Common. Wet meadows, woods, marshes
Hybrid Avens *Geum rivale x urbanum (G. x intermedium)* Uncommon. Wet woodland. Boondreigh
Herb Bennet *Geum urbanum* Very Common. Woods, banks, scrub
Agrimony *Agrimonia eupatoria* Scarce. Roadsides, scrub. Boondreigh Foot
Lady's-mantle *Alchemilla vulgaris agg* Common. Grassland, difficult to distinguish. The recorded segregates are:
Alchemilla xanthochlora Uncommon, *Alchemilla filicaulis ssp. vestita* Common, *Alchemilla glabra* Common
Parsley-piert *Aphanes arvensis* Uncommon. Arable, bare ground.
Slender Parsley-piert *Aphanes inexspectata* Common. Rocky or sandy ground
Burnet Rose *Rosa pimpinellifolia* Scarce. Moorland, shingle, scrub. Wheel Burn. Airhouse.
Dog Rose *Rosa canina agg* Common. (comprising *R. canina, R. caesia* and their hybrid) Woods, scrub, hedgerows
Soft Downy-rose *Rosa mollis* Uncommon. Scrub, hedgerows
Sherard's Downy-rose *Rosa sherardii* Rare. Huntingdon, near Dod Mill 1966
Blackthorn *Prunus spinosa* Common. Hedgerow, scrub
Wild Plum *Prunus domestica* Rare/Extinct. * Planted in banks, woods. 1960
Wild Cherry *Prunus avium* Common. Local in deans. Also planted widely.
Bird Cherry *Prunus padus* Uncommon. Moist woods. Leader, burns
Pear *Pyrus communis* Scarce. * Planted. Near Carfraemill
Apple *Malus domesticus.* Scarce. * Hedgerows, scrub. Blackburn
Rowan *Sorbus aucuparia* Common. Dry woods, usually acid, rocks

Swedish Whitebeam *Sorbus intermedia* Scarce. * A68 south of Lauder
Wall Cotoneaster *Cotoneaster horizontalis* Uncommon. * Walls
Himalayan Cotoneaster *Cotoneaster simonsii* Uncommon. * Scrub and waste
Hawthorn *Crataegus monogyna* Very Common. Scrub, hedgerow. Widely planted.

Fabaceae
Kidney Vetch *Anthyllis vulneraria* Rare/Extinct. Calcareous grassland. 1960
Common Bird's-foot-trefoil *Lotus corniculatus* Very Common. Grassland, roadsides
Large Bird's-foot-trefoil *Lotus pedunculatus* Common. Damp meadows, marshes
Tufted Vetch *Vicia cracca* Very Common. Hedges, woodland border, scrub
Hairy Tare *Vicia hirsute* Uncommon. Banks, grassland
Bush Vetch *Vicia sepium* Very Common. Woods, banks, scrub
Narrow-leaved Vetch *Vicia sativa ssp. nigra* Scarce. Hedges, banks, grassland, scrub. Boondreigh, Lauder, Longmuir Moss
Bitter-vetch *Lathyrus linifolius* Common. Banks, scrub, heath, upland woods
Meadow Vetchling *Lathyrus pratensis* Very Common. Banks, grassland scrub
Common Restharrow *Ononis repens* Rare/Extinct. Calcareous grassland, scrub. 1960.
Black Medick *Medicago lupulina* Uncommon. Grassland, roadsides. Boondreigh, Lauder.
White Clover *Trifolium repens* Very Common. Grassland
Alsike Clover *Trifolium hybridum* Scarce. * Waste, sometimes sown. Lauder, Howlet's Ha'
Hop Trefoil *Trifolium campestre* Uncommon. Dry grassland, roadsides. Spottiswoode.
Lesser Trefoil *Trifolium dubium* Uncommon. Dry grassland, roadsides
Red Clover *Trifolium pratense* Common. Grassland, except on higher ground.
Zigzag Clover *Trifolium medium* Uncommon. Basic grassland, sometimes on higher ground.
Broom *Cytisus scoparius* Common. Scrub on dry, acid soils
Petty Whin *Genista anglica* (LBAP) Rare. Dry moorland. Hogs Law, Wheelburn
Gorse *Ulex europaeus* Very Common. Rough grassland, scrub, moorland.

Halogaraceae
Spiked Water-milfoil *Myriophyllum spicatum* Scarce. Base-rich water. Spottiswoode Loch
Alternate Water-milfoil *Myriophyllum alterniflorum* Local. Base-poor water. Leader and burns.

Onagraceae
Great Willowherb *Epilobium hirsutum* Very Common. Marshes, ditches, river banks
Hoary Willowherb *Epilobium parviflorum* Rare. Burnsides, marshes, waste. Houndslow
Broad-leaved Willowherb *Epilobium montanum* Very Common. Woods, hedges, walls, gardens
Short-fruited Willowherb *Epilobium obscurum* Common. Moist woods, marshes, wet pasture
American Willowherb *Epilobium ciliatum* Uncommon. * Woods, gardens, waste.
Marsh Willowherb *Epilobium palustre* Common. Acid marshes, ditches.
New Zealand Willowherb *Epilobium brunnescens* Uncommon. * Upland burnsides
Rosebay Willowherb *Chamerion angustifolium* Very Common. Waste, woods, gardens, cleared plantations
Enchanter's-nightshade *Circaea lutetiana* Scarce. Shady woods, basic soil. Brunta Burn

Onagraceae
Red-osier Dogwood *Cornus sericea* Scarce. * Policy woodland. Thirlestane

Aquifoliaceae
Holly *Ilex aquifolium* Uncommon. Woods, scrub, hedges. Limited to a few woods.

Buxaceae
Box *Buxus sempervirens* Scarce. * Policy woodland. Spottiswoode, Thirlestane.

Euphorbiaceae
Dog's Mercury *Mercurialis perennis* Uncommon. Basic, often ancient woodland
Sun Spurge *Euphorbia helioscopia* Uncommon. Arable weed. Lauder, Carfraemill
Petty Spurge *Euphorbia peplus* Rare/Extinct. Arable, waste. 1960
Cypress Spurge *Euphorbia cyparissias* Rare. * Garden escape. Lauder

Linaceae
Fairy Flax *Linum catharticum* Uncommon. Upland grassland, flushes.

Polygalaceae
Common Milkwort *Polygala vulgaris* Rare. Calcareous grassland. Soonhope Burn 1983

Heath Milkwort *Polygala serpyllifolia* Common. Acid grassland, moorland.

Hippocastanaceae
Horse-chestnut *Aesculus hippocastanum* Uncommon. *Policy woodland.

Aceraceae
Norway Maple *Acer platanoides* Scarce. * Policy woodland. Thirlestane, Pickie Moss
Sycamore *Acer pseudoplatanus* Common. * Invasive and planted.

Oxalidaceae
Wood-sorrel *Oxalis acetosella* Very Common. Shady woods, and among rocks.

Geraniaceae
French Crane's-bill *Geranium endressii* Rare. * Garden escape. Lauder
Wood Crane's-bill *Geranium sylvaticum* Uncommon. Burnsides, damp woods.
Meadow Crane's-bill *Geranium pratense* Uncommon. Grassland, roadsides (esp. calc. soils)
Cut-leaved Crane's-bill *Geranium dissectum* Uncommon. Arable, waste, banks. Lauder, Oxton, Addinston.
Dove's-foot Crane's-bill *Geranium molle* Uncommon. Dry grassland, waste, arable. Lauder, Thirlestane, Addinston
Herb-robert *Geranium robertianum* Very Common. Woods, banks.
Common Stork's Bill *Erodium cicutarium* Rare/Extinct. Waste, arable. 1960

Araliaceae
Common Ivy *Hedera helix* Uncommon. Dry woods, climbing on trees, walls, rocks.
Irish Ivy *Hedera helix 'Hibernica'* Uncommon. * Spottiswoode

Apiaceae
Marsh Pennywort *Hydrocotyle vulgaris* Rare. Marshes and fens. Houndslow, Lauder Hill 1902
Sanicle *Sanicula europaea* Scarce. Woods. Whitlaw, Brunta Burn
Rough Chervil *Chaerophyllum temulum* Rare. Banks, roadsides. Thirlestane 1982
Cow Parsley *Anthriscus sylvestris* Very Common. Banks, roadsides.
Sweet Cicely *Myrrhis odorata* Scarce. * Meadows, roadsides. Airhouse Wood, Newbigging
Pignut *Conopodium majus* Very Common. Dry woods, old grassland
Burnet-saxifrage *Pimpinella saxifraga* Uncommon. Dry grassland, often calcareous. Burnsides
Ground-elder *Aegopodium podagraria* Common. * Banks, woodland, gardens.
Hemlock *Conium maculatum* Uncommon. Waste. Carfraemill, Hillhouse, Rachan Burn
Lesser Marshwort *Apium inundatum* Rare. Water margins. Muircleuch
Cowbane *Cicuta virosa* Rare. Waters fens. Everett Moss
Wild Angelica *Angelica sylvestris* Common. Damp meadows, boggy areas, wet woods.
Hogweed *Heracleum sphondylium* Very Common. Banks, woodland, grassland.
Giant Hogweed *Heracleum mantegazzianum* Scarce. * River and burn sides. Lauder Burn
Upright Hedge-parsley *Torilis japonica* Uncommon. Roadsides. Brunta Burn, Airhouse, Carfrae
Wild Carrot *Daucus carota* Rare/Extinct. Basic grassland, roadsides. 1960

Apocynaceae
Lesser Periwinkle *Vinca minor* Rare/Extinct. * Woods. 1960

Convolvulaceae
Field Bindweed *Convolvulus arvensis* Rare. * Waste, arable, gardens. Lauder Burn, Whitlaw 1960
Hedge Bindweed *Calystegia sepium* Uncommon. * Hedgebanks, scrub, waste.
Large Bindweed *Calystegia silvatica* Rare. * Hedges, waste. Howlet's Ha'

Menyanthaceae
Bogbean *Menyanthes trifoliate* Uncommon. Still or slow water. Threepwood, Longmuir Moss, Gullett Pond, Wheel Burn

Boraginaceae
Lungwort *Pulmonaria officianalis* Rare. * Woods. Thirlestane 1982
Russian Comfrey *Symphytum asperum x officinale (S. x uplandicum)* Uncommon. * Roads, banks, woods, riversides. Oxton, Carfrae, Wooplaw
Tuberous Comfrey *Symphytum tuberosum* Uncommon. Woods, riversides. Dowiedean Burn, Washing Burn, Thirlestane.
Green Alkanet *Pentaglottis sempervirens* Uncommon. * Banks, waste. Houndslow, Thirlestane,

Spottiswoode.
Water Forget-me-not *Myosotis scorpioides* Common. Marshes, burns, ponds.
Creeping Forget-me-not *Myosotis secunda* Common. Upland burnsides, boggy areas.
Tufted Forget-me-not *Myosotis laxa* Common. Boggy areas, burnsides.
Wood Forget-me-not *Myosotis sylvatica* Common. * Policy and other woodlands
Field Forget-me-not *Myosotis arvensis* Very Common. Dry woods, arable, banks, roadsides.
Early Forget-me-not *Myosotis ramosissima* Rare/Extinct. Dry, open grassland. 1960
Changing Forget-me-not *Myosotis discolor* Uncommon. Dry grassland. Upland burnsides.

Lamiaceae
Hedge Woundwort *Stachys sylvatica* Very Common. Banks, woods
Hybrid Woundwort *Stachys palustris x sylvatica (S x ambigua)* Scarce. Woods, burnsides.
Standalane Plantation
Marsh Woundwort *Stachys palustris* Common. Marshes, burnsides.
White Dead-nettle *Lamium album* Common. Banks, roadsides, waste.
Red Dead-nettle *Lamium purpureum* Common. Arable, waste, banks.
Northern Dead-nettle *Lamium confertum* Scarce. Arable. Addinston area, Birkenside.
Hen-bit Dead-nettle *Lamium amplexicaule* Scarce. Arable, waste. Boondreigh Water, Raiway
cutting at Oxton, Addinston, Birkenside
Large-flowered Hemp-nettle *Galeopsis speciosa* (LBAP) Common. Arable, waste
Common Hemp-nettle *Galeopsis tetrahit* Uncommon. Arable, banks, woods, mosses
Bifid Hemp-nettle *Galeopsis bifida* Uncommon. Arable, mosses. Spottiswoode, Raecleuch,
Wiseburn, near Pickie Moss
Wood Sage *Teucrium scorodonia* Common. Dry woods, grassland, moorland.
Bugle *Ajuga reptans* Very Common. Damp woods.
Ground-ivy *Glechoma hederacea* Common . Woods, banks.
Selfheal *Prunella vulgaris* Very Common. Grassland, woods, waste.
Wild Thyme *Thymus polytrichus* Common. Dry moorland, rocky outcrops
Corn Mint *Mentha arvensis* Rare/Extinct. Arable. Oxton 1960
Whorled Mint *Mentha aquatica x arvensis (M. x verticillata)* Rare. Burnsides. Brunta Burn
Bushy Mint *Mentha arvensis x spicata (M. x gracilis)* Rare. * Damp ground. Airhouse Wood,
Annfield
Water Mint *Mentha aquatica* Common. Burn sides, marshes, ponds.
Spear Mint *Mentha spicata* Rare/Extinct. * Ditches, roadsides. Oxton 1960
Peppermint *Mentha aquatica x spicata (M. x piperita)* Uncommon. * River and burnsides.
Leader and tributaries.

Hippuridaceae
Mare's-tail *Hippuris vulgaris* Rare. Marshes, water margins. Threepwood Moss, Oxton 1960

Callitrichaceae
Annual Water-Starwort *Callitriche hermaphroditica* Uncommon. Burns and still water. Brunta
Burn, Wheel Burn, Spottiswoode, Muircleuch, Earnscleuch.
Common Water-Starwort *Callitriche stagnalis* Common. Leader and tributaries.
Various-leaved Water-Starwort *Callitriche platycarpa* Scarce. Corsbie Bog, Spottiswoode Loch
Intermediate Water-Starwort *Callitriche hamulata* Scarce. Leader, Boondreigh Water,
Spottiswoode Loch.

Plantaginaceae
Greater Plantain *Plantago major* Very Common. Arable, waste, roadsides.
Ribwort Plantain *Plantago lanceolata* Very Common. Grassland, waste, roadsides.

Oleaceae
Ash *Fraxinus excelsior* Very Common Woods, hedgerows. Widely planted.
Lilac *Syringa vulgaris* Rare. * Planted. Overhowden 1982
Wild Privet *Ligustrum vulgare* Rare. * Mostly planted. Thirlestane, Boondreigh Water.

Scrophulariaceae
Great Mullein *Verbascum thapsus* Scarce. Waste, dry banks, open woods. Leader at Thirlestane,
East Mains, Railway cutting, Oxton.
Common Figwort *Scrophularia nodosa* Uncommon. Woods, banks.
Monkeyflower *Mimulus guttatus* Common. * River banks. Leader and tributaries.

Hybrid Monkeyflower *Mimulus guttatus x luteus (M. x rober-sii)* Uncommon. * Leader, burns, Spottiswoode
Coppery Monkeyflower *Mimulus cupreus x guttatus (M. x burnetii)* Rare. * Leader near Carfraemill
Small Toadflax *Chaenorhinum minus* Rare/Extinct. * Waste. arable, railways. 1960
Ivy-leaved Toadflax *Cymbalaria muralis* Common. * Walls, rocks.
Italian Toadflax *Cymbalaria pallida* Rare. * Garden escape. Lauder
Common Toadflax *Linaria vulgaris* Rare. Grassland, scaurs, waste, arable. Near Old Thirlestane 1982
Purple Toadflax *Linaria purpurea* Rare. * Waste. Railway cutting, Oxton and near Airhouse, Lauder.
Pale Toadflax *Linaria repens* Rare/Extinct. * Waste, banks.1960
Foxglove *Digitalis purpurea* Very Common. Woods, upland rocks, banks.
Thyme-leaved Speedwell *Veronica serpyllifolia* Common. Grassland, moorland, waste.
Heath Speedwell *Veronica officinalis* Very Common. Grassland, moorland, open woods.
Germander Speedwell *Veronica chamaedrys* Very Common. Woods, banks, grassland.
Wood Speedwell *Veronica Montana* Uncommon. Woods
Marsh Speedwell *Veronica scutellata* Uncommon. Marshes, damp moorland.
Brooklime *Veronica beccabunga* Common. Burns, ponds, wet woods.
Blue Water-speedwell *Veronica anagallis-aquatica* Scarce. Burns, ponds, wet woods. Earnscleuch Water, Leader, Boon Bridge
Pink Water-speedwell *Veronica catenata* Rare. Burns. Brunta Burn
Wall Speedwell *Veronica arvensis* Common. Dry grasslands, arable, walls
Green Field-speedwell *Veronica agrestis* Scarce. Arable. Addinston, St. Leonards
Common Field-speedwell *Veronica persica* Common. * Arable, waste.
Slender Speedwell *Veronica filiformis* Common. * Grassland, gardens, river banks.
Ivy-leaved Speedwell *Veronica hederifolia* Common. Woods, arable, banks, waste.
Eyebright *Euphrasia officinalis agg.* Common. Moorland, dry grassland - difficult to tell apart. Recorded segregates are:
Euphrasia arctica ssp. borealis Common, *Euphrasia nemorosa* Uncommon, *Euphrasia confusa* Common, *Euphrasia micrantha* Uncommon, *Euphrasia scottica* Rare
Common Cow-wheat *Melampyrum pratense* Rare. Woods, moorland. Soonhope Burn 1983
Red Bartsia *Odontites vernus* Uncommon. Arable, waste, grassland. Blackburn, Wooplaw, Burn Mill
Yellow-rattle *Rhinanthus minor* Uncommon. Grassland. Longmuir, Threepwood, Pickie Mosses, Colmslie
Marsh Lousewort *Pedicularis palustris* Uncommon. Mosses, upland burnsides, marshy areas.
Lousewort *Pedicularis sylvatica* Common . Moorland

Lentibulariaceae
Common Butterwort *Pinguicula vulgaris* Common. Base-rich flushes. Boondreigh, Wheel and Whalplaw Burns

Campanulaceae
Giant Bellflower *Campanula latifolia* Uncommon. Woods, banks. Tower Wood, West Mains, Muircleuch
Harebell *Campanula rotundifolia* Very Common. Moorland, dry grassland.

Rubiaceae
Field Madder *Sherardia arvensis* Rare. Arable, waste. Set-aside near Carfraemill
Woodruff *Galium odoratum* Scarce. Ancient woodland. Boondreigh Water, Brunta Burn.
Fen Bedstraw *Galium uliginosum* Common. Marshes and bogs.
Common Marsh-bedstraw *Galium palustre* Common. Marshes, ditches, ponds.
Lady's Bedstraw *Galium verum* Common. Grassland, basic rock outcrops.
Heath Bedstraw *Galium saxatile* Very Common. Heath, grassland, woods on acid soil.
Cleavers *Galium aparine* Very Common. Banks, waste, arable, gardens.
Crosswort *Cruciata laevipes* Common. Woods, scrub, banks, grassland.

Caprifoliaceae
Red-berried Elder *Sambucus racemosa* Scarce. * Naturalised in woods. Mountmill and Whalplaw Burns, Thirlestane.

Elder *Sambucus nigra* Common. Woods, scrub, waste.
Guelder-rose *Viburnum opulus* Uncommon. Woods, scrub. Boondreigh Foot, Tower Wood.
Snowberry *Symphoricarpos albus* Common. * Introduced in hedges and woods.
Honeysuckle *Lonicera periclymenum* Uncommon. Woods and rocky places.

Adoxaceae
Moschatel *Adoxa moschatellina* Rare. Ancient woodland. Old Thirlestane, Airhouse Wood,
Wheel Burn

Valerianaceae
Common Valerian *Valeriana officinalis* Uncommon. Marshy areas, wet woods, riversides.
Marsh Valerian *Valeriana dioica* (LBAP) Uncommon. Marshes. Whalplaw Burn, Muircleuch,
Boondreigh, Longmuir

Dipsacaceae
Field Scabious *Knautia arvensis* Rare/Extinct. Dry grassland, roadsides. 1960
Devil's-bit Scabious *Succisa pratensis* Common. Grassland, meadows, damp woods.

Asteraceae
Lesser Burdock *Arctium minus* Common. Woods, scrub, banks, roadsides, waste.
Welted Thistle *Carduus crispus* Uncommon. Open woods, banks, waste. Thirlestane, Addinston,
Carfraemill, Hillhouse Burn.
Spear Thistle *Cirsium vulgare* Common. Waste, roadsides, grassland, open woods.
Melancholy Thistle *Cirsium heterophyllum* Uncommon. Grassland, open woods. Airhouse
Wood, Houndslow West Wood.
Marsh Thistle *Cirsium palustre* Common. Marshes, damp grassland, open woods.
Creeping Thistle *Cirsium arvense* Very Common. Grassland, arable, roadsides, waste.
Milk Thistle *Silybum marianum* Rare/Extinct. * Waste. 1960
Perennial Cornflower *Centaurea montana* Rare. * Introduced, waste. Oxton and railway cutting
near Oxton.
Cornflower *Centaurea cyanus* Rare. * Arable, waste. Cleekhimin Burn
Common Knapweed *Centaurea nigra* Very Common. Grasslands, roadsides, waste.
Nipplewort *Lapsana communis* Common. Banks, roadsides, waste, woods.
Cat's-ear *Hypochaeris radicata* Common. Grassland, roadsides.
Autumnal Hawkbit *Leontodon autumnalis* Common. Grassland, roadsides.
Goat's-beard *Tragopogon pratensis* Rare/Extinct. Roadsides, waste, arable. 1960
Rough Hawkbit *Leontodon hispidus* Uncommon. Calcareous grassland. Brunta Burn, Oxton,
Boondreigh
Perennial Sow-thistle *Sonchus arvensis* Uncommon. Arable, waste, roadsides. High Cross,
North of Oxton
Smooth Sow-thistle *Sonchus oleraceus* Uncommon. Arable, waste. Carfrae, Lauder.
Prickly Sow-thistle *Sonchus asper* Common. Arable, waste, open woods, banks.
Common Blue-sow-thistle *Cicerbita macrophylla* Rare. * Roadsides. Allanbank.
Dandelion *Taraxacum officinale agg.* Very Common. Grassland, roadside, waste.
Marsh Hawk's-beard *Crepis paludosa* Uncommon. Moist grassland. Damp woods. Basic flushes.
Northern Hawk's-beard *Crepis mollis* (Nationally Scarce, LBAP) Uncommon. Basic woodland-
edge grassland. Brunta Burn, Edgarhope Wood 1853
Rough Hawk's-beard *Crepis biennis* Rare. * Grassland, roadsides. Threepwood Bridge.
Smooth Hawk's-beard *Crepis capillaries* Uncommon. Grassland, waste, roadsides. Mountmill,
railway cutting, Boondreigh Foot.
Mouse-ear-hawkweed *Pilosella officinarum* Common. Grassland, rock outcrops.
Fox-and-cubs *Pilosella aurantiaca* Scarce. * Waste, roadsides. Railway cutting, Oxton.
Hawkweed *Hieracium murorum* Uncommon. Burnsides, rocks, woodland edges. Several
segregates present.
Mountain Everlasting *Antennaria dioica* Rare/Extinct. Moorland, dry grassland. Blythe Moors
1951
Heath Cudweed *Gnaphalium sylvaticum* Rare/Extinct. Open woods, moorland, acid grassland.
1960
Marsh Cudweed *Gnaphalium uliginosum* Uncommon. Damp arable, grassland. Mountmill,
Raecleuch, near Crib Law
Goldenrod *Solidago virgaurea* Uncommon. Rocks and steep banks. Blythe water, Edgarhope
moor, Earnscleuch

Confused Michaelmas-daisy *Aster novi-belgii* Rare. * Garden escape. Lauder Barns.
Daisy *Bellis perennis* Very Common. Grassland, gardens, waste.
Feverfew *Tanacetum parthenium* Scarce. * Banks, walls, waste, roadsides. Lauder, Railway at Oxton, Spottiswoode
Tansy *Tanacetum vulgare* Scarce. * Roadsides, waste, river banks. Mountmill, Lauder, Whalplaw
Mugwort *Artemisia vulgaris* Rare/Extinct. Waste, roadsides, arable. 1960
Sneezewort *Achillea ptarmica* Uncommon. Wet grassland, moorland, mosses.
Yarrow *Achillea millefolium* Common. Grassland, roadsides, banks.
Oxeye Daisy *Leucanthemum vulgare* Common. Grassland, roadsides
Scented Mayweed *Matricaria recutita* Rare. * Arable, waste High Cross.
Pineappleweed *Matricaria discoidea* Common. * Waste, roadsides, arable.
Scentless Mayweed *Tripleurospermum inodorum* Uncommon. Arable, waste. Railway cutting, Oxton, Annfield.
Common Ragwort *Senecio jacobaea* Common. Grasslands, roadsides, waste.
Marsh Ragwort *Senecio aquaticus* Scarce. Marshes, wet meadows. Longmuir Moss, Threepwood, Corsbie Bog
Oxford Ragwort *Senecio squalidus* Scarce. * Waste, roadsides, walls. Lauder
Groundsel *Senecio vulgaris* Common. Roadsides, sandy grassland.
Heath Groundsel *Senecio sylvaticus* Uncommon. Acid grassland, rock outcrops, open woods. Lauder Burn, Mountmill Burn, Spottiswoode, Hillhouse Burn
Sticky Groundsel *Senecio viscosus* Scarce. Waste, railway lines. Oxton, Lauder, Threepwood Bridge.
Colt's-foot *Tussilago farfara* Common. River banks, waste, arable.
Butterbur *Petasites hybridus* Common. River banks, wet pasture, roadsides.
Perennial Sunflower *Helianthus rigidus x tuberosus (H. x laetiflorus)* Rare. * Walls. Lauder.

Liliidae
Alismataceae
Water-plantain *Alisma plantago-aquatica* Scarce. Ponds, slow-moving water. Wooplaw. Leader.
Arrowhead *Sagittaria sagittifolia* Rare * Ponds. Gullett Pond.

Hydrocharitaceae
Canadian Waterweed *Elodea canadensis* Common. * Running and still water

Juncaginaceae
Marsh Arrowgrass *Triglochin palustre* Uncommon. Mainly upland wet areas. Boondreigh Burn, Mountmill Burn, Longmuir Moss, Threepwood, Spottiswoode.

Potamogetonaceae
Broad-leaved Pondweed *Potamogeton natans* Uncommon. Still and slow-moving water. Brunta Burn, Raecleugh
Bog Pondweed *Potamogeton polygonifolius* Uncommon. Shallow, peaty water, bogs. Longmuir Moss, Pickie Moss, Threepwood, Whalplaw Burn.
Red Pondweed *Potamogeton alpinus* Rare. Muircleugh 1997
Small Pondweed *Potamogeton berchtoldii* Rare. Still and slow-moving water. Oxbow pool below Cleekhimin Bridge
Fennel Pondweed *Potamogeton pectinatus* Rare. Still and running water. Spottiswoode Loch.

Araceae
Lords-and-ladies *Arum maculatum* Uncommon. * Woods and policies, banks. Thirlestane

Lemnaceae
Common Duckweed *Lemna minor* Common. Still or slow-moving water.

Juncaceae
Heath Rush *Juncus squarrosus* Common. Moorland
Toad Rush *Juncus bufonius* Common. Bogs, wet heath, damp, bare ground. e.g. Brunta Burn, Whalplaw
Jointed Rush *Juncus articulatus* Common. Acid, wet pasture and boggy areas.
Sharp-flowered Rush *Juncus acutiflorus* Common. Less-acid moorland, bogs, wet flushes and grassland.

Bulbous Rush *Juncus bulbosus* Uncommon. Bogs, wet moorland. e.g. Raecleugh, Boondreigh Burn, Longmuir Moss
Hard Rush *Juncus inflexus* Scarce. Damp, basic pasture. Thirlestane, Spottiswoode.
Soft Rush *Juncus effuses* Very Common. Wet grassland, bogs, damp woods
Compact Rush *Juncus conglomerates* Common. Wet grassland, damp woods, moorland
Hairy Wood-rush *Luzula pilosa* Common. Dry woods, moorland banks.
Great Wood-rush *Luzula sylvatica* Uncommon. Woodland or moorland banks with acid soil, indicative of former oak or birch woods. e.g. Airhouse Wood, Wooplaw, Whalplaw Burn
White Wood-rush *Luzula luzuloides* Scarce. * Policies. Thirlestane, Harryburn.
Field Wood-rush *Luzula campestris* Common. Grassland, moorland
Heath Wood-rush *Luzula multiflora* Common. Moorland, acid grassland and woods.

Cyperaceae
Common Cottongrass *Eriophorum angustifolium* Common. Moorland and mosses
Broad-leaved Cottongrass *Eriophorum latifolium* Scarce. Base-rich flushes. Whalplaw Burn
Hare's-tail Cottongrass *Eriophorum vaginatum* Common. Peaty moorland and mosses
Deergrass *Trichophorum cespitosum* Common. Peaty moorland. The rare ssp. *cespitosum* can be found at Longmuir Moss.
Common Spike-rush *Eleocharis palustris* Common. Water margins, wet grassland, upland burns, Spottiswoode
Few-flowered Spike-rush *Eleocharis quinqueflora* Rare. Base-rich flushes. Boondreigh Burn, Whalplaw Burn
Bristle Club-rush *Isolepis setacea* Scarce. Moorland edges. Cleekhimin Burn, Wheel Burn, Lauder Common
Greater Tussock-sedge *Carex paniculata* (LBAP) Scarce. Peaty soils, marshes, wet woods. Corsbie Bog, Pickie Moss, Mountmill Burn, Longmuir Moss
Lesser Tussock-sedge *Carex diandra* (LBAP) Rare. Watery mosses. Longmuir Moss, Threepwood
Prickly Sedge *Carex muricata ssp. lamprocarpa* Rare. Rocky grassland, acid soils. Brunta Burn
Grey Sedge *Carex divulsa ssp. leersii* Rare. * Shady places. Castle Hill, Thirlestane, 1975
Brown Sedge *Carex disticha* Common. Upland burnsides and mosses.
Remote Sedge *Carex remota* Rare/Extinct. Damp woods and shady places. Whitlaw 1960
Oval Sedge *Carex ovalis* Common. Moorland, damp grassland, woodland rides on acid soils.
Star Sedge *Carex echinata*. Common. Upland burns and marshy areas, on acid soils
Dioecious Sedge *Carex dioica* Scarce. Moorland, basic flushes. Boondreigh, Whalplaw and Wheel Burns
White Sedge *Carex curta* Uncommon. Raised mosses and other areas of peat. Threepwood, Pickie, Longmuir and Jordanlaw Mosses
Hairy Sedge *Carex hirta* Uncommon. Damp grassland, lowland burns. Lauder Burn.
Lesser Pond-sedge *Carex acutiformis* Scarce. Boggy areas, by ponds and burns. Pickie Moss, Thirlestane, Boondreigh Foot
Bottle Sedge *Carex rostrata* Common. Swamps, water edges, peaty areas.
Pendulous Sedge *Carex pendula* Scarce. * Garden escape. Harryburn.
Wood-sedge *Carex sylvatica* Scarce. Woodland tracks. Wooplaw, Thirlestane, Brunta Burn
Glaucous Sedge *Carex flacca* Common. Calcareous damp grassland, bogs.
Carnation Sedge *Carex panicea* Common. Moorland, boggy areas.
Smooth-stalked Sedge *Carex laevigata* Uncommon. Damp, shady woodland. Blythe Water, Boondreigh Burn, Brunta Wood.
Green-ribbed Sedge *Carex binervis* Common. Moorland in acid soils. Lauder Common, Longmuir, Threepwood.
Tawny Sedge *Carex hostiana* Uncommon. Moorland in basic flushes. Boondreigh, Whalplaw and Wheel Burns, Raecleugh.
Long-stalked Yellow-sedge *Carex viridula ssp. brachyrrhyncha* Uncommon. Moorland in basic flushes. Longmuir Moss, Boondreigh and Whalplaw Burns, Blythe Water
Common Yellow-sedge *Carex viridula ssp. oedocarpa* Uncommon. Moorland. Blythe Water, Boondreigh and Whalplaw Burns, Raecleugh
Pale Sedge *Carex pallescens* Rare. Open woods and damp grassland. Brunta Burn, Spottiswoode
Spring Sedge *Carex caryophyllea* Scarce. Basic rock outcrops. Lauder. Brunta and Whalplaw Burns, Longmuir Moss

Pill Sedge *Carex pilulifera* Uncommon. Moorland on acid soil. Lauder Common, Corsbie Bog, Longmuir Moss, Upland Burns.

Common Sedge *Carex nigra* Common. Moorland, boggy places.

Flea Sedge *Carex pulicaris* Uncommon. Moorland, in basic flushes, burnsides. Threepwood, Longmuir Moss

Poaceae

Mat-grass *Nardus stricta* Common. Locally dominant on moors.

Meadow Fescue *Festuca pratensis* Uncommon. Grassland with heavy or neutral soils. Whitlaw, Muircleuch, Threepwood, Longmuir

Tall Fescue *Festuca arundinacea* Uncommon. Road verges and grassy areas. Brunta, Mountmill Burns, Oxton railway, Boondreigh Foot.

Giant Fescue *Festuca gigantean* Rare. Woods, indicative of ancient woodland. Boondreigh Water

Red Fescue *Festuca rubra* Very Common. Pasture and grassy places.

Sheep's-fescue *Festuca ovina* Very Common. Dry grassland, moors.

Fine-leaved Sheep's-fescue *Festuca filiformis* Scarce. Acid soils. Pickie Moss, Muircleuch

Perennial Rye-grass *Lolium perenne* Very Common. Extensively sown for fodder and pasture.

Italian Rye-grass *Lolium multiflorum* Rare * Rarely sown. Whitlaw 1965

Crested Dog's-tail *Cynosurus cristatus* Common. Pastures.

Reflexed Saltmarsh-grass *Puccinellia distans* Scarce. * Roadsides. Dod Mill, near Corsbie Moor, west of Houndslow

Quaking-grass *Briza media* Uncommon. Upland grassland, often calcareous. Lauder Common, Threepwood, Longmuir Moss

Annual Meadow-grass *Poa annua* Very Common. Bare and disturbed ground.

Rough Meadow-grass *Poa trivialis* Very Common. Grassy areas, often damp and shady locations.

Spreading Meadow-grass *Poa humilis* Common. Upland gressland. Lauder Common, Oxton railway cutting.

Smooth Meadow-grass *Poa pratensis* Uncommon. Drier grassland.

Broad-leaved Meadow-grass *Poa chaixii* Rare. * Policy woods, planted ornamentally. Thirlestane

Wood Meadow-grass *Poa nemoralis* Scarce. Woods and walls. Boondreigh Water, Brunta Burn, Lauder, Thirlestane

Cock's-foot *Dactylis glomerata* Very Common. Usually lowland pasture. Native and sown.

Whorl-grass *Catabrosa aquatica* Rare. Mud by shallow pools. Everett Moss, Corsbie Bog

Floating Sweet-grass *Glyceria fluitans* Common. Running and still water, bogs.

Small Sweet-grass *Glyceria declinata* Uncommon. Freshwater margins. Blythe Water, Lauder, Brunta and Mountmill Burns, Longmuir Moss

Plicate Sweet-grass *Glyceria notata* Rare Damp areas and freshwater margins. Railway cutting at Oxton, Burnfoot, Corsbie Bog

Wood Melick *Melica uniflora* Rare. Dry woods and shady banks. Brunta Burn

Meadow Oat-grass *Helictotrichon pratense* Uncommon. Dry, rocky grassland. Whalplaw Burn, Whitlaw

False Oat-grass *Arrhenatherum elatius* Common. Roadsides, pasture, if not excessively grazed, waste.

Yellow Oat-grass *Trisetum flavescens* Uncommon. Calcareous grassland. Carfrae, Railway cutting at Oxton, Whitlaw, Boondreigh Burn

Crested Hair-grass *Koeleria macrantha* Uncommon. Dry, calcareous grassland. Whalplaw Burn.

Tufted Hair-grass *Deschampsia caespitosa* Very Common. Damp woods and grassland, marshes.

Wavy Hair-grass *Deschampsia flexuosa* Very Common. Dominant in dry moorland on acid soil.

Yorkshire-fog *Holcus lanatus* Very Common. Pasture, waste.

Creeping Soft-grass *Holcus mollis* Very Common. Open woods, banks. Dominant in sites of ancient oakwoods.

Silver Hair-grass *Aira caryophyllea* Rare. Dry, bare places. Whitlaw area.

Early Hair-grass *Aira praecox* Common. Dry, bare ground on acid soils. Lauder, Mountmill, Whalplaw and Brunta Burns, Edgarhope Moor, Blythe Water.

Sweet Vernal-grass *Anthoxanthum odoratum* Very common. Meadows, pastures, moorland.

Reed Canary-grass *Phalaris arundinacea* Common. River and burnsides, marshes, damp woods.

Common Bent *Agrostis capillaris* Very Common. Pasture and meadows, acid grassland.
Creeping Bent *Agrostis stolonifera* Common. Pasture, waste and disturbed ground
Velvet Bent *Agrostis canina* Uncommon. Damp moorland
Brown Bent *Agrostis vinealis* Uncommon. Moorland, generally drier than for Velvet Bent.
Meadow Foxtail *Alopecurus pratensis* Common. Pasture and meadow, neutral soils.
Marsh Foxtail *Alopecurus geniculatus* Common. Wet grassy places and in shallow, still water.
Timothy *Phleum pratense* Uncommon. Pasture, native and sown.
Smaller Cat's-tail *Phleum bertolonii* Scarce. Dry grassland. Spottiswoode, Blythe Water, Blackburn
Soft-brome *Bromus hordeaceus ssp. hordeaceus* Scarce. Road verges. Railway cutting at Oxton, Lauder, Boon Hill
Hairy Brome *Bromopsis ramose* Rare. Woods, shady banks. Boondreigh Water, near Boon
Barren Brome *Anisantha sterilis* Rare. Roadsides, waste. Lauder
False-brome *Brachypodium sylvaticum* Rare. Woods, banks, indicative of ancient woodland. Brunta Burn
Bearded Couch *Elymus caninus* Scarce. Damp, shady places - by rivers in woods. Brunta Burn, Boondreigh Burn
Common Couch *Elytrigia repens* Common. Pasture and arable weed waste.
Foxtail Barley *Hordeum jubatum* Rare. * Waste and roadsides. A68 near Channelkirk
Heath-grass *Danthonia decumbens* Uncommon. Dry, acid moorland edges. Whalplaw, Lauder Burns and Blythe Water, Longmuir Moss
Purple Moor-grass *Molinia caerulea* Common. Wet moorland on acid soil.

Sparganiaceae
Branched Bur-reed *Sparganium erectum* Common. Still and moving water. Leader and slower tributaries
Unbranched Bur-reed *Sparganium emersum* Scarce. Still and moving water. Muircleuch

Typhaceae
Bulrush (Common Reedmace) *Typha latifolia* Uncommon. Swamps, still or slow-moving water. Pond at Thirlestane, Pickie Moss

Liliaceae
Bog Asphodel *Narthecium ossifragum* Uncommon. Wet moorland, Sphagnum bog. Lauder Common, Threepwood, Longmuir Moss
Garden Solomon's-seal *Polygonatum multiflorum x odoratum (P. x hybridum)* Rare. * Garden escape. Carfraemill
Pyranean Squill *Scilla lilio-hyacinthus* Rare. * Escape. Lauder
Bluebell *Hyacinthoides non-scripta* (UKBAP, WCA Schedule 8) Uncommon. Woodland. Often confused with garden hybrids. Airhouse, Boondreigh Water, Brunta Burn, Tower wood.
Hybrid Bluebell *Hyacinthoides hispanica x non-scripta* Uncommon. * Dowiedean Burn, Thirlestane Castle.
Few-flowered Garlic *Allium paradoxum* Common. * Woodland, roadsides and spreading along riversides.
Ramsons *Allium ursinum* Uncommon. Damp old woodland, policies. Thirlestane, Washing Burn
Snowdrop *Galanthus nivalis* Uncommon. * Policy woodland. Thirlestane
Daffodil *Narcissus spp.* Uncommon. * Policy woodland, river banks.

Iridaceae
Yellow Iris *Iris pseudacorus* Common. River and burnsides, marshy places.
Montbretia *Crocosmia x crocosmiiflora (C. aurea x pottsii)* Rare. * Garden escape. Lauder

Orchidaceae
Broad-Leaved Helleborine *Epipactis helleborine* Rare. Woods. Thirlestane Castle, 1982
Common Twayblade *Listera ovata* Rare. Woods, grassland. Spottiswoode
Lesser Twayblade *Listera cordata* (LBAP) Rare. Moorland, peaty bogs. Longmuir and Threepwood Mosses, Rushy Grain
Fragrant Orchid *Gymnadenia conopsea* Rare. Dry, calcareous grassland. Brunta Burn
Common Spotted-orchid *Dactylorhiza fuchsii* Common. Grassland, scrub, woods.
Heath Spotted-orchid *Dactylorhiza maculata* Common. Moorland, bogs, acid grassland. Good display at Colmslie.

Hybrid Marsh-orchid *Dactylorhiza x formosa (D. maculata x purpurella)* Rare. Longmuir Moss
Early Marsh Orchid *Dactylorhiza incarnata* Rare. Marshes, wet meadows. Threepwood Moss
Northern Marsh-orchid *Dactylorhiza purpurella* Uncommon. Damp pasture. Longmuir, Threepwood, Thirlestane, Lauder Common, Whitlaw

Plants not recorded since the publication of Lauder and Lauderdale in 1902.

Flat-sedge	*Blysmus compressus*	Thirlestane	1902
Frog Orchid	*Coeloglossum viride*	Muircleuch	1902
Parsley Fern	*Cryptogramma crispa*	Chester Hill	1902
Pencilled Crane's-bill	*Geranium versicolor*	Allanbank nr Lauder	1902
Henbane	*Hyoscyamus niger*	Longcroft Water	1902
Martagon Lily	*Lilium martagon*	Thirlestane	1902
Musk Mallow	*Malva moschata*	Leadervale	1902
Tall Melilot	*Melilotus altissima*	Newmills	1902
Royal Fern	*Osmunda regalis*	Flass Wood	1902
Hoary Plantain	*Plantago media*	Thirlestane Castle Lawn	1902
Lesser Butterfly-orchid	*Platanthera bifolia*	Thirlestane	1902
Mountain Currant	*Ribes alpinum*	Thirlestane	1902
Sweet-briar	*Rosa rubiginosa*	Nr Lauder	1902
Monks' Rhubarb	*Rumex pseudoalpinus*	Earnscleugh Water	1902
Shepherd's-needle	*Scandix pecten-veneris*	Lauderdale	1902
Pepper-saxifrage	*Silaum silaus*	Fir Stell nr Lauder	1902
Field Woundwort	*Stachys arvensis*	Crofts nr Lauder	1902
Wood Bitter-vetch	*Vicia orobus*	Nr Lauder	1902
Wood Vetch	*Vicia sylvatica*	Road Lauder to Stow	1902
Squirrel-tail Fescue	*Vulpia bromoides*	Manse Road Lauder	1902
Prickly Sedge	*Carex muricata ssp. muricata*	Thirlestane Castle	1878
Wood Millet	*Milium effusum*	Thirlestane	1874
Field Gentian	*Gentianella campestris*	Lauder Common	1873
Adder's-tongue	*Ophioglossum vulgatum*	Lauder Common	1873
Chickweed Wintergreen	*Trientalis europaea*	Spottiswoode	1870

INVERTEBRATES

The list of invertebrates entirely reflects the recording effort in the area in the recent past, and is not a good representation of what is actually present in Lauderdale. The only group that has received anything like comprehensive coverage has been the butterflies. Moths have been poorly recorded, as have other conspicuous groups such as bees and dragonflies. Most of the moth records here were collated by A.G. Long in the 1960's, and were largely from his own traps at Spottiswoode in the 1950s. Within the moth list taken from Albert Long's records are several from George Bolam's work, *The Lepidoptera of Northumberland and the Eastern Borders* (published from 1925 to 1927), some of which may refer back to Andrew Kelly's original list, and therefore should be treated with caution. David Long has contributed more recent records from the last decade at Spottiswoode House. With the exception of the above, most invertebrate records have been collected from Threepwood on behalf of Scottish Natural Heritage (formerly NCC). These include moth records from Keith Alexander and Andrew Buckham, beetle records from Magnus Sinclair, Keith Alexander and M Collet, dance fly and miscellaneous invertebrate records from Keith Alexander and spider records from Jim Stewart.

Other records of interest include a significant contribution from Magnus Sinclair relating to water beetles from Longmuir Moss, and to the aquatic life of a horse trough near Stow! ("Towards Stow" in list below). Dipteran records from Lauder Common were collected by Mr. R. Crossley, trichopteran records again by A.G.Long, aquatic hemipteran records from Thirlestane farm pond and the Kelphope Burn by T. Huxley, and water beetle records from the Kelphope Burn by Dr. G.N. Foster. Other contributors with several records include Ross Spalding, Jon and Angela Mercer, Dan Watson and Richard Buckland.

References

The Millennium Atlas of Butterflies of Great Britain. 2002. Butterfly Conservation

Long, A.G. and McNeill, S. 1970. The Macro-Lepidoptera, Trichoptera and Heteroptera of Berwickshire; VC.81. From History of the Berwickshire Naturalists' Club, Vols. 34-38, 1956-1970 (kindly loaned by D.G.Long)

Prys-Jones, O.E. & Corbet, S.A. (1991) Bumblebees

Common Name *Species* (National Status) Local Status Distribution/Locality

Invertebrates

Mollusca
Arionidae
Great Black Slug *Arion ater* (Common) Threepwood Moss
Dusky Slug *Arion subfuscus* (Common) Threepwood Moss

Diplopoda (Millipedes)
Blaniulidae
Snake Millipede *Proteroiulus fuscus* (Common) Threepwood Moss

Julidae
Blunt-tailed Snake Millipede *Cylindroiulus punctatus* (Common) Threepwood Moss

Odonata (Dragonflies and Damselflies)
Coenagriidae
Large Red Damselfly *Pyrrhosoma nymphula* (Common, LBAP) Uncommon. Spottiswoode, Wooplaw
Blue-tailed Damselfly *Ischnura elegans* (Common) Common. Spottiswoode, Wooplaw
Common Blue Damselfly *Enallagma cyathigerum* (Common) Common. Spottiswoode, Wooplaw
Azure Damselfly *Coenagrion puella* (Common) Uncommon. Wooplaw

Lestidae
Emerald Damselfly *Lestes sponsa* (Common) Common. Wooplaw

Aeshnidae
Common Hawker *Aeshna juncea* (Common)Uncommon. Harryburn, Wooplaw

Orthoptera (Grasshoppers and Crickets)
Acrididae
Common Green Grasshopper *Omocestus viridulus* (Common) Lauder

Dermaptera (Earwigs)
Common Earwig *Forficula auricularia* (Common) Threepwood Moss

Hemiptera (Bugs)

Miridae
Bracken Bug *Monalocoris filicis* (Common) Threepwood Moss
a plantbug or grassbug *Bryocoris pteridis* (Common) Threepwood Moss
a plantbug or grassbug *Mecomma ambulans*(Common) Threepwood Moss

Gerridae
Common Pondskater *Gerris lacustris* (Common) Most still or slow-moving water

Notonectidae
Common Water-boatman *Notonecta glauca*(Common) Thirlestane, Kelphoe, Harryburn

Corixidae
a waterboatman *Callicorixa praeusta* (Common) Thirlestane
Punctate Corixa *Corixa punctata* (Common) Thirlestane
a waterboatman *Arctocorisa germari* (Common) Thirlestane
a waterboatman *Sigara dorsalis* (Common) Thirlestane, Kelphope Burn
a waterboatman *Sigara distincta* (Common) Thirlestane
a waterboatman *Sigara falleni* (Common) Thirlestane
a waterboatman *Sigara lateralis* (Common) Thirlestane

Cercopidae
Cuckoo-spit Insect *Philaenus spumarius* (Common) Threepwood Moss

Cicadellidae
a leafhopper *Ulopa reticulata* (Common) Threepwood Moss

Coleoptera (Beetles)

Carabidae
Snail Hunter *Cychrus caraboides* (Common) Wooplaw
a ground beetle *Leistus rufescens* (Common) Threepwood Moss
a ground beetle *Trechus obtusus* (Common) Threepwood Moss
a ground beetle *Pterostichus niger* (Common) Threepwood Moss
a ground beetle *Pterostichus nigrita* (Common) Threepwood Moss
a ground beetle *Synuchus nivalis* (Local) Threepwood Moss
a ground beetle *Agonum gracile* (Local) Longmuir Moss
a ground beetle *Trichocellus placidus* (Local) Threepwood Moss

Dytiscidae (LBAP)
a water beetle *Hydroporus discretus* (Local) Towards Stow
a water beetle *Hydroporus incognitos* (Local) Kelphope Burn
a water beetle *Hydroporous elongatulus* (RDB – Rare) Longmuir Moss
a water beetle *Hydroporous erythrocephalus* (Common) Longmuir Moss
a water beetle *Hydroporous gyllenhaali* (Common) Longmuir Moss
a water beetle *Hydroporous longicornis* (Notable/Nb) Longmuir Moss
a water beetle *Hydroporous obscurus* (Common) Longmuir Moss
a water beetle *Hydroporous plaustris* (Common) Longmuir Moss
a water beetle *Hydroporous pubescens* (Common) Longmuir Moss
a water beetle *Hydroporous striola* (Common) Longmuir Moss
a water beetle *Hydroporus memnonius* (Common) Towards Stow
a water beetle *Hydroporus nigrita* (Common) Towards Stow
a water beetle *Oreodytes sanmarki* (Common) Kelphope Burn
a water beetle *Oreodytes septentrionalis* (Local) Kelphope Burn
a water beetle *Laccornis oblongus* (RDB – Rare) Longmuir Moss
a water beetle *Platambus maculates* (Common) Kelphope Burn
a water beetle *Agabus bipustulatus* (Common) Longmuir Moss, Kelphope Burn
a water beetle *Agabus congener* (Local) Longmuir Moss
a water beetle *Agabus guttatus* (Common) Kelphope Burn
a water beetle *Agabus paludosus* (Local) Kelphope Burn
a water beetle *Agabus sturmii* (Common) Longmuir Moss
a water beetle *Ilybius fuliginosus* (Common) Kelphope Burn

Hydrophilidae
a scavenger water beetle *Helophorus aequalis* (Common) Longmuir Moss
a scavenger water beetle *Helophorus brevipalpis* (Common) Longmuir Moss, Kelphope Burn, Towards Stow
a scavenger water beetle *Helophorus flavipes* (Common) Longmuir Moss
a scavenger water beetle *Megasturnum obscurum* (Common) Longmuir Moss
a scavenger water beetle *Anacaena globules* (Common) Longmuir Moss, Towards Stow
a scavenger water beetle *Laccobius bipunctatus* (Common) Longmuir Moss, Kelphope Burn
a scavenger water beetle *Chaetarthria seminulum* (Notable/Nb) Longmuir Moss

Hydraenidae
a small water beetle *Ochthebius exsculptus* (Notable/Nb) Kelphope Burn
a small water beetle *Hydraena gracilis* (Local) Kelphope Burn
a small water beetle *Limnebius truncatellus* (Common) Kelphope Burn

Silphidae
a carrion beetle *Nicrophorus sp.* Thirlestane
Red-breasted carrion beetle *Oiceoptoma thoracicum* (Local) Wooplaw

Scaphidiidae
a shining fungus beetle *Scaphisoma agaricinum* (Local) Threepwood Moss

Staphylinidae
a rove beetle *Omalium oxyacanthae* (Local) Threepwood Moss
a rove beetle *Omalium rivulare* (Common) Threepwood Moss
a rove beetle *Stenus pubescens* Longmuir Moss
a rove beetle *Philonthus nigrita* (Local) Longmuir Moss
a rove beetle *Quedius fuliginosus* (Common) Threepwood Moss
a rove beetle *Lordithon lunulatus* (Common) Threepwood Moss
a rove beetle *Lordithon thoracicus* (Common) Threepwood Moss
a rove beetle *Gymnusa variegata* (Notable) Longmuir Moss
a rove beetle *Atheta graminicola* Longmuir Moss

Scirtidae
a marsh beetle *Cyphon coarctatus* (Common) Threepwood Moss
a marsh beetle *Cyphon hilaris* (Local) Threepwood Moss
a marsh beetle *Cyphon ochraceus* (Common) Threepwood Moss
a marsh beetle *Cyphon phragmiteticola* (Local) Threepwood Moss

Elmidae
a riffle beetle *Elmis aenea* (Common) Kelphope Burn
a riffle beetle *Esolus parallelepipedus* (Common) Kelphope Burn
a riffle beetle *Limnius volckmari* (Common) Kelphope Burn

Elateridae
a click beetle *Denticollis linearis* (Common) Threepwood Moss
a click beetle *Dalopius marginatus* (Common) Threepwood Moss
a click beetle *Ampedus balteatus* (Local) Threepwood Moss

Cantharidae
a soldier beetle *Cantharis figurate* (Local) Threepwood Moss
a soldier beetle *Cantharis nigra* (Common) Threepwood Moss
a soldier beetle *Cantharis paludosa* (Local) Threepwood Moss
a soldier beetle *Rhagonycha lignose* (Common) Threepwood Moss
a soldier beetle *Rhagonycha limbata* (Common) Longmuir Moss
a soldier beetle *Malthodes mysticus* (Local) Threepwood Moss

Rhizophagidae
a narrow bark beetle *Rhizophagus dispar* (Common) Threepwood Moss
a narrow bark beetle *Rhizophagus nitidulus* (Notable/Nb) Threepwood Moss

Cerylonidae
a cerylonid beetle *Cerylon ferrugineum* (Local) Threepwood Moss

Coccinellidae

Two-spot Ladybird *Adalia bipunctata* (Common) Lauder
Seven-spot Ladybird *Coccinella 7-punctata* (Common) Common. Harryburn
Cream-spot Ladybird *Calvia quattuordecimguttata* (Common) Common. Threepwood Moss
14-spot Ladybird *Propylea quattuordecimpunctata* (Common) Uncommon.
Orange Ladybird *Halyzia 16-guttata* (Local) Uncommon. Wooplaw

Scraptiidae
a tumbling flower beetle *Anaspis maculata* (Common) Threepwood Moss

Cerambycidae
a longhorn beetle *Strangalia quadrifasciata* (Local) Threepwood Moss

Chrysomelidae
a reed beetle *Plateumaris discolor* Longmuir Moss
Mustard beetle *Phaedon cochleariae* (Common) Longmuir Moss
Small Turnip Flea Beetle *Phyllotreta undulata* (Common) Threepwood Moss

Attelabidae
a leafroller weevil *Rhynchites nanus* (Local) Threepwood Moss
Birch Leaf Roller *Deporaus betulae* (Common) Threepwood Moss
a leafroller weevil *Deporaus mannerheimi* (Local) Threepwood Moss

Apionidae
White Clover Seed Weevil *Protapion fulvipes* (Common) Threepwood Moss
a seed weevil *Perapion curtirostre* (Common) Threepwood Moss
a seed weevil *Perapion violaceum* (Common) Threepwood Moss
a seed weevil *Eutrichapion ervi* (Common) Threepwood Moss
a seed weevil *Eutrichapion viciae* (Common) Threepwood Moss

Curculionidae
Silver-green Leaf Weevil *Phyllobius argentatus* (Common) Threepwood Moss
a weevil *Anoplus plantaris* (Common) Threepwood Moss
Small Heather Weevil *Micrelus ericae* (Common) Threepwood Moss
Strawberry Blossom Weevil *Anthonomus rubi* (Common) Threepwood Moss

Scolytidae
a bark or ambrosia beetle *Scolytus ratzeburgi* (Notable/Nb) Threepwood Moss

Trichoptera (Caddis Flies)

Rhyacophilidae
A caddis fly *Rhyacophila dorsalis* (Common) Earnscleuch Water, Dye Water

Psychomyiidae
A caddis fly *Psychomyia pusilla* (Common) Spottiswoode Loch
A caddis fly *Tinodes waeneri* (Common) Spottiswoode Loch

Limnephilidae
A caddis fly *Halesus radiatus* (Common) Spottiswoode Loch
A caddis fly *Chaetopteryx villosa* (Common) Spottiswoode Loch
A caddis fly *Anabolia nervosa* (Common) Spottiswoode Loch

Leptoceridae
A caddis fly *Athripsodes aterrimus* (Common) Spottiswoode Loch

Lepidoptera (Butterflies and Moths)

Hepialidae
Ghost Swift *Hepialus humuli* (Common) Spottiswoode House
Map-Winged Swift *Hepialus fusconebulosa* (Common) Spottiswoode House

Incurvariidae
a longhorn moth *Phylloporia bistrigella* (Unknown) Threepwood Moss
a longhorn moth *Lampronia fuscatella* (pRDB3) Threepwood Moss

Yponomeutidae
a small ermine moth *Swammerdamia caesiella* (Unknown) Threepwood Moss

Coleophoridae
a micro-moth *Coleophora serratella* (Common) Threepwood Moss
Tortricidae
Flax Tortrix *Cnephasia interjectana* (Common) Threepwood Moss
a tortrix moth *Olethreutes olivana* (Notable/Nb) Threepwood Moss

Pyralidae
a pyralid moth *Crambus lathoniellus* (Common) Threepwood Moss
Pearl-band Grass Veneer *Catoptria margaritella margaritella* (Local) Threepwood Moss

Pieridae
Clouded Yellow *Colias croceus* (Migrant) Rare, Lauder, 2000.
Large White *Pieris brassicae* (Common) Very Common, Widespread
Green-veined White *Pieris napi* (Common) Very Common, Widespread
Small White *Pieris rapae* (Common) Common, Widespread
Orange Tip *Anthocharis cardamines* (Common) Common, Widespread

Lycaenidae
Small Copper *Lycaena phlaeas* (Common) Uncommon, Spottiswoode
Common Blue *Polyommatus icarus* (Common, LBAP) Uncommon, Whalplaw Burn, Wooplaw
Northern Brown Argus *Aricia artaxerxes* (Local, LBAP) Uncommon, Lauder Burn, Woodheads

Nymphalidae
Red Admiral *Vanessa atalanta* (Migrant) Common, Widespread
Painted Lady *Cynthia cardui* (Migrant) Uncommon, Blainslie, Spottiswoode
Small Tortoiseshell *Aglais urticae* (Common) Very Common, Widespread
Peacock *Inachis io* (Common) Common, Widespread
Small Pearl-bordered Fritillary *Boloria selene* (Local) Rare, Threepwood Moss
Dark Green Fritillary *Argynnis aglaja* (Local) Uncommon, Colmslie Junipers, Thirlestane

Satyridae
Meadow Brown *Maniola jurtina* (Common) Very Common, Widespread
Small Heath *Coenonympha pamphilus* (Common) Common, Widespread in moorland
Large Heath *Coenonympha tullia* (Local, LBAP) Rare, Corsbie Bog, Jordonlaw Moss (probably extinct at latter site)
Large Heath *Coenonympha tullia polydama* (Notable/Nb) Rare, Corsbie Bog, Threepwood Moss
Ringlet *Aphantopus hyperantus* (Common) Common, Widespread

Lasiocampidae
December Moth *Poecilocampa populi* (Common) Spottiswoode House
Pale Eggar *Trichiura crataegi* (Local) Byrecleuch

Saturniidae
Emperor *Pavonia pavonia* (Common) Threepwood Moss, Tollis Hill

Thyatiridae
Peach Blossom *Thyatira batis* (Common) Spottiswoode
Yellow Horned *Achlya flavicornis* (Common) Spottiswoode House

Geometridae
Large Emerald *Geometra papilionaria* (Common) Threepwood Moss, Spottiswoode House
Maiden's Blush *Cyclophora punctaria* (Regionally Notable) Lauderdale 1927 - possibly before (Bolam)
Wood Carpet *Epirrhoe rivata* (Regionally Notable) Lauder 1927
Common Carpet *Epirrhoe alternata* (Common) Spottiswoode
Silver Ground Carpet *Xanthorhoe montanata* (Common) Spottiswoode House
Yellow Shell *Camptogramma bilineata bilineata* (Common) Airhouse Wood, Spottiswoode House
Water Carpet *Lampropteryx suffumata* Spottiswoode House
Grey Mountain Moth *Entephria caesiata* (Common) Whalplaw Burn
Purple Bar *Cosmorhoe ocellata* (Common) Whalplaw, Whitlaw, Spottiswoode
Chevron *Eulithis testate* (Common) Spottiswoode House
Red Green Carpet *Chloroclysta siterata* (Common) Harryburn

Autumn Green Carpet *Chloroclysta miata* (Local) Spottiswoode House, Harryburn
Common Marbled Carpet *Chloroclysta truncata* (Common) Spottiswoode, Harryburn
Grey Pine Carpet *Thera obeliscata* (Common) Spottiswoode, Harryburn
Mottled Grey *Colostygia multistrigaria* Spottiswoode House
July Highflyer *Hydriomena furcata* (Common) Harryburn
May Highflyer *Hydriomena impluviata* (Common) Brunta Burn
Winter Moth *Operophtera brumata* (Common) Spottiswoode
Small Rivulet *Perizoma alchemillata* (Common) Spottiswoode
Dwarf Pug *Eupithecia tantillaria* (Local) Spottiswoode
Wormwood Pug *Eupithecia absinthiata* (Common) Spottiswoode
Satyr Pug *Eupithecia satyrata* (Local) Byrecleuch
Tawny-Speckled Pug *Eupithecia icterata* (Common) Spottiswoode
Treble Bar *Aplocera plagiata* (Local) Spottiswoode
Chimney Sweeper *Odezia atrata* (Common) Threepwood Moss, Airhouse, Brunta Burn, Wooplaw
Brimstone Moth *Opisthograptis luteolata* (Common) Spottiswoode House
Canary-Shouldered Thorn *Ennomos alniaria* (Common) Upper Blainslie, Harryburn
Lunar Thorn *Selenia lunularia* (Local) Spottiswoode House
Scalloped Hazel *Odontopera bidentata* (Common) Spottiswoode House
Scalloped Oak *Crocallis elinguaria* (Common) Spottiswoode
Feathered Thorn *Colotois pennaria* (Common) Lauder 1927, Harryburn
Pale Brindled Beautty *Apocheima pilosaria* (Common) Spottiswoode House
Dotted Border *Agriopis marginaria* (Common) Spottiswoode, 1996
Mottled Umber *Erannis defoliaria* (Common) Spottiswoode House
Mottled Beauty *Alcis repandata* (Common) Spottiswoode
Engrailed *Ectropis bistortata* (Common) Spottiswoode House
Common White Wave *Cabera pusaria* (Common) Spottiswoode
Light Emerald *Campaea margaritata* (Common) Spottiswoode, Harryburn
Barred Red *Hylaea fasciaria* (Common) Spottiswoode

Sphingidae
Poplar Hawk-moth *Laothoe populi* (Common) Spottiswoode
Humming Bird Hawk-moth *Macroglossum stellatarum* (Migrant) Lauder 1947, Spottiswoode House
Elephant Hawk-moth *Deilephila elpenor* (Local in Scotland) Spottiswoode House

Notodontidae
Iron Prominent *Notodonta dromedarius* (Common) Woodheads
Coxcomb Prominent *Ptilodon capucina* (Common) Spottiswoode House
Small Chocolate-tip *Clostera pigra* (Notable/Nb) Legerwood 1927

Arctiidae
Wood Tiger *Parasemia plantaginis* (Local) Lauder 1925
Clouded Buff *Diacrisia sannio* (Regionally Notable) Oxton & Lauderdale 1925

Noctuidae
Flame Shoulder *Ochropleura plecta* (Common) Spottiswoode
Large Yellow Underwing *Noctua pronuba* (Common) Spottiswoode, Harryburn
Lesser Broad Bordered Underwing *Noctua janthe* (Common) Spottiswoode
True Lover's Knot *Lycophotia porphyrea* (Common) Spottiswoode
Ingrailed Clay *Diarsia mendica mendica* (Common) Spottiswoode
Small Square-Spot *Diarsia rubi* (Common) Spottiswoode
Great Brocade *Eurois occulta* (Regionally Notable) Spottiswoode
Dog's Tooth *Lacanobia suasa* (Regionally Notable) Lauderdale 1927
Antler *Cerapteryx graminis* (Common) Spottiswoode, Harryburn
Small Quaker *Orthosia cruda* (Common) Spottiswoode House
Clouded Drab *Orthosia incerta* (Locally common) Spottiswoode
Twin-Spotted Quaker *Orthosia munda* (Local) Lauderdale 1927
Hebrew Character *Orthosia gothica* (Common) Spottiswoode House
Brindled Ochre *Dasypolia templi* (Local) Spottiswoode House, Harryburn
Grey Chi *Antitype chi* (Common) Spottiswoode

Chestnut *Conistra vaccinii* (Common) Spottiswoode House, Harryburn
Dark Chestnut *Conistra ligula* (Common) Lauderdale 1927
Red-Line Quaker *Agrochola lota* (Common) Lauder 1927, Harryburn
Yellow-Line Quaker *Agrochola macilenta* (Common) Lauder 1927, Spottiswoode House, Harryburn
Lunar Underwing *Omphaloscelis lunosa* (Local) Lauder 1927
Sallow *Xanthia icteritia* (Common) Lauder 1927
Confused *Apamea furva britannica* (Local)   Spottiswoode
Dusky Brocade *Apamea remissa* (Common) Spottiswoode
Small Clouded Brindle *Apamea unanimis* (Common) Lauder 1927
Clouded-Bordered Brindle *Apamea crenata* (Common) Spottiswoode House
Dark Arches *Apamea monoglypha* (Common) Spottiswoode, Harryburn
Middle-Barred Minor *Oligia fasciuncula* (Common) Spottiswoode
Double Square-Spot *Xestia triangulum* (Common) Spottiswoode
Dotted Clay *Xestia baja* (Common) Spottiswoode
Six-Striped Rustic *Xestia sexstrigata* (Common) Spottiswoode
Angle Shades *Phlogophora meticulosa* (Common) Harryburn
Pink-Barred Sallow *Xanthia togata* Spottiswoode House
Coronet *Craniophora ligustri* (Regionally Notable) Lauder 1927
Burnished Brass *Diachrysia chrysitis* (Common) Spottiswoode House
Gold Spot *Plusia festucae* (Common) Spottiswoode
Gold Spangle *Autographa bractea* (Common) Spottiswoode
Plain Golden Y *Autographa jota* (Common) Spottiswoode
Silver Y *Autographa gamma* (Common) Spottiswoode House
Scarce Silver Y *Syngrapha interrogationis* (Local) Spottiswoode
Mother Shipton *Callistege mi* (Common) Spottiswoode, Brunta Burn, Raecleuch Farm

Diptera (True Flies)

Stratiomyidae
a soldier fly *Beris geniculata* (Common) Threepwood Moss

Rhagionidae
a snipe fly *Symphoromyia crassicornis* (Local) Threepwood Moss
a snipe fly *Rhagio lineola* (Common) Threepwood Moss
a snipe fly *Rhagio tringarius* (Common) Threepwood Moss

Tabanidae
a horse fly *Haematopota pluvialis* (Common) Oxton

Asilidae
a robber fly *Dioctria rufipes* (Local) Lauder Common, Threepwood

Empididae
a dance fly *Platypalpus notatus* (Common) Lauder Common
a dance fly *Bicellaria spuria* (Local) Lauder Common
a dance fly *Empis (Pachymeria) tessellata* (Common) Lauder Common
a dance fly *Hilara chorica* (Common) Lauder Common
a dance fly *Hilara litorea* (Common) Lauder Common

Dolichopodidae
a dolichopodid fly *Dolichopus discifer* (Common) Lauder Common, Threepwood
a dolichopodid fly *Dolichopus lepidus* (Local) Lauder Common, Threepwood
a dolichopodid fly *Dolichopus plumipes* (Common) Lauder Common
a dolichopodid fly *Dolichopus vitripennis* (Local) Lauder Common
a dolichopodid fly *Hercostomus nigripennis* (Local) Lauder Common
a dolichopodid fly *Sympycnus desoutteri* (Common) Lauder Common

Syrphidae
a hoverfly *Melanostoma mellinum* (Common) Lauder Common
a hoverfly *Platycheirus angustatus* (Common) Lauder Common
a hoverfly *Chrysogaster hirtella* (Common) Lauder Common

a hoverfly *Eristalis arbustorum* (Common) Lauder Common
a hoverfly *Eristalis horticola* (Common) Lauder Common
a hoverfly *Helophilus pendulus* (Common) Lauder Common
a hoverfly *Sericomyia silentis* (Common) Lauder Common
a hoverfly *Volucella bombylans* (Common) Thirlestane

Sciomyzidae
a snail-killing fly *Tetanocera hyalipennis* (Common) Lauder Common

Hymenoptera (Ants, Bees and Wasps)

Siricidae
Greater Horntail *Urocerus gigas* (Uncommon) Spottiswoode House, Wooplaw

Cimbicidae
a clubhorned sawfly *Trichiosoma lucorum* (Local) Threepwood Moss

Diprionidae
a sawfly *Diprion pini* Edgarhope 1947

Formicidae
Red Ant *Myrmica rubra* (Common) Threepwood Moss
an ant *Myrmica ruginodis* (Common) Threepwood Moss
Slender Ant *Leptothorax acervorum* (Common) Threepwood Moss
an ant *Formica lemani* (Local) Threepwood Moss

Apidae
White-tailed Bumble Bee *Bombus lucorum* (Common) Widespread
Buff-tailed Bumble Bee *Bombus terrestris* (Common) Widespread
Red-tailed Bumble Bee *Bombus lapidarius* (Common) Widespread
a social bee *Bombus magnus* NT55
Mountain Bumble Bee *Bombus monticola* (Local) NT55
Small Garden Bumble Bee *Bombus hortorum* (Common) Widespread in gardens
Common Carder Bee *Bombus pascuorum* (Common) Widespread
Four Coloured Cuckoo Bee *Psithyrus sylvestris* (Common) NT55

Amphipoda (Amphipods)

Gammaridae
a freshwater shrimp *Gammarus pulex* (Common) All running water

Isopoda (Woodlice)

Oniscidae
Common Shiny Woodlouse *Oniscus asellus* (Common) Threepwood Moss
Porcellionidae
Common Rough Woodlouse *Porcellio scaber* (Common) Threepwood Moss

Araneae (Spiders)

Dictynidae
a mesh webbed spider *Dictyna arundinacea* (Common) Threepwood Moss

Lycosidae
a wolf spider *Pardosa nigriceps* (Common) Threepwood Moss
a wolf spider *Pirata piraticus* (Local) Threepwood Moss

Theridiidae
a comb-footed spider *Theridion sisyphium* (Common) Threepwood Moss

Araneidae
an orb-weaver spider *Araneus quadratus* (Common) Threepwood Moss

Linyphiidae
a money spider *Ceratinella brevipes* (Common) Threepwood Moss

a money spider *Hypomma cornutum* (Common) Threepwood Moss
a money spider *Maso sundevalli* (Common) Threepwood Moss
a money spider *Pelecopsis mengei* (Local) Threepwood Moss
a money spider *Cnephalocotes obscurus* (Local) Threepwood Moss
a money spider *Lepthyphantes mengei* (Common) Threepwood Moss
a money spider *Linyphia triangularis* (Common) Wooplaw

VERTEBRATES

Large, visible animals are relatively easy to spot and identify, and this is reflected in the coverage of the vertebrate species.

Although adders have been recorded in Lauderdale, they are almost certainly a lot more common than records suggest. Similarly, slow worms and common lizards almost certainly occur, but have not been recorded.

Frogs and toads are relatively abundant, but there are no records of newts, again probably a consequence of under-recording.

A comprehensive programme of sampling the rivers and burns of the Tweed catchment using electro-fishing techniques has been undertaken by the Tweed Foundation for almost 20 years. This has ensured that the list of fish species, whilst relatively short, is almost certainly complete. Thanks must be offered to Dr. Ron Campbell of the Tweed Foundation for his efforts in this respect. Salmon spawn in large numbers in the Leader in the late autumn, although the number of trout has probably declined over the last century.

Birds are well recorded through national schemes run by the British Trust for Ornithology and the Scottish Ornithological Club, and we have several active members in the area. Special mention should be made of Ray Murray who edits the annual Borders Bird report, and was also a major contributor to the Breeding Birds of South East Scotland, both of which have been widely consulted in the preparation of the current lists. Of special note is the relative increase in raptors over the second half of the 20th.Century. In particular, buzzards are now a common sight, largely due to changes in attitude towards persecution, together with a decline in the fortunes of the sporting estates. Other birds have shown a surprising increase, such as the oystercatcher, now almost a defining feature of the Leader haughs. Lauderdale remains relatively well off for farmland birds in decline elsewhere, such as skylark, song thrush and lapwing. 'New' birds such as the nuthatch are increasing their range northwards; this species can now be seen at Spottiswoode, and in Lauder

Mammals somewhat surprisingly fare rather worse in the recording stakes. Hardly any records exist of small rodents, albeit they are certainly abundant. Similarly there is very little information about bat species, other than pipistrelle and long-eared bat. A welcome change in the fauna has been the steady increase in otter numbers, signs of which can be found throughout Lauderdale. A less welcome addition has been the Sika deer, which wreaks havoc in forestry together with the burgeoning population of roe deer. Grey squirrels are also now common, whilst the red squirrel is in serious decline, with strongholds probably only in the larger conifer plantations such as Edgarhope.

References:

Murray, R.D, Holling, M, Dott, H.E.M. and Vandome, P. (1998) The Breeding Birds of South-east Scotland. A Tetrad Atlas 1988-1994. Scottish Ornithological Club

Murray, R.D. (2002) Borders Bird Report 2000.

Common Name *Species* **(National Status)** **Local Status** **Distribution/ Locality**

Vertebrates

Fish

Hyperoartia

Petromyzonidae
Lamprey species *Lampetra sp.* (LBAP) Uncommon, Leader, Boondreigh Burn and Brunta Burn, mostly in larval form

Isospondyli

Salmonidae
Atlantic Salmon *Salmo salar* (LBAP) Common, Leader and tributaries are important spawning areas
Sea Trout *Salmo trutta* (LBAP) Common, Leader and tributaries
Brown Trout *Salmo trutta fario* (LBAP) Very Common, Leader and all tributaries
Rainbow Trout *Salmo gardenerii* Local, May be in lower stretches of Leader as Tweed stocked at Galashiels. Stocked in still waters.

Ostariophysi

Cyprinidae
Minnow *Phoxinus phoxinus* Common, Leader - prefers larger bodies of water

Cobitidae
Stone Loach *Noemacheilus barbatulus* Common, Leader Water, Boondreigh, Brunta and Lauder Burns

Apodes

Anguillidae
Eel *Anguilla anguilla* Very Common, Throughout all bodies of water

Thoracostei

Gasterosteidae
Three-spined Stickleback *Gasterosteus aculeatus* Common, Leader and most larger burns

Amphibians and Reptiles

Anura (Amphibians)

Bufonidae
Common Toad *Bufo bufo* Common, Common in damp places

Ranidae
Common Frog *Rana temporaria* (LBAP) Common, Throughout the area

Squamata (Snakes and lizards)

Lacertidae
Common Lizard *Lacerta vivipara* Uncommon, No records, but likely to be present on moorland, stane dykes.

Anguidae
Slow Worm *Anguis fragilis* (LBAP) Scarce, No records, but likely to be present on moorland

Viperidae
Adder *Vipera berus* (LBAP) Common, Moorland. Few records from Lammermuirs, but under-recorded.

Birds

Podicipediformes
Podicipedidae
Little Grebe *Tachybaptus ruficollis* Uncommon, Spottiswoode, occasional

Ciconiiformes
Ardeidae
Grey Heron *Ardea cinerea* Common, Fishes throughout Lauderdale. Only small nesting colonies, plantations
 e.g. at Addinston, Thirlestane

Anseriformes
Anatidae
Whooper Swan *Cygnus cygnus* Scarce, Occassional winter visitor. Spottiswoode 1999
Mute Swan *Cygnus olor* Uncommon, Few pairs only. Spottiswoode, Leader, Addinston
Pink-footed Goose *Anser brachyrhyncus* Uncommon, Passage, may feed over winter
Greylag Goose *Anser anser* (LBAP) Uncommon, Occassional breeder. Winter visitor
Canada Goose *Branta Canadensis* Scarce, Occasional breeder
Teal *Anas crecca* Uncommon, Probably common breeder in upland sites
Mallard *Anas platyrhynchos* Common, Breeds throughout area
Pochard *Aythya ferina* Uncommon, Occasional visitor, Spottiswoode
Tufted Duck *Aythya fuligula* Uncommon, Occasional visitor, Spottiswoode
Goldeneye *Bucephala clangula* Uncommon, Winter visitor to Leader
Goosander *Mergus merganser* Common, Breeds on Leader and upland sites, larger numbers in winter
Ruddy Duck *Oxyura jamaicensis* (Naturalised) Uncommon, Occasional visitor to Spottiswoode

Accipitriformes
Accipitridae
Red Kite *Milvus milvus* Rare, Seen 2000 and 2001 around Lauder, Lauder Common and Wooplaw, may breed in future.
Hen Harrier *Circus cyaneus* (LBAP) Rare, Breeds in small numbers in Lammermuirs
Goshawk *Accipiter gentiles* Rare, Rare breeder. Spottiswoode 1996
Sparrowhawk *Accipiter nisus* Common, Woodland and hedges
Buzzard *Buteo buteo* Common, Has become very common over last 10 years throughout area.
Rough-legged Buzzard *Buteo lagopus* Rare, Spottiswoode

Pandionidae
Osprey *Pandion haliaetus* Rare, Wooplaw, 2002

Falconiformes
Falconidae
Kestrel *Falco tinnunculus* Common, Farmland. Often seen on overhead wires.
Merlin *Falco columbarius* (LBAP) Scarce, Breeds in small numbers in Lammermuirs. May be seen on lower ground in winter.
Peregrine *Falco peregrinus* Scarce, Breeds in small numbers in upland sites and old quarries

Galliformes
Phasianidae
Red Grouse *Lagopus lagopus* Common, Moorland breeder, not as widespread as used to be
Black Grouse *Tetrao tetrix* (LBAP) Uncommon, Declining, still reasonable numbers in eastern part of Lauderdale, small numbers on Lauder Common
Red-legged Partridge *Alectoris rufa* Common, Widely introduced in last 5 years.
Grey Partridge *Perdix perdix* (LBAP) Uncommon, Declining, arable and mixed farmland.

Quail *Coturnix coturnix* Scarce, Records from East Mains in 1999 and Blackburn area 2000
Pheasant *Phasianus colchicus* Very Common, Widely introduced for shooting each year.

Gruiformes

Rallidae
Moorhen *Gallinula chloropus* Common, Breeds by both still and running water
Coot *Fulica atra* Uncommon, Occasional breeder, Spottiswoode

Charadriiformes

Haematopodidae
Oystercatcher *Haematopus ostralegus* Common, Widespread - a harbringer of spring in Lauderdale.

Charadriidae
Dotterel *Charadrius morinellus* Rare, Passage migrant. Records from Lauder Common and fields near Westruther.
Golden Plover *Pluvialis apricaria* Uncommon, Breeds in small numbers in the Lammermuirs and Dun Law
Lapwing *Vanellus vanellus* (LBAP) Common, Breeds throughout region

Scolopacidae
Dunlin *Calidris alpinus* Uncommon, Breeds in small numbers in the Lammermuirs
Snipe *Gallinago gallinago* Common, Reasonably frequent in marshy areas
Woodcock *Scolopax rusticola* Common, Woodland. Breeds at Wooplaw, Spottiswoode, Thirlestane. More in winter.
Curlew *Numenius arquata* (LBAP) Common, Common in all upland areas and rough pasture.
Whimbrel *Numenius phaeopus* Rare, Winter visitor. Spottiswoode 1998.
Redshank *Tringa tetanus* Common, Common breeder along Leader and tributaries, uplands
Greenshank *Tringa ochropus Linnaeus* Uncommon, Occasional passage migrant
Common Sandpiper *Actitis hypoleucos* Common, Breeds along Leader and tributaries

Laridae
Black-headed Gull *Larus ridibundus* Very Common, Possibly one colony, common visitor to Leader.
Common Gull *Larus canus* Uncommon, Winter visitor to Leader and upland sites
Lesser Black-backed Gull *Larus fuscus* Uncommon, Some summer non-breeders
Herring Gull *Larus argentatus* Common, Non-breeding birds on Leader
Great Black-backed Gull *Larus marinus* Uncommon, A few birds appear on Leader late autumn, coinciding with salmon spawning.

Columbiformes

Columbidae
Feral Pigeon *Columba livia (feral)* Uncommon, Urban and farmland areas.
Stock Dove *Columba oenas* Uncommon, Under-recorded, confined largely to improved farmland.
Woodpigeon *Columba palumbus* Very Common, Throughout the area.
Collared Dove *Streptopelia decaocto* Common, Improved farmland and lower ground.

Cuculiformes

Cuculidae
Cuckoo *Cuculus canorus* Uncommon, Upland areas, but may be heard throughout Lauderdale.

Strigiformes

Tytonidae
Barn Owl *Tyto alba* (LBAP) Uncommon, Leader haughs, Carfraemill, Wooplaw.

Strigidae
Little Owl *Athene noctua* Scarce, A few records from Whitslaid, Lauder, Carfraemill
Tawny Owl *Strix aluco* Common, Wood and farmland
Long-eared Owl *Asio otus* Uncommon, Conifer plantations, under-recorded.
Short-eared Owl *Asio flammeus* (LBAP) Scarce, Occasional. Lauder Common, Spottiswoode.

Apodiformes

Apodidae
Swift *Apus apus* (LBAP) Common, Built-up areas

Coraciiformes

Alcedinidae
Kingfisher *Alcedo atthis* (LBAP) Uncommon, Occasional breeder on Leader

Piciformes

Picidae
Green Woodpecker *Picus viridis* Scarce, Woodland edges. Thirlestane, Oxton
Great Spotted Woodpecker *Dendrocopos major* Common, Broad-leaved woodland

Passeriformes

Alaudidae
Skylark *Alauda arvensis* (LBAP) Common, Upland pasture and moorland

Hirundinidae
Sand Martin *Riparia riparia* Common, Sand banks mainly by Leader
Swallow *Hirundo rustica* Common, Throughout Lauderdale
House Martin *Delichon urbica* Common, Built up areas, congregate over water to feed

Motacillidae
Tree Pipit *Anthus trivialis* Uncommon, Open land, often felled woodland / new plantations. Spottiswoode.
Meadow Pipit *Anthus pratensis* Very Common, Moorland and rough pasture.
Grey Wagtail *Motacilla cinerea* Common, Along Leader and burns.
Pied Wagtail *Motacilla alba yarrellii* Common, Throughout area.

Bombycillidae
Waxwing *Bombycilla garrulous* Uncommon, Occasional winter visitor

Cinclidae
Dipper *Cinclus cinclus* Common, Along Leader and burns.

Troglodytidae
Wren *Troglodytes troglodytes* Very Common, Throughout area.

Prunellidae
Dunnock *Prunella modularis* Very Common, Woodland, gardens. Throughout lower-lying parts.

Turdidae
Robin *Erithacus rubecula* Very Common, Throughout lower-lying parts.
Redstart *Phoenicurus phoenicurus* Uncommon, Open and riverine woodland. Spottiswoode.
Whinchat *Saxicola rubetra* Uncommon, Grassland and scrub. Spottiswoode.
Stonechat *Saxicola torquata* Scarce, Scub and rough ground, often on gorse. Lauder Burn, Spottiswoode
Wheatear *Oenanthe oenanthe* Common, Throughout upland areas.
Ring Ouzel *Turdus torquatus* (LBAP) Uncommon, Higher parts of uplands, rocky cleuchs.
Blackbird *Turdus merula* Very Common, All but highest ground
Fieldfare *Turdus pilaris* Common, Widespread winter visior on pasture, woodland. Occasional breeder.
Song Thrush *Turdus philomelos* Common, Throughout area except on higher land.
Redwing *Turdus iliacus* Common, Widespread winter visior on pasture, woodland
Mistle Thrush *Turdus viscivorus* Common, Woodland, policies and gardens

Sylviidae
Grasshopper Warbler *Locustella naevia* Scarce, Thick herb layer. Spottiswoode, Longmuir
Sedge Warbler *Acrocephalus schoenobaenus* Common, Reed and tall herb, us. Associated with water. Banks of Leader.
Lesser Whitethroat *Sylvia curruca* Rare, Scrub. Whitslaid and Dod Mill areas.
Whitethroat *Sylvia communis* Common, Hedges, scrub, thick ground cover. Lower ground.
Garden Warbler *Sylvia borin* Uncommon, Deciduous woodland, gardens. Under-recorded.

Blackcap *Sylvia atricapilla* Common, Woodland
Wood Warbler *Phylloscopus sibilatrix* Scarce, Deciduous woodland. Wooplaw.
Willow Warbler *Phylloscopus trochilus* Very Common, Woodland, tall scrub. Ubiquitous.
Chiffchaff *Phylloscopus collybita* Uncommon, Mainly deciduous woodland.
Goldcrest *Regulus regulus* Common, Coniferous woodland.

Muscicapidae
Spotted Flycatcher *Muscicapa striata* (LBAP) Common, Deciduous woodland, gardens.
Pied Flycatcher *Ficedula hypoleuca* Rare, Old deciduous woodland. Airhouse, Whitslaid, Spottiswoode.

Aegithalidae
Long-tailed Tit *Aegithalos caudatus* Common, Deciduous woodland, increasingly common in gardens.

Paridae
Marsh Tit *Parus palustris* (LBAP) Rare, Deciduous woodland gardens. Blainslie, Spottiswoode.
Coal Tit *Parus ater* Very Common, Coniferous woodland
Blue Tit *Parus caeruleus* Very Common, Deciduous woodland, gardens
Great Tit *Parus major* Very Common, Deciduous woodland

Sittidae
Nuthatch *Sitta europaea,* Uncommon, Deciduous woodland. Expanding northwards. Spottiswoode, Lauder

Aegithalidae
Treecreeper *Certhia familiaris* Common, Deciduous or mixed woodland

Corvidae
Jay *Garrulus glandarius* Scarce, Woodland. Spottiswoode, Pickie Moss, Thirlestane
Magpie *Pica pica* Scarce, Farmland, woods, parks and gardens. Oxton, Edgarhope
Jackdaw *Corvus monedula* Very Common, Urban areas, most habitats
Rook *Corvus frugilegus* Very Common, Tilled farmland
Carrion crow *Corvus corone corone* Very Common, All types of countryside
Raven *Corvus corax* Scarce, Upland. Sightings from Headshaw, Edgarhope, Carfrae Common.

Sturnidae
Starling *Sturnus vulgaris* Common, Urban areas and farmland

Passeridae
House Sparrow *Passer domesticus* (LBAP) Common, Urban areas and farm buildings
Tree Sparrow *Passer montanus* (LBAP) Scarce, Lowland farmland. Leader vale, Spottiswoode.

Fringillidae
Chaffinch *Fringilla coelebs* Very Common, Woodland, scrub, gardens. Ubiquitous.
Brambling *Fringilla montifringilla* Uncommon, Winter visitor, farmland, with chaffinch.
Greenfinch *Carduelis chloris* Very Common, Woodland-edge, farmland, gardens
Goldfinch *Carduelis carduelis* Common, Farmland, scrub and tall herbs
Siskin *Carduelis spinus* Common, Coniferous woodland. Increasingly common on garden feeders.
Linnet *Carduelis cannabina* Common, Farmland, hedges and scrub
Redpoll *Carduelis flammea* Common, Birch, alder and confers.
Twite *Carduelis flavirostris* Scarce, Winter visitor, farmland. Thirlestane, High Cross.
Common Crossbill *Loxia curvirostra* Uncommon, Coniferous woodland. Edgarhope
Bullfinch *Pyrrhula pyrrhula* (LBAP) Common, Farmland, gardens
Hawfinch *Coccothraustes coccothraustes* Locally extinct? Policy woodland, gardens. North of Lauder 1977.

Emberizidae
Yellowhammer *Emberiza citrinella* (LBAP) Common, Farmland, hedgerows, scrub
Reed Bunting *Emberiza schoeniclus* (LBAP) Uncommon, Farmland, scrub, us. Associated with water or marshy ground
Corn Bunting *Milaria calandra* Locally extinct? Farmland. Whitslaid area 1992.

Mammals

Insectivora
Erinaceidae
Hedgehog *Erinaceus europaeus* (Common) Uncommon, Farmland, woods, gardens. Under-recorded

Talpidae
Mole *Talpa europaea* (Common) Very Common, Highly visible throughout area!

Soricidae
Common Shrew *Sorex araneus* (Common) Common, Under-recorded.
Water Shrew *Neomys fodiens* (Common) Uncommon, Close to water. Thirlestane

Chiroptera
Vespertilionidae
Pipistrelle *Pipistrellus pipistrellus* (Common) Common, Throughout lowland areas.
Brown Long-eared Bat *Plecotus auritus* (Common, LBAP) Common, Under-recorded. Blainslie, Spottiswoode.

Lagomorpha
Leporidae
Rabbit *Oryctolagus cuniculus* (Common) Very Common, Farmland, sometimes reaching plague proportions.
Brown Hare *Lepus capensis* (Common, LBAP) Common, Farmland, extending to moorland. Still relatively abundant.
Mountain Hare *Lepus timidus* Uncommon, Upland areas. Reintroduced in 19th century.

Rodentia
Sciuridae
Red Squirrel *Sciurus vulgaris* (Local, LBAP) Uncommon, Coniferous woodland. Declining. Edgarhope
Grey Squirrel *Sciurus carolinensis* (Naturalised) Common, Mixed woodland, gardens. Increasing.

Cricetidae
Bank vole *Clethrionomys glareolus* (Common) Common, Grassland.
Short-tailed vole *Microtus agrestis* (Common) Very Common, Grassland
Water vole *Arvicola terrestris* (Local, LBAP) Scarce, Water edges. Almost exterminated by mink. Recent records from Allan Water at Wooplaw. May be upland populations.

Muridae
Field mouse *Apodemus sylvaticus* (Common) Common, Grassland, woodland
House mouse *Mus musculus* (Common) Common, Urban and farms
Brown Rat *Rattus norvegicus* (Common) Common, Farms

Carnivora
Canidae
Fox *Vulpes vulpes* (Common) Common, Throughout area, controlled for shooting interests.

Mustelidae
Weasel *Mustela nivealis* (Common) Common, Seldom reported.
Stoat *Mustela erminea* (Common) Common, Throughout area. Individuals in ermine over winter.
American Mink *Mustela vison* (Naturalised) Common, Associated with water. Along Leader and tributaries.
Ferret *Mustela furo* (Naturalised) Rare (escapees?), Occasional road casualties seen around Lauder and Oxton.
Badger *Meles meles* (Common) Common, All areas - wood, moor and farmland. Several known setts.
Otter *Lutra lutra* (Local, LBAP) Common, Throughout area along Leader and tributaries.

Artiodactyla
Cervidae
Sika Deer *Cervus nippon* (Naturalised) Uncommon, Woodland. Sightings from Wooplaw
Roe Deer *Capreolus capreolus* (Common) Common, Woodland. Increasing in numbers.

Appendix 1:
Giles County Directory

Lauder 1896

R.S.O Berwickshire

Royal Burgh:	James IV 1494
Population:	Burgh 719 Parish 158
Chief Magistrate:	Robert Symington 1891 to 1894
Chairman of Parochial Board:	R. Symington
	(tel hours 7.30 a.m to 8 p.m. Sun 9 to 10 a.m.)
Town Clerks:	Robert Romanes, George Rankin
Clergy:	Est. Church: Rev. Thomas Martin M.A.
	Free Church: Rev. Duncan Turner
	U.P. Church: Rev. Thomas Keir M.A.
Notaries to Public:	George Rankin and R. Romanes
Solicitor:	G.L. Broomfield
Medical Practitioners:	D. Skinner, R.S. Gibb
Bank:	Bank of Scotland
	R. Romanes and G. Rankin (agent)

Inspector of Poor and Clerk to School board: G.L Broomfield

Registrar:	William Moore	
Hotels:	Black Bull:	John Sanderson
	Eagle:	Robert Smart
	Commercial:	Thomas Wilson
Inn:	Annfield:	James Robertson
Sub Post Master:	J.H. Scroggie	
Station:	Stow (N.B.R.)	
Member of Parliament:	Harold John Tennent,The Glen, Innerleithen.	

Lauder 1902

Population:	Burgh: 803
	Municipality: 724
	Parish: 1461
Tel hours 8 a.m. to 8 p.m.	
Provost:	William Moore

Chairman of Parish Council:	R.Dickinson (Longcroft)
Town Clerk:	George Rankin
Clergy:	Est. Church: Rev. Thomas Martin
	U.F. Church: Rev. Duncan Turner, U.P. Church: Rev. Thomas Keir
Sol. and Notaries to Public:	G. Rankin, Sol. G. L. Broomfield
Medic. Pract.:	D. Skinner (M.O.), W. A. Skinner, J. Hamilton
Bank:	Bank of Scotland George Rankin (agent)
Inspector of Poor and clerk to the School Board:	G. L. Broomfield
Registrar:	William Moore

Hotels:	Black Bull:	P.E. Shepherd
	Commercial:	Alex Moodie
	Eagle:	Allan Davidson
	Lauderdale Temperance:	Geo. Bowie

Sub Postmaster:	J. H. Scroggie
Station:	Stow (N.B.R.)

Lauder Trades 1927

McDonalds Directory

Town Officials

Provost	G. W. Anderson
Baillies:	J. Stevenson, A. Trotter
Councillors:	A.G. Shirra-Gibb, D. Donaldson, J.Gillespie, R. Cossar, J.H. Scroggie, J. Rutherford
Town Clerk:	A.G. Doughty, Solicitor
Burgh Treasurer:	G. L. Broomfield, Solicitor
Burgh Surveyor:	R. Pauling
Burgh Analyst:	A Scot Dodd B.Sc. F.I.C. F.C.S. Edinburgh
Bakers:	J. M.Graham, High St., John Hislop, Market Place, Also teas and refreshments
Banks:	Bank of Scotland
Blacksmiths:	A. Fairbairn, Westruther, A.Y. Fairbairn, Houndslow. P. Reid, Oxton. James Park, Blainslie, C. Murray, Lauder.
Boot and Shoe Makers:	J. Cowan, Oxton D. & W. Harvey, High St., Lauder, P. & P. J. Lothian, High St.
Butcher:	Alexander Brodie, High St., D. S. Donaldson, Market Place, Lauder.

Chemist & Pharmacy:	John H. Scroggie. Post Office
China Dealer:	James McLaughlan, High St.
Coach and Carriage Hire:	George R.Todd Miss L.Wood, Porties, Governess carts, cars and motor for hire
Confectioners:	Miss H. Anderson, High St., Also Fruiterer and Newsagent. B. Pow, High St. Robert John Prentice, Mid Row A. Trotter.
Contractors:	J. & G. Campbell, Oxton. J.Middlemiss.
Drapers:	James Cossar and Son, High St. William Smith, High St. Mrs H. Swanston, Oxton.
Grocers & General Merchants:	T. Cockburn, Oxton. T. Gill, Westruther. J. N. Graham, High St. A. Lothian, Houndslow. G. C. McQueen, High St. R. W. Mathewson, Oxton. A.& J. Rutherford, High St. J. Stoddart, High St. R. Tait, High St.
Hotels:	Black Bull Hotel, High St. Carfrae Mill Hotel, Oxton. Eagle Hotel, Market Place. Family and Commercial Hotel, J. Wilson, Licencee Lauderdale Temperance Hotel. Thistle Hotel, Westruther
Plumbers:	Robert Watson and Son, High St., also slaters
Joiners and Cart Wrights:	G. Anderson. P. Carfrae and Son, High St. A. Mercer and Sons Houndslow. J. Ramage, Westruther. Alexander Scott, Boghall, Oxton.
Motor Car Hirers:	J.M. Broomfield, High St., Phone No.13. George Deans, Lauderdale Garage cars for hire, 14 seat omnibus for Public Hire. Pratts Petrol Pump, repairs and accessories, Phone No. 10. H. J. McDonald, High St., Mrs N. Wilson, Black Bull Stables. closed & open cars also Motor Hearse & a char-a-banc owner, Phone No. 8
Motor Engineers:	J. N. Broomfield, High St., Phone No 13, Robson and Oliver, West End Garage, also motor and general engineers.

Motor Garages:	Robson and Oliver, West End Garage also motor and general engineers car and motor vehicle overhauls & speciality accessories stocked also car for hire.
Painters and Paper Hanger:	Lindsay and Son
Posting Establishments:	Nellie Wilson, Lauder, Phone No. 8
Solicitors:	G. L. Broomfield, A.G. Doughty
Spirit Dealers:	W. Mayne, Commercial Inn, High St., Miss Walker, Carfrae Mill.
Tailors:	John Melrose, Oxton. William Walkinshaw, Oxton. James Murray, West End.

Lauder, Berwickshire, Royal and Police Burgh 7 miles from Earlston. It has R.S. and P.O. with M.O. and T. Depts. of Berwickshire

Pop. 759 Lauder Parish acres 33,617 Pop. 1,369

By 1956 in McDonald's Directory

Lauder, Berwickshire, Royal and Police Burgh 7 miles from Earlston. It has P.O. with M.O. and T. Depts. of Berwickshire

Pop. 623 Parish 1,190 Area 33,617.

Town Officials

Provost:	H.J.C. Crombie-Smith
Baillies:	D.W.Harvey / I.R.Pitman
Councillors:	G.K. Fleming, A.R.Jolly, K.Miller, J.H.G.Scott, A.L. Thomson
Hon. Treasurer:	A. McNeilage
Town Clerk:	A.Y.Henry
Burgh Chamberlain:	D.T. Watson
Burgh Surveyor:	J.W.Benton M.B.E.; AM. Inst. C.E. Duns
Burgh Assessor:	D.C. Hannah, 21 Duke St., Edinburgh
Burgh Analyst:	A. Scott Dodd, B.Sc. P.l.C. P.C.S. Edinburgh
Sanitary Inspector:	J.S. Beedie, Duns
Medical Officer:	Dr Allan, Duns
Post Master:	P. Mathieson Thomson

Trades

Baker:	J.M. Bell, Oxton also confectioners
Bank:	Bank of Scotland, R.J. Wight, Manager
Boot and Shoe Retailers:	J. Hardie, 13 East High St , also repairs country wear.

Builders:	Thomas Murray, Dawson's Brae, 51 West High Street. R. & A. Redpath, 2 The Loan
Building Society:	Scottish Amicable Building Society, Market Place
Butchers:	H. Scott, 29a West High St. Thos Shaw, Market Place
Chemist:	Galashiels United Co-operative Society, Market Place
China Dealer:	Jas McClachlan, High St.
Confectioners:	Miss M Archibald, Oxton. H & M Anderson, High St., W, J. Brown, High St., (also bakers) H. J. McDonald, 20 Market Place, Joseph Sidonio, High St., Mrs Threadgall, 57 West High St.
Contactors:	J. Middlemiss and Son, 16 Market Place.
Farming:	Contractors, J. & G. Campbell, Oxton, R.& A. Redpath, 2 The Loan.
Dairies:	Wyndhead Dairy, Prop. J.P.Finlayson
Drapers:	J.Cossar and Son, Prop. A. Thomson, Market Place.
Fried Fish Shop:	Joseph Sidonio, High St.
Fruiterers:	Mrs Threadgall, 57 West High Street
Grocers and General Merchants:	Miss Douglas, Westruther. Andrew B. Brown, West High St. Galashiels United Co-operative Society, West High St. A.&J. Rutherford, Market Place.
Hairdresser:	H.E.C. Mitchell, 7a Market Place, Ladies and Gents Hairdresser
Hotels:	Black Bull Hotel, James F. Scott Prop. Eagle Hotel, Prop. W. Brotherstone, Market Place. Harryburn House Hotel. Tower Hotel, Prop. J. Thorburn
Joiners:	G. Cossar and Son. High St. James A. Middlemiss, 1East High St.
Motor Engineers and Agents:	J. M. Broomfield, High St. James Shiel and Son, Leadervale Garage, Morris Dealer and Breakdown service
Motor Hirer:	J. M. Broomfield, High St. H.J. McDonald, 20 Market Place, T. B. Wilson, 55 West High St.
Painters:	Miller and Murray, High St., also at Galashiels.

Pig Breeders:	J. & W. Hume, Burnfoot, Breeder of Large whites Pedigree Pigs
Plasterers:	R. & A. Redpath, 2 The Loan
Provision Merchant:	A. B. Brown, 5 High St.
Public House:	Commercial Inn, 4 High St., (Walter Hogarth)
Radio and Television:	A.R. Jolly, 22-24 West High St.
Solicitors:	Romanes and Rankin, Bank of Scotland Buildings

Appendix 2:
Elections since 1979

European Elections

Elections to the European Parliament are held every five years. The European Parliament was directly elected for the first time in 1979. On 10 June 1999 voters in Britain elected MEPs under a proportional representation system for the first time. The European Parliamentary Elections Act, which received Royal Assent on 14th January 1999, introduced a regional list system with seats allocated to parties in proportion to their share of the vote. Britain is divided into eleven electoral regions with between 4 and 11 MEPs representing each region. Scotland elects eight MEPs.

The system used in Britain is similar to the ones used in France, Germany, Greece, Portugal and Spain to elect their MEPs. The introduction of proportional representation in Britain means all 626 MEPs in the European Parliament are elected under some form of proportional representation.

June 1999 Candidates

SNP

1. Ian Hughton, MEP
2. Professor Neil MacCormick
3. Dr Anne Lorne Gillies
4. Dr Gordon Wilson
5. Janet Law
6. Kris Murray Browne
7. Ian Goldie
8. Josephine Docherty

LABOUR

1. David Martin, MEP
2. Bill Miller, MEP
3. Catherine Taylor
4. Christine May
5. Hugh McMahon, MEP
6. James Paton
7. John Clifford
8. Jeanette Bradley

SCOTTISH CONSERVATIVE

1. Struan Stevenson
2. John Purvis
3. Anne Harper
4. Cameron Buchanan
5. Sebastian Leslie
6. Iain Mitchell
7. Peter Ramsey
8. Anthony Gilbey

SCOTTISH LIBERAL DEMOCRAT PARTY

1. Elspeth Attwood
2. Robert Aldridge
3. Neil Mitchison
4. Heather Lyall
5. Clive Sneddon
6. Danus Skene
7. Karen Freel
8. Jayne Struthers

SCOTTISH GREEN PARTY

1. Marion Coyne
2. Eleanor Scott
3. Phil O'Brien
4. Graeme Farmer
5. Linda Hendry
6. Chris Ballance
7. Kay Allan
8. Alastair Whitelaw

UK INDEPENDENCE

1. Alistair McConnachie
2. Donald Mackay
3. James McKenna
4. Stuart Brown
5. Matthew Henderson
6. Joseph Smith
7. Peter Nielson
8. John Mumford

PRO EURO CONSERVATIVE

1. Paul Dwyer
2. Joanna Lavender
3. Douglas McConchie
4. Richard Ashurst
5. Neasa MacEarlean
6. Oliver Grant
7. Alexander Skinner
8. James Waters

NATURAL LAW

1. James McKissock
2. George Stidolph
3. Diana Kras
4. Kenneth Blair
5. David Pettigrew
6. Iain Petrie
7. Anna Rawlinson
8. Thomas Pringle

Elspeth Attwooll
Ian Hughton
Nell MacCormick
Oavid Martin
Bill Miller
John Purvis
Struan Stevenson
Catherine Taylor

BRITISH NATIONAL PARTY

1. Kenneth Smith
2. Scott McClean
3. Russell Bradley
4. Mark Allen
5. Paul Wilkinson
6. Robert Currie
7. David Kerr
8. James Mills

SOCIALIST LABOUR PARTY

1. Louise McDaid
2. Christopher Herriot
3. Katharine McGavigan
4. Stephen John Mayes
5. Patricia Graham
6. Colin Turbett
7. Margaret Stead
8. James Galloway

(Scottish Liberal Democrat)
(SNP)
(SNP)
(Labour)
(Labour)
(Scottish Conservative and Unionist)
(Scottish Conservative and Unionist)
(Labour)

SCOTTISH SOCIALIST PARTY

1. Hugh Kerr
2. Rosie Kane
3. Harvey Duke
4. Catherine Stewart
5. Colin Fox
6. Shareen Blackall
7. Steve Arnott
8. Frances Curran

INDEPENDENT - ACCOUNTANT FOR LOWER TAXES

Charles Lawson

Party	Number of votes	Percentage of votes
Labour	283,490	28.68
SNP	268,528	27.17
Scottish Conservative	195,296	19.76
Scottish Liberal Democrat	96,971	9.81
Scottish Green	57,142	5.78
Scottish Socialist	39,720	4.02
Pro Euro Conservative	17,781	1.8
UK Independence	12,549	1.27
Socialist Labour	9,385	0.95
British National	3,729	0.38
Natural Law	2,087	0.21
Accountant for Lower Taxes	1,632	0.17

Total of votes:	988,310
Turnout:	24.7%
Electorate:	3,999,623

June 1994

Candidate	Party	Votes	Votes %	Change %
A Smith	Labour	90,750	45.2	5.4
A Hutton	Conservative	45,595	22.7	-9.5
C Creech	SNP	45,032	22.4	5.5
D Millar	LiberaI Democrat	13,363	6.7	1.6
J Hein	Liberal	3,249	1.6	-
L Hendry	Green	2,429	1.2	-4.5
G Gay	NLP	539	0.3	-
Electorate	500,643			
Turnout	200,957 (40.1%)			

June 1989

Candidate	Party	Votes	Votes%	Change %
A Smith	Labour	81,366	39.8	4.7
A Hutton	Conservative	65,673	32.2	-4.8
M Brown	SNP	35,155	17.2	3.7
J McKerchar	Democat	11 ,658	5.7	-9.3
J Button	Green	10,368	5.1	-
Electorate	497,108			
Turnout	204,220 (41.1%)			

June 1984

Candidate	Party	Votes	Votes%	Change %
A Hutton	Conservative	60,843	37.0	-6.0
R Stewart	Labour	57,7O6	35.1	7.4
E Buchanan	LIberal/SDP	23,598	14.4	3.6
I Goldie	SNP	22,242	13.5	-5.0
Electorate	484,760			
Turnout	164,389 (33.9%)			

June1979

Candidate	Party	Votes	Votes%
A Hutton	Conservative	66,816	43.0
P Foy	Labour	43,145	27.7
I MacGibbon	SNP	28,694	18.5
J Wallace	Liberal	16,825	10.8
Electorate	450,761		
Turnout	155,480 (34.5%)		

1999   Tweeddale Ettrick & Lauderdale

Candidate	Party	Votes	Votes %
Ian Jenkins	Liberal Democrat	12,078	35.82
Christine Creech	SNP	7,600	22.54
George McGregor	Labour	7,546	22.38
John Campbell	Conservative	6,491	19.25
Electorate	51,577		
Turnout	33,715		65.37

South Of Scotland Regional Seat

Labour	6 seats
Liberal Democrat	2 seats
SNP	1 seat

Additional Members Elected South of Scotland

Regional Vote	%
Labour	31.04
SNP	25.15
Conservatives	21.64
Liberal Democrat	11.99

Phil Gallie	Conservative
David Mundell	Conservative
Murray Tosh	Conservative
Alex Ferguson	Conservative
Michael Russell	SNP
Adam Ingram	SNP
Christine Creech	SNP

Index of People and Places

Jones, G I; 50
J P Court; 139

Kay family; 253
Kay, A; 248
Kay, D; 248
Kedzlie; 119, 262
Keir, Rev. Thomas; 122
Kellett, Bill; 183
Kelly, Alexander; 26, 322
Kelly, Andrew; 322, 345
Kelly, Mr R; 18, 23, 41
Kelly; Thomson; 345
Kelphope; 53, 190, 200, 248, 270, 271
Kelso; 62, 86, 130, 153, 214, 277, 278, 294, 297, 340
Kelso Ice Rink; 62
Ker, Mr; 251
Ker, Jean; 62
Kerr, Alister; 78
Kerr, Mrs J; 71
Kerr, R A; 50
Kilmarnock Dairy School; 85
King Alexander III; 339
King David1; 1, 213, 339
King Charles II; 21
King George V; 49
King James IV; 210
King James VI; 213
Kinghorn, James; 283
Kinnon, John; 322
Kirkcaldy; 101, 219
Kirktonhill; 246, 247, 248, 251, 255, 278
Kirkwood, James; 283
Knight, Jim; 114
Knox, Alexander; 59
Knox, Miss; 343

Laidlaw, James; 322
Laidlaw, Margaret; 224
Laidlaw, Mr; 64, 67
Laing, Jimmy; 269
Lamb, Rev. Walter; 120, 121, 122
Lambie, John; 328
Lambie, Thomas; 328
Lammermuirs; 54, 187, 201, 246, 268, 271, 345
Lanark; 253
Landells, Robert; 316
Landells, A; 50
Landells, Jean; 40
Landells, M; 248
Landells, R B; 50
Landells, R E; 50
Landells, R T; 50
Langshaw; 96
Lascelles, Major; 255

Lauder: Allanbank; 158, 176, The Avenue; 19, 39, 176, 177, Black Bull Hotel; 19, 35, 58, 73, 74, 76, 73, 160, 164-165, 220, Brownsmuir Park; 92. 140, 178, Burnmill; 178, Castle Haugh; 49, Castle Riggs; 49, Castle Wynd; 76, 118 Church Wynd; 26, Cottesbrook; 177, Crofts Road; 158, Eagle Hotel; 76, 101, 113, 144, East High St.; 22, 92, 119, 135, 136, 147, 160, 161, 219, 220, 221, Factors Park; 61, 63,77, 158, 220, 221, The Glebe; 119, Harryburn; 43, High St.; 14, 36, 49, 144, 177, 178, Kirk Hall; 76, Kirk Wynd; 116, 118, 136, Lauder Old Manse; 119, Lauderdale Drive; 178, Lauderdale Hotel; 64, 75, 76, 79, 117, 118, 130, 136, 280, The Loan; 21, 59, 64, 176, Loanside; 220 Lockuphouse; 144, 147, Mace Shop; 22, Manse Road; 95, Market Place; 22, 158, 160, 165, 177, 220, Mid Row; 25, 54, 144, 158, 166, 1687 Mill Wynd; 16, 142, 158, 160, 167-168, 176, 339, Millburn Park; 61, 158, 178 Old Causeway; 24, 105, Old Station Yard; 92, 178 Peatman Corner; 92; The Red House; 101, 102, 119, 219, 220, The Row; 92, 130, 168-169, 176, Rutherford's Shop; 138, 220, Scott Road; 178, Session House; 76, 158, South Gardens; 158, Station Road; 95, 158 Smiddy; 24, 35, 36, 39, 52 105, 127, Stow Road; 24, 176, 219, Temperance Hotel; 63, Territorial Hall; 61, 63, 77, Tolbooth; 141, Tower; 339, Under Loan Park; 81, 178, Upper Loan Park; 158, Upper Vennel; 176 War Memorial; 160, 162, 308, 312, West Church Hall; 76, West High St.; 22, 66, 76, 123, 126, 135, 136, 137, 169, 170, 177, 219, Woodcote House; 66,
Lauder After School Club; 55
Lauder Amateur Dramatic Society; 55-58
Lauder, Sir Andrew Dick; 339
Lauder and Lauderdale; 1, 9, 43, 49, 67, 75, 117, 135,162, 67, 243
Lauder Barns; 98, 237, 246, 247, 248, 293
Lauder Bowling Club; 19, 24, 59-60, 120
Lauder Bridge; 160, 172, 224
Lauder, Burgh of; 1, 2, 3, 8, 15, 50, 55, 63, 76, 79, 81, 82, 92, 93, 94, 96, 97, 98, 99, 101, 102, 105, 107, 108, 111, 114, 120, 123, 129, 130,135, 139, 140, 141, 142, 143, 145, 146,147, 148, 149, 150, 176, 177, 178, 181, 187, 193, 199, 201, 202, 209, 210, 219, 231, 234, 247, 250, 260, 261, 265, 277, 278, 280, 281, 289, 292, 293,294, 297, 303.312, 325, 332, 334, 340, 343, 344
Lauder Burn; 115
Lauder Cemetery; 133-134, 209
Lauder Church Guild; 120
Lauder, Common; 1, 5, 6, 11, 12, 13, 43-48, 49, 53, 59, 68, 90, 113, 209